MEMOIRS

OF

THE JACOBITES

OF 1715 AND 1745.

BY MRS. THOMSON,

AUTHOR OF

"MEMOIRS OF THE COURT OF HENRY THE EIGHTH, "
"MEMOIRS OF SARAH, DUCHESS OF MARLBOROUGH, " ETC.

VOLUME III.

1845.

Memoirs of the Jacobites of 1715 and 1745 - Volume III

Mrs. Thomson

DODO PRESS

PREFACE.

In completing this work, I have to repeat my acknowledgments to those friends and correspondents to whom I expressed my obligations in the Preface to the first volume; and I have the additional pleasure of recording similar obligations from other channels.

I beg to testify my gratitude to Sir William Maxwell, Bart., of Montreith, for some information regarding the Nithsdale family; which, I hope, at some future time, to interweave with my biography of the Earl of Nithsdale; and also to Miss Charlotte Maxwell, the sister of Sir William Maxwell, whose enthusiasm for the subject of the Jacobites is proved by the interesting collection of Jacobite airs which she is forming, and which will be very acceptable to all who can appreciate poetry and song.

To Sir John Maxwell, Bart., of Pollock, and to Lady Matilda Maxwell, I offer my best thanks for their prompt and valued suggestions on the same subject.

I owe much to the courtesy and great intelligence of Mrs. Howison Craufurd, of Craufurdland Castle, Ayrshire: I have derived considerable assistance from that lady in the life of the Earl of Kilmarnock, and have, through her aid, been enabled to give to the public several letters never before published. For original information regarding the Derwentwater family, and for a degree of zeal, combined with accurate knowledge, I must here express my cordial thanks to the Hon. Mrs. Douglass, to whose assistance much of the interest which will be found in the life of Charles Radcliffe is justly due.

I have also to acknowledge the kindness of Mons. Amedée Pichot, from whose interesting work I have derived great pleasure and profit; and to Madame Colmache, for her inquiries in the Bibliothéque du Roi, for original papers relating to the subject. To W. E. Aytoun, Esq., of Edinburgh, I beg also to express my acknowledgments for his aid in supplying me with some curious information regarding the Duke of Perth. The kindness with which my researches, in every direction, have been met, has added to my task a degree of gratification, which now causes its close to be regarded with something almost like regret.

One advantage to be gained by the late publication of this third volume, is the criticism of friends on the two former ones. Amid many errors, I have been admonished, by my kind adviser and critic, Charles Kirkpatrick Sharpe, Esq., of having erred in accepting the common authorities in regard to the celebrated and unfortunate Lady Grange. Whatever were the sorrows of that lady, her faults and the provocation she gave to her irritated husband, were, it appears, fully equal to her misfortunes. Since the story of Lady Grange is not strictly connected with my subject, I have only referred to it incidentally. At some future time, the singular narrative of her fate may afford me a subject of further investigation.

I beg to correct a mistake into which I had fallen, in the first volume, respecting those letters relating to the Earl of Mar, for which I am indebted, to Alexander Macdonald, Esq. These, a distinct collection from that with which I was favoured by James Gibson Craig, Esq., were copied about twelve years ago, from the papers then in the possession of Lady Frances Erskine. They have since passed into the possession of the present Earl of Mar.

An interesting letter in the Appendix of this work, will be found relative to the social state of the Chevalier St. George, at Rome. For permission to publish this I am indebted to the valued friendship of my brother-in-law, Samuel Coltman, Esq., in whose possession it is, having been bequeathed, with other MSS. to his mother, by the well-known Joseph Spence, author of the "Anecdotes", and of other works.

LONDON, *28th March, 1846.*

CONTENTS OF THE THIRD VOLUME.

LORD GEORGE MURRAY

JAMES DRUMMOND, DUKE OF PERTH

FLORA MACDONALD

WILLIAM BOYD, EARL OF KILMARNOCK

CHARLES RADCLIFFE

With Portraits of Flora Macdonald, Prince Charles, and Lord Balmerino.

LORD GEORGE MURRAY.

This celebrated adherent of the Chevalier was born in the year 1705. He was the fifth son of John Duke of Atholl, and the younger brother of that Marquis of Tullibardine, whose biography has been already given.

The family of Atholl had attained a degree of power and influence in Scotland, which almost raised them out of the character of subjects. It was by consummate prudence, not unattended with a certain portion of time-serving, that, until the period 1715, the high position which these great nobles held had been in seasons of political difficulty preserved. Their political principles were those of indefeasible right and hereditary monarchy. John, first Marquis of Atholl, the father of Lord George Murray, married Amelia Stanley, daughter of Charlotte De la Tremouille, Countess of Derby, whose princely extraction, to borrow a phrase of high value in genealogical histories, was the least of her merits. This celebrated woman was remarkable for the virtue and piety of her ordinary life; and, when the season of trial and adversity called it forth, she displayed the heroism which becomes the hour of adversity. Her well-known defence of Latham House in 1644 from the assaults of the Parliamentarian forces, and her protracted maintenance of the Isle of Man, the last place in the English dominions that submitted to the Parliament, were followed by a long and patient endurance of penury and imprisonment.

The Marquis of Atholl was consistent in that adherence to the Stuarts which the family of his wife had professed. He advocated the succession of James the Second, and was rewarded with the royal confidence. Indeed, such was the partiality of the King towards him, that had the Marquis "in this sale of favour, " as an old writer expresses it, "not been firm and inflexible in the point of his religion, which he could not sacrifice to the pleasure of any mortal, he might have been the first minister for Scotland. "[1] After the Revolution, the Marquis retired into the country, and relinquished all public business; thus signifying his opinion of that event.

He bequeathed to his son, John second Marquis of Atholl, and the father of Lord George Murray, as great a share of prosperity and as many sources of self-exultation as ordinarily fall to the lot of one man. To the blood of the Murrays, the marriage with Lady Amelia

Stanley had added a connection in kindred with the Houses of Bourbon and Austria, with the Kings of Spain and Duke of Savoy, the Prince of Orange, and most of the crowned heads in Europe. Upon the extinction of the descendants of John the seventh Earl of Derby, commonly called the loyal Earl of Derby, and of his wife Charlotte De La Tremouille, "all that great and uncommon race of royal and illustrious blood, " as it has been entitled, centred in the descendants of the Marquis of Atholl. In 1726, the barony of Strange devolved upon the Duke of Atholl; and the principality of the Isle of Man was also bequeathed to the same House by William ninth Earl of Derby. This was the accession of a later period, but was the consequence of that great and honourable alliance of which the family of Atholl might justly boast.

The father of Lord George Murray adopted every precaution, as we have seen, [2] to preserve the acquisitions of dignity and fortune which the lapse of years had added to his patrimonial possessions. Sixteen coats of arms, eight on the paternal side, and eight on the maternal side, had composed the escutcheon of his father, John Marquis of Atholl. Among those great names on the maternal side, which graced a funeral escutcheon, which has been deemed the pattern and model of perfect dignity, and the perfection of ducal grandeur, was the name of the Prince of Orange. [3] This plea of kindred was not thrown away upon the Marquis of Atholl; he declared himself for King William, and entered early into the Revolution. For this service he was rewarded with the office of High Commissioner to represent his Majesty in the Scottish parliament. But subsequent events broke up this compact, and destroyed all the cordiality which subsisted between William and the head of the House of Atholl. The refusal of the King to own the African Company was, it is said, the reason why the Marquis withdrew himself from Court, and remained at a distance from it during the lifetime of William.

The accession of Anne brought, at first, fresh honours to this powerful Scottish nobleman. He was created in 1704 a Duke, and was made Privy Seal: but the politics of the Court party changed; the Duke of Atholl was dismissed from the Ministry, and he became henceforth a warm opponent of all the Government measures. He spoke with boldness, yet discretion, against the Union; and protested against a measure which, as he conceived, gave up all the dignity and antiquity of the kingdom.

During his proud career, a marriage with Katherine, the daughter of William Duke of Hamilton, a lady of great prudence, and of eminent piety and virtue, added to the high consideration of the Duke of Atholl. Of this nobleman, certain historians have left the highest character. "He was, " says Nisbet, "of great parts, but far greater virtues; of a lively apprehension, a clear and ready judgment, a copious eloquence, and of a very considerable degree of good understanding. "[4] It is difficult to reconcile this description with the intrigues and bitterness which characterise the Duke of Atholl, in Lovat's narrative of their rivalry; nor would it be easy to reconcile the public report of many men with the details of their private failings. That, however, which has impugned the consistency and sincerity of the Duke of Atholl far more than the representations of Lovat, is the belief that, whilst his feelings were engaged in one cause, his professions were loud in upholding the other; that he was double and self-interested; and that he saved his vast estates from forfeiture by an act of policy which might, in some bearings, be regarded as duplicity, in proof of which it is asserted, that, whilst he pretended to condemn the conduct of his eldest son in joining the Rebellion of 1715, he was the chief instigator of that step. [5] Such was the father to whom Lord George Murray owed his birth.

During the unbroken prosperity of his House, the future General of the Jacobite army was born. He was the fifth son of eight children, borne by the first Duchess of Atholl, and was born in the year 1705. Of these, John the eldest, and presumptive heir to the dukedom, had been killed at the battle of Mons, or Malplaquet, in 1709. He was a youth of great promise, and his death was a source of deep lamentation to his father; a sorrow which subsequent events did not, perhaps, tend to alleviate. William, Marquis of Tullibardine, was therefore regarded as the next heir to all the vast possessions and ancestral dignities of his House. His faithful adherence to the Chevalier St. George, and the part which he adopted in the Rebellion of 1715, produced a revolution in the affairs of his family, which, one may suppose, could not be effected without some delicacy, and considerable distress.

In 1716 the Marquis of Tullibardine was attainted by an act passed in the first year of George the First; and by a bill, which was passed in the House of Commons relating to the forfeited estates, all these estates were vested in his Majesty from and after the twenty-fourth of January 1715. [6] Upon this bill being passed, the Duke of Atholl, who had been residing for many years with the splendour and state of a prince at his Castle at Blair Atholl, journeyed to London, and, being graciously received by George the First, he laid his case before that monarch, representing the unhappy circumstances of his son, and pointing out what effect and influence this might have, in the event of his own death, on the succession of his family, if his estate and honour were not vested in law upon his second son, Lord James Murray, who had performed very signal service to his Majesty in the late rebellion. This petition was received, and a bill was brought into parliament for vesting the honours of John Duke of Atholl in James Murray, Esq., commonly called Lord James Murray; and, as a reward of his steady loyalty, a law was passed, enacting that the act of attainder against William Marquis of Tullibardine should not be construed to extend to Lord James Murray or his issue. In consequence of this bill, on the death of the Duke of Atholl, in 1724, Lord James Murray succeeded to all those honours and estates, which had thus been preserved through the prudence of his father, and the clemency or policy of the King.

In this divided House was Lord George Murray reared. It soon appeared that he possessed the decision and lofty courage of his ancestry; and that his early predilections, in which probably his father secretly coincided, were all in favour of the Stuarts, and that no considerations of self-interest could draw him from that adherence.

The events of 1715 occurring when Lord George Murray was only ten years of age, his first active exertions in the cause of the Stuarts did not take place until a later period. In the interim, the youth, who afterwards distinguished himself so greatly, served his first apprenticeship to arms in the British forces in Flanders. In 1719, when only fourteen years of age, a fresh plan of invasion being formed by Spain, and the Marquis of Tullibardine having again ventured to join in the enterprise, Lord George showed plainly his attachment to the Jacobite cause. He came over with the Marquis, with a small handful of Spaniards, and was wounded at the battle of Glenshiels on the tenth of June. Of his fate after that event, the following account has been given by Wodrow, [7] who prefaces his statement with a congratulatory remark that several of the Jacobites were by their sufferings converted from their error. "At Glenshiels, " he writes, referring to Lord George Murray, "he escaped, and with a servant got away among the Highland mountains, and lurked in a hut made for themselves for some months, and saw nobody. It was a happy Providence that either he or his servant had a Bible, and no other books. For want of other business, he carefully read that neglected book, and the Lord blessed it with his present hard circumstances to him. Now he begins to appear abroad, and it is said is soon to be pardoned; and he is highly commended not only for a serious convert from Jacobitism, but for a good Christian, and a youth of excellent parts, hopes, and expectations. "

It appears, however, that Lord George, however he might be changed in his opinions, did not consider himself safe in Scotland. He fled to the Continent, and entered the service of Sardinia, then, in consequence of the quadruple alliance, allotted to the possessions of the Duke of Savoy.

Meantime, through the influence of his family, and, perhaps, on the plea of his extreme youth when he had engaged in the battle of Glenshiels, a pardon was obtained for the young soldier. His father, as is related in the manuscript account of the Highlands before quoted, "had found it his interest to change sides at the accession of George the First. " His second brother, as he was now called, James Murray, or Marquis of Tullibardine, was a zealous supporter of the Hanoverian Government, although it proved no easy matter to engage his Clan in the same cause.

During many succeeding years, while Lord George Murray was serving abroad, cultivating those military acquirements which afterwards, whilst they failed to redeem his party from ruin, extorted the admiration of every competent judge, the progress of events was gradually working its way towards a second great attempt to restore the Stuarts.

Notwithstanding the apparent tranquillity of the Chevalier St. George, he had been continually though cautiously maintaining, during his residence at Albano, as friendly an intercourse with the English visitors to Rome as circumstances would permit. Most young men of family and condition travelled, during the time of peace, in Italy; many were thus the opportunities which occurred of conciliating these youthful scions of great and influential families. As one instance of this fact, the account given by Joseph Spence, the author of the "Anecdotes" and of "Polymetis, " affords a curious picture of the eagerness evinced by James and his wife, during the infancy of their son, to ingraft his infant image on the memory, and affections of the English. Mr. Spence visited Rome while Charles Edward was yet in his cradle. He was expressly enjoined by his father, before his departure from England, on no account to be introduced to the Chevalier. Yet such were the advances made to him, as his own letter[8] will show, that it was almost impossible for him to resist the overture: and similar overtures were made to almost every Englishman of family or note who visited Rome at that period.

In addition to these efforts, a continual correspondence was maintained between James and his Scottish adherents. The Chevalier's greatest accomplishment was his art of writing letters; and he appears eminently to have excelled in that power of conciliation which was so essential in his circumstance.

Meantime Charles grew up, justifying, as he increased in stature, and as his disposition revealed itself, the most ardent expectations of those who wished well to his cause. One failing he very early evinced; that remarkable devotion to certain favourites which marked the conduct of his ancestors; and the partiality was more commonly built upon the adulation bestowed by those favourites than founded in reason.

It was in the year 1741 that the royal youth, then scarcely nineteen years of age, became acquainted with a man whose qualities of mind, and attractions of manner, exercised a very considerable influence over his destiny; and whose character, pliant, yet bitter, intriguing and perfidious, came afterwards into a painful collision with the haughty overbearing temper, and manly sincerity, of Lord George Murray.

It was in consequence of the practice adopted by some of the hangers-on of the Chevalier's court, of luring young English or Scottish strangers to its circles, that John Murray of Broughton, afterwards Secretary to Prince Charles, was first introduced to the young Chevalier. Murray was the son of Sir David Murray, Bart., by his second wife, a daughter of Sir David Scott of Ancrum: he was at this time only twenty-three years of age, and he had lately completed his studies at Edinburgh, where he had gone through a course of philosophy, and studied the civil and municipal laws. The report which prevailed that Mr. Murray had been educated with the young Chevalier was untrue; it was by the desire of his mother, Lady Murray, that he first, in 1741, visited both France and Italy, and perfected himself in the language of those countries, then by no means generally attained by Scotchmen.

Mr. Murray had been brought up in the principles of the Episcopal Church, and therefore there was less reason, than there would have been in the case of a Roman Catholic, to apprehend his being beguiled into an intimate connection with the exiled Stuarts. He had not, however, been long in Rome before he was asked by an acquaintance whether he had seen the Santi Apostoli, as the palace of the Chevalier was called. On answering in the negative, he was assured that, through a knowledge of some of the servants, a sight might be obtained of the palace; and also of the Protestant chapel, in which, as Mr. Murray heard with great surprise, the Chevalier allowed service to be performed for such of the retinue of the young Prince as were of the Protestant persuasion. It was also alleged that this indulgence was with the cognizance of the Pope, who, in order to remove the barrier which prevented the Stuarts from enjoying the crown of England, was willing to allow Charles Edward to be brought up as a Protestant. This assertion was further confirmed by the fact, that the noblemen, Lord Inverness and Lord Dunbar, who had the charge of Charles Edward, were both Protestants; a choice on the part of James which had produced all that contention between himself and the Princess Clementina, with the details of which the Courts of Europe were entertained.

The family and retinue of the Chevalier St. George being then at Albano, Mr. Murray was able to gratify his curiosity, and to inspect the chapel, which had neither crucifix, confessional, nor picture in it, —only an altar, —and was not to be distinguished from an English chapel; and here English divines officiated. Here, it is said, whilst at his devotions, a slight accident occurred, which nourished a belief in presages in the mind of Charles Edward. A small piece of the ceiling, ornamented with flowers in fretwork, fell into his lap; it was discovered to be a thistle: soon afterwards, another of these ornaments became detached, and fell also into his lap; this proved to be a rose. Such omens, coupled with the star of great magnitude which astronomers asserted to have appeared at his nativity, were, it was thought, not without their effect on the hopes and conduct of the young Prince. One can hardly, however, do him so much injustice as to suppose that such could be the case.

Mr. Murray expressed, it is affirmed, a considerable degree of curiosity to see the Chevalier and his two sons, who were both highly extolled for their natural gifts and graces; the wish was communicated, and, acting upon the principle of attracting all comers to the Court, was soon realised: a page was sent, intimating that Mr. Murray's attendance would be well received, and he was, by an order from the Chevalier, graciously admitted to kiss hands. Such was the commencement of that acquaintance which afterwards proved so fatal to the interests of Prince Charles, and so disgraceful to the cause of the Jacobites. Such was the introduction of the young Prince to the man who subsequently betrayed his companions in misfortune. This step was shortly followed by an intimacy which, probably in the commencement, was grounded upon mutual good-will. Men become perfidious by slow degrees; and perform actions, as they advance in life, which they would blush to reflect on in the day-dawn of their honest youth.

This account is, however, derived from the statements of an anonymous writer, evidently an apologist for the errors of Mr. Murray, [9] and is contradicted so far as the sudden conversion of the young Scotchman to the cause of the Stuarts, by the fact that he had all his life been a violent Jacobite. [10] On the other hand, it is alleged by Mr. Murray's champion, that his feelings and affections, rather than his reason, were quickly engaged in the cause of the Chevalier, from his opportunities of knowing intimately the personal qualities of the two royal brothers, Charles Edward and Henry Benedict. He was, moreover, independent of circumstances; being in the enjoyment of a fortune of three or four hundred a year, which was considered a sufficient independence for a younger brother, and therefore interest, it is alleged, could not have been an inducement to his actions.

Whether from real admiration, or from a wish to disseminate in Scotland a favourable impression of the Stuart Princes, it is difficult to decide; but Mr. Murray, in 1742, dispatched to a lady in Scotland, who had requested him to describe personages of so great interest to the Jacobites, the following, perhaps, not exaggerated portrait of what Charles Edward was in the days of his youth, and before he had left the mild influence of his father's house.

"Charles Edward, the eldest son of the Chevalier de St. George is tall, above the common stature; his limbs are cast in the exact mould, his complexion has in it somewhat of an uncommon delicacy; all his features are perfectly regular, well turned, and his eyes the finest I ever saw; but that which shines most in him, and renders him without exception the most surprisingly handsome person of the age, is the dignity that accompanies his every gesture; there is, indeed, such an unspeakable majesty diffused throughout his whole mien and air, as it is impossible to have any idea of without seeing, and strikes those that do with such an awe, as will not suffer them to look upon him for any time, unless he emboldens them to it by his excessive affability.

"Thus much, madam, as to the person of this Prince. His mind, by all I can judge of it, is no less worthy of admiration; he seems to me, and I find to all who know him, to have all the good nature of the Stuart family blended with the spirit of the Sobieskys. He is, at least as far as I am capable of seeing into men, equally qualified to preside in peace and war. As for his learning, it is extensive beyond what could be expected from double the number of his years. He speaks most of the European languages with the same ease and fluency as if each of them were the only one he knew; is a perfect master of all the different kinds of Latin, understands Greek very well, and is not altogether ignorant of Hebrew; history and philosophy are his darling entertainments, in both which he is well versed; the *one* he says will instruct him how to govern *others*, and the *other* how to govern *himself*, whether in *prosperous* or *adverse* fortune. Then for his courage, that was sufficiently proved at the siege of Gaità, where though scarcely arrived at the age of fifteen, he performed such things as in attempting made his friends and his enemies alike tremble, though for different motives. What he is ordained for, we must leave to the Almighty, who alone disposes all; but he appears to be born and endowed for something very extraordinary. "[11]

It was not long before Mr. Murray perceived that, although James Stuart had given up all hopes of the English crown for himself, he still cherished a desire of regaining it for his son. Scotland was of course the object of all future attempts, according to the old proverb:

> "He that would England win,
> Must with Scotland first begin."

The project of an invasion, if not suggested by Murray, as has been stated, was soon communicated to him; and his credit attained to such an extent, that he was appointed by the Chevalier, at the request of Prince Charles, to be secretary for Scottish affairs. At the latter end of the year 1742 he was sent to Paris, where he found an emissary of the Stuarts, Mr. Kelly, who was negotiating in their behalf at the Court of France. Here Murray communicated with Cardinal Tencin, the successor of Cardinal Fleury, in the management of the affairs of the Chevalier, and here he met the exiled Marquis of Tullibardine, who, notwithstanding his losses and misfortunes in the year 1715, was still sanguine of ultimate success. Here, too, was the unfortunate Charles Radcliffe, who, with others once opulent, once independent, were now forced to submit to receive, with many indignities in the payment, pensions from the French Government. It was easy to inflame the minds of persons so situated with false hopes; and Murray is said to have been indefatigable in the prosecution of his scheme. After a delay of three weeks in Paris, he set off on that memorable undertaking to engage the Clans, which ultimately ended in the insurrection of 1745.

Lord George Murray, meantime, had returned to his native country, where he was presented to George the Second, and solicited, but ineffectually, a commission in the British army. This was refused, and the ardour in the Stuart cause, which we may presume to have wavered, again revived in its original vigour.

Previous to the Insurrection of 1745, Lord George Murray married Amelia, the only surviving child and heiress of James Murray of Glencarse and Strowan, a lady who appears, both from the terms of affection and respect expressed towards her by the Marquis of Tullibardine, and from the tenour of her own letters, to have coincided warmly in the efforts of her husband for the restoration of the Stuarts. [12] Five children were the issue of this marriage.

The course which public affairs were now taking checked, however, completely all hopes of domestic felicity. After several unsuccessful negotiations in Paris attempted by the agents of James Stuart, and in London by Lord Elcho, the scheme of invasion languished for some time. Whilst all was apparently secure, however, the metropolis was the scene of secret cabals and meetings of the Jacobites, sometimes at one place, sometimes at another; but unhappily for their cause, the party generally wanted compactness and discretion. "The little Jacobites, " as those who were not in the secret of these manoeuvres were called, began to flatter themselves that a large army would land in England from France that summer. Nor was it the policy of Government to check these reports, which strengthened the hands of the ministry, and procured a grant of the supplies with alacrity. The Jacobites, meantime, ran from house to house, intoxicated with their anticipated triumphs; and such chance of success as there might be was thus rendered abortive.

The year 1743 ended, however; and the visions of the Jacobites vanished into air. Donald Cameron of Lochiel, the elder, who visited Paris for the purpose of ascertaining what were the real intentions of the French cabinet, found that even the Cardinal Tencin did not think it yet time for the attempt, and he returned to Scotland disheartened. The death of the Cardinal Fleury in 1743 added to the discomfiture of his hopes. [13] Above all, the reluctance of the English Jacobites to pledge themselves to the same assurances that had been given by the Scotch, and their shyness in conversing with the people who were sent from France or Scotland on the subject, perplexed the emissaries who arrived in this country, and offered but a faint hope of their assistance from England.

But, in the ensuing year, the affairs of the Jacobites brightened; France, which had suspended her favours, once more encouraged and flattered the party. A messenger was dispatched to the palace of Albano, to acquaint the Chevalier that the day was now arrived when his views might be expected to prosper; whilst at the same time the utmost pains were taken by the French Government to appear to the English averse to the pretensions of James Stuart. It affords, indeed, another trait of the unfortunate tendency of the Stuart family to repose a misplaced confidence, that they should have relied on professions so hollow and so vague as those of France. But the dependent and desolate situation of that Prince may well be supposed to have blinded a judgment not ripened by any active participation in the general business of life, and narrowed within his little Court. Besides, there remained some who, after the conflict at Culloden was over, could even view the enterprise as having been by no means unauspicious. "Upon the whole, " writes Maxwell of Kirkconnel, "the conjuncture seemed favourable; and it is not to be wondered that a young Prince, naturally brave, should readily lay hold of it. There was a prospect of recalling his father from an exile nearly as long as his life, saving his country from impending ruin, and restoring both to the enjoyment of their rights."[14]

Great preparations were in fact actually made by the French Government for the invasion of Great Britain. The young Prince, who was forthwith summoned from Rome, was to land in the Highlands and head the Clans; Lord John Drummond, it was arranged, should make a descent on the southern part of the island, and endeavour to join the young Chevalier, and march towards Edinburgh. Twelve thousand French were to pour into Wales at the same time, under the command of a general who was never named, and to join such English insurgents as should rally to their assistance.

This scheme, had it been executed with promptness, might perhaps have prospered better than, in these later times, in the security of an undisturbed succession, we are inclined to allow. General discontents prevailed in England. The partiality which had been shown to the Hanoverian troops in preference to the English at the battle of Dettingen had irritated, if not alienated, the affections of the army. The King and the Duke of Cumberland were abroad, and a small number of ships only guarded the coast. Parliament was not sitting; and most of the members both of the Lords and Commons, and of the Privy Council, were at their country-seats. But the proper moment for the enterprise was lost by delays, and the same opportunity never again occurred.

Meantime, the young Prince who was to influence the destiny of so many brave men, accompanied by his brother, left Rome furtively, under pretext of going to hunt at Cisterna. A tender affection, cemented by their adversities, existed between James Stuart and his sons. As they parted from each other with tears and embracings, the gallant Charles Edward exclaimed, "I go to claim your right to three crowns: If I fail, " he added earnestly, "your next sight of me, sir, shall be in my coffin! " "My son, " exclaimed the Chevalier, "Heaven forbid that all the crowns in the world should rob me of my child! "[15] Mr. Murray of Broughton was present at this interview; the prelude to disasters and dangers to the ardent young man, and of anxieties and disappointments to his father, feelingly depicted in the Chevalier's touching letters to his children. [16]

By a stratagem the young Prince effected his journey from Rome without its becoming known, and eleven days after his departure from that city elapsed before it was made public. He was accompanied by Henry Benedict, who was at this time a youth of great promise. He is described as having had, as well as his brother, a very fine person, though somewhat shorter in stature than that ill-fated young man, and of a less delicate complexion. He seems to have been, perhaps, better constituted for the career of difficulty which Charles Edward encountered. He was of a robust form, with an unusual fire in his eyes. Whilst his brother united the different qualities of the Stuart and the Sobieski, Henry Benedict is said to have been more entirely actuated by the spirit of his great ancestor,

King John of Poland; by whom, and the handful of Christians whom he headed, a hundred and fifty thousand Turks were defeated. Even when only nine years of age, the high-spirited boy, whose martial qualities were afterwards subdued beneath the taming influence of a Cardinal's hat, resented the refusal of his father to allow him to accompany his brother to assist the young King of Naples in the recovery of his dominions; and could only be pacified by the threat of having his garter, the beloved insignia of English knighthood, taken from him as well as his sword. [17][18]

It soon became evident that the designs of France were not unknown at St. James's. The celebrated Chauvelin, Secretary of State to Louis the Fifteenth, had long been employing his influence over the Cardinal Fleury to counteract the wishes of the English. By a slight accident his designs were disclosed to Queen Caroline. Chauvelin had, unintentionally, among other papers, put into the hands of the Earl of Waldegrave, then ambassador in France, a letter from the Chevalier. Lord Waldegrave immediately sent it to Queen Caroline. This involved a long correspondence between Sir Robert Walpole and Waldegrave on the subject. "Jacobitism, " to borrow the language of Dr. Cox, "at this time produced a tremor through every nerve of Government; and the slightest incident that discovered any intercourse between the Pretender and France occasioned the most serious apprehensions. "[19] The spirit of insurrection and discontent had long pervaded not only the capital, which was disturbed by frequent tumults, but the country; and the murder of Porteous in Edinburgh, in 1736, was proved only to be the result of a regular systematic plan of resistance to the Government. [20]

The death of Queen Caroline deprived the oppressed Jacobites in both kingdoms of their only friend at Court. The unfortunate of all modes of faith met, indeed, with protection and beneficence from that excellent Princess. Those Roman Catholics, whose zeal for the Stuart cause had exposed them to the rigour of the law, were succoured by her bounty; large sums were sent by her to the indigent and ruined Jacobite families; and Sir Robert Walpole, who was greatly disturbed at this show of mercy to the delinquent party, truly exclaimed, "that the Jacobites had a ready access to the Queen by the backstairs, and that all attempts to suppress them would be ineffectual. "[21]

The last efforts of Walpole, then Lord Orford, were exerted to warn the country of the danger to be feared in that second invasion, for prognosticating which he had so often been severely ridiculed. He alluded to "the greatest power in Europe, which was setting up a Pretender to the throne; the winds alone having hindered an invasion and protected Britain. " He warned the Lords, that the rebellion which he anticipated would be "fought on British ground. " The memorable oration in which he unfolded these sentiments, which were delivered with great emotion, touched the heart of Frederic Prince of Wales; who arose, quitted his seat, and, taking Lord Orford by the hand, expressed his acknowledgments. [22] That warning was the last effort of one sinking under an excruciating disease, and to whose memory the tragedy of 1715 must still have been present.

Charles Edward, to whose ill-omened attempts to sail from Dunkirk, Walpole had thus alluded, had borne that disastrous endeavour with a fortitude which augured well for his future powers of endurance. Mr. Maxwell[23] thus describes his commencement of the voyage. "Most of the troops, " he says, "were already embarked, when a furious storm dispersed the ships of war, and drove the transports on the coast: the troops already embarked were glad to gain the shore, having lost some of their number. It is hardly possible to conceive a greater disappointment than that which the Prince met with on this occasion. How severely soever he might feel it, he did not seem dejected; on the contrary, he was in appearance cheerful and easy; encouraged such of his friends as seemed most deeply affected, telling them Providence would furnish him with other occasions of delivering his father's subjects, and making them happy. Immediately after this disaster the expedition was given up, and the Prince returned to Paris, where he lived incognito till he set out for Scotland. Not long after his return to Paris, war was declared betwixt France and England, which gave him fresh hopes that something would be undertaken. But after several months, seeing no appearance, he grew very impatient, and began to think of trying his fortune with such friends as would follow him: he was sick of the obscure way he was in; he thought himself neglected by the court of France, but could not bear the thoughts of returning to Rome. He had heard much of the loyalty and bravery of the Scotch Highlanders; but the number of those Clans he could depend upon was too inconsiderable to do anything effectual. While he was thus perplexed and fluctuating, John Murray of Broughton arrived from Scotland. "

In this emergency, the flattering representations of Murray of Broughton found a ready response in the young Prince's heart. Notwithstanding the assertions of that individual in his evidence at Lovat's trial, that he had used every means to dissuade the Prince from going to Scotland, [24] it is expressly stated by Mr. Maxwell, [25] that he "advised the Prince, in his own name, to come to Scotland at any rate; it was his opinion that the Prince should come as well provided and attended as possible, but rather come alone than delay coming; that those who had invited the Prince, and promised to join him if he came at the head of four or five thousand regular troops, would do the same if he came without any troops at all; in fine, that he had a very strong party in Scotland, and would have a very good chance of succeeding. This was more than enough to determine the Prince. The expedition was resolved upon, and Murray despatched to Scotland with such orders and instructions as were thought proper at that juncture. "

Mr. Murray may therefore be considered as in a great measure responsible for the event of that proceeding, which he afterwards denounced as a "desperate undertaking. " He found, unhappily, ready instruments in the unfortunate Marquis of Tullibardine, in Mr. Radcliffe, and others, whose fate he may thus be considered to have hastened by his alluring representations of the prospects of success.

When it was decided that Charles Edward should throw himself on the loyalty of the Clans, and intimation was given of the whole scheme, Lord George Murray prepared for action. The landing of the Prince, the erection of a standard at Glenfinnin, the march through Lochiel, and the encampment between Glengarry and Fort Augustus, were events which he did not personally aid by his presence. He was, indeed, busily employed in assembling his father's tenantry; and it was not until the Prince arrived at Perth that Lord George Murray was presented to him; he was almost immediately created a Lieutenant-General in the Prince's service. His power in the Highlands was, indeed, of a far greater extent than that military rank would seem to imply; for, although the Marquis of Tullibardine was the nominal commander in the North, to Lord George Murray was entrusted the actual management of affairs; an arrangement with which the modest and conscientious Tullibardine willingly complied.

The character of Lord George might be considered as partly sobered by time; since, at the commencement of the Rebellion of 1745, he was forty years of age. He was in the full vigour, therefore, of his great natural and intellectual powers, which, when at that period of life they have been ripened by exercise and experience, are perhaps at their zenith. The person of Lord George was tall and robust; he had the self-denial and energy of his countrymen. He slept little, and entered into every description of detail; he was persevering in everything which he undertook; he was vigilant, active, and diligent. To these qualities he united a natural genius for military operations; and his powers were such, that it was justly thought, that, had he been well instructed in military tactics, he would have formed one of the ablest generals of the day. As it was, the retreat from Derby, ill-advised as it may be deemed, is said to have sufficiently manifested his skill as a commander.

In addition to these attributes, Lord George was brave to the highest degree; and, in all engagements, was always the first to rush sword in hand into danger. As he advanced to the charge, and looked round upon the Highlanders, whose character he well understood, it was his practice to say, "I do not ask you, my lads, to go before; but only to follow me. "[26] It cannot be a matter of surprise, that, with this bold and resolute spirit, Lord George was the darling of the Highland soldiers; and that his strong influence over their minds should have enabled him to obviate, in some measure, the deficiencies of discipline. "Taking them, " as a contemporary writer asserts, "merely as they came from the plough, he made them perform prodigies of valour against English armies, always greatly superior in number to that of the Prince Charles Edward, although the English troops are allowed to be the best in Europe. " Thus endowed, Lord George Murray showed how feeble are the advantages of birth, compared with those of nature's gift. In rank, if not in family connections, and in an hereditary hold upon the affections of his countrymen, the Duke of Perth might be esteemed superior; but, brave and honourable as he was, that amiable nobleman could never obtain the confidence of the army as a general. It is not, however, to be supposed that any commander would ever have obtained an influence over a Highland army, if he had not added high birth to his other requisites. The Clansmen were especially aristocratic in their notions; and the names which they had honoured and loved from their birth, were alone those to which they would eagerly respond.

To counterbalance the fine, soldierly characteristics which graced the lofty and heroic Lord George Murray, some defects, of too stern a nature to be called weaknesses, but yet indicative of narrowness of mind, clouded his excellent qualities. Unlike most great men, he was not open to conviction. That noble candour, which can bear counsels, or receive even admonition with gratitude, was not a part of his haughty nature. A sense of superiority over every human being rendered him impatient of the slightest controul, and greedy of exclusive power. He was imperious and determined; and was deficient in the courtesy which forms, combined with honesty, so fine an attribute in a soldier's bearing. "He wanted, " says one who knew him well, "the sole ordering of everything. "[27]

At Perth, Lord George Murray met with the famous Chevalier Johnstone, whom he soon adopted into his service. This young soldier, whose pen has supplied memoirs of the Rebellion of 1745, and upon whose statements much of the reported merits of Lord George Murray rests, was the only son of a merchant in Edinburgh, and the descendant of an ancient and well-connected family. By the marriage of his sister he was nearly related to the House of Rollo; and, from these and other circumstances, he mingled with the best society in his native city.

Having been educated in Jacobite and Episcopalian principles, young Johnstone hailed with delight the arrival of Prince Charles: he resolved instantly to join his standard. Escaping from Edinburgh, he hastened to Duncrub, the seat of Lord Rollo, near Perth. Here he awaited the arrival of the young Chevalier; and here he was introduced by his cousins, the daughters of Lord Rollo, to the Duke of Perth and to Lord George Murray. The Chevalier Johnstone was one of the first Low-countrymen that joined the standard of Charles Edward.

Lord George Murray very soon discovered that the requisites for forming a good soldier and an active partizan were centred in young Johnstone. For the former he was qualified by an open and impetuous character, generally combined with a desperate courage. The jollity and licence of the Cavalier school, which characterized Johnstone, did not materially detract from, but added rather to the popularity of his character. As a partizan, he has proved his zeal by his Memoirs, which afford a sample of much heat and prejudice, and which have, in upholding Lord George Murray, done an injury to the memory of Charles Edward, of which the adversaries of his cause have not failed to take advantage. To many errors of character, and to some egotism, the Chevalier Johnstone, as he came to be called in after-life, united a kind heart and an enthusiastic disposition. He acted for a considerable time as aide-de-camp to Lord George Murray, and afterwards in the same capacity with the Prince. But his liveliest admiration appears to have been directed towards the general who has been classed with Montrose and Dundee, [28] and no subsequent service under other masters ever effaced his impression of respect and confidence to Lord George Murray. After the battle of Preston-Pans Johnstone received a captain's commission from the Prince: and, exhausted with his duties as aide-de-camp, he formed a company, with which he joined the Duke of Perth's regiment. His history, mingled up as it is with that of the General under whom he first served, must necessarily be incorporated with the following narrative.

Lord George Murray continued, for some time, busily engaged in rallying around him his brother's vassals. The Duke of Atholl is partly proprietor, partly superior, of the country which bears his name. That region is inhabited by Stuarts and Robinsons, none of the Duke's name living upon his estates. Of these, several have fiefs or mortgages of the Atholl family, and command the common people of their respective Clans; but, like other Highlanders, they believe that they are bound to rise in arms when the chief of their whole Clan requires it. The vassals on the Atholl territory were well-affected to the Stuarts, great pains having been taken by the father of Lord George Murray, notwithstanding his efforts to appear loyal to the Government, to infuse the spirit of Jacobitism among them. [29]

Of the events which succeeded his joining the Prince's standard at Perth, until the commencement of the retreat from Derby, Lord George Murray has left a succinct relation. It is written, as are his letters, in a plain, free, manly style, which dispels all doubt as to the sincerity of the narrator.

"I joined the standard at Perth, "[30] he begins, "the day his Royal Highness arrived there. As I had formerly known something of a Highland army, the first thing I did was to advise the Prince to endeavour to get proper people for provisors and commissaries, for otherwise there would be no keeping the men together, and they would straggle through the whole country upon their marches if it was left to themselves to find provisions; which, beside the inconveniency of irregular marches, and much time lost, great abuses would be committed, which, above all things, we were to avoid. I got many of the men to make small knapsacks of sacking before we left Perth, to carry a peck of meal each upon occasion; and I caused take as many threepenny loaves there as would be three days' bread to our small army, which was carried in carts. I sent about a thousand of these knapsacks to Crieff, to meet the men who were coming from Atholl. "

The difficulties which Lord George encountered were, it is evident, considerable. Upon the arrival of Charles Edward at Perth, his army amounted only to two thousand men, [31] until he was joined by Lord George Murray, by the Duke of Perth, and by Lord Nairn, and other persons of distinction. [32] There were few persons in that army who were capable, by being versed in military affairs, of giving Lord George Murray any advice or assistance. The Highland chiefs possessed the most heroic courage; but they knew no other manoeuvre but that of rushing, sword in hand, upon an enemy. The Irish officers were equally deficient in experience and knowledge; and, with the exception of Mr. Sullivan, are stated "to have had no more knowledge than the whole stock of subalterns, namely, the knowing how to mount and quit guard. " Such is the description given of the collected forces by Johnstone. But, although not trained as regular soldiers, and accustomed chiefly to the care of herds of black cattle, whom they wandered after in the mountains, the Highlanders had a discipline of their own. Their chiefs usually kept about them several retainers experienced in the use of arms; and a meeting of two or three gentlemen was sure to bring together a little army, for the habits of the clansmen were essentially military. It was, some considered, a circumstance favourable to Lord George Murray, that, being unprepared by an early military education, he was unfettered by its formal rules, and therefore was more calculated to lead an undisciplined army of Highlanders, whose native energies he knew how to direct better than a skilful tactician would have ventured to do. [33] During his stay at Perth, the Highlanders, so prone to irregularities when not in active service, were tranquil under the strictest military rule. [34]

It was here, however, that the first seeds of dissension were sown between Charles Edward and Lord George. Sir Thomas Sheridan, the tutor of the Prince, who was allowed to "have lived and died a man of honour, " but who was manifestly incapable of the great charge intrusted to him, both in the education of the young Princes and as their adviser in after-life, added to his other deficiencies a total ignorance of the British constitution and habits of thinking. The Prince, of course, was equally ill-informed. They were therefore in the practice, in conversation, of espousing sentiments of arbitrary power, which were equally impolitic and unbecoming. Sincere and shrewd, Lord George Murray lost no time in expressing to Charles Edward his decided disapproval of this tone of discourse. His motives in these expostulations were excellent, but his overbearing manner nullified all the good that might have been effected. He offended the Prince, who repressed indeed his secret indignation, but whose pride, fostered by circumstances, could ill brook the assumption of his General. [35]

It was not until the Prince reached Edinburgh that a regular Council was formed; consisting of the Duke of Perth, Lord George Murray, Lord Elcho, Secretary Murray, Sir Thomas Sheridan, and Mr. Sullivan, the Highland chiefs, and afterwards of all the colonels in the army. But, among the advisers of the Prince, an "ill-timed emulation, " as Mr. Maxwell calls it, now crept in, and bred great dissension and animosities. "The dissensions, " he states, "began at Edinburgh: " according to Sir Walter Scott, they had an earlier origin, and originated at Perth.

They were aggravated, as in the Council at Perth in the time of Lord Mar, by the base passions of an individual. Detesting the weak and crooked policy of Mar and viewing from his calm position as an inferior actor, with a fiendish pleasure, the embarrassments and mistakes of him whom he hated, stood the Master of Sinclair. Blinded by a selfish jealousy of power over the mind of him whom he afterwards betrayed to the ruin which he was working, and "aiming at nothing less than the sole direction and management of everything, the Secretary Murray sacrificed to this evil passion, this thirst for ascendancy, all the hopes of prosperity to Charles Edward—all present peace to the harassed and perplexed young man whom his counsels had brought to Scotland. It was he, " strongly, and perhaps bitterly, writes Mr. Maxwell, "that had engaged the Prince to make this attempt upon so slight a foundation, and the wonderful success that had hitherto attended it was placed to his account. "

By some the sincerity of Murray's loyalty and good-faith were even credited. The Duke of Perth, among a few others, judged of Murray's heart by his own, went readily into all his schemes, and confirmed the Prince in the opinion which he had imbibed of his favourite. After Kelly had left the Prince, Murray contrived to gain over Sullivan and Sir Thomas Sheridan, and by that means effectually governed Charles Edward. The fearless, lofty, honest character of Lord George Murray alone offered an obstacle to the efforts of the Secretary to obtain, for his own purposes, an entire controul; he cherished towards the General that aversion which a mean and servile nature ever feels to one whose dealings are free from fraud or deceit. He also feared him as a rival, and it became his aim to undermine him, and to lay a plot for the chief stay and prop of the undertaking. It was naturally to be supposed that Lord George Murray's age, his high birth, his experience and influence, and his great capacity, would have given him an advantage over his dastardly rival, and have gained the first consideration with the Prince. But Murray of Broughton, unhappily, had acquired an early influence over the credulous mind of the young adventurer. His acquaintance beneath the roof of the Santi Apostoli had secured an unhappy confidence in his fidelity and worth. He shortly took advantage of the sentiments which ought to have ensured the nicest honour, the most scrupulous truth, in return, to deceive and to mislead his young master. [36]

Unfortunately there was one point upon which the honour of Lord George Murray was to be suspected. He "*was said*" to have solicited a commission in the English army. [37] Upon this supposed early defection of Lord George to the Hanoverian party, Murray grounded his accusations.

"He began by representing Lord George as a traitor to the Prince; he assured him that he had joined on purpose to have an opportunity of delivering him up to Government. It was hardly possible to guard against this imposture. The Prince had the highest opinion of his Secretary's integrity, and knew little of Lord George Murray. So the calumny had its full effect. Lord George soon came to know the suspicion the Prince had of him, and was affected, as one may easily imagine; to be sure, nothing could be more shocking to a man of honour, and one that was now for the third time venturing his life and fortune for the royal cause. The Prince was partly undeceived by Lord George's gallant behaviour at the battle; and, had Lord George improved that opportunity, he might perhaps have gained the Prince's favour, and get the better of the Secretary: but his haughty and overbearing manner prevented a thorough reconciliation, and seconded the malicious insinuations of his rival. "

Another anecdote is related, on the authority of Murray of Broughton: On the tenth of October the Chevalier issued a manifesto, dated from Holyrood House. This document is acknowledged, even by the opposite party, to have been remarkably well written: [38] but it was not completed without some heart-burnings, arising from the distrust of many members of the Kirk, who conceived that it did not contain assurances for the security of their manner of Divine worship. A grand council was therefore held, concerning the alterations which were necessary to conciliate the good opinion of the Presbyterians. Mr. Kelly, who had drawn up the manifesto, was very tenacious of his performance; but the majority of those who were present were of opinion that the manifesto would prosper better if a promise of putting the penal laws against Papists into effect were added to it. Upon this proposition the young Chevalier was observed to change countenance, doubtless reflecting that it would be ungrateful to depress those who had been such real friends to his father. He had, however, the prudence to say but little, and to maintain a neutral position during the debate, which was carried on with much bitterness on both sides of the question. It is remarkable that the Duke of Perth, Sullivan, and O'Neil, who were all Papists, voted for the addition; whilst many who were of the Reformed Church opposed it. Amongst these was Lord George Murray, who, starting up and turning to Charles Edward, exclaimed, with an oath, "Sir, if you permit this article to be inserted, you will lose five hundred thousand friends; " meaning that there were that number of Papists in England. On this, the Prince arose from his chair and withdrew, offended, as it was thought, by the vehemence and overbearing advice of Lord George. As he left the room, he said, "I will have it decided by a majority. " But the freedom with which he had been treated appears to have rankled in his mind. The additional clause was negatived, and the manifesto remained in the same state as when it came from Mr. Kelly's hands. [39]

There were, indeed, times when Lord George endeavoured to retrieve mistakes of which he was conscious, and upon some occasions he subdued his lofty temper so far as to be "very obsequious and respectful, but had not temper to go through with it. " "He now and then broke into such violent sallies as the Prince could not digest, though the situation of his affairs forced him to bear with them. [40] The Secretary's station and favour had attached to him such as were confident of success, and had nothing in view but making their fortunes. Nevertheless, Lord George had greater weight and influence in the Council, and generally brought the majority over to his opinion; which so irritated the ambitious

Secretary, that he endeavoured to give the Prince a bad impression of the Council itself, and engaged to lay it entirely aside. "

It was not only in regard to Lord George Murray that the influence of the Secretary was prejudicial to the Prince's interests; neither was Lord George the only person whom he dreaded as a rival. Having access to the most intimate communication with Charles Edward, he abused the youth and inexperience of the ill-fated man to inspire him with a distrust of many gentlemen of good family and of integrity, whose fidelity he contrived to whisper away. All employments were filled up at the Secretary's nomination; and he contrived to bestow them upon his own creatures, who would never thwart his measures. Hence it followed that places of trust were bestowed on "insignificant little fellows, " while there were abundance of gentlemen of merit who might have been of great use, had they met with the confidence of their Prince. "Those that Murray had thus placed, " continues Mr. Maxwell, "seconded his dirty little views; and it was their interest, too, to keep their betters at a distance from the Prince's person and acquaintance. "

Until a very short time before Charles Edward left Perth, he appears to have felt the most unqualified admiration for the Highland character, which he had carefully studied. [41] He thus expressed himself to his father: "I have occasion every day to reflect on your Majesty's last words to me, —that I should find power, if tempered with justice and clemency, an easy thing to myself, and not grievous to those under me. 'Tis owing to the observance of this rule, and to my conformity to the customs of these people, that I have got their hearts, to a degree not easy to be conceived by those who do not see it. One who observes the discipline which I have established, would take my little army to be a body of picked veterans; and, to see the love and harmony that reigns amongst us, he would be apt to look upon it as a large well-ordered family, in which every one loves another better than himself. "

He even applauded the rude climate of Scotland. "I keep my health better in these wild mountains than I used to do in the Campagna Felice; and sleep sounder, lying on the ground, than I used to do in the palaces at Rome. "

In this happy temper the Prince set out on his march from Perth to Edinburgh. The march was made in the most perfect good order, and the strictest discipline prevented any depredations. As the insurgent army passed by Stirling, the standard of the Chevalier was saluted by some shot from the castle. Nevertheless, Lord George Murray sent into the town, and the gates were opened; and bread, cheese, and butter sent out to sell, near to Bannockburn, where the army halted. On the seventeenth of September the city of Edinburgh was taken.

In the description of the courtly scenes of Holyrood, it does not appear that Lord George Murray took any conspicuous part. His sphere was the council-room, or the camp, or the battle-field; and of his proceedings in these different occupations he has left a very particular account, written with the same manly spirit and fearless tone which he displayed in ordinary life.

When the Prince's Council had received accounts of Sir John Cope's landing at Dunbar, they left Edinburgh and lay upon their arms at Duddingstone, and on the twentieth marched to meet the enemy. Lord George commanded the van, and, whilst passing the south side of Pinkie Gardens, he heard that Cope was at or near Preston, and that he would probably gain the high ground at Fawside. There was no time to deliberate or to wait for orders. Well acquainted with the ground, Lord George struck off through the fields, without keeping to any road. He went without being even preceded by the usual escort to choose the ground where to halt. In less than half an hour, by marching quickly, he gained the eminence; he slackened his pace and waited for the rear, still proceeding slowly towards Tranent, always fronting the enemy. General Cope's army was drawn up on the plain between Preston Grange and Tranent, with deep broad ditches between them. After much reconnoitring and some firing, on the part of the enemy, from these ditches, at the Highlanders, who they thought had never seen cannon, and would therefore be intimidated, the English army was drawn up on the east side of the village of Tranent, where, on a dry stubble-field, with a small rising in front to shelter them, they lay down to repose in rank and file.

"It was now night, " writes Lord George Murray; [42] "and when all the principal officers were called together, I proposed the attacking the enemy at break of day. I assured them that it was not only practicable, but that it would, in all probability, be attended with success. I told them I knew the ground myself, and had a gentleman or two with me who knew every part thereabouts: there was indeed a small defile at the east end of the ditches, but, once that was past, there would be no stop; and though we should be long on our march, yet, when the whole line was past the defile, they had nothing to do but to face to the left, and in a moment the whole was formed, and then to attack. The Prince was highly pleased with the proposal, as indeed the whole officers were; so, after placing a few pickets, everybody lay down at their posts; and supped upon what they had with them. At midnight the principal officers were called again, and all was ordered as was at first proposed. Word was sent to the Atholl brigade to come off their post at two in the morning, and not to make the least noise. "

Before four in the morning the army began to march, and an arrangement of the first line, which had been previously agreed upon, was now put into execution. Those who had had the right the day before, were to have the rear and the left; and this alteration was made without the least noise or confusion. The Duke of Perth therefore went into the front, Lord George giving up his guides to him. No horse marched at that time, for fear of being discovered. When the army had advanced within a hundred paces of the ditches, they marched on to the attack, Lord George calling on Cameron of Lochiel to incline to the left. As the enemy discovered their approach, the noise of the cannon announced that the engagement had begun. Notwithstanding that Lord George Murray's regiment was the last to pass the defile towards the enemy, it was the first to fire. "Our whole first line, " writes the gallant soldier, "broke through the enemy. Some of them were rallying behind us; but when they saw our second line coming up, they then made the best of their way. "

Lord George pursued the enemy to the walls of Bankton House, the residence of Colonel Gardiner; and here a party of the enemy got over the ditch, and fired at the Highland foe. This little company, brave as it was, was composed of only fourteen men, headed by a Lieutenant-Colonel. "I got before a hundred of our men, " writes Lord George, "who had their guns presented to fire upon them, and at my desire they kept up their fire, so that those officers and soldiers surrendered themselves prisoners; and nothing gave me more pleasure that day than having it in my power to save those men, as well as several others. " This declaration was perhaps necessary, to rescue the memory of Lord George from the opprobrium of cruelty; since it has been asserted, that at the battle of Culloden he issued orders to give no quarter, and that such a document to that effect, in the handwriting of Lord George, was in the possession of the Duke of Cumberland. [43] This stigma on the fame of Lord George Murray may have originated from the desperate character of that last effort: his haughty temper may have been exasperated in the course of the fatal contest. It is a charge which can now only be repelled by the previous character of the individual against whom it is made, since it was never fairly made out, nor satisfactorily contradicted.

After the action was partially over, Lord George Murray perceived that a number of people were gathered together on the height near to Tranent. Mistaking them for the enemy, the General marched with his regiment, accompanied by Lochiel, who had kept his men together in good order, back to the narrow causeway that led up to Tranent. Here he found that the supposed enemy were only country-people and servants. From them, however, he learned that the enemy were at Cokenny, only a mile and a half distant; and he instantly determined on pursuing them. His energy and valour in thus doing so, after the events of that harassing and exhausting day, cannot but be admired. He found on arriving at Cokenny, a force of about three hundred Highlanders, a volunteer company recently embodied at Inverness by President Forbes. These soon surrendered; between sixteen and seventeen hundred prisoners were taken that day, among whom were seventy officers. [44] "His Royal Highness, " adds Lord George Murray in giving this his personal narrative, "took the same care of their wounded as of his own. I do not mention the behaviour of all our officers and men that day; their actions shewed it. I only take notice of those two that were immediately under my eye, which was Lochiel's regiment and the Stewarts of Appin. " As the enemy's foot-soldiers had made little or no resistance during the battle of Preston-Pans, they might have been all cut to pieces had it not been for the interposition of Prince Charles and his officers, who gained that day as much honour by their humanity as by their bravery. The Prince, when the rout began, mounted his horse, galloped all over the field, and his voice was heard amid that scene of horror, calling on his men to spare the lives of his enemies, "whom he no longer looked upon as such. " Far from being elated with the victory, which was considered as complete, the care of the kind-hearted and calumniated young man was directed to assist the wounded. Owing to his exertions, eighty-three of the officers were saved, besides hundreds of soldiers. "The Prince, " writes Mr. Maxwell, "had a livelier sense of other people's misfortunes than of his own good-fortune. "

This spirit of humanity was extended to the two Lieutenants-General. The conduct of the Duke of Perth was ever consistent with his mild character. On that occasion, at all events, Lord George participated in the noble clemency which usually characterized the Jacobites.

"In the evening, " he writes, [45] "I went with the officer prisoners to a house in Musselburgh that was allotted for them. Those who were worst wounded were left at Colonel Gardiner's house, where surgeons attended them; the others walked, as I did, along with them without a guard (as they had given me their parole); and to some, who were not able to walk, I gave my own horses. It was a new-finished house that was got for them, where there was neither table, bed, chair, nor chimney grate. I caused buy some new-thrashed straw, and had by good-fortune as much cold provisions and liquor of my own as made a tolerable meal to them all; and when I was going to retire, they entreated me not to leave them; for, as they had no guard, they were afraid that some of the Highlanders, who had got liquor, might come in upon them and insult or plunder them. "

Beside these suffering men Lord George lay on a floor all night, having given up the minister's house in Musselburgh, which had been destined as his quarters, to those who were valetudinary. On the following day those officers who were tolerably well were removed to Pinkie House, where Prince Charles was staying. Lord George then returned to the field of battle, to give directions about the cannon, and to see about the other wounded prisoners. He afterwards repaired to Pinkie House, the gardens of which were thronged that night with the prisoners, privates, to whom provisions were sent; "and the night before, " as Lord George relates, "I got some of their own provisions carried from Cokenny to Colonel Gardiner's courts and gardens for their use. In these things I ever laid it down as a maxim, to do by others as I would wish they would do by me, had I been in their place, and they in mine. " Such is the spirit in which the unfortunate were regarded by the victors of that day; and these two accounts, that of Lord George Murray and that of Maxwell of Kirkconnel, written without any mutual compact, and at different times, and even in different countries, disprove the following gross and improbable statement of Henderson's of that which occurred after the day at Preston was fought and won.

According to his account, professedly that of an eye-witness, the conduct of the young Chevalier (who, he acknowledges, had, by the advice of the Duke of Perth, sent to Edinburgh for surgeons,) was, in the highest degree, unfeeling and indecent. He stood by the road-side, his horse near him, "with his armour of tin, which resembled a woman's stays, affixed to the saddle; he was on foot, clad as an ordinary captain, in a coarse plaid, and large blue bonnet, a scarlet waistcoat with a narrow plain lace about it; his boots and knees were much dirtied (the effect of his having fallen into a ditch, as I afterwards understood); he was exceeding merry, and twice said, 'My Highlanders have lost their plaids, ' at which he laughed very heartily, being in no way affected when speaking of the dead or wounded. Nor would his jollity have been interrupted, if he had not looked upon seven standards that had been taken from the dragoons; on which he said, in French, (a language he frequently spoke in,) 'We have missed some of them. ' After this, he refreshed himself upon the field, and, with the utmost composure, ate a piece of cold beef and drank a glass of wine, amidst the deep and piercing groans of the poor men who had fallen victims to his ambition. "[46]

After this flippant and hard-hearted conduct, as it is described, the Prince is said to have ridden off to Pinkie House, leaving the bulk of the wounded on the field that day, to be brought in carts to Edinburgh. "Few, " he says, "recovered; and those who did, went begging through the streets, their heads tied about with bandages, but obtaining no relief from their conquerors. The property of the prisoners, the fine linen of the officers, their gold and silver hilted swords, their watches and rings, were worn by the lowest among the soldiery almost before their eyes. "[47]

The battle of Preston, which was magnified by Lord Lovat as a "glorious victory not to be paralleled in history, " although not meriting such extravagant remarks, produced the most important consequences to the Jacobite cause. Among not the least important was the acquisition of all the arms of the whole body of foot, and even of the volunteers. These went to supply the recruits whom the Marquis of Tullibardine and others were sending daily to the camp. No enemy was left in the field to oppose the progress of Charles Edward's victorious troops. [48] When, having, as the Chevalier Johnstone asserts, escaped from the field of battle by placing a white cockade on his head, Cope arrived at Coldstream with his troops in great disorder, he was greeted by Lord Mark Ker, one of a family who had long had hereditary claims to wit as well as courage, with the bitter remark, that "he believed he was the first general in Europe that had brought tidings of his own defeat. "

"The Prince, " writes Maxwell of Kirkconnel, "was now, properly speaking, master of Scotland. " The militia, which had been raised in some parts of Scotland for the service of Government, was dismissed; and the Chevalier's orders were obeyed in many places far from his army. These advantages were, however, rather glaring than solid and permanent.

After the battle of Preston, it became a serious and important question what step was to be taken. It was the Prince's earnest desire to push the advantages thus gained by an immediate invasion of England, before the Hanoverians had time to recover from their surprise. But this spirited and, as the event proved, sagacious opinion was objected to on the score of the smallness of the forces, and the probability of an accession of strength before marching southwards. Lastly, the fatal hope of aid from France, that *ignis fatuus* which had misled the Jacobite party before, and on which it was their misfortune to depend, was adduced as an argument. The Prince yielded to his counsellors, and consented to remain some time in Edinburgh. Upon this decision Lord George Murray offers no opinion.

The castle of Edinburgh remained still unsubdued; and the Prince, upon his return to that city, resolved on blockading the fortress. This was a very unpopular step, but Charles had no alternative; since it was of vital importance to reduce a place of so great strength and consequence. Accordingly a proclamation was issued, forbidding, under pain of death, that any provisions should be sent up to the castle; and the management of this blockade was entrusted to Lord George Murray. [49]

This able General now proposed to place guards in such a manner as should prevent the garrison in the castle marching out to surprise him, but his exertions were baffled by the want of judgment and incompetency of those beneath him in command. The guard was placed near the weigh-house at the foot of the Castle-rock, so that the battery of the half-moon, as it was termed, near the Castle-gate, bore upon it, and many of the guard within would have perished upon the first firing. This was not the only mistake. Mr. O'Sullivan, one of Prince Charles's officers, one day placed a small guard near the West Kirk, which was not only exposed to the enemy's fire, but conveniently situated near the sally-port, whence the besieged might issue and take the party there prisoners; for no relief could be sent to them in less than two hours' time, owing to its being necessary to pass round the whole circumference of the castle to arrive at that point. "I never, " says Lord George Murray, "knew of that guard's being placed there, until they were taken prisoners. " So severe a service was this blockade, that it was found necessary to relieve the guards, which were thus placed, by different corps who could not know the risk which they encountered. Desertions from the Jacobite army were among the most formidable evils with which Lord George had to contend. It was therefore important not to discourage the soldiery. In the midst of difficulty the high-minded Cameron of Lochiel came forward to offer his own person, and to risk his own regiment in this service. He agreed to take all the guards, and to relieve them with the soldiers of his own regiment, who were quartered for that purpose in the outer Parliament House. "I was with him, " writes Lord George, [50] "when the guards were relieved, and the men did their duty exceedingly, especially when there was danger; and, when the fire was hottest from the castle, they kept their post with much resolution and bravery. Lochiel and I being much with them, gave them a heartiness that hindered them from complaining of a duty which was so hard, and which the rest of the army had not in their turns. We even placed new guards to keep the castle from sallying, as they seemed disposed; and Keppoch's regiment was brought into town to take some of the guards and support them. I lay in town for some nights, and was constantly visiting the guards and sentinels. "

The castle, nevertheless, seated on the precipitous rocks, which, steep as they are, have yet been "scaled by love and ambition, "[51] defied the blockaders. The Highlanders continued to keep guard in the weigh-house, and, stationing themselves in the Grass-market, the Smithfield as well as the Hay-market of Edinburgh, lying on the south side of the Castle-hill, awaited there the proceedings of the enemy.

On the twenty-ninth of September, a letter was sent to the Provost of Edinburgh by General Guest, intimating, that, unless a communication were kept up between the city and the castle, he should be under the necessity of using cannon to dislodge the Highlanders. It was said that Guest had an order from the Government, signed by the Marquis of Tweedale, empowering him to lay the city in ashes if the citizens did not remove the Highlanders from their quarters. A message was dispatched from the Provost to General Guest obtaining a respite for that night; but, meantime, the utmost consternation prevailed in the town. Twelve o'clock at night was the hour fixed upon for the execution of this threat of the enemy; and, although many who reasoned did not believe in the existence of the order, the lower classes were seized with a panic, and the streets were crowded with women and children running towards the gates, and with people removing their property to more secure quarters. When the clocks struck twelve, the hour fixed in General Guest's message, the noise of the cannon was heard firing upon the principal streets; but the Highlanders were all under shelter, and only a few poor inhabitants were injured. Nothing was heard except imprecations on that Government which had issued so cruel an order, since it was quite out of the power of the citizens to dislodge the Highlanders from their quarters. But the firing was soon intermitted; and whether the garrison had private orders only to threaten, or whether they found it impossible to execute so barbarous an order, is unknown. They spared the city generally, and only directed their fire to any place where they fancied that they saw a Highlander.

On the following morning a deputation of citizens waited on the Chevalier, and showed him General Guest's letter. He immediately replied, that he was surprised and concerned at the barbarity of the order, but that if, out of compassion for the city, he were to remove his guards, the castle might with equal reason summon him to quit the town, and abandon all the advantages of which he was possessed. A respite of a day was afterwards obtained; and subsequently for six days, in case the Highlanders would abstain from firing at the castle; and a dispatch to London was sent to obtain a mitigation of the order in council.

Meantime, on the first of October, the Highlanders fired; whether at some people who were carrying provisions to the castle, or at the castle itself, is uncertain. Reprisals were instantly made by a heavy cannonading and small shot. The firing continued for some days, bringing terror to the hearts of those who lived remote from the scene of danger; whilst the aged and infirm were carried out of that noble city, thus threatened with destruction. Sir Walter Scott observes, that the generation of his own time alone can remember Edinburgh in peace, undisturbed by civil commotion. The fathers of that generation remembered the days of 1745—*their* fathers the disturbances of 1715. The fathers of those who had witnessed the rebellion of 1715 could remember the revolution of 1688.

The merciful temper of the young Chevalier saved the city of Edinburgh. At first he resolved to continue the blockade; and he renewed his former orders, prohibiting any person from going to the castle without a pass from his secretary, and threatening any one who was disobedient to this proclamation with instant death. But, when he beheld the distress to which the firing had already reduced the city, —then, let it be remembered, comprised within boundaries of very moderate extent, —he issued another proclamation, expressing his deep concern for the many murders which were committed upon the innocent inhabitants of the city, so contrary to the laws of war, to the truce granted to the city, and even exceeding the powers given. His humanity had, therefore, yielded to the barbarity of his enemy; the blockade of the castle was taken off, and the threatened punishment suspended. [52]

The army of Charles Edward was now increasing daily; and, in consequence of the reports which were circulated in the metropolis, a panic spread there, of which no estimate can be made without consulting the newspapers of that time. Among other writers who employed their talents in inveighing against the cause of James Stuart, was the celebrated Henry Fielding, whose papers in the *True Patriot* upon the subject present a curious insight into those transient states of public feeling, which perished almost as soon as expressed. The rapidity of the progress made by the insurgents is declared by his powerful pen to have been unprecedented. "Can History, " he writes, "produce an instance parallel to this, —of six or seven men landing in a powerful nation, in opposition to the inclination of the people, in defiance of a vast and mighty army? (For, though the greater part of this army was not then in the kingdom, it was so nearly within call, that every man of them might, within the compass of a few days, or weeks at farthest, have been brought home and landed in any part of it.) If we consider, I say, this handful of men landing in the most desolate corner, among a set of poor, naked, hungry, disarmed slaves, abiding there with impunity till they had, as it were, in the face of a large body of his Majesty's troops collected a kind of army, or rather rabble, together, it will be extremely difficult to assign any adequate cause whatsoever, for this unexampled success, without recurring to one, of whose great efficacy we have frequent instances in sacred history: I mean, the just judgment of God against an offending people. " The state of public morals, Fielding considers, to have drawn down upon society this signal visitation of Providence. "Indeed, such monstrous impieties and iniquities have I both seen and heard of, within these last three years, during my sojourning in what is called the world, particularly the last winter, while I tarried in the great city, that, while I verily believe we are the silliest people under Heaven in every other light, we are wiser than Sodom in wickedness. "[53] The consternation of the sister kingdom had now, indeed, become general; on the slightest report of foreign ships being seen in the Downs, the dismay of the London citizens was extreme: and such was the liberality, or such were the fears of the inhabitants of the county of York, the capital of which may almost have been deemed, in those days, a northern metropolis, that forty thousand pounds were subscribed for its defence, after a grave and mournful address of the archbishop of that diocese. [54]

When the Prince had determined to take off the blockade, and indeed had actually resolved to evacuate Edinburgh and to march southwards, he sent orders to Lord George Murray to nail the cannon upon the city walls, and to retire to Musselburgh and Dalkeith. But the sagacious Lord George, apprehending no further cannonading from the castle, begged permission not to make a precipitate retreat, and obtained leave to continue three weeks longer in Edinburgh, during which time the town remained in a much quieter state than it had been heretofore.

Whilst Lord George Murray was quartered in Edinburgh, he communicated frequently with his wife, the Lady Emilia, who remained with her children at Tullibardine. That lady seems to have taken a deep interest in the events which so deeply concerned her family. She was the first to communicate to the Marquis of Tullibardine the intelligence of the victory of Preston-Pans. "I pray God, " she says in her postscript, "to prosper his Royal Highness's arms, and congratulate your Grace upon his happy success. " A gentleman, who had seen her husband after the battle, had brought to the anxious wife the tidings of his success.

Towards the end of October the Prince resolved to march into England, without waiting any longer for the landing of French auxiliaries, or even for the arrival of the friendly Clans of Frasers and Mackintoshes, who were ready to march from the north to join Charles Edward. By some of the Chevalier's advisers he was recommended to go to Berwick; but this was a scheme counteracted by the counsels of Lord George Murray, who, in the presence of the principal officers, represented it as "a thing at least of great difficulty, and of not so great use as to lose time, which is precious. "

Lord George therefore proposed marching into England by the other road; but, to conceal their design, he advised that the army should be divided into three columns; one to go by Kelso, the second by Moffat, and a third by Galashiels, Selkirk, and Hawick; so that all the columns should join on an appointed day near Carlisle. The plan was approved; and, the secret being very well kept, on the thirty-first of October the army prepared to march. [55] It is remarkable, that, during the whole period of their stay in Edinburgh, no general review of the Jacobite forces had taken place. The consequent uncertainty of what was really the amount of those forces, which existed in England, fostered the general panic. "Abundance of people, " writes Mr. Maxwell, "friends as well as enemies, had made it their business to find out the number of the Prince's army, but to no purpose. Great pains had been taken to conceal its weakness."[56]

In order to conceal the design upon England, a scheme was formed, allowing three days to elapse between the marching of the two great divisions of the army; and accordingly the Prince, attended by Lord George Murray, took up his abode at the palace of Dalkeith, and here he remained until the third of November. In this princely abode the young representative of the Stuart line may have remembered the adverse fortunes of Queen Mary, and the bold character of the Regent Morton, to whom the castle of Dalkeith belonged, when it had acquired from the character of its owner the name of the "Lion's Den. " After the death of Morton, the barony of Dalkeith was included in the attainder; and the castle had been considered, during many years, as public property, and was inhabited by General Monk during the usurpation of Cromwell.

But, long before Charles Edward made it his temporary residence, Dalkeith had been repaired and beautified by Anne Duchess of Buccleugh and Monmouth, the widow of the unfortunate Duke of Monmouth. It was, as it is now, an appropriate residence for royalty. The more ancient part of the building has, it is true, lost its castellated appearance; but the beautiful site on the steep banks of the Eske, and the thickness of the walls, are still proofs of former strength and great importance, to which the contiguity of Dalkeith to Edinburgh conduce; whilst the junction of the north and south Esk in the park add to the beauties of this noble demesne.

The Chevalier Johnstone was still aide-de-camp to Lord George Murray, and remained to accompany the General on his march. Among those with whom the exertions of Lord George were frequently united was Mr. O'Sullivan, an Irish officer, and the object of Charles Edward's partiality and confidence, and he was a man of considerable abilities. Having received his education in a Romish college abroad, O'Sullivan had originally entered into priest's orders. It was his lot to be recommended as a tutor to the son of Marshal Maillebois, who, perceiving in the young ecclesiastic proofs of a genius better adapted to the use of the sword than to the gravity of the gown, encouraged him to apply himself to the profession of arms. There were not wanting in those days opportunities of cultivating a military turn, and Corsica was the scene of Mr. O'Sullivan's first exploits. Here he acted as secretary to Marshal Villebois; an office of no slight responsibility, for the Marshal was tainted with the prevalent vice of the day, and scarcely ever left the dinner-table in a state fit for public business. O'Sullivan, therefore, in the course of those oppressions which the French inflicted on the inhabitants of Corsica, acquired not only great experience in business, but also in military affairs; as well as knowledge in what is termed the art of making irregular war. To this acquirement he afterwards added another; for, having served a campaign on the Rhine, it was said by a French General, under whom he fought, that his knowledge of the regular art of war was equal to that of any General in Europe. To his abilities were attributed much of the rapid success of those whom it was the fashion of the newspapers of the day to describe as "a handful of savages, " but whom the loungers about the English court soon learned to dread. [57]

It is now necessary, before entering into details of fresh operations, to review the proceedings of Lord George Murray during the last few weeks, and to give some notion how he exercised the functions of his generalship. His chief sources of annoyance, besides the intrigues in the Prince's council, were the deserters from the Jacobite army. Before leaving Edinburgh, Lord George Murray had despatched a number of prisoners to Logierait; and the following letter shows how rigid were the instructions which he peremptorily sent to his brother, the Marquis of Tullibardine, at Perth. The correspondence of Lord George Murray proves him to have been a man of a stern, hard nature; and effaces much of the impression produced by his united valour and clemency in the field of battle.

"Dear Brother,

"Things vary so much from time to time that I can say nothing certain as yet, but refer you to the enclosed letter; but depend upon having nothing express from me with you before Monday night. But, in the mean time, you must resolve to be ready to march on Tuesday morning, by Keinacan and Tay Bridge, so as to be at Crieff on Wednesday; and even that way, if you do your best, you will be half a march behind: but you will be able to make up that on Thursday, when I reckon we may meet at Dunblane or Doun: but of this more fully in my next. It is believed for certain that Cope will embark at Aberdeen.

"I hope the meal was with you before this—thirty-five bolls—for it was at Inuar last night. It shall be my study to have more meal with you on Monday night, for you must distribute a peck a man; and, cost what it will, there must be pocks to each man, to contain a peck or two for the men to have always with them. Buy linen, yarn, or anything; for these pocks are of absolute necessity—nothing can be done without them. His Royal Highness desires you to acquaint Glenmoriston and Glencoe, if they come your way, of this intended march, so that they may go by Tay Bridge (if you please, with you); and what meal you can spare, let them have. You may please tell your own people that there is a project to get arms for them.

"Yours, adieu! "GEORGE MURRAY. "

"Saturday, nine at night. "

"For God's sake! " he adds in another part of his letter, "cause some effectual measures to be taken about the deserters: I would have their houses and crops destroyed, for an example to others, and themselves punished in a most rigorous manner. "

Another source of anxiety was connected with the prisoners of war. It was difficult to know how to dispose of them. The island in the Loch of Clunie, not far from Dunkeld, was afterwards considered by the Marquis as the most suitable place for the reception of the prisoners; and was conceded by Lady Ogilvy, the daughter of Lord Airlie, for that purpose, in her father's absence. In a letter addressed by Tullibardine to the Earl of Airlie, to whom the Loch of Clunie belonged, a spirit of kindness and consideration is shown, very different to the stern mandates of Lord George Murray. "I presume, " writes the Marquis, "your Lor'ship will not only cheerfully make everything be carefully prepared for their reception, but also contribute what's possible to prevent any dangerous mutiny or escape among them. " Although describing these prisoners as a "troublesome and dangerous set of people, " he recommends no harsh measures, except precautionary vigilance. [58] Beef, mutton, and meal were provided and paid for by the Marquis, who, ultimately, was obliged to quarter a considerable number of the prisoners in barns and other outhouses near Logierait. This charge appears to have been very unwelcome to the good old Tullibardine, who talks to his sister in law, Lady Emilia Murray, of "ane unworthy pack of prisoners that is sent us. "[59]

Meantime, the want of money for the supply of the garrison at Perth was another source of uneasiness to Lord George Murray. Many disappointments, on this score, occurred. "I told you, " Lord George writes to his brother, "that some gentlemen had promised to his Royal Highness some money in loan, more besides what they already gave; but it is to their ladies you will please to write, as they appear to do the thing, and not the husbands. "[60] "I have been as pressing, " he says in another letter to the Marquis, "about money to be sent to you, both formerly and now, as if my life depended upon it. There is three hundred pounds sent at present, mostly in specie. You are desired to write to people in the country to advance money, particularly to Lady Methven; which if they do not immediately, their corn and other effects will be seized. "[61]

Previously to his march southwards, Prince Charles appointed Viscount Strathallan Governor, and Deputy Governor of Perth, and Commander-in-chief during the absence of the Marquis of Tullibardine, whom Lord George Murray now summoned to join him, considering that the addition of the Marquis's tenantry to the army was of the utmost importance. "I am extremely anxious, " he writes, "to have our men here, at least as many as would make Lord Nairn's battalion, and mine, five hundred each; for at present I could get them supply'd with guns, targets, tents, and, those who want them, shoes also: but if they be not here soon, them that come first, will be first serv'd. "

These directions were reiterated, and were also repeated by the pen of Lady Emilia Murray, to whom her lord sent immediate accounts of all that occurred. This spirited and indefatigable help-meet resided generally at Tullibardine. "These, " she writes, "were his words, 'I entreat, for God's sake, that the Duke of Atholl send off the men here immediately, or they will be too late for arms, targets, tents, &c. ; nay, for our march, which begins on Thursday. " All this haste and impetuosity was meekly but decidedly resisted by the slow Marquis of Tullibardine. He thus writes in reply to one of his brother's most urgent entreaties:

"About ten o'clock in the afternoon I received your express, dated the fourth, four o'clock, afternoon, and am very much concerned to find that it is morally impossible for me, or any of the men in these parts, to be up with you against Thursday night, the day you say it is resolved, in a Council of War, to march southward. Did any of us endeavour to make too much haste to join the Prince, I am afraid we should be like a good milk cow, that gives a great pail of milk, and after, kicks it down with her foot. Forgive the comparison. "[62]

Other apprehensions also increased the desire of Lord George to begin his march. "I am desired to let you know, " he writes to the Marquis of Tullibardine, "that there is one Kimber, an anabaptist, who came from London with a design to assassinate the Prince; he is about twenty-seven years old, black hair, of a middling stature, and talks fluently and bluntly about his travels in the West Indies. " This man, it was suspected, afterwards changed his name to Geffreys. He was supposed to have even been received by the Marquis of Tullibardine at his table, and to have obtained a pass from him; but nothing more was disclosed, as far as the correspondence informs us, touching this attempt.

Lord George continued in a fever of vexation and anxiety at the delay of his brother, upon whose arrival at the camp, the march to England was to begin. Public affairs in England favoured, as he justly thought, the most decisive measures. "Everything, " he writes to his brother, "is in great confusion in England, particularly in London, where credite is at a stand. The greatest banquiers have stopt payment; all would go to our wish, if we could but march instantly. If you delay longer, " Lord George adds, "it will be the utter ruine of the cause. You should wait for nobody but your own men. " The arrival of supplies from France, of arms and ammunition, though they were represented as being very inferior in quantity to what had been expected, gave encouragement to the hopes of the sanguine; and re-assured in some degree, even the anxious mind of Lord George Murray.

Before finally quitting Perth, the Marquis of Tullibardine received a compliment from the gentlemen prisoners of war there, which proved how soldierlike and courteous his conduct towards them had been. They inquired whether he would have morning levees, since they wished "to wait upon him. " To this the Marquis replied, with his thanks, that, although not fond of ceremonious visits, he would always be "glad to cultivate an acquaintance with gentlemen whose actions show they are true Britons, by standing up for and supporting the ancient constitution and liberties of well-born subjects, whose honour is engaged to shake off the slavery of a foreign yoke. "[63]

Notwithstanding all the remonstrances of Lord George, who had reiterated his entreaties during the whole of the month of October, the winter was far advanced before the Marquis left his castle of Blair to proceed southwards. [64]

On the thirty-first of October, a considerable force took the road to Duddingstone, a small village at the foot of Arthur's Seat; presenting, before the Highland army poured in upon its serene precincts, a scene of repose and quiet beauty, finely contrasted with the clamour of the city, and the grandeur of the rugged hill.

Foremost rode Lord Elcho, commanding the first troop of horse-guards, consisting of sixty-two gentlemen, and their servants, under five officers, forming altogether a troop of a hundred and twenty horse. A smaller troop, not amounting to more than forty horse, followed under the command of Arthur Elphinstone, afterwards Lord Balmerino. Then came a little squadron of horse grenadiers, with whom were incorporated the Perthshire gentlemen, in the absence of their own commander, Lord Strathallan, who was left Governor of Perth. The whole of this squadron did not amount to a hundred. It was commanded by William Earl of Kilmarnock, the representative of an ancient and noble family, which, as an historian remarks, "sometimes matched with the blood-royal. " "He was, " adds the same writer, "in the flower of his age, being about forty years old. The elegance of his person, and comeliness of his features, which were every way handsome, bespake internal beauties. "[65] It is remarkable, that, at this very time, the young Lord Boyd, Lord Kilmarnock's son, held a commission in the British army and fought against the Jacobites.

The Aberdeen and Bamffshire gentlemen, amounting with their servants to a hundred and twenty, with seventy or eighty hussars, were commanded by Lord Pitsligo; but Mr. Murray, "who would have a share at least of everything, " was their colonel. [66]

The infantry consisted of thirteen little battalions, for the Highlanders would not be commanded by any but their own chiefs; and it was necessary therefore to have as many regiments as there were Clans.

On the third of November, the Prince marched from Dalkeith on foot, at the head of the Clans, who were commanded under him by Lord George Murray. The acclamations of the people of Edinburgh, who flocked in crowds to witness the departure of the army, were loud and friendly. Yet it is remarkable, that in spite of his long residence in that city, in spite of his hereditary claims on its inhabitants, and of the popularity of his manners, the party of the Prince in that capital never increased in proportion to his expectations. This indifference to the cause of Charles Edward has with much reason been attributed to the strong and unalterable distrust entertained by all zealous Presbyterians of any approach to Popery: the firmness of the Scottish character to a principle may be plainly read in the reluctance of the Lowlanders to hazard, even for a Stuart, the safety of what they esteem to be their vital interests. [67]

It was, however, a fine, although a mournful sight, when the Clans taking the road to London left Dalkeith. It was indeed only after long and anxious deliberation, that these brave men had resolved to risk an advance to England, without any certain expectation of a rising in that country; yet there were many among the chiefs who went forth that day, and among these were some of the bravest and the most determined who "trusted in themselves alone. "[68] Among those who were declared secretly to have desponded of success, and yet to have gone on in the career from a sense of honour, was Lord George Murray.

The march to England was very judiciously planned and well executed. "It resembled, " observes the Chevalier Johnstone, "on a small scale, that of Marshal Saxe some years before, when he advanced to lay siege to Maestricht. " The Prince went day after day on foot, contrary to general expectation; for it was thought that he would only have done so at the beginning to encourage the soldiers: but in dirty lanes, and in deep snow, the youth reared in seclusion and luxury took his chance with the common men, and could scarcely ever be prevailed upon even to get on horseback to ford a river. "It's not to be imagined, " writes his affectionate partisan and historian Maxwell, "how much this manner of bringing himself down to a level with the men, and his affable behaviour to the meanest of them, endeared him to the army. "[69] On arriving at Lauder, hearing that some of the Highlanders had remained behind with a view, it was thought, of deserting, Charles got on horseback before it was light, rode back two or three miles, and brought the stragglers with him. [70] On the fourth instant he reached Kelso. Such was the success of this well-contrived march, and such the secrecy with which it was made, that Marshal Wade, who was at Newcastle with eleven thousand men, continued to cover and protect that place, without an idea of advancing to intercept the Highland troops. Indeed, the secret was so well kept, that hardly any subordinate officer in the Prince's service knew where the junction of the columns was intended to take place. [71]

Arduous as the Prince's march had been to Kelso, it was enlivened by some incidents in which the stern and haughty Lord George Murray must have participated, as well as the gallant young Chevalier. On passing through Preston Hall gate, the first morning of his march, the Prince found breakfast there prepared for him by order of the Duchess of Gordon, for which act that lady was deprived of a yearly pension of one thousand pounds, given to her in consideration of her Grace's having educated her family in the Protestant religion. [72] As he passed Fala Danes, the ladies of Whitborough, who were the sisters of a zealous adherent of the Prince, Robert Anderson, entertained Charles and his chief officers with a collation in the open air. The royal guest, being asked to leave some memorial of his visit, cut from the hilt of his sword a piece of crimson velvet, which is still preserved at Whitborough. At Lauder, Charles took up his abode in Hurlestane castle, the seat of the Earl of Lauderdale. From Kelso, Charles dispatched the guards across the Tweed; not so much to reconnoitre, as to amuse the enemy: they went some miles into the country, and, when they came to any English villages, made inquiries as to what reception and accommodation the army might meet with on arriving there. The object of this manoeuvre was to keep General Wade in suspense as to the movements of the army, and to prevent his marching towards Carlisle. Such was the success of these artifices, that Wade, who had decided on a march to Berwick, countermanded that order. On the sixth of November the Jacobite forces crossed the Tweed: that river was scarcely fordable; but the Highlanders were elated beyond measure, and, even when bathed in the water, expressed their delight by discharging their pieces and uttering cries of joy. Such was their humour, that they gave the horses which were taken from the enemy the name of General Cope, by way of expressing their contempt for the fugitive Englishman.

Amid indications of homage, especially from the women of the town of Jedburgh, who ran forth to kiss the young hero's hand, Charles entered Jedburgh, and took up his residence at an inn in the centre of the town, called the Nag's Head. On the following day he led his troops over the Rule water, famous for the warriors of old who dwelt near its banks; and over the Knot o' Gate into Liddiesdale, "noted in former times for its predatory hands, as in more recent times for its primitive yeomen and romantic minstrelsy. "[73] After a march of twenty-five miles, the Prince arrived at Haggiehaugh, upon Liddel water; here he slept, the Highlanders finding their quarters for the night as well as they could in barns, or byres, or houses, as their fortune might be. On the eighth of November Charles Edward, proceeding down the Liddel water, met the column of horse which had taken the middle road by Selkirk and Hawick. They joined him at Gritmill Green upon the banks of the Esk, four miles below Langholm. Shortly afterwards the first division of the Prince's army crossed the river, which here separates the two kingdoms, as the Tweed does at Berwick, and trod upon English ground. That event was signalized by a loud shout, whilst the Highlanders unsheathed their swords. But soon a general panic was spread among the soldiery, by the intelligence that Cameron of Lochiel, in drawing his sword, had drawn blood from his hand. [74] This was regarded as an omen of mournful import. What was of much more vital consequence was the incessant desertion of the troops, especially from the column which the Prince commanded. Arms were afterwards found flung away in the fields, and the roads to Lanarkshire and Stirlingshire were crowded with these renegades. This circumstance Lord George Murray accounted for in these terms, when, upon a subsequent occasion, he wrote to his brother, complaining of the fact: "We are quite affronted with the scandalous desertion of our men: it was the taking money instead of the best men, which is the occasion of all the evil; for good men, once coming out, would have been piqued in honour, and not deserted us on the point of fighting the enemy. "[75]

Such was the skill and secrecy with which the whole of this march had been planned, chiefly by the suggestions of Lord George Murray, that the forces were very much surprised on finding that all the three columns arrived nearly at the same time, on a heath in England, about two miles distant from the city of Carlisle. The plan was executed with such precision, that there was not an interval of two hours between the junction of the columns. [76]

It was now resolved to invest Carlisle. Few cities in England have been the scenes of more momentous events than that which was now the object of the Chevalier's efforts. Long the centre of border hostilities, it was the fate of Carlisle to be at once the witness of the insurrection of 1745, and the scene of punishment of those who were concerned in that movement.

In modern times, the importance of Carlisle as a fortress has inevitably declined; and it is at present regarded as a venerable relic of former strength, rather than as a place of defence. But, in ancient days, the Warden of the Marches, selected from among the nobles of tried fidelity and courage, attracted to the castle of Carlisle a host of youthful aspirants for military renown, who there sought to be trained to arms, amid contests not depending upon a single achievement, but requiring watchfulness, patient labour, and skill, slowly and painfully to be acquired.

Founded by William Rufus, who restored the city after it had lain two hundred years in ruins, owing to the depredations of the Danes; and improved and enlarged successively by Richard the Third and Henry the Eighth; the castle had received the unhappy Mary Stuart: and here she was treated with an insidious respect which soon threw off the mask. In the time of Queen Elizabeth, the citadel, which was entirely built by Henry the Eighth, fell into decay; and after the prohibition of all incursions on England on the part of King James the Sixth, Carlisle ceased to be of so much importance as a military possession; and its position, as one of the keys of England, did not avail to secure any great attention to its dilapidated state. At the time of Charles Edward's arrival in Cumberland, the fortifications of the City had been neglected for several centuries; but it still bore the outward aspect of former strength.

The works, which had thus been left to moulder away, were in the form of a triangle, and were separated from the town by a deep ditch. Upon the east angle, which is also cut off from the Parade by a ditch, is seated the Castle, properly so called, though the whole generally goes by that name. These works consist of a dungeon, the walls of which are twelve feet in thickness; a tower, called the Captain's Tower; two gates, one to each ward; there being an inward and an outward ward. In the castle there is a great chamber, and a hall, but no storehouse for ammunition. In the walls of the town, three gateway towers, a semi-circular bastion called Springeld Tower, and the citadel, complete the fortifications: unless we comprise several square towers with which the city walls are furnished; especially one at the west sally-port, and the Tile Tower, both of considerable strength. [77]

The foreground of the castle is formed of green and level meadows washed by the river Eden; and, in modern days, two fine stone bridges add to the beauty of the scene. The hanging banks are crowned with the village and church of Stanwix, and the mountains of Bewcastle form the distance. "To the south, " to use the words of Hutchinson in his History of Cumberland, "you command the plains towards Penrith, shut in on either side with a vast range of mountains, over which Crossfell and Skiddaw are distinctly seen greatly eminent. To the east a varied tract of cultivated country, scattered over with villages and hamlets, mingle beautifully with woodlands on the extensive landscape; the distant horizon formed by the heights of Northumberland. To the west, the Solway Frith sparkles out, a shining expanse of waters, flowing along a cultivated tract of land on the English coast; on the other, the bold heights of Weffel and a chain of mountains extend towards the sea. "[78]

When Charles Edward spread out his forces before Carlisle, the garrison within its mouldering walls was composed of a company of invalids, under the command of Colonel Durand; but the Cumberland militia were almost all collected within the city walls. Colonel Durand, however, as well as the Mayor of the place, showed a spirit of defence; and the latter issued a proclamation informing the inhabitants that he was not Paterson, a Scotchman, but Pattieson, a true-born Englishman, who was determined to hold out the city to the last. Since Charles had no battering cannon, it appeared impossible to reduce the castle if it were well-defended; but it was resolved to make the attempt. Whilst he was meditating an attack, the news that Wade's army was marching from Newcastle drew him for some days from continuing these operations. The report proved, however, to be groundless; and the Duke of Perth was sent, therefore, with several regiments to begin the siege.

The Jacobite army had all crossed the river Eden at Rowcliff, four miles below Carlisle; and next day they marched to Harraby, Blackhall, and Boutcherby, to the southward of Carlisle. At Harraby Lord George Murray remained, in order to cover the siege; that place being most contiguous to Carlisle, and on the highway to Penrith: the other troops under his command lay in the adjoining villages. The Duke of Perth had the direction of the trenches. It was here that an event occurred, which shortly afterwards excited the greatest discontent among the followers of Charles Edward. [79]

The attack upon the city was made from Stanwix Bank; the Marquis of Tullibardine, who had at length joined the insurgent army, with his tenantry, assisting the Duke of Perth. As it was market-day on the ninth, when the Jacobites made their appearance within a quarter of a mile of Carlisle, the Highland soldiers were mingled with the market-people returning home, so that the garrison dared not fire upon them. On the following day, the city was attacked in three places; but the Marquis of Tullibardine, who commanded a four-gun battery, planted at the entrance of a lane, was heard to say to his followers, "Gentlemen, we have not metal for them; retreat. " After three days' attack, however, the courage of Mr. Pattieson, and the strength of the garrison, gave way. The valiant Mayor forgot his English birth so far as to hang out a white flag, and to request a capitulation for the town. The garrison and townsmen of Carlisle, in the opinion of the writers of the day, merited no more credit than that of Edinburgh, in their defence and capitulation. In the siege, the Highland army had only one man killed, and another wounded; and the reduction of Carlisle gave great, but not lasting, lustre to their arms.

On entering Carlisle, Lord George Murray is said, in the newspapers of the day, to have encountered an old friend, who asked him how he could be so rash as to lend himself to the aid of a hopeless and futile invasion. To this Lord George is declared to have replied, that he was well aware that the cause was hopeless; but that, having once engaged to maintain it, honour compelled him to continue his exertions. [80] It was not, however, long before those fatal dissensions appeared which effectually defeated all that valour or fidelity could effect to save Charles Edward from defeat.

It was, perhaps, the well-earned popularity of the Duke of Perth, his forbearance, and the gratitude evinced towards him by the inhabitants of Carlisle, as he rode triumphantly through their city, that first roused the jealousy of Lord George Murray's proud nature. The disinterested conduct of the Duke of Perth, as soon as he became informed of the sentiments entertained towards him by Lord George Murray, was worthy of himself. That brave and excellent young man modestly withdrew from a rivalry which, he justly concluded, must be injurious to the cause of that Prince whose interests he had espoused; for few men could cope with the natural abilities, the force of character, and the experience of Lord George. He was by far the most able general that appeared in either of the two insurrections in the cause of the Stuarts. "His personal hardihood and bravery, " remarks Lord Mahon, "might be rivalled by many others; but none could vie with him in planning a campaign, providing against disasters, or improving victory. "

Whilst the Jacobite forces lay encamped near Carlisle, certain differences of opinion arose in the Council. There were some who had even thought that it would be desirable, before investing Carlisle, to return to Scotland to collect a greater force. Lord George Murray, seconded by the Duke of Perth, had opposed this cautious proposal; and recommended that part of the army should stay at Brampton, and the rest go to blockade Carlisle. The Duke of Perth had seconded this scheme, and it had accordingly been decided that Lord George should command the blockade, whilst the Duke conducted the battery. The result has been seen; and the Prince was now master of Carlisle.

A few days after he had taken possession of the town, a council of war was called, to consider what was next to be done. Some of the officers proposed returning to Scotland; others were in favour of encamping near Carlisle, and waiting to see whether there would be any rising in England. Others advised marching forwards, by the west of England; arguing, that having Carlisle, happen what might, they had a safe retreat. Charles Edward declared himself to be of the last-mentioned opinion, and his inclinations were seconded by Lord George to a certain extent. He stated the advantages and disadvantages of both propositions; but added, that, although he could not venture to advise the Prince to march into England without more encouragement than they had hitherto received, yet he was persuaded that if his Royal Highness marched south, his army, though but small, would follow him. Upon this, Charles immediately said these words, "I will venture it. " "I spoke, " adds Lord George, "with the more caution, since some things had happened about the time of the blockade of Carlisle, and a little before, which had made me desirous to serve only as a volunteer, and not as a general officer; but, as all the other officers were very pressing with me, I soon laid that thought aside. "[81]

What those circumstances were, Lord George explains in the following letter to his brother. His difficulties, owing to the want of arrangements, such as his skill and experience might have suggested, had he been first in command, appear to have been sufficiently trying. Yet, in the extract from a letter dated Nov. 15, from Harraby, Lord George does ample justice to the exertions of the Duke of Perth. This epistle was written whilst the blockade and battery were going on.

"I am sorry to find that it is impossible to go on so quick with the battery of cannon as would have been wished. By the report of those I sent there, the ground is marshy, and vastly too much exposed; and, notwithstanding all the pains taken by the Duke of Perth, who is indefatigable in that service, and who meets with innumerable difficulties, I suspect the place pitched upon will not answer. But, if the thing be prosecuted, I think it my duty to tell you, so as you may represent it to his Royal Highness, that the men posted upon the blockade of Carlisle will not expose themselves, either in trenches, or all night in the open air, within cannon-shot, or even musket-shot of the town, except it be in their turn with the rest of the army, and that it be decided by lot who is to mount the guard, first night, second, and so on. The way I would propose, if it be approved of by a council of war, is as follows: —that fifty men be draughted out of each of the battalions that are at Brampton, with proper officers, and at least two majors out of the six battalions, and be sent to quarter at Butcherby, which, I believe, is within a mile of the battery; and, as I suppose, one hundred and fifty men will mount guard at the battery. These six battalions will furnish two guards; your men will furnish one, General Gordon and Lord Ogilvie's one, which, in the whole, makes four guards, or reliefs; and I think, by that time, the town will be either taken or the blockade removed. I don't mention the Duke of Perth's regiment, because they have more than their turn of the duty already, besides furnishing workmen, &c. And for Colonel Roy Stuart's regiments, I suppose they have the guard of the equipage, &c. ; and they will, perhaps, be able to furnish some workmen. If anything be done of this nature, the sooner I hear of it the better. I ever am, dear brother, your most affectionate brother, and faithful humble servant,

"GEORGE MURRAY. "[82]

This advice was disregarded. A court-martial was held to consider of the plan suggested by Lord George. By this council the detachments proposed by Lord George for the relief of the battery were refused, upon the plea that those corps had lately encountered all the fatigue of the blockade at Edinburgh, and that it would not be fair to put them again upon that service. On the day after receiving this decision, in the hand-writing of Secretary Murray, Lord George addressed the following letter to the Prince. His conduct upon this occasion shows the proud and fiery spirit of this able commander.

"15th November, 1745.

"Sir,

"I cannot but observe how little my advice as a General officer has any weight with your Royal Highness, ever since I had the honour of a commission from your hands. I therefore take leave to give up my commission. But as I ever had a firm attachment to the royal family, and in particular to the King my master, I shall go on as a volunteer, and design to be this night in the trenches as such, with any others that will please to follow me, though I own I think there are full few on this post already. Your Royal Highness will please order whom you think fit to command on this post, and the other parts of the blockade. I have the honour to be, sir, your Royal Highness's most faithful and most humble servant,

(Signed) "GEORGE MURRAY. [83]

"Lord Elcho has the command till you please to appoint it otherwise."

To his brother, the Marquis of Tullibardine, Lord George wrote still more fully. In this letter, after informing the Marquis that he had given up his commission of Lieutenant-General, Lord George complains of a want of confidence on the part of the Prince, in regard to the terms which were to be accepted or rejected in the surrender of Carlisle. Touching these, Charles Edward, who was now almost completely under the controul of Secretary Murray, acted in a weak and vacillating manner. When pressed by Lord George Murray to give him full instructions, he hesitated; Lord George entreated him, if he could not decide during his presence in the camp, that the Prince would send instructions after him. [84] "When he would not come to any fixed resolution before I came away, I begged his Royal Highness would send his intentions and instructions after me, that I might conduct myself by them; but his secretary told me plainly, he took that matter to be his province, as he seems indeed to take everything upon him both as to civil and military. There are many other things which have determined me to wish to have no command; and it is some time past since I observed things must go into utter confusion. I shall show, as a volunteer, that no man wishes more success to the cause; and I can be of more use charging in the first rank of your Atholl men than as a general, where I was constantly at a loss to know what was doing. I am of opinion you should reduce your men to two battalions; one for Lord Nairn, the other Mr. Mercer. When you are quartered anywhere, if you have a hole to spare, I shall be as often with you as I can; at other times, I shall lye with the men in a barn, which I doubt not will hearten them much. In every thing, as a volunteer, I shall do all I can to advance the service; but am determined never to act as an officer. I have several things to say at meeting. If you have occasion for tent or horses, they are at your service, for I design to keep none, but make presents of them all.

"Adieu! Yours, GEORGE MURRAY. "

"Haroby, 15th Nov. 1745. "

* * * * *

Not only were the seeds of disunion thus sown between the Prince and the Generals, but also between the Marquis of Tullibardine and Lord George Murray.

"I did expect, " writes Lord George to the Marquis, "that you would have upon occasion stood my friend; but I find you are too apt to hearken to designing people, by your being so ready to blame me before I was heard; and, except you show some regard for me, how can I expect it of others? I told his Royal Highness that you had acquainted me that he desired to see me. He said, No, he had nothing particular to say to me. I told him I should be as ready to serve in a private station, and as a volunteer, in the first rank of your men, as ever I could be in any other. He said I might do so. Nothing else passed. I spoke a good time to Sir Thomas Sheridan, and told him in particular, that if anything was taken amiss in my letter, as having expressed my attachment to the King, without having mentioned his Royal Highness, it was very injurious to me; for having mentioned the King and royal family, (and designing my letter to be short,) I thought it needless to be more particular; for surely, next to the King, I would serve none on earth before his Royal Highness: which, after what I have shown, and all my actions since I joined the standard, could not be called in question. I mentioned several particulars, wherein I showed that I had no authority in the station I was in, and that others acted as General who had not any call, but used his Royal Highness's name. That in the drudgery, I was employed, but anything of moment was done without my participation. That, in short, I had ventured my all—life, fortune, family—every thing, my honour; which last I had some to lose, but none to gain, in the way things were managed, and therefore resolved upon a private station. "[85]

The concluding paragraph of this painful letter is written with a force and bitterness which show how deeply this ardent servant of a failing cause was wounded by what he justly deemed unmerited caprice and disrespect. "I wish you would be careful of the Atholl men, that they be not slighted; which never should have happened as long as I had any command. I find scarce any of them have got even thanks for venturing life and fortune, and even the gallows; and, which is worse, (I don't know how it is come about,) they are not thought equally good with other men. If you would send me the notes, that were made out, of the way of modelling them into two different regiments, I would do, now that I have time to do it, as much as possible for the good of the service and general comfort. I always am, dear brother, your most faithful and humble servant and affectionate brother,

"GEORGE MURRAY. "[86]

"Haroby, 16th Nov. 1745. "

* * * * *

There was also another source of complaint, which, though appearing on the surface to have originated with the Duke of Perth, was clearly traceable to the Prince, or rather to his adviser, Secretary Murray. A marked slight had been passed on Lord George Murray on the very night on which the battery on Carlisle was opened. He had gone into the trenches; and, seeing the Duke of Perth there, he had desired him, in case of anything extraordinary happening, to let him know, and that he would aid him by every means in his power. What private orders the Duke had was not known; but, far from applying to Lord George for aid or counsel, he sent to Brampton, seven miles' distance, whenever any difficulty occurred, and acquainted the Prince with it, but took no notice of Lord George, although he was an older officer than himself, and had been sent to Harroby to cover the siege. Upon this, Lord George, who thought he was entitled to know what had passed in the trenches, complained, but received no satisfactory answer: and thus aggrieved, and, as he conceived, insulted, he sent that letter to the Prince, which has justly been censured as making an invidious distinction between the young Chevalier and his father. [87]

These acts of indiscretion and intemperance were followed by another proceeding still less worthy of the soldier and the man of honour: Lord George Murray indeed lowered himself, when, at the same time that he wrote to the Prince, he set on foot a petition praying Charles that he would dismiss all Roman Catholics from his councils. This was aimed at the Duke of Perth and Sir Thomas Sheridan; nor can we assign to it any better motive than that it was intended to re-instate Lord George Murray in the command. Some allowance may, nevertheless, be made for the prejudices of a Presbyterian, acting on the determined and overbearing nature of a high-spirited man. But the vital principles of our Christian faith tend to soften animosities, to humble pride, and to accord to others the same intention to act rightly as that of which we ourselves are prone to boast. A sincere, a truly pious member of the Christian church cannot be an intolerant partizan of certain modes of faith. There dwells within his breast a deeper sentiment than that which is inspired by the worldly and sublunary distinctions of sect. And Lord George Murray, seeing his young and blameless rival, the Duke of Perth, brave, honourable, and moderate, had shown greater zeal for true religion had he not availed himself of an unworthy plea to base upon it an invidious and covert insinuation.

He was reproved by the magnanimity of the man whom he desired to remove from the Prince's councils. Although the Duke of Perth did not profess to acquiesce in the opinion that it was unreasonable that he should have the chief command, although he did not pretend to acknowledge the justice of the claim, he nobly gave up, for the sake of a Prince whom he loved, the superiority to Lord George Murray. His conduct on this occasion recalls the generous sentiments of the knight and soldier in ancient times; unhappily it failed in producing that unanimity which it was intended to effect. The rancour between Lord George Murray and the Secretary still remained, although it did not break out on every occasion, and sometimes gave way to the common cause when the interests of all were at stake. [88]

At Carlisle the forces were reviewed and were found to amount to above five thousand foot, with five hundred[89] on horseback, mostly low-country gentlemen followed by their servants, under the name of guards, hussars, &c. [90] After a few days rest, and after completing every arrangement for the preservation of Carlisle, the army marched to Penrith; Lord George preceding the rest of the forces at the head of six regiments and some horse. This was an adventurous undertaking with so small a force; for there were now in England above sixty thousand men in arms including the militia and the newly raised regiments; but the Prince, observes Mr. Maxwell, "had hitherto had a wonderful run of success. " He was still buoyed up with hopes of a landing of French troops, and of an insurrection in his favour. [91]

On the twenty-fourth of November the Prince marched from Carlisle to Penrith, and thence to Lancaster, which he reached on the twenty-fifth, at the head of the vanguard of his army. He was dressed in a light plaid belt, with a blue sash, a blue bonnet on his head, decorated with a white rose, the sound of the bagpipes, and the drum playing "The King shall have his own again; " the banners, on which were inscribed the words "Liberty and Property, Church and King, " failed, nevertheless, to inspire the cold spectators who beheld them with a corresponding enthusiasm.

The army advanced towards Preston, Lord George Murray commanding the van; and on the twenty-sixth of November, the whole force assembled before that town, the very name of which struck terror into Scottish breasts. Nor were the English Jacobites without their fears, nor devoid of associations with the name of a place in which the hopes of their party had been blighted in 1715, and their banners steeped in blood. The walls of Preston recalled to many of the volunteers of Lancashire the prison in which their fathers had died of fever, or starvation, or of broken hearts. It is remarkable, as one of the newspapers of the day observes, that many of those who joined the Chevalier's ranks were the sons of former insurgents. "Hanging, " adds the coarse party writer, "is hereditary in some families. "[92] Lord George Murray, in order to avoid the "freit, " or, in other words, to humour the superstition of the Highlanders, who had a notion that they never should get beyond Preston, crossed the Ribble bridge, and landed a great many of his men on the other side of the water, about a mile from the town, where they halted the next day, waiting for some intelligence, of which it is presumed, says Lockhart, "they were disappointed. " Here it was necessary to divide even this little army for the convenience of quarters. [93] At Preston the Prince was received with enthusiastic cheers, but when officers were ordered to beat up for recruits, no one enlisted. The tents which had been provided had been left on the road from Moffat to Edinburgh; and the season was so severe, that it was impossible even for Highlanders to sleep in them; the town was too small to receive them; the same arrangement that had been begun at Carlisle was still pursued, and the army went in two great divisions, though with scarcely a day's march between them. Lord George Murray commanded what was called the low-country regiments; but the greater part of these was, observes Mr. Maxwell, "Highlanders by their language, and all were in their dress, for the Highland garb was the uniform of the whole army. "

One can easily conceive what must have been the effect of this gallant force, unbroken by fatigue or privation, and glorying in their enterprise, as they entered into the friendly county of Lancaster, filled with Roman Catholic gentry, who gathered around the standard of the Prince. The colours of the Tartan, which was worn, as we have seen, by the whole of the army, both Highlanders and Lowlanders, although denominated by a writer in the *Scots' Magazine* as a "vulgar glare, " never offend the eye, but are, according to a high authority, "beautifully blended and arranged. " "Great art, " observed the celebrated Mr. West, "(that is to say, much knowledge of the principles of colouring with pleasing effect,) has been displayed in the composition of the tartans of several Clans, regarding them in general as specimens of national taste, something analogous to the affecting but artless strains of the native music of Scotland. "

This garb, which excited the attention and admiration of Napoleon at the battle of Waterloo, consisted of the truis, the kilted plaid, and philibeg. The truis, be it observed, for the benefit of the dwellers in the south, were used by gentlemen on horseback, and by others according to their choice; but the common garb of the people was the plaid and kilt; and this was the usual dress down to the passing of the act for suppressing the garb. The tartan is said to have been known in Flanders; and the tartan and kilt to have been adopted in the Lowlands before their adoption among the mountains. [94] Without attempting to meddle in the dangerous and intricate question of antiquity, it must be acknowledged that the Highland dress is well adapted to the habits of a pastoral people, as well as being extremely graceful and picturesque. It is also admirably fitted to oppose the inclemency of those regions in which, among the other habits which characterise the peculiar people who wear it, it is still regarded as a loved and revered badge of national distinction. In the various campaigns in Holland, the Highlanders suffered far less than other nations in that damp and chilly climate; in the retreat to Corunna, under the hero Sir John Moore, their plaids bound lightly round their bodies, they experienced the convenience of that simple form of dress in a rapid and protracted march. Light and free, the mountaineer could pursue, without restraint, the most laborious occupations; he could traverse the glens, or ascend mountains which offer a hopeless aspect to the inhabitants of more civilized spheres. But it was not only as a convenient and durable mode of apparel that the kilt and philibeg were advantageous. The Highland costume, when it formed a feature among English or foreign regiments, cemented a spirit which was felt and feared by foes. It bound those who wore it in a common bond, not to dishonour the garb which their chiefs and their forefathers had worn, by an act of cowardice, or by deeds of cruelty. [95]

Little did the English Government, or the inhabitants of the metropolis, or probably the country in general, know the character of the brave, ill-fated band of Highlanders, who were now advancing into the very heart of the country. It was the custom, especially among those who wished to gain preferment at Court, or who affected to be fashionable, to speak of the Highlanders as low, ignorant savages; semi-barbarians, to whom the vulgar qualities of personal courage and hardihood might be allowed, but who had neither any urbanity to strangers, nor refined notions of honour. The word "rebel, " was a mild name for those who were following Prince Charles's standard as it was borne southwards. The hardened villains, "the desperadoes, rabble, thieves, banditti! "[96] are the terms usually employed in expressing the sovereign contempt felt by ignorance for an honourable, religious, and primitive people. It seems also to have been thought only necessary for the Duke of Cumberland to show his face in the north, to put to flight a beggarly handful of undisciplined men, whose moral character, if we might credit certain passages in the Magazines of the day, was as low as their military acquirements. By other nations besides their own sister country, the same erroneous notions concerning the Scottish Highlanders prevailed. In Germany it was conceded that they might be capable of becoming "good and useful subjects when converted from heathenism. " The French, too, presumed to look upon them with contempt, until they met them, when acting as auxiliaries to other powers, so often in battle, and beheld them so generally in the front, that they verily believed at last, there were twelve battalions in the army instead of two; and one of their Generals, Broglio, in after times remarked, that "he had often wished to be a man of six feet high, but that he became reconciled to his size after he saw the wonders performed by the little mountaineers. "[97]

It is scarcely now necessary to allude to these errors at that time prevalent regarding the valour of the Scottish host. Tributes from every known country have long elevated this brave and oppressed people into a proud and honourable position. Instead, however, of the undisciplined savages who were supposed to be traversing the country, it was sooner found than acknowledged, that the intrepidity of the Highlanders was united to humanity, and to upright principles. To their noble qualities was added a deep sense of religion. In after-times it was remarked, that no trait in the character of the Highlanders was more remarkable than the respect which was paid by the different regiments which were eventually employed in the British service, to their chaplains. The men when they got into any little scrape were far more anxious, writes General Stuart, "to conceal it from their chaplain than from their commanding officer. "

But, however the public prints might revile, and the polite society at St. James's ridicule, and misunderstand the Highlanders, the General whose lot it was to conquer the unfortunate Jacobites knew well of what materials their forces were composed. The Duke of Cumberland, at the battle of Fontenoy, had been so much pleased with the conduct of the famous Black Watch, that he had offered them any favour which they chose to ask, or which he could grant, to mark his approbation. The answer to this proof of approbation was worthy of those valiant auxiliaries, who are described by the French as "Highland furies, who rushed in upon us with more fury than ever did a sea driven by a tempest. " The Highlanders replied, after thanking the Royal Duke for his courtesy, "that no favour he could bestow on them would gratify them so much as to pardon a soldier of their regiment, who lay under a sentence of court martial, by which he was decreed to incur a heavy corporal punishment; the infliction of which would, " they said, "bring dishonour on themselves, their friends, and their country. " The request was granted. It was, nevertheless, the countrymen of these Highlanders, men as heroic as true, as nice in their sense of honour as the Black Watch, upon whom the Duke wreaked the utmost of his vengeance after Culloden, whom he hunted with bloodhounds, —whose honest hearts he broke by every possible indignity, though their gallant spirits could never be subdued.

As the army advanced, a great multitude assembled to gaze upon the singular spectacle. The very arms borne by the Highlanders were objects of curiosity and surprise, no less than of alarm, to the populace, who stood by the way-side expressing their good-will to the expedition, but who, when asked to join the insurgents, declined, saying, "they did not understand fighting. "[98] The formidable weapons with which the Highlanders contrived to make themselves terrible to their enemies, consisted of a broad-sword, girded on the left side, and a dirk or short thick dagger on the right, used only when the combat was so close as to render the broadsword useless. In ancient times, these fierce warriors brandished a small short-handled hatchet or axe, for the purpose of a close fight. A gun, a pair of pistols, and a target, completed their armour, except when ammunition failed, when they substituted for the gun, the lochaber axe; this was a species of long lance, or pike, with a formidable weapon at the end of it, adapted either for cutting or stabbing. The lochaber axe had fallen into disuse since the introduction of the musket; but a rude, yet ready substitute had been found for it, by fixing scythes at the end of a pole, with which the Highlanders resisted the attacks of cavalry. Such had been their arms in the early part of the Insurrection of 1745, and such they continued until, at the battles of Falkirk and Preston Pans, they had collected muskets from the slain on the battle-field. In addition to these weapons, the gentlemen sometimes wore suits of armour and coats of mail; in which, indeed, some of the principal Jacobites have been depicted; but, with these, the common men never incumbered themselves, both on account of the expense, and of the weight, which was ill-adapted to their long marches and steep hills. [99]

A distinguishing mark which the Highland Clans generally adopted, was the badge. This was frequently a piece of evergreen, worn on the bonnet, and placed, during the insurrection of 1745, beside the white cockade. When Lord Lovat's men assembled near the Aird, they wore, according to the evidence given on the State Trials, sprigs of yew in their bonnets. [100] These badges, although generally considered to have been peculiar to the clans, were, observes a modern writer, [101] "like armorial bearings, common to all countries in the middle ages; and shared by the Highlanders among the general distinctions of chivalry, were only peculiar to them when disused by others. " Thus, the broom worn by Geoffrey Plantagenet, Count D'Anjou; —and the raspberry by Francis the First of France, were only discontinued as an ornament to the head when transferred to the habit, or housings; but the Highland Clans, tenacious of their customs, wore the plant not only upon their caps, but placed them on the head of the Clan standard. The white cockade was now regarded as the peculiar badge of the party; yet it seems not, at all events among the Clan Fraser, to have superseded the evergreen. Some few traces are left, in the present day, to certify, nevertheless, that they were worn during the contest of 1745. "Lord Hardwicke's Act, and continual emigration, " remarks John Sobieski Stuart, "have extirpated the memory of these distinctions once as familiar as the names of those who bore them; and all of whom I have been able to collect any evidence are, the Macdonalds, the Macphersons, the Grants, the Frasers, the Stuarts, and the Campbells. " "The memory of most, " mournfully remarks the same writer, "has now perished among the people; but, within a recent period, various lists have been composed—some by zealous enthusiasts, who preferred substitution to loss, and some by the purveyors of the carpet Highlanders, who once a-year illuminate the splendour of a ball-room with the untarnished broadswords and silken hose, never dimmed in the mist of a hill, or sullied in the dew of the heather."[102]

The Macdonalds, until a very short period before the rebellion of 1715, were known by the heather bow. "Let every man, " said one of their chiefs of old, looking round on a field of blooming heather, "put over his head that which is under his feet. " The destined sufferers of Glenco were marked by their "having a fair busk of heather, well spread and displayed over the head of a staff. " The Clan Macgregor wore the fir; and the Clan Grant assumed a similar badge; whilst the badge of the Frasers is said to have been supplied for ages by a yew of vast size, in Glen-dubh, at the head of Strath Fearg. The badge assigned to the Macphersons was the water lily, which abounds in the Lochs of Hamkai, upon the margin of which was the gathering place of the Clan Chattan. Some of these distinctions appear to have been used during the year 1745, as we see in the case of the Frasers, but all to have emerged into the one general distinction of the Jacobites, the white rose, first worn by David the Second, at the tournament of Windsor in 1349, when he carried the "*Rose argent*. " This badge had been almost forgotten in

Scotland, until the year 1715, when it was worn by the adherents of James Stuart, on his birthday, the tenth of June. "By the Irish Catholics, " observes the Editor of the "Vestiarium Scoticum, " "it is still worn on the same day; but in Scotland its memory is only retained in the ballads of '15, and '45. "

The Muses, who, as Burns has remarked, are all Jacobites, have celebrated this badge in these terms: —

"O' a' the days are in the year,
The tenth o' June I lo' maist dear,
When our *white roses* a' appear,
For the sake o' Jamie the Rover."[103]

The Highland host, after marching through Preston, to the sounds of the bagpipes, which played "The King shall have his own again, " took the road through Wigan, towards Manchester. The Prince was informed that the English troops had broken down the bridge at Warrington; and that circumstance, which decided him to go through Wigan, somewhat encouraged his naturally sanguine temper, as it showed fear on the part of the enemy. During this march, the kind-hearted young man went on foot, except occasionally, when we find notice of his riding a fine horse in the public prints of the day. He usually, however, gave up his carriage to the venerable Lord Pitsligo, and marched at the head of one of the columns. He never took dinner, but ate a hearty supper; and then, throwing himself upon a bed, slept until four in the morning, when he arose, to prosecute the fatigues of another day, fatigues which youth, a sound constitution, and, above all, a great degree of mental energy, enabled him to endure.

Wigan, which the Chevalier's forces now approached, had been, in the time of Queen Elizabeth, agitated by religious differences; and the Queen's Commission for promoting the ordinances of the Reformed Church had been there met with a vigorous resistance. During the civil wars, this town, both from its vicinity to Latham House, and from its attachment to Charles the First, took a distinguished part, and obtained the characteristic designation of the "faithful and loyal town of Wigan. " After the insurrection of 1715, the oaths of supremacy and allegiance to the reigning family had been, in vain, strongly urged upon the inhabitants of Lancashire, and a large mass of landed estates were, in consequence, put in jeopardy; although it does not appear that the owners were dispossessed of their estates, or that any other use was made of the register taken of all the landed properties in the county, except to assist the magistrates in the suppression of the insurrection in the north. Nevertheless, the expectation which Charles might naturally entertain of a general rising in Lancashire was not realized. "Nothing, " observes Mr. Maxwell, "looked like a general concurrence until he came to Manchester. "[104] This was remarkable, for Manchester had been the head-quarters of many of the Parliamentary party in Lancashire during the civil wars; whilst Preston and Wigan had both been royalist boroughs. But a singular alteration had taken place in the people of Manchester, who had changed from Roundheads to Jacobites. [105]

During the whole of the preceding march the Highland army had levied the public revenue with great accuracy; but no extortion, nor any attempts at plunder, had disgraced their cause, nor reflected on Lord George Murray as their General. [106]

At Manchester, the first organized force raised in England for the Chevalier joined Charles Edward. It was a regiment of two hundred men, commanded by Colonel Townley, a gentleman who had been in the French service; and was called the Manchester Regiment. It was composed of young men of the most reputable families in the town, of several substantial farmers and tradesmen, and of about one hundred common men. The accession of this troop gave great encouragement to the Prince; yet there were still many who thought very badly of the enterprise, and the advice afterwards given by Lord George Murray at Derby, to retreat, was also whispered at Manchester, Lord George being resolved to retreat, should there be no insurrection in England, nor landing from France. "At Manchester, one of his friends told Lord George, " relates Maxwell, "that he thought they had entered far enough into England, since neither of these events had happened. " To this Lord George replied that they might make a farther trial, and proceed to Derby; where, if there should be no greater encouragement to go on, he should propose a retreat to the Prince. [107]

The reception of Prince Charles at Manchester, was celebrated with demonstrations of enthusiastic joy. As he marched on foot into the town, at the head of the clans, halting to proclaim the Chevalier St. George, King, the bells rang, and preparations were made for illuminations and bonfires in the evening. The Prince was attended by twelve Scottish and English noblemen: from these he was distinguished by wearing the white cockade on the top of his cap, in the centre, instead of on the side, as did his general officers. Peculiarly formed to grace such occasions as a triumphal entry into an important and friendly town, Charles Edward quickly won the good will of the female part of the community; and the beauty and grace of the kingdom were soon, to use a phrase of a contemporary writer, enlisted in his behalf.

To the personal attributes of the Prince, "joining the good nature of the Stuarts with the spirit of the Sobieski, " Charles Edward added one accomplishment which the monarch then on the throne of England did not possess: he spoke English well, although with a foreign accent: in this last respect, he resembled some of those around him, more especially the Duke of Perth, who, having been long abroad, in vain endeavoured to conceal the French idiom and pronunciation by affecting a broad Scottish dialect. [108]

Still, in spite of these advantages, and notwithstanding the known predilection of the Lancastrians for the cause of the Stuarts, the lowest populace alone joined the standard of Charles. One melancholy, though admirable exception has been already referred to in the person of Colonel Francis Townley. This gentleman was a member of an ancient family, and the nephew of Mr. Townley, whose seat in Townley Hall, Lancashire, lays claim to high antiquity; and yet, is modern in comparison with a former residence, once seated on what is still called the Castle Hill. Francis Townley was a man of literary acquirements, which, indeed, eminently distinguished his relative, the celebrated Charles Townley, who formed at Rome, and afterwards brought to London, the well-known collection of marbles which was bought by the Trustees of the British Museum for twenty thousand pounds; (supposed to be a sum far beneath its actual value,) and which still graces that national structure.

The family of Townley had been remarkable for their fidelity to the Stuarts long before Colonel Francis Townley raised a troop for the Chevalier. The grandfather of this unfortunate man, had been tried for rebellion, in 1715, but acquitted; it was therefore very unlikely that when his accomplished descendant espoused the same ill-starred cause, there would be any mercy shown to a family so deeply implicated in Jacobitism. Francis Townley was afterwards taken prisoner, and tried with other persons, chiefly captains in the Manchester regiment. Of these the greater number were hung on

Kennington Common. The head of Colonel Townley was severed from his body, according to sentence, after death, and was placed upon Temple Bar; but those of most of his brothers in arms were preserved in spirits, and sent into the country, to be placed in public situations in Manchester and Carlisle. [109]

Prince Charles now prepared to proceed on his march to Macclesfield, while Lord George Murray was sent with his division to Congleton. The accompaniments of the Jacobite army, if we can venture to believe a letter inserted in the Gentleman's Magazine for 1745, and purporting to be written by a lady in Preston to her friend in London, formed a singular spectacle. Four ladies of some distinction are stated in this letter to have marched with the army. These were Lady Ogilvie, Mrs. Murray of Broughton, a lady of great beauty and spirit, the celebrated Jenny Cameron, and another female, unknown, but who is supposed to have been the mistress of Sir Thomas Sheridan. The populace, nevertheless, mistook Sheridan for a priest, and assigned to him the nick-name of the "Archbishop of Canterbury. " The first two ladies went in a chariot by themselves; the others were in a coach and six with the young Chevalier, to whose dejection and weariness as he passed through Preston, Jenny Cameron is said to have administered cordials. By the same writer the Jacobite army are described as looking like "hunted hares. " Such is a specimen of one of the ephemeral slanders of the day; and the circumstance of the coach and six tends to disprove the whole letter. The Prince, it is evident from every isolated account, marched on foot until he entered Derby. [110] It was, however, perfectly true that Mrs. Murray of Broughton and Lady Ogilvie, whose husbands were both with the army, attended the movements of the Highland force.

And now were the merits of Lord George Murray as a General, certain very soon to be called into active play; for, on the twenty-sixth of November, William Augustus, Duke of Cumberland, had left London at the head of an army, to oppose the insurgents.

On the character of the royal individual who, in his twenty-fifth year came forward to rescue his country, as it was said, from the yoke of a foreign invader; and whose promising, but immature talents, backed by a great military force, were effectual in defeating the skill of an experienced General, some reflections will naturally arise.

William, Duke of Cumberland, was born in the year 1721. He very early demonstrated that predilection for military affairs which obtained for him from Walpole the praise of having been "one of the five only really great men whom he had ever seen. " He very soon, also, betrayed that cruel and remorseless spirit which was wreaked on the brave and the defenceless; that indifference to suffering which too aptly was repaid by an indignant people with the name of "the Butcher; "—that thirst for blood which we read of in Heathen countries, before the commandments of the God of Israel, or the beautiful commentary of a Saviour of Mercy upon those sacred commandments, had chastened and humanized the people. Those tendencies which, whilst England was elate with success, and when she gloried in a suppressed rebellion, raised the Duke of Cumberland to a hero; —and, when reflection came, sank him to a brute; were manifested in the dawn of youth. In after years, (what extreme of odium could be greater?)—even children instinctively feared him. One day, when playing with his nephew, afterwards George the Third, a child, the Duke drew a sword to amuse him. The incident occurred long after the mouldering bones upon the field of Culloden were whitened in the sun; long after the brave Balmerino had suffered, and vengeance had revelled in the doom of the beloved Kilmarnock. But the sins of the remorseless Cumberland cried to Heaven. They were registered in the mind of a child. The boy turned pale and trembled, and acknowledged that he thought his "uncle Cumberland was going to kill him. " The Duke shocked and deeply hurt, referred to popular prejudice the impression which was the result of crime.

Imperious, aspiring, independent, the grasping and able intellect of the Duke soon imbibed a knowledge of affairs beyond his years. When scarcely out of the nursery he loved the council chamber, and delighted in the recitals of foreign wars. As he reached manhood, he affected a lofty and philosophical coldness; a dangerous attribute in youth, and one which either springs from a frigid disposition, or else infallibly contracts the heart. But, in the case of the Duke of Cumberland, it concealed a proud and selfish spirit, which could ill brook the superiority of his elder brother, Frederic, Prince of Wales, or bear with temper the popularity of another. When, in after years, his brother's death was communicated to him, those jealous and disdainful feelings broke forth. "It is a great blow to the country, " he said, sarcastically; "but I hope, in time, it will recover it. " That want of faith in human nature, of reverence for good motives, that absence of a generous confidence which one can suppose strongly characterise the lost angels, were among the many odious features in the character of this truly bad man. The prevailing feeling of his mind was, contempt for everything and everybody; —a contempt for renown; —a contempt, in after life, for politics, which he conceived were below his attention; a contempt for women, whom he lowered by a sort of preference consistent with the rest of his coarse character, but whose modest virtues he mistrusted. With this affectation of superiority, the Duke combined the littleness of envy. When he had attained the height of his popularity, his satisfaction was tarnished by the reputation of Admiral Vernon, who was the idol of the public. As a General, his acknowledged and eminent qualities were sullied by the German puerilities of an exact attention to military trifles; any deficiency in etiquette was punished like a crime: the formation of a new pattern of spatterdashes was treated as an important event. Nor was this all. He introduced into an army of Englishmen the German notions of military severity; he fostered a system which it has taken nearly a century of great efforts, and good works in the humane, to annul. "He was, " says Horace Walpole, "a Draco in legislation; " adding, "that in the Duke's amended mutiny bill the word 'Death' occurred at every clause. "[111]—Such is the general colouring of his public character. A strong and sensitive feeling with regard to the national honour; a devoted reverence for the sovereign authority; which were the only principles and institutions which he seemed to respect, are the milder traits. In private, he countenanced, by his own practice, most of those vices which scarcely existed with greater impunity, or with less inconvenience from public opinion, in the days of Charles the Second, than in those in which Cumberland flourished, and left a finished model of a character without one redeeming excellence.

As a soldier, however, the merits of the Duke, if merits those can be called which were the natural effects of animal courage, and of a strong, remorseless mind, must be, at all events, acknowledged. He behaved with great gallantry in his first campaign with his royal father, and was wounded at the battle of Dettingen. At too early an age, in 1744, he was placed at the head of a great army, in order to oppose Marshal Saxe; and the event of the battle of Fontenoy proved the error. But, in that engagement, the valour of the young General was admitted on all hands. "His Royal Highness, " relates the author of "The Conduct of the Officers at Fontenoy considered, " "was everywhere, and could not without being on the spot have cheered that Highlander who with his broad sword killed nine men, and making a stroke at the tenth, had his arm shot off, —by a promise of something better than the arm which he, the Duke, saw drop from him. "[112]

It was with the hope of retrieving the lost reputation of the Duke at Fontenoy, and in order to remedy the glaring defects of General Hawley, that this young man, old in hardened feelings, but full of ardour and courage, was sent to repel the forces of the Chevalier. It was also thought by the Government that the placing a prince of the blood-royal at the head of the army would have a powerful influence on the minds of the people, and neutralize the counter-influence of Charles Edward. [113] The Duke therefore assumed the command of an army ten thousand strong, and set out from London to intimidate the enemy.

The Duke of Cumberland was by no means so ignorant of the force which he was now destined to attack, as were most of the other "good people of England, who knew as little of their neighbours of the Scottish mountains, as they did of the inhabitants of the most remote quarter of the globe. "[114] In the battle of Fontenoy, the Duke of Cumberland had become acquainted with the peculiar mode of fighting practised by the Highlanders, in the manoeuvre of the "Black Watch, " or 42nd; and had shown his judgment in allowing them to fight in their own way. This gallant regiment, in which many of the privates were gentlemen, were exempted at this time from the service of crushing the rebellion, only to have a duty, perhaps more cruel and more unwarrantable, forced upon them, after the battle of Culloden. By a singular circumstance, the Black Watch was commanded by Lord John Murray, a brother of Lord George Murray's, Sir Robert Munro officiating as acting colonel. [115]

At Macclesfield, Prince Charles gained the intelligence that the Duke of Cumberland had taken the command of Ligonier's army, and that he was quartered at Lichfield, Coventry, Stafford, and Newcastle-under-Line. The Prince then resolved to go direct to Derby; and it was to conceal his design, and to induce the Duke to collect his whole army at Lichfield, that Lord George Murray marched with a division of the army to Congleton, which was the road to Lichfield. Congleton, being on the borders of Staffordshire, was sufficiently near Newcastle-under-Line for Lord George to send General Ker to that place to gain intelligence of the enemy. General Ker advanced to a village about three miles from Newcastle, and very nearly surprised a body of dragoons, who had only time to make off. He took one prisoner, a man named Weir, who was a noted spy, and who had been at Edinburgh during the whole of the Prince's stay there, and had since always kept within one day's march of the army. It was proposed to hang him; but Charles could not be brought to consent to the measure, and insisted that Weir was not, strictly speaking, a spy, since he wore no disguise. "I cannot tell, " observes Mr. Maxwell, "whether the Prince on this occasion was guided by his opinion or by his inclination: I suspect the latter, because it was his constant practice to spare his enemies when they were in his power. I don't believe there was an instance to the contrary to be found in this expedition. "[116]

Upon the third of December, Lord George Murray with his division of the army marched by Leek to Ashbourn; and the Prince, with the rest of the forces, came from Macclesfield to Leek, where, considering the distance of the two columns of his army, and the neighbourhood of the enemy, he naturally considered his situation as somewhat precarious. It was possible for the enemy, by a night-march, to get betwixt the two columns; and, contemplating this danger, the Prince set out at midnight to Ashbourn, where it was conceived that the forces should proceed in one body towards Derby. "Thus, " remarks a modern historian, "two armies in succession had been eluded by the Highlanders; that of Wade at Newcastle, in consequence of the weather or the old Marshal's inactivity, and that of Cumberland through the ingenuity of their own leaders. "[117]

Charles Edward and his officers slept at Ashbourn Hall, now in the possession of Sir William Boothby, Baronet; into whose family the estate passed in the time of Charles the Second. [118]

The young Prince had now advanced far into that county which has no rival in this Island in the beauty and diversity of its scenery, in the simple, honest character of its fine peasantry, or in the rank and influence of its landed proprietors. The history of these families is connected with the civil, and foreign wars of the kingdom; and already had the moors and valleys of Derbyshire been the scene of contest which had the Restoration of the Stuarts for their aim and end. In 1644, a battle was fought near Ashbourn, in which the Royalists were defeated; in 1645, just a century before Charles Edward entered Ashbourn, Charles the First had attended service in the beautiful gothic church of Ashbourn, as he marched his army through the Peak towards Doncaster.

The inhabitants of the district retained some portion of their ancient loyalty to the Stuarts. As Prince Charles ascended the height, from which, leading towards Derby, a view of the town of Ashbourn, seated in a deep valley, and of the adjacent and romantic country, may be seen, the roads were lined with peasantry, decorated with white cockades, and showing their sentiments by loud acclamations, bonfires, and other similar demonstrations. "One would have thought, " remarks Mr. Maxwell, [119] "that the Prince was now at the crisis of his adventure; that his fate, and the fate of the three kingdoms, must be decided in a few days. The Duke of Cumberland was at Lichfield; General Wade, who was moving up with his army along the west side of Yorkshire, was about this time at Ferry Bridge, within two or three days' march. So that the Prince was, with a handful of brave, indeed, but undisciplined men, betwixt two armies of regular troops, one of them above double, the other almost double, his number. " It was owing to the skill and prudence of Lord George Murray that this gallant but trifling force was enabled to return to Scotland, for scarcely ever was there a handful of valiant men placed in a situation of more imminent peril.

Derby, which is fifteen miles from Ashbourn, was thrown into the utmost confusion and disorder when the news that the vanguard of the insurgent army was approaching it became generally known. "The hurry, " says a contemporary writer, "was much increased by the number of soldiers, and their immediate orders to march out of town, and nothing but distraction was to be read in every countenance. The best part of the effects and valuables had been sent away or secreted some days before, and most of the principal gentlemen and tradesmen, with their wives and children, were retiring as fast as possible. "[120]

The borough of Derby, although by no means so opulent when Charles Edward and his friends visited it as in the present day, presented, perhaps, a far more appropriate scene for the faint and transient shadow of a Court, than it now affords. It had, even within the memory of man, an aspect singularly dignified, important, and antique in its streets; and it still possesses many residences which are adapted for the higher orders, rather than for the industrious burgesses of a town. These are chiefly seated on the outside of the town. They were, so late as 1712, and perhaps much later, "inhabited by persons of quality, and many coaches were kept there. " To the west, King's Mead, where formerly there was a monastery of the Benedictine order, is now graced by a series of stately detached residences, which, under the modernized name of Nun's Green, constitute the court end of Derby. But, interspersed in the streets, there are still many ancient tenements in which Prince Charles and his high-born adherents might find suitable accommodation.

Party feeling ran high in Derby, and most of its leading and principal denizens were Tories, and even Jacobites. It was in Derby that Henry Sacheverell preached his famous sermon, on "Communication of Sin. " This literary firebrand was first thrown out to the High-Church party in 1709, when the High Sheriff, George Sacheverell, of Callow, was attended by Dr. Henry Sacheverell as his chaplain, and the walls of All Saints Church resounded with the denunciations of that vehement, and ill-judging man. The seed that was thus sown fell into a land fertile in High Church propensities; the Grand Jury intreated Dr. Sacheverell to print his discourse; and, eventually, when they considered that, by the mild sentence given against their Preacher on his trial, they had gained a triumph, bonfires proclaimed their joy, in the market-place of that town, where the warfare of Sacheverell had first begun.

On the accession of George the First, and when the Chevalier landed in Scotland, fresh manifestations of the Jacobite party broke forth. The Church of All Saints was again the scene of its display. Three principal clergymen in the town openly espoused the Stuart cause. Sturges, the Rector of All Saints, prayed openly for "King James"—but, after a moment's pause, said, "I mean King George. " "The congregation became tumultuous; the military gentlemen drew their swords, and ordered him out of the pulpit, into which he never returned. "[121] Perhaps the event which tended most to quiet the spirit of Jacobitism among the lower classes in the town, was the erection of silk mills, in 1717. Nothing tranquillises extreme views in politics more surely than employment; few things attach men's minds to a Government more, than efforts crowned with success. Notwithstanding the memory of Sacheverell, a Whig member had been returned, in the last election, for the borough; the great merits and influence of the House of Cavendish overpowering the uproarious Tories, who, in vain, broke windows, and attacked their enemies. But discontent again broke forth. The winter of 1745 found the whole nation in a state of suffering and discontent; and many of the constitutional securities for liberty and property had been given up, in order to secure the stability of the throne. Taxation had been imposed, in the worst and most unpopular form, that of excise duties, in order to maintain an expensive Court, and to pay for Continental wars, which were maintained to preserve the hereditary German possessions of the King. Yet, in spite of these crying evils, such is the difficulty of inducing Englishmen to incur the risk of forfeiture and disaster, that even the town of Derby had diligently provided itself with a defence against the Chevalier's divided forces, on hearing of their approach.

During the month of September 1745, in consequence of instructions from London, the Duke of Devonshire, attended by the greatest appearance of gentlemen ever seen in the town before, assembled the clergy, in order to consider of such measures as were necessary for the support of the Government. An association was entered into, and sums were liberally contributed, after a splendid dinner, at that ungrateful inn, the George, which, during the sojourn of Charles Edward at Derby, changed its sign, into the safe and ambiguous title of the King's Head. Two companies of volunteers, of six hundred men each, were raised by the association. A proposal to call out the county militia was vehemently negatived, probably from that spirit of distrust which pervaded the councils of King George's Government. By an order in council, passed in the previous September, all Roman Catholics had been prohibited from keeping a horse of above five pounds in value, and restrained from going five miles from their dwellings. It was, therefore, deemed advisable to select the volunteer forces from the well-affected, and not to employ the militia of a county so manifestly disposed to foster the young adventurer as Derbyshire was at that time considered. During the month of November, a great degree of alarm had disturbed the burgesses of Derby; and from the communications of the Duke of Devonshire, then Lord-Lieutenant of the county, to the Mayor, it appears that the young Chevalier completely baffled the Duke of Cumberland and General Wade, by his rapid movement into the very heart of England. [122]

So late as the twelfth of December, the Duke of Devonshire and his eldest son, the Marquis of Hartington, were stationed at the George Inn, to watch the event of the coming storm, and to concert means for averting the threatened danger. Some days previously, the Duke had reviewed a company of six hundred volunteers, together with one hundred and twenty men raised at his own expense; and those townsmen, who were not Jacobites, were in high spirits, concluding that the Duke of Cumberland must have overtaken and attacked the insurgents. On the evening of the twelfth, the soldiers were summoned to the market-place, where they stood for some hours; they were then sent to quarters to refresh themselves; about ten the drums beat to arms, and, being again drawn out, these valiant defenders of the Borough marched out of the town, by torch-light, towards Nottingham, headed by the Duke of Devonshire.

On the following morning, about eleven, two of the vanguard of the insurgent army rode into the town; and, after seizing a very good horse, belonging to a Mr. Stamford, went to the George Inn, and there inquiring for the magistrates, they demanded billets for nine thousand men, or more.

In a short time afterwards, the vanguard itself rode into the town; this detachment consisted of about thirty men; they are described in the account of a cotemporary writer, probably an eye witness, as "likely men, " making a good appearance, in blue regimentals faced with red, with scarlet waistcoats trimmed with gold lace. They posted themselves in the Market-place, where they rested for two or three hours; at the same time bells were rung, and bonfires made upon the pretext of "preventing any resentment" from the rebels that might ensue upon a cold reception. About midday, Lord George Murray, Lord Elcho, and several other chiefs arrived, with troops to the number of one hundred and fifty, the flower of the army, who made "a fine show. " Soon afterwards the main body marched into the town in tolerable order, six or eight abreast, with about eight standards, most of them having a white flag with a red cross. But the appearance of the main body was totally different to that of the vanguard, and justified the contemptuous opinion and expectations formed by the loyal inhabitants of Derby, of their coming foe. As they marched along, the sound of their bagpipes was heard, for the first time, in the crowded and ancient streets of the borough; but the dress and bearing of these brave, but ill-accoutred men excited the derision of the thriving population of an important country town. They were, says the writer in the *Derby Mercury* of the day, "a parcel of shabby, pitiful looking fellows, mixed up with old men and boys, dressed in dirty plaids, and as dirty shirts, without breeches, and wore their stockings, made of plaid, not half way up their legs, and some without their shoes, or next to none, and numbers of them so fatigued with their long march, that they really commanded our pity more than our fear. "[123]

About five in the evening, when it was nearly dark, the Prince, with the other column, arrived. He walked on foot, attended by a great body of men, to a house appointed for his reception, belonging to Lord Exeter, and seated in Full-street. Here guards were placed around the temporary abode of the Prince; and here, during his stay at Derby, he held his councils.

"Every house, " adds the writer before quoted, "was pretty well filled (though they kept driving in till ten or eleven at night), and we thought we should never have seen the last of them. The Duke of Atholl had his lodgings at Thomas Gisborne's, Esq. ; the Duke of Perth at Mr. Rivett's; Lord Elcho at Mr. Storer's; Lord Pitsligo at Mr. Meynell's; Lord George Murray at Mr. Heathcote's; Old Gordon, of Glenbucket, at Mr. Alderman Smith's; Lord Nairn at Mr. John Bingham's; Lady Ogilvie, Mrs. Murray, and some other persons of distinction at Mr. Francey's; and their chiefs and great officers were lodged in the best gentlemen's houses. [124] Many ordinary houses both public and private, had forty or fifty men each, and some gentlemen near one hundred. "

The Prince, upon his arrival at Derby, resolved to halt for one day, and to take the advice of his council what was to be done at this juncture. His hopes were high, and his confidence in the good-will of the people of England to his cause was unabated. He continued to entertain the notion that George the Second was an usurper, for whom no man would willingly draw his sword; that "the people of England, as was their duty, still nourished that allegiance for the race of their native Princes which they were bound to hold sacred, and that if he did but persevere in his daring attempt, Heaven itself would fight in his cause. " His conversation, when at table, beneath the roof of Exeter House, turned on the discussion "how he should enter London, whether on foot, or on horseback, or whether in Highland or in Lowland garb. "[125] Nor was Charles Edward singular in his sanguine state of mind. It was observed, says Mr. Maxwell, "that the army never was in better spirits than while at Derby. "[126]

The judgment which Lord George Murray had formed at Manchester, remained, however, unaltered by all these expectations. On the following morning, when the council met, he represented to the Prince that they had marched so far into the country, depending on French succours, or on an insurrection, neither of which had taken place; that the Prince's army, by itself, was wholly unprepared to face the troops which the "Elector of Hanover, " as Lord George denominated him, had assembled. Besides General Wade's army, which was coming to oppose them, and that of the Duke of Cumberland, forming together a force of between seventeen and eighteen thousand strong, there was a third army, encamped on Finchley Common, of which George the Second was going to take the command in person. Even supposing that the Prince should be successful in an engagement with one of these armies, "he might be undone by a victory. " The loss of one thousand or fifteen hundred men would incapacitate the rest of his small force from another encounter; and supposing that he was routed in that country, he and all his friends must unavoidably be killed. On the whole, including the army formed at London, there would be a force of thirty thousand men to oppose an army of five thousand fighting men; that before such a host, pursued Lord George, [127] "it could not be supposed one man could escape; for the militia, who had not appeared much against us hitherto, would, upon our defeat, possess all the roads, and the enemy's horse would surround us on all hands; that the whole world would blame us as being rash and foolish, to venture a thing that could not succeed, and the Prince's person, should he escape being killed in the battle, must fall into the enemy's hands. "

"His Royal Highness, " continues Lord George Murray in his narrative, "had no regard to his own danger, but pressed with all the force of argument to go forward. He did not doubt but the justness of his cause would prevail, and he could not think of retreating after coming so far; and he was hopeful there might be a defection in the enemy's army, and that several would declare for him. He was so very bent on putting all to the risk, that the Duke of Perth was for it, since his Royal Highness was. At last, he proposed going to Wales, instead of returning to Carlisle, but every other officer declared his opinion for a retreat, which some thought would be scarce practicable. I said all that I thought of to persuade the retreat, and, indeed, the arguments to me seemed unanswerable; and for the danger, though I owned an army upon a retreat did not fight with equal valour as when they advanced, yet, if the thing were agreed to, I offered to make the retreat, and be always in the rear myself; and that each regiment would take it by turns till we came to Carlisle; and that the army should march in such order, that if I were attacked, I might be supported as occasion required, and without stopping the army (except a very great body of the enemy should be upon me), I would send aide-de-camps to desire such assistance as I should judge the occasion would require; but that I really believed there would be no great danger; for, as we were informed, the Duke of Cumberland was at Stafford, and would in all appearance, that night or next morning, be drawing near London to intercept us, so that if our design were not mentioned till next morning that it should be put in execution, we would be got to Ashbourn before he could have certain information of our design to retreat. "

The Prince, who was naturally bold and enterprising, and who had been hitherto successful in every thing, was indignant at this. Since he had set out from Edinburgh, he had never had a thought but of going on, and fighting everything in his way to London. He had the highest idea of the bravery of his own men, and a despicable opinion of his enemies, and hitherto with good reason; and he was confirmed in these notions by some of those that were nearest his person; these sycophants, more intent upon securing his favour than promoting his interest, "were eternally saying whatever they thought would please, and never hazarded a disagreeable truth. "[128]

A connected narrative of the proceedings in council has been given by Lord Elcho; and, at the risk of some recapitulations, it is here inserted, not having been previously published entire.

"The fifth, in the morning, Lord George Murray, and all the commanders of battalions and squadrons, waited on the Prince, and Lord George told him that it was the opinion of every body present that the Scots had now done all that could be expected of them. That they had marched into the heart of England, ready to join any party that would declare for him. That none had done so, and that the counties through which the army had passed had seemed much more enemies, than friends, to his cause. That there were no French landed in England; and that if there was any party in England for him, it was very odd that they had never so much as either sent him money or intelligence, or the least advice what to do. But if he could produce any letter from any person of distinction, in which there was an invitation for the army to go to London, or to any other part of England, that they were ready to go; but if nobody had either invited them, or meddled in the least in their affairs, it was to be supposed that there was either no party at all, or, if there was, they did not choose to act with them, or else they would ere now have let him know it. Suppose even the army marched on and beat the Duke of Cumberland, yet, in the battle they must lose some men; and they had, after that, the king's own army, consisting of seven hundred men, near London to deal with. On the contrary, if either of these armies beat them, there would not a man escape; as the militia, although they durst never face the army while in a body, yet they would have courage enough to put an end to them if ever they were routed; and so the people that were in armies in Scotland would fall an easy sacrifice to the fury of the Government. Again, suppose the army was to slip the King's and Duke's army, and get into London, the success of the affair would entirely depend on the mob's declaring for or against it; and that if the mob had been much inclined to his cause since his march into England, to be sure some of his friends in London would have fallen upon some method to let him know it; but if the mob was against the affair, four thousand five hundred men would not make a great figure in London. Lord George concluded by saying, that the Scots army had done their part; that they came into England at the Prince's request, to join his English friends, and to give them courage by their appearance to take arms and declare for him publicly, as they had done, or to join the French if they had landed. But as none of these things had happened, that certainly four thousand five hundred Scots had never thought of putting a king on the English throne by themselves. So he said his opinion was, they should go back and join their friends in Scotland, and live and die with them.

"After Lord George had spoken, all the rest of the gentlemen present spoke their sentiments, and they all agreed with Lord George except two (the Duke of Perth and Sir William Gordon), who were for going to Wales to see if the Welsh would join.

"The Prince heard all these arguments with the greatest impatience, fell into a passion, and gave most of the gentlemen that had spoke very abusive language; and said they had a mind to betray him. The case was, he knew nothing about the country, nor had the smallest idea of the force that was against him, nor how they were situated. " Fully convinced that the regular army would never dare to fight against him, and trusting to the consciences of men more than to the broad sword of his army, he always believed that he should enter St. James's with as little difficulty as he had done Holyrood-house. "He continued, " says Lord Elcho, "all that day positive he would march to London. The Irish in the army were always for what he was for, and were heard to say, that day, 'that they knew if they escaped being killed, the worst that could happen to them was a few months imprisonment.'"

The reluctance of the unfortunate and brave young Chevalier was increased by the evident ardour which his men, in the expectation of an engagement with the Duke of Cumberland, were at that very instant displaying, whilst the arguments which sealed Charles

Edward's fate, resounded within the walls of Exeter-house. The Highlanders, whose heroism balanced the inequality of the respective forces, breathed nothing but a desire for the combat. They were to be seen, during all that eventful day, in crowds before the shops of the cutlers, quarrelling who should be the first to get their swords sharpened. [129] In the very midst of the discussions, a courier arrived from Lord John Drummond, informing the Prince that he had landed at Montrose with his regiment, the Scottish Brigade, newly raised in France, and some pickets of the Irish Brigade, the rest of which would probably be in Scotland before the letter reached the Prince. [130] But this favourable intelligence, far from lessening the desire of Lord George to secure a retreat, rather increased his determination to uphold that resolution; and emboldened him to unfold to Charles Edward a plan for a Scottish campaign, which, he thought, might be prosecuted with advantage. In retreating to Scotland, the Prince, he argued, would have the advantage of retiring upon his reinforcements, which included the Highlanders at Perth, and the succours brought by Lord John Drummond. He concluded his address by a request, in the name of the persons present, that they should go back and join their friends in Scotland, to live or die with their countrymen.

Two councils were held upon this important subject, for in the afternoon the Prince convened another, to consider of the advices which the courier sent by Lord John Drummond had brought. "The debates, " observes the Chevalier Johnstone, "were very keen. " The Prince obstinately insisted upon giving battle to the Duke of Cumberland on the next day, the sixth; but he stood alone in that opinion. The Chiefs of Clans, who, since the council held at Perth, had never opposed the Prince in anything, feeling that they had now advanced too far to retreat, nevertheless opposed the march to London. They pointed to the coldness with which the insurgent army had hitherto been received; and asked how, supposing by some miracle the forces were to reach London, an army of four thousand men would appear among a population of a million people? The Prince still insisted upon marching to London; he even opposed the retreat, on the ground of the immense risk. The Duke of Cumberland, he contended, would pursue them hotly, and be always at their heels. Marshal Wade, he remarked, would certainly receive orders to intercept the army, so that they would "be placed between two fires, and caught as it were, in a net. "

This argument was met by the assurances which have been already stated in Lord George Murray's own language—that he would manage the retreat, taking always the rear. That he ably and effectually fulfilled that promise, was shown in the result.

At length the Prince, finding the greater part of the council was of Lord George's opinion, and deserted even by the Duke of Perth, who, after for long time resting his head on the fire-place in silence, accorded loudly with the Clans, consented to the retreat. This assent, wrung from him, was given with these bitter words, —"Rather than go back, " exclaimed the high-spirited young man, "I would wish to be twenty feet under ground. [131] Henceforth, " he added, haughtily, "I will hold no more Councils, for I am accountable to no one for my actions, except to my father. "

The usual double-dealing, and factious contention of party, succeeded this painful scene in the council. "After the council was dismissed, " says Mr. Maxwell, [132] "some of those who had voted against the retreat, and the Secretary, who had spoken warmly for it in private conversation with the Prince, condemned this resolution, and endeavoured to instil some suspicion of the courage and fidelity of those who had promoted it. The Prince was easily persuaded that he had been too complaisant in consenting to a retreat, but would not retract the consent he had given, unless he could bring back those to whom he had given it over to his own sentiments; which he hoped he might be able to do, since the Secretary had altered his opinion. With this view he called another meeting of the Council, in the evening, but found all the rest, to a man, firm in their former sentiments; upon which, the Prince gave up a second time his own opinion and inclination, to the advice and desire of his Council. "

The character of one individual was, however, elicited in this affair. "From this time, " observes Mr. Maxwell, [133] "the Secretary ceased to be in odour of sanctity with those that were not highly prejudiced in his favour. The little knave appeared plainly in his conduct on this occasion. He argued strenuously for the retreat, because he thought it the only prudent measure, till he found it was carried by a great majority, and would certainly take place; and then he condemned it, to make his court to the Prince, to whom it was disagreeable, and lay the odium upon other people, particularly Lord George, whom he endeavoured to blacken on every occasion. " Some people will wonder that this bare-faced conduct did not open the Prince's eyes as to the baseness of Secretary Murray's heart; "but, " says Maxwell, "if we consider that Murray was in the highest degree of favour, the steps by which he rose to it, and the arts he used to maintain himself and exclude everybody that could come in competition with him, he will easily conceive how he got the better of any suspicions his behaviour might have created at this time. "

The question, whether the arguments of Lord George Murray were guided by wisdom, or whether they might be better characterised as the result of a cold, and, in this case, unworthy prudence, has been very differently canvassed.

"There are not a few, " observes Mr. Maxwell, "who still think the Prince would have carried his point had he gone on from Derby; they build much upon the confusion there was at London, and the panic which prevailed among the Elector's troops at this juncture. [134] It is impossible to decide with any degree of certainty, whether he would or would not have succeeded, —that depended upon the disposition of the Army and of the City of London, ready to declare for the Prince. What could he do with four thousand four hundred men, suppose he got to London, whatever were the dispositions of the Army and the City? It is certain the Prince had no intelligence from either. This leads me to examine the conduct of the Prince's friends in England. The cry was general against them about this time in the Prince's army, and they are still exclaimed against by foreigners, who, having but a very superficial knowledge of these affairs, conclude that either the English are all become Hanoverians, or, if there are still some that have an English heart, they must be strangely degenerated, since they did not lay hold of this opportunity of shaking off the German yoke. Though I am convinced the Prince had a great many well-wishers in England, and though it is my opinion he would have succeeded had they all declared for him, nevertheless I cannot join in the cry against them, no more than I can condemn abundance of his friends in Scotland who did not join him. I have told elsewhere upon what a slender foundation this expedition was undertaken. Murray had imposed upon the Prince, and hurried him into it, without concerting anything with England. The English had always insisted upon a body of regular troops, not under seven and not above twelve thousand effective men. They saw the Prince in England with a handful of militia, which they could never think a match for thirty thousand regular troops. It is true the English have, in former times, taken arms upon less encouragement and less provocation than they had met with of late; but in those days the common people were accustomed to arms, and the insurgents were as good soldiers as any that could be brought against them. "

Such is the reasoning of an eye-witness. One thing is certain, contemporary writers appear to have generally acquiesced in the propriety of the retreat; and that circumstance constitutes the strongest evidence in favour of the step. Yet, viewing events at this distance of time, and taking into account the panic which seized, not only the public mind, but which affected the heads of the Government on hearing of the bold and rapid march of the insurgents, our faith in the wisdom of a retreat is weakened. In the night when it was announced in the fashionable circles of St. James's that the Prince had reached Derby, a general consternation was diffused throughout society. A lady of the highest rank, who was in one of the assemblies of the day, related to one of her descendants that upon the intelligence reaching the party where she was, the rooms were instantly cleared, and on the following morning there was not a carriage to be seen in London.

Nor were these apprehensions confined to any particular sphere. [135] The arrival of the troops at Derby was known in London on the ninth of December, henceforth called by the English "Black Monday. " Many of the inhabitants fled in terror from the metropolis, taking their treasures with them; the shops were closed: people thronged to the bank to obtain payment of its notes, and it only escaped bankruptcy by the following stratagem. Those who came first being entitled to priority of payment, the managers of the bank took care to be surrounded by agents with notes, to whom their pretended claims were paid in sixpences to gain time. These agents went out by one door and came back by another, so that the *bona fide* holders of notes could never get near enough to present them; and the bank stood out by these means until the panic had died away. King George even embarked all his most precious effects on his yachts, which were stationed in the Tower-quay, in readiness to convey him away, should the dreaded Highlanders, as it now began to be generally expected, march to London in a few days. The "moneyed corporations, " according to Smollett, were all in the deepest dejection; they reflected that the Highlanders, of whom they had conceived a most terrible idea, were within four days' march of the capital; they anticipated a revolution ruinous to their own prosperity, and were overwhelmed with dismay.

"I was assured, " writes the Chevalier Johnstone, (who differed from his General, Lord George,) "on good authority, when I was in London, some time after our unfortunate defeat, that the Duke of Newcastle, then Secretary of State for the War Department, remained inaccessible in his own house the whole of the 6th of December, weighing in his mind the part which it would be most prudent for him to take, and even uncertain whether he should not instantly declare himself for the Pretender. It was even said at London, that fifty thousand men had actually left that city to meet the Prince and join his army, and every body in the capital was of opinion, that, if we had beaten the Duke of Cumberland, the army of Finchley Common would have dispersed of its own accord, and that by advancing rapidly to London, we might have taken possession of that city without the least resistance from the inhabitants, and without exchanging a single shot with the soldiers. Thus a revolution would have been effected in England, so glorious for the few Scotchmen by whom it was attempted, and altogether so surprising, that the world would not have comprehended it. It is true, the English were altogether ignorant of the number of our army, from the care we took in our marches to conceal it; and it was almost impossible for their spies ever to discover it, as we generally arrived in the towns at nightfall, and left them before the break of day. In all the English newspapers our numbers were uniformly stated as high as twelve or fifteen thousand men. Under such circumstances, some temporary advantages might have been gained by marching southwards; for it is now believed that the Jacobite party in England were much more numerous than we have generally understood; and that thousands would have flocked to the standard of Charles Edward had he been accompanied by a sufficient force to authorise the expectation of his success. "

The British administration was, it is true, devoid of men of talent or principle, and discontent and distress prevailed in the country. In the City of London, the Jacobite party was very strong; its member was Alderman Heathcote, who, with Sir Watkin Williams Wynn, had announced to Lord Temple his determination to rise immediately upon a landing of troops from France. [136] The prevalence of Jacobite principles among the English gentry is supposed to have infected many officers in the royal army, who might have avowed them at any crisis in the public affairs; many were, at all events, suspected of Jacobite principles; "and the mere suspicion, " remarks Lord Mahon, "would have produced nearly the same effects as the reality, —bewilderment, distrust, and vacillation in the chiefs. "

"Had, then, the Highlanders combined to push forward, " observes this able writer, "must not the increasing terror have palsied all power of resistance? Would not the little army at Finchley, with so convenient a place for dispersing as the capital behind it, have melted away at their approach? "

In confirmation of this surmise may be quoted an anecdote which is related of a company of the celebrated Black Watch, which had been exempted during the insurrection of 1745 from serving against their countrymen; more than three hundred of the regiment having brothers and relations engaged in the Jacobite army. [137] But it was afterwards employed on a service which might well have been assigned to others; —to execute the decrees of burning, and to lay waste the districts where the forefathers of these brave men had lived. On marching one company of this famous regiment out of London, the Highlanders, on arriving at Hounslow, suddenly became immovable; they halted, and refused to proceed, or to bear arms against their countrymen. Their commanders, in dismay, turned to the chaplain of the regiment, to use his influence. The clergyman then in office happened to be Ferguson, the celebrated astronomer. He mounted on a temporary rostrum or pulpit, harangued the Highlanders, and, after an emphatic address, prevailed on them to march forward.

Such were some of the difficulties which the English Government encountered. To this may be added, the defenceless state of the coasts of Kent and Essex. The French ministers were now in "the very crisis of decision as to their projected expedition. " The preparations at Dunkirk were completed; and had Charles Edward, by advancing, shown that such aid was only a secondary matter in his favour, their fleet would have set sail. Besides, the Jacobites in England were by no means in so apathetic and subdued a condition as that which has been generally represented. [138]

"I believe then, " emphatically remarks Lord Mahon, "that had Charles marched onward from Derby he might have gained the British throne; but I am far from thinking that he would long have held it. "

"Whether he (Charles Edward), " says Sir Walter Scott, "ought ever to have entered England, at least without collecting all the forces which he could command, is a very disputable point; but it was clear, that whatever influence he might for a time possess, arose from the boldness of his advance. The charm, however, was broken the moment he showed, by a movement in retreat, that he had undertaken an enterprise too difficult for him to achieve. "[139]

In the opinion of the Chevalier Johnstone, whose judgment was formed under the influence of Lord George Murray, much of the failure of the expedition was owing to the inactivity of Lord John Drummond, who ought, according to his statement, to have advanced by forced marches to the assistance of Prince Charles. Nor was this the only error of that zealous, but inexperienced general: through his representations, the false intelligence that an army of ten thousand men was awaiting him in Scotland, was conveyed to the Prince; the disembarkation of this force was continually and confidently expected. "The first thing we did in the morning, " says Chevalier Johnstone, "was to see whether the wind was favourable; " and this delusive expectation had a very great influence in deciding the resolution taken at Derby to retreat to Scotland.

Whatever were the reasons which actuated the council of war, the result was, in the first instance, both painful to those who promoted the decision of the question, and highly obnoxious to the army. Arrangements were, however, made to keep the proposed retreat as secret as possible, both in order to baffle the Duke of Cumberland and not to irritate the Highlanders. Yet the design was soon penetrated by those who were intent upon every movement of their superiors. Lord George Murray, in his journal, describes the sensation which the projected retreat occasioned, in the following terms. [140] "Our resolution was to be kept secret, as it was of great consequence the enemy should have the intelligence of our march as late as possible. Yet, in the afternoon, one Sir John Macdonald, an Irish officer in the French service who had come over with the Prince, came where Lochiel, and Keppoch and I were talking together, and railed a great deal about our retreat. 'What! ' says he to Keppoch, 'a Macdonald turn his back? ' and to Lochiel, 'For shame; a Cameron run away from the enemy! Go forward, and I'll lead you. ' This gentleman was old, and had dined heartily, for he was much subject to his bottle: we endeavoured to persuade him that he was mistaken, but he still insisted, and said he had certain information of it. To tell the truth, I believe he liked his quarters and entertainment better in England than in Scotland, and would rather have been taken than return; for he thought, as he was in the French service, he did not run the same risk as others did. Some people, seeing the Prince so much cast down about the retreat, to ingratiate themselves, blamed the resolution; and though they had in the morning, as much as any body, given their hearty concurrence in the measure, and had exprest themselves so; yet, as they saw the retreat would certainly be put in execution, though they appeared against it, they thought proper to say that their reason for agreeing to it was because they knew the army would never fight well when the officers were against it. Sir Thomas Sheridan and his Royal Highness's secretary acted this part. And the Duke of Atholl, who had not been present in the morning, when the Prince sent for him in the afternoon, and spoke to him, seemed much for going forwards. In the evening, when this was understood by the rest of the officers, they told his Royal Highness that they valued their lives as little as brave men ought to do; and if he inclined to go forward they would do their duty to the last, but desired that those that advised his Royal Highness to go forward would sign their opinion, which would be a satisfaction to them. This put a stop to all underhand dealings, and the Duke of Atholl when he heard others upon the same subject, was fully satisfied as to the necessity of the measure. "

The town of Derby presented, during its occupation by the Jacobites, a singular scene. The Highlanders, hitherto maintaining a character for good order, now broke loose upon the townsmen of a city, which they, perhaps, began to consider as their own. They took the opportunity of replenishing themselves with gloves, buckles, powder-flasks, handkerchiefs, &c., which they demanded from the tradespeople, whose shops they entered. Being refreshed with a good night's rest, they ran about from house to house, until the town looked as if it were the resort of some Highland fair. "If they liked a person's shoes better than their own, " relates a contemporary writer, "nothing was more common for them than to demand them off their feet, and not to give them anything, or what they asked for them. " This insolence grew upon the forbearance of the townsmen, who dared not to resist martial law. Even the medical profession did not escape an unwilling participation in the concerns of the Jacobites. Dr. Hope, a physician residing in the town, and a member of the highly-respectable family there, was summoned to attend one of the sojourners in Exeter-house. The tradition which has preserved this anecdote among the descendants of Dr. Hope, has not specified the name of the invalid. The physician was told that he must go instantly: he was blindfolded, and led by armed men into the presence of his patient, without knowing whither he was conducted; a precaution, it may be presumed, adopted to prevent a refusal.

The church of All Saints witnessed what its Protestant ministers must have viewed with indignation and sorrow. Prayers were ordered to be said at six o'clock in the evening, when a Roman Catholic clergyman entered the sacred edifice, and performed the service according to the ritual of his church. [141]

In addition to these impolitic acts of a short-lived power, proclamations were made by the Town Crier, levying the excise duties; and a demand of one hundred pounds was made upon the post-office. In other quarters, even these forms were omitted, and plunder and outrage, which, says the author of the Derby Mercury, "were they to be stated would fill our paper, " were mercilessly committed. Nevertheless, such was the tendency of the town of Derby to Jacobite principles, that, among the higher orders, the brief appearance of the young and unfortunate adventurer was long remembered with interest, and his fate recalled with regret. The ladies of Derby vied with each other in making white cockades, of delicate and costly workmanship, to present to the hero of the day. To some of these admiring votaries he presented his picture, a dangerous gift in after-times, when a strict system of scrutiny prevailed; and when even to be suspected of Jacobite principles was an effectual barrier to all promotion in offices, and a severe injury to those in trade. One of these Jacobite ladies[142] is known by her family to have kept the portrait of the Prince behind the door of her bedchamber, carefully veiled from any but friendly inspection.

Early on the morning of Friday, the sixth of December, the drums beat to arms, and the bagpipes were heard playing in different parts of the town: the forces, it was expected by the townsmen, were thus summoned to continue their march to Loughborough, a town full of Jacobites, who were known to have been pledging the young adventurer's health on their bare and bended knees. [143] The retreat was begun in such haste, and attended with such confusion, that many of the Highlanders left their arms behind them, where they were quartered.

At nine o'clock, Prince Charles, in deep dejection, was seen mounted on a black horse, which had belonged to the brave Colonel Gardiner; —to quit Exeter-house, and, crossing the market-place, to proceed to Broken-row; he then turned through Sadler Gate, towards Ashbourn; he was followed by the main body of his army. Before eleven o'clock, Derby, so lately resembling, in its busy streets, the animated scene of a Highland fair, was totally cleared of all the Highland troops. But the consternation of the inhabitants paralyzed them. On that day no market was held, as usual; nor did the bells toll to church on the next Sunday; nor was divine service performed in any of the numerous and fine churches which grace the town. [144]

The retreat, thus begun under such inauspicious circumstances, was left solely to the guidance of the General who had so earnestly recommended it; and Lord George Murray took the sole management of it. In the dawn of the morning, when some of the troops had begun their march, the Highlanders did not perceive in which direction they were marching; they believed that they were going to give the Duke of Cumberland battle. When they discovered that they were in retreat, a murmur of lamentation ran through the ranks. "The inferior officers, " Lord Elcho relates, [145] "were much surprised when they found the army moving back, and imagined some bad news had been received; but, when they were told everything, and found the army had marched so far into England without the least invitation from any Englishman of distinction, they blamed their superiors much for carrying them so far, and approved much of going back to Scotland. They had all along imagined they were marching to join the English, and were acting in concert with them. To the common men it was given out the army was going to meet their friends from Scotland, and to prevent Marshal Wade from getting in between them, whose army was at Wetherby and Doncaster. "

The influence, however, of these contradictory reports upon the common men was soon conspicuous. The march was at first regular enough; but the whole bearing of the Highlanders was changed. Dispirited and indignant, they became reckless in their conduct: they lingered on the way, and committed outrages of which but few instances had been heard during their march southwards. Lord George Murray found it difficult to keep his army together. "In the advance, " observes Sir Walter Scott, "they showed the sentiments of brave men, come, in their opinion, to liberate their fellow-citizens; in the retreat, they were caterans, returning from a creagh. " The cause which they had adopted, had lost, from this moment, all hope, though the mournful interest attached to it still remained, perhaps, with increasing force.

In order to conceal the retreat as long from the enemy as possible, a party of horse was ordered to advance some miles in the direction of Lichfield, where the Duke of Cumberland was posted; and, to keep up the delusion, powder was distributed among the army. It was also insinuated that Wade was at hand, and that they were going to fight him; but when the soldiers found themselves on the road to Ashbourn they suspected the truth, and became still more sullen and dejected. Another artifice adopted to raise their spirits was a report, circulated purposely among them, that the reinforcements expected from Scotland were on their road, and that having met these, near Preston the army would resume its march southwards. This project, however distasteful to Lord George Murray, was, it seems, seriously entertained by the Prince.

And now commenced the difficulties of that undertaking in which Lord George had pledged himself to conduct an army of little more than six thousand men, in the depth of winter, in safety to Scotland, although in the neighbourhood of two great armies. The management of this retreat has been a subject of admiration to all competent judges of military affairs; it has conferred lasting honour on the capacity of Lord George Murray as a General.

It was of the greatest importance, under his circumstances, that Lord George should know of the movements and intentions of the enemy; and such was his system, such his address, in employing spies and emissaries, that he was always informed of what took place in the armies of the Duke and General Wade. One of his principal agents was Hewett, a butcher in Derby; who, from his local knowledge, could tell many particulars of the country-gentlemen, as well as of the movements of the Duke and his formidable forces. [146]

The Highland army arrived on the night of the sixth at Ashbourn, on the following day they reached Leek, on the ninth they arrived at Manchester, where a great revulsion of feeling had taken place. The "Hanoverian mob, " to use the expression of Mr. Maxwell, were determined to dispute the Prince's entrance; but when his vanguard appeared, these noisy heroes were instantly silenced. [147] From Manchester the Prince proceeded to Wigan, and thence to Preston, where he halted on the twelfth. Here the disappointed young man recurred to his cherished project, that of having reinforcements sent from Scotland, under Viscount Strathallan, who had been left in command at Perth, and those also under Lord John Drummond. Upon his arrival at Preston, he sent the Duke of Perth into Scotland to bring them with the utmost expedition. He was resolved to retire no further until he met them, and then to march directly for London, casting his whole chance of success upon the event of that step.

Among the generals and chiefs of this army a different sentiment had now arisen. A safe retreat was their object, and the subject of universal attention. Hitherto there had been little or no danger; it was impossible for the enemy to overtake the army before it had reached Preston; but between Preston and Carlisle it was practicable for the enemy's cavalry to come up with the Prince's army during that march. There was even a greater danger to be apprehended than the pursuit of the Duke. Marshal Wade had left his position at Newcastle-upon-Tyne, having been ordered by the Duke to place himself between the insurgent forces and Scotland, in order to cut off the retreat. There were in those days but few roads, or even passes in the mountainous regions of Cumberland and Westmoreland, by which a regular army could march. There was, however, an excellent road from Newcastle to Penrith, a town through which Wade might march his army, and where he could arrive a day or two before the Prince, and intercept his retreat.

On the fifteenth the Prince arrived at Kendal, and here Lord George Murray, taking a body of life-guards, went in person to reconnoitre the position of the enemy. He brought back several prisoners, who gave him all the information of which he was desirous. From what was thus gathered, Lord George perceived that the whole cavalry of Wade's army might possibly overtake the Highland forces before they could reach Carlisle; he therefore represented to the Prince the propriety of sacrificing the cannon and heavy baggage to the safety of the men; since the mountainous journey from Kendal to Penrith rendered the transit of such carriages very difficult. But the Prince was determined that his retreat should have the air of retiring, not of flying; he was resolved not to leave a single piece of his cannon; he would rather fight both armies than give such a proof of weakness. He issued peremptory orders that the march should be continued as before, and that not a single carriage should be left at Kendal.

The dissensions between Charles Edward and Lord George Murray had now ripened into reproaches on the one hand, answered by something not unlike taunts on the other. The former had cherished a predilection for battles ever since his victory at Glandsmuir, and he often broke out into expressions of anger towards his General, for his having prevented his fighting the Duke of Cumberland at Derby. As they quitted Kendal, Lord George observed to Charles, "Since your Royal Highness is always for battles, be the circumstances what they may; I now offer you one, in three hours from this time, with the army of Marshal Wade, who is only three miles distant from this place. " The Prince made no reply, but mounted into his carriage. All his ardour in marching at the head of the Clans was gone; he had become listless, careless, and dejected since the retreat. The army were dispirited by his gloomy and mournful aspect; and a still greater degree of difficulty and responsibility devolved therefore upon their General. On the sixteenth of December the army slept at Shap, and on the seventeenth the Prince arrived at Penrith; but the artillery, and the regiment of the Macdonalds of Glengarry, could only reach Shap by nightfall.

On the following morning Lord George proceeded towards Penrith. Scarcely had he begun his march when he saw a number of the enemy's light horse hovering about, but not venturing within musket-shot. About midday, as the Highland army began to ascend an eminence about half-way between Shap and Penrith, they discovered cavalry riding two and two abreast on the top of the hill. These instantly disappeared, but the noise of the kettle-drums and trumpets announced that they were only on the other side of the hill, and that they were probably forming in order of battle. Lord George was in the rear of the Highland army.

The advanced guard stopped at the foot of the hill, when suddenly they formed a resolution to advance sword in hand on the enemy, without informing Lord George of their resolution. On arriving at the summit of the hill, the party whose kettle-drums and trumpets had caused such an alarm, were found to be only three hundred light horse and chasseurs, who instantly fled. One prisoner only was made, a man who fell from his horse. It was desirable, on all accounts, to have preserved the life of this person, but the fury of the Highlanders was such that he was instantly cut to pieces.

After this alarm, this detachment of the Highland army resumed their march: the appearance of the light horse had, however, begotten an impression that Wade's forces were not far distant. The Chevalier Johnstone, more especially, had strong misgivings on the subject; his fears were confirmed by his serjeant Dickson, who called his attention to something black on a hill about three miles distant. This appearance, which every one else regarded as bushes, was soon found to be the English army, slowly but surely advancing. Before the vanguard could recover the surprise, the Duke of Cumberland, who had pursued them with forced marches, fell upon the Macdonalds, who were in the rear, with fury. Fortunately the road running between thorn hedges and ditches, the English cavalry could not act in such a manner as to surround the army, nor present a larger front than the breadth of the road.

The Highlanders instantly ran to the enclosures in which the English were, fell on their knees, and began to cut down the hedges with their dirks. This precaution was necessary, for their limbs were unprotected by anything lower than their kilts. During this operation, they sustained the fire of the English with admirable firmness. As soon as the hedges were cut down, they jumped into the enclosures sword in hand, and broke the English battalions. A fierce and deadly contest ensued. The English were nearly cut to pieces without quitting their ground. Platoons might, indeed, be seen, composed of forty or fifty men falling beneath the Highlanders, yet they remained firm, closing up their ranks, as fast as an opening was made by the broad-swords of the Highlanders. This remarkable attack was made in person by Lord George Murray, at the head of the Macphersons, whom he ordered to charge. At length the English dragoons were driven from their posts, and closely pursued until they arrived at the moor where their main body was planted. In this "scuffle" the Macphersons lost only twelve men; about one hundred of the English were killed or wounded. A footman in the service of the Duke of Cumberland was the only prisoner made by the Highlanders. This man declared that his royal master would have been killed, if the pistol, with which a Highlander took aim at his head, had not missed fire. Prince Charles, with much courtesy, sent him back instantly to the Duke. [148]

Such is a brief account of the engagement which Lord George Murray calls a "little skirmish, " but which must have afforded, at all events, some notion of Highland valour to the Duke of Cumberland and his dragoons. But, independent of the dauntless bravery of the Macphersons, to the skill of Lord George Murray may be attributed much of the success of the action. Before the firing began, he contrived, by rolling up his colours, and causing them to be carried half open to different places, to deceive the enemy with regard to the numbers of the Highland force; and to make them conclude that the whole of the army was posted in the village of Clifton. With about a thousand men in all, he contrived to defeat five hundred dragoons, backed by a great body of cavalry, all well disciplined troops. The moon, which was in its second quarter, appeared at intervals during the close of the action, and gave but a fitful light, being often over-clouded, so that the combatants fought almost in gloom, except for a few minutes at a time. The English, being all on horseback, were just visible to their foes, but the "little Highlanders" were in darkness. "We had the advantage, " observes Lord George, "of seeing their disposition, but they could not see ours. "[149] This encounter had the effect of saving the Prince and the whole army. "It was lucky, " calmly remarks Lord George Murray, "that I made that stand at Clifton, for otherwise the enemy would have been at our heels, and come straight to Penrith, where, after refreshing two or three hours, they might have come up with us before we got to Carlisle. "[150]

Lord George was in imminent danger during the action at Clifton. Fortunately, an old man, Glenbucket, who was very infirm, remained at the end of the village on horseback. He entreated Lord George to be very careful, "for if any accident happened, he would be blamed. " "He gave me, " relates Lord George, "his targe; it was convex, and covered with a plate of metal, which was painted; the paint was cleared in two or three places, with the enemy's bullets; and, indeed, they were so thick about me, that I felt them hot about my head, and I thought some of them went through my hair, which was about two inches long, my bonnet having fallen off. "[151]

In this skirmish Lord George commanded the Glengarry regiment, who had remained, at the General's request, in the rear, to guard the baggage. The officers, observes Lord George, "behaved to my wish, and punctually obeyed the orders they received. That very morning, however, the Glengarry regiment had told Lord George that they would not have stayed three days behind the rest of the army to guard the baggage for any man but himself. " The Stewarts, of Appin, were also among the most valiant of the combatants; but the most signal instances of courage were shown by Macpherson of Clunie, and his fierce band.

This unfortunate chief was engaged in the insurrection of 1715; that circumstance had been overlooked by Government; and, in the very year 1745, he had been appointed to a company in Lord Loudon's regiment, and had taken the oaths to Government. His clan were, however, anxious to espouse the cause of Charles Edward. Whilst Clunie wavered, his honour requiring the fulfilment of his oaths, his affections, and his hereditary principles leading him to follow Charles, his wife, although a stanch Jacobite, and a daughter of Lord Lovat, entreated him not to break his oaths, and represented that nothing would end well which began with perjury. She was overruled by the friends of Clunie, and he hastened to his ruin. [152]

The victorious General remained at Clifton half an hour after all the other officers had proceeded to Penrith. This circumstance disproved a statement given in the English newspapers, which intimated that the Highlanders had been beaten from their post at Clifton. On the contrary, "I heard, " observed Lord George, "that the enemy went a good many miles for quarters, and I am persuaded they were as weary of that day's fatigue as we could be. "

Upon arriving at Penrith, Lord George found the Prince much pleased with what had occurred. He was, however, just taking horse for Carlisle. On the next day, after staying a very short time at Penrith to refresh, Lord George joined Charles Edward in that city, which had yielded so short a time previously to his arms; and here various circumstances occurred which sufficiently show the discord which prevailed in the councils of the young Chevalier.

During the march, the young Prince had manifested a lofty sense of his own honour; but it was combined with a great degree of obstinacy in some respects, almost accompanied by puerility. Disgusted with the retreat, indignant with the promoter of that step, bent upon returning to England, unhappy, discouraged, and distracted by evil counsels, the Prince had plainly shown, that he would controvert the opinions of Lord George in every possible instance. He had lingered so late in the morning before leaving his quarters, as to detain the rear, which that General commanded, long after the van. This was a great inconvenience, and difficult for an impetuous temper to tolerate. The Prince not only refused to allow the army to be eased of any of the ammunition, being resolved "rather to fight both their armies than to give such a proof of his weakness; "[153] but he carried that order to an extreme, behaving as a petulant young man, who exerts power more in anger than from reflection. The march thus encumbered had been made with a degree of difficulty and fatigue which tried the patience of the soldiers, who were obliged, in one instance, to drag, like horses, the heavy waggons, in order to get them through a stream of water where there was a narrow pass, and a steep ascent. [154]

No enemy had molested the troops after they left Penrith; and it appeared evident that, at that time, the Duke of Cumberland had no intention of coming to a pitched battle, but intended only to take advantage of the disorder which he might suppose would have attended the retreat of an army of militia.

On arriving at Carlisle, a council of war was held. Lord George Murray was in favour of evacuating Carlisle, but his influence was overruled. "I had been so much fatigued, " he remarks, "for some days before, that I was very little at the Prince's quarters that day. " It was, however, determined to leave a garrison in Carlisle, for Prince Charles had set his heart upon returning to England. He, therefore, placed in the castle Mr. Hamilton, whilst the unfortunate Mr. Townley commanded the town.

"This, " remarks Mr Maxwell, [155] "was perhaps the worst resolution that the Prince had taken hitherto. I cannot help condemning it, though there were specious pretexts for it. " It would, indeed, have been highly advantageous for the Prince to have retained one of the keys of England; and he might have hoped to return before the place could be retaken. Of this, however, he could not be certain; and he was undoubtedly wrong in exposing the lives of the garrison without an indispensable necessity, which, according to Maxwell, did not exist; for "blowing up the castle, and the gates of the town might equally have given him an entry into England. "

The day after the Prince had arrived in Carlisle, he left it, and proceeded northwards. One cause of this, apparently, needless haste was, the state of the river Esk, about seven miles from Carlisle; it was, by a nearer road, impassable. This stream, it was argued, might be swollen by a few hours rain, and then it could not be forded. The Prince might thus be detained at Carlisle; and he had now become extremely impatient to know the exact state of his affairs in Scotland; to collect his forces, in order to return to England. Letters from Lord John Drummond had re-assured him of the good will of the Court of France—that delusive hope was not even then extinct. Advice from Viscount Strathallan had imparted excellent accounts of the army in Scotland. Under these circumstances, Charles hastened forward, and encountered the difficult passage over the Esk. Hope again gladdened the heart of one for whose errors, when we consider the stake for which he fought, and the cherished wishes of his youth, too little allowance has been made. But, in the eyes of others, the prospect of the young Chevalier's return to England was regarded as wholly visionary; and the planting a garrison in the dilapidated fortress of Carlisle, was deemed indifference to the fate of his adherents who remained, unwillingly, and certain of their doom. "The retreat from Derby was considered throughout England, " observes Sir Walter Scott, "as the close of the rebellion: as a physician regards a distemper to be nearly overcome, when he can drive it from the stomach and nobler parts, into the extremities of the body."[156]

The army, after marching from three o'clock in the morning until two in the afternoon, arrived on the borders of the Esk. This river, which is usually shallow, had already been swollen by an incessant rain of several days, to the depth of four feet. It was, therefore, necessary to cross it instantly, for fear of a continuation of the rain, and an increase of the danger. The passage over the Esk was admirably contrived; it could only have been effected by Highlanders. The cavalry formed in the river, to break the force of the current, about twenty-five paces above the ford where the infantry were to pass. Then the Highlanders plunged into the water, arranging themselves into ranks of ten or twelve a-breast, with their arms locked in such a manner as to support one another against the rapidity of the river, leaving sufficient intervals between their ranks for the passage of the water. "We were nearly a hundred men a-breast, " writes Lord George Murray; [157] "and it was a very fine show. The water was big, and most of the men breast-high. When I was near across the river, I believe there were two thousand men in the water at once: there was nothing seen but their heads and shoulders; but there was no danger, for we had crossed many waters, and the ford was good; and Highlanders will pass a water where horses will not, which I have often seen. They hold by one another, by the neck of the coat, so that if one should fall, he is in no danger, being supported by the others, so all went down, or none. "

The scene must have been extremely singular. "The interval between the cavalry, " remarks an eyewitness, "appeared like a paved street through the river, the heads of the Highlanders being generally all that was seen above the water. Cavalry were also placed beneath the ford, to pick up all those who might be carried away by the current. In an hour's time the whole army had passed the river Esk; and the boundary between England and Scotland was again passed. "[158]

Lord George Murray had, on this occasion, assumed the national dress. "I was this day, " he says "in my philibeg. " Well might he, in after times, when reviewing the events of the memorable campaign of 1745, dwell with pride on the hardihood of those countrymen from whom he was for ever an exile when he composed his journal. "All the bridges that were thrown down in England, " he remarks, "to prevent their advancing in their march forwards, never retarded them a moment. " Nor was the philibeg assumed merely for the convenience of the passage over the Esk. "I did not know, " writes Lord George, "but the enemy might have come from Penrith by Brampton, so shunned the water of Eden, to have attacked us in passing this water of Esk; and nothing encouraged the men more, than seeing their officers dressed like themselves, and ready to share their fate. "

Some ladies had forded the river on horseback immediately before the Highland regiments. These fair, and bold equestrians might have given intelligence; but luckily they did not. The General who had provided so carefully and admirably for the safety of his troops, knew well how to temper discipline with indulgence. Fires were instantly kindled to dry the men as they quitted the water. The poor Highlanders, when they found themselves on Scottish ground, forgot all the vexation of their retreat, and broke out into expressions of joy; —of short lived continuance among a slaughtered and hunted people. It was near night; yet the bagpipes struck up a national air as the last of the Highland host passed the river: and the Highlanders began dancing reels, "which, " relates Lord George, "in a moment dried them, for they had held up the tails of their short coats in passing the river; so when their legs were dry, all was right. " This day, forming an epoch in the sorrowful narrative of the insurrection of 1745, was the birthday of Prince Charles, who then attained his twenty-fifth year. Many mercies had marked the expedition into England, fruitless as it had proved. After six weeks' march, and sojourn, in England, amid innumerable enemies, threatened by two formidable armies in different directions, the Jacobite forces, entering England on the eighth of November, and quitting it on the twentieth of December, had returned without losing more than forty men, including the twelve killed at Clifton Wall. They had traversed a country well-peopled with English peasantry, without any attacks except upon such marauders as strayed from their main body.

As soon as the army had passed the river, the Prince formed it into two columns, which separated; the one, conducted by Charles Edward, took the road to Ecclefechan; the other, under the command of Lord George Murray, marched to Annan. In the disposition of these routes, the principal object was to keep the English in a state of uncertainty as to the direction in which the Jacobite army intended to go, and the towns which they purposed to occupy: and the end was answered; for no just notion was given of the movements of the Highlanders until after the subsequent junction of the two columns; and time was thus gained.

There being no town within eight or ten miles from the river Esk, the army were obliged to march nearly all night. The column conducted by the Prince had to cross mossy ground, under a pouring rain, which had continued ever since the skirmish at Clifton Wall. The guides who conducted Lord George's division led them off the road; this was, however, a necessary precaution in order to shun houses, the lights from which might have tempted the drenched and hungry soldiers to stray, and take shelter. Then the hardy and energetic general of his matchless forces first felt the effects of this laborious march in unusual debility, and fever.

At Moffat, this column halted; and divine service was performed in different parts of the town, all the men attending. "Our people, " remarks Lord George, "were very regular that way; and I remember, at Derby, the day we halted, as a battle was soon expected, many of our officers and people took the sacrament. "[159]

On the twenty-fifth of December, Lord George arrived at Glasgow, having passed through the towns of Hamilton and Douglas, and here, on the following day, Charles Edward also arrived, with the other column. Lord Elcho, who had conducted the cavalry through Dumfries, preceded the two great divisions. It was resolved to give the army some days' rest after the excessive fatigue which the men had uncomplainingly sustained. The spirits of Charles Edward were now recruited, and his example contributed not a little to the alacrity and energy of his force. Small, indeed, did it appear, when he reviewed it on Glasgow-green, and found how little he had suffered during his expedition into England. Hitherto Charles had carefully concealed his weakness; but now, hoping in a few days to double his army, he was not unwilling to show with what a handful of men he had penetrated into England, and conducted an enterprise, bold in its conception, and admirable in its performance.

At Glasgow, the melancholy fate of the brave garrison in Carlisle became known to the Jacobite army. Two days after the Prince had left, the Duke of Cumberland invested it, and began to batter that part of the wall which is towards the Irish gate. The governor of the Castle, Mr. Hamilton, determined to capitulate even before a breach had been made in the walls; and his proposal was vainly resisted by the brave Francis Townley and others, who were resolved to defend themselves to the last extremity. "They were in the right. "[160] They might have held out for several days, and perhaps obtained better terms; but the governor persisted in surrendering to the clemency of

King George, promised by his inhuman and dishonourable son. Assurances of intercession were given by the Duke of Cumberland, and the garrison of three hundred men surrendered. On the Duke's return to London, it was decided by the British government that he was not bound to observe a capitulation with rebels. The brave, and confiding prisoners perished, twelve of the officers by the common hangman, at Kennington; others, at Carlisle—many died in prison. Their fate reflected strongly upon the conduct of Charles Edward; but the general character of that young Prince, his hatred of blood, his love of his adherents, prove that it was not indifference to their safety which actuated him in the sacrifice of the garrison of Carlisle. He was possessed with an infatuation, believing that he should one day, and that day not distant, re-enter England; he was surrounded by favourites, who all encouraged his predilections, and fostered the hereditary self-will of his ill-starred race. The blood of Townley, and of his brave fellow-sufferers, rests not as a stain on the memory of Lord George Murray; and the Prince alone must bear the odium of that needless sacrifice to a visionary future. "We must draw a veil, " says the Chevalier Johnstone, "over this piece of cruelty, being altogether unable either to discover the motive for leaving this three hundred men at Carlisle, or to find an excuse for it. "[161]

On arriving at Glasgow, the Prince sent a gentleman to Perth to procure a particular account of the state of affairs in that part of the country; and on finding that his forces were so widely scattered that a considerable time must elapse before they could reassemble, he gave up the hope of returning to England, and determined upon the sieges of Edinburgh and Stirling. On the fourth of January he marched from Glasgow to Bannockburn, where he took up his quarters; and Lord George Murray, with the clans, occupied Falkirk. Before the twelfth of the same month, General Hawley, who had now formed a considerable army in Edinburgh, resolved upon raising the siege of Stirling, before which the trenches were opened.

Lord George Murray was, however, resolved to make a strong effort to prevent this scheme of General Hawley's from taking effect. Hearing that there was a provision made of bread and forage at Linlithgow for General Hawley's troops, he resolved to surprise the town and to carry off the provisions. He set out at four o'clock in the morning; was joined by Lord Elcho and Lord Pitsligo, with their several bodies of horse, and before sunrise Linlithgow was invested. The Jacobites were disturbed, however, in their quarters by a party of General Hawley's dragoons; and a report which prevailed that another body of horse and foot were also approaching, induced Lord George to return to Falkirk. On the following day he returned to Stirling; and the clans were quartered in the adjacent villages. The reinforcements which had been so long expected from the north were now near at hand; so that they could scarcely fail to arrive before an engagement began. The clans were augmented in number, and what was almost of equal importance, they had regained confidence and health on returning to their native land. All were in high spirits at the prospect of an engagement.

The Prince employed the fifteenth day of the month in choosing a field of battle; on the sixteenth he reviewed the army. The plan of the engagement was drawn out by Lord George Murray, according to his usual practice. The army of the insurgents amounted to nine thousand men. On that evening he learned that General Hawley had encamped on the plain between that town and the river Carron: upon which a council was called, and it was resolved the next day to attack the enemy.

The sympathies of the modern reader can scarcely fail to be enlisted in the cause of the Jacobites, who appear henceforth in the character of the valiant defenders of their hills and homes, their hereditary monarchy, their national honour and rights. Whatever an Englishman may have felt on beholding the incursions of a Highland force in his own country, the sentiment is altered into one of respect and of compassion when he views the scene of the contest changed, and sees the hopeless struggle fought on Scottish ground.

Never were two parties more strongly contrasted than the Hanoverians and the Jacobites. The very expressions which each party used towards the other, as well as their conduct in the strife, are characteristic of the coarse insolence of possession, and the gallant contest for restoration. Nothing could present a more revolting contrast than that between the individuals who headed the armies of Government, and the unfortunate Prince Charles and his brave adherents. In opposition to his generosity and forbearance stood the remorseless vengeance of the Duke of Cumberland. In comparison with the lofty, honest, fearless Lord George Murray, was the low instrument of Cumberland, the detestable Hawley. One blushes to write his name an English word. Succeeding General Wade, whose feeble powers had become nearly extinct in the decline of age, General Hawley was the beloved officer, the congenial associate of the young and royal commander-in-chief, who even at his early age could select a man without love to man, or reverence to God, for his General. These two were kindred spirits, worthy of an union in the task of breaking the noblest hearts, and crushing and enslaving the finest people that ever blessed a land of sublime beauty. Perhaps, if one may venture to make so strong an assertion, the General was more odious than his patron. It is, indeed, no easy point to decide towards which of these two notorious, for I will not call them distinguished men, the disgust of all good minds must be excited in the greater degree. In contempt for their fellow men, in suspicion and distrust, they were alike. In the directions for Hawley's funeral, he wrote in his will: "The priest, I conclude, will have his fee: let the puppy take it. I have written all this with my own hand; and this I did because I hate priests of all professions, and have the worst opinion of all members of the law. "

To this low and ignorant contempt for the members of two learned professions, Hawley added an utter disregard of every tie of honour; he was wholly unconscious of the slightest emotion of humanity; he revelled in the terrors of power. The citizens beheld, with disgust, gibbets erected on his arrival there, to hang up any rebels who might fall into his hands: the very soldiers detested the General who had executioners to attend the army. The generous nature of Englishmen turned against the man, who, as it has been well remarked, "deserved not the name of soldier. " They gave him the nick-name of the "Chief Justice; " and hated him as a man unworthy to cope with brave and honourable foes.

General Hawley had all the contempt, fashionable in those days, for Highland valour. "Give me but two regiments of horse, " he said, "and I will soon ride over the whole Highland army. " He quickly, however, learned his mistake; his contempt was, therefore, changed into a fiendish abhorrence, exhibited in the most horrible forms of unmitigated revenge.

It was decided by Charles and his Generals, in a council held on the evening preceding the battle of Falkirk, to attack the Hanoverian troops by break of day. The Tor Wood, formerly an extensive forest, but much decayed, lay between the two armies. The high road from Stirling to Falkirk, through Bannockburn, passes through what was once the middle of the wood. About eleven in the morning the Jacobite army was seen, marching in two columns, and advancing to the rising ground. Scarcely had they begun their march than the sky was overcast, and a violent storm blinded their enemy, who were, on the other hand, marching with their bayonets fixed; the fury of the tempest was such, that they could hardly secure their pieces from the rain.

Lord George Murray, with his drawn sword in his hand, and his target on his arm, conducted the Macdonalds of Keppoch. This clan regiment advanced very slowly that they might keep their ranks until they had gained possession of the ground they wanted; they then turned their backs to the wind, and formed into the line of battle. The field which they intended to occupy was skirted by a deep morass as they came foot by foot, within pistol shot of the enemy.

Meantime, General Ligonier, with three regiments of dragoons, began to move towards the Highlanders: whilst Lord George Murray, riding along the ranks of the Macdonalds, was forbidding them to fire until he gave orders. The English came at last, on full trot, almost close up to the line: then Lord George Murray gave the word of command to fire; the dragoons were instantly repulsed and fled back; upon which Lord George commanded the Macdonalds to keep within ranks, and stand firm. A total rout of the King's troops ensued; and the field of battle presented a strange spectacle. The English troops were, during the whole of the battle, severely incommoded by the storm of wind and rain, which almost blinded the enemy; but, independent of this accidental cause, their usual valour was, on this day, called into question. They fled in every direction. This famous battle did not last more than twenty minutes from the first fire of the Macdonalds to the retreat of the last regiment of dragoons. Before it grew dark General Hawley gave orders that his tents should be burned; he then retreated to Linlithgow.

Many brave English officers fell in this ill-conducted engagement, and their defeat was attributed at once to the arrogant confidence of Hawley, and to the courage and discipline of the Macdonalds of Keppoch, who, under the skilful command of Lord George Murray, are considered to have won the day. "If the bravery of the Macdonald regiments were put out of view, " observes Mr. Chambers, "it might be said that the storm had gained the Jacobites the battle. "

But the rain, which lasted during the whole of the battle, prevented a full advantage of the defeat being taken. The Highlanders, who do not use cartridges, were unable to load again, but were forced to have recourse to their broadswords; they were, however, out-lined by one-half of the enemy's infantry, and one of the battalions wheeling about, they were thrown into disorder by the force of a flank fire. They retreated up the hill, and before they could be rallied, the English, who could not be prevailed upon to stand a second attack of the Highland broadswords, had begun an orderly retreat. Had the whole of the Jacobite army been at hand, to rush headlong upon the enemy the moment they turned their backs, few of their infantry would have escaped being killed or taken. [162]

Lord George Murray, advancing with the Atholl men, who had kept the line in perfect order, pursued the retreating army towards Falkirk. He had arrived at the foot of the hill just as the English troops entered the town, which was at the distance of a musket-shot from the place where he stood. It was then proposed by most of the officers to retire towards Dunnipace, in order to shelter the men from the incessant rain; but Lord George opposed this proposition. He had observed the disorder of the English: "Let them not have time, " he remarked, "to rally, and to line the houses, and clean their guns, so as to defend the town of Falkirk; there is not a moment to be lost. " He concluded with the expression of Count Mercy at the battle of Parma—"I will either lie in the town, or in Paradise. "

Prince Charles coming up at the instant, approved of the resolution. A singular difficulty now occurred; there were no bag-pipes to inspirit the men with a warlike air; the pipers, as soon as a battle began, were in the practice of giving their pipes into the keeping of boys, who had to take care of themselves, and often disappeared with the instruments. "The pipers, who, " as Lord George remarks, "were commonly as good men as any, " then charged with the rest. This circumstance, which might appear trifling, was in fact the cause why the Macdonalds and other Clans had not rallied from the first. [163] Such was the importance of the national music at this critical moment. In ancient days the bards shared the office of encouragement to the Clans. It was their part to stimulate valour, and, before the battle began they passed from tribe to tribe, giving exhortations, and expatiating on the dishonour of retreat. They familiarized the people with a notion of death, and took from it, in one sense, its sting. When their voices could no longer be heard, they were succeeded by the pipes, whose wailing and powerful strains kept alive the enthusiasm which languished when those notes ceased to be heard. [164]

Lochiel, Lord Ogilvy, Colonel Roy Stewart, and several other chiefs, followed Lord George Murray into the town. On the ensuing day Charles and most of the army entered it. All were disappointed not to overtake the enemy; and Lord George Murray has left on record proofs of his bitter disappointment at the fruitless issue of this gallant encounter, much of which he attributes to want of decision and arrangement. Early on the morning of the battle, he had given the Prince a scroll of the line of battle, which was approved; he had requested that it might be filled in with the names of officers appointed to command. "I never, " he observes, "heard that there was any appointment made that day. " When it was agreed to march towards the enemy between twelve and one, he asked the Prince whether, since there was no other Lieutenant-General there, he should march at the head of the army? He was answered in the affirmative, after which he never received any other instructions until the action was over. The difficulties which Lord George had, therefore, to encounter, without knowing who were to command in the different stations; with only two aides-de-camp, both on foot, whilst his personal enemies were near the Prince in the time of the action, and did little to advise or suggest, are strongly insisted upon in his narrative. "I believe, " he adds, after firmly but dispassionately stating all these unhappy mistakes, "that my conduct was unexceptionable, and that in the advantages we gained I had a considerable share. "[165]

The day succeeding the victory of Falkirk was passed by the insurgents in burying the slain, and in collecting the spoils. A deep pit was dug by the country people, into which the English soldiers and the Highland clansmen were precipitated into one common grave. The former were easily distinguished by the frightful gashes of the broad-swords on their breasts and limbs. The tomb contained a heap of human bodies; and long after the event the spot of this rude sepulchre might be traced by a deep hollow in the field. [166]

Charles Edward had now arrived at another crisis of his singular destiny. The fate of a single day had once more rendered him victorious, but it requires a superior and matured judgment to profit by success. "One thing is certain, " remarks an eye-witness of this contest, and that is, "that the vanquished will always have great resources in the negligence of the victorious party. "

The battle of Falkirk struck terror into every English heart, and the panic of the Black Monday again spread like a contagion throughout the country. After the retreat from Derby, the higher ranks of society in England, who had betrayed an unwonted degree of alarm, concluded that they had nothing more to fear even from "a band of men so desperately brave who had done so much with such little means. " The victory at Falkirk was, therefore, received with redoubled alarm; and at court, during a ball which was held instantly after the event, only two persons appeared with calm and cheerful countenances. These were the King, whose personal courage was undoubted, and General Cope, who rejoiced that Hawley's failure might in some measure excuse his own. [167]

Under these circumstances, and being assured that the panic in Edinburgh equalled that in London, Prince Charles was strongly advised to repair to Edinburgh and to resume the possession of the capital. He hesitated, and the delay proved fatal to his interests. There was no time to be lost; —the conduct of Hawley had inspired universal contempt not only for his abilities, but for his cowardice. "General Hawley, " wrote General Wightman to Duncan Forbes, "is much in the same situation as General Cope, and was never seen in the field during the battle; and everything would have gone to wreck in a worse manner than at Preston, if General Huske had not acted with judgment and courage, and appeared everywhere. "

Lord George Murray remained at Falkirk with the Clans until apprised, through the secretary Murray, that the Duke of Cumberland was expected at Edinburgh on the twenty-eighth of the month; and that it was Charles's intention to attack him as soon as he arrived at Falkirk. At the first news of the project, Lord George seemed to approve of it; he drew up a plan of the battle, which he submitted to the ardent young Chevalier, who was delighted to think that he was to have to oppose the Duke of Cumberland in person. But this hope was transient; for on the very same evening, a representation, signed at Falkirk, by Lord George Murray and all the commanders of Clans, begging him to retreat, was presented to the disappointed and indignant Charles Edward. The great desertions which were daily taking place since the battle, was made the chief plea of this unexpected address; two thousand men, it was alleged, had gone off since that action, whilst the army of the enemy was reinforced. Some of the battalions were said to be one-third weaker than before the engagement at Falkirk.

The Prince received this address with a dissatisfaction even more apparent than that which he had shown at Derby, when persuaded to retreat. He dashed his head against the wall with violence, exclaiming, "Good God! have I lived to see this? " As the event showed, it had perhaps been wiser to have risked the event of an action at that time, than to have awaited the mournful catastrophe of Culloden. At length, although he never could be brought to approve of the step, Charles gave a reluctant and sorrowful consent to that which all his chieftains called upon him to adopt. The burden of the censure which was afterwards cast upon this decision, was thrown upon the Lieutenant-General. "I was told, " writes Lord George, "that I was much blamed for it. I really cannot tell who was the first that spoke of it, but this I am sure, every one of us were unanimously of the same opinion. " The siege of Stirling had proved, indeed, wholly unsuccessful; that very morning the battery, although it had been long in preparation, was silenced in a few hours after it began to play. It was therefore determined to abandon it; and it was decided that the time of the army would be more profitably employed in driving Lord Loudon from Inverness, and in taking the forts in the north, than in a rash engagement, or a hopeless siege. The spirit of the enterprise was, indeed, gone; otherwise such a retreat could never have been proposed and entertained. It was, however, fully determined on. The deepest dejection prevailed among the army when it was announced.

The Prince still remained at Bannockburn. On the thirty-first of the month it was determined to have a general review of the troops; the retreat was not to begin until ten o'clock. Early in the morning Charles Edward, still hoping that the desertions were not so numerous as had been represented, and that the "odious retreat" might be prevented, came out to view his troops. There was hardly the appearance of an army to receive him. On hearing the decision of the Prince, the men had risen at day-break and had gone off to the Frews, many of them having arrived by that time at that ford. There was nothing to be done; Lord George Murray, who had now joined the Prince from Falkirk, and who was quartered with some troops in the town of Stirling, was summoned. The Prince marched off with some of the chiefs and the few troops he had with him, and Lord George brought up the rear. A great portion of the artillery was left behind; the heaviest pieces being nailed up and abandoned. The retreat was thus precipitately commenced, and presented a very different aspect to the withdrawal of the Prince's troops from Derby.

Of this disorderly and disreputable march, Lord George Murray knew nothing until it was begun. The very morning on which it took place, the church of St. Ninian's, where the powder was lodged, was blown up. Lord George Murray was in his quarters when he heard the great noise of the explosion, and thought it was a firing from the Castle. "My surprise, " he thus writes, "is not to be expressed. [168] I knew no enemy was even come the length of Falkirk; so that, except the garrison of Stirling Castle, nothing could hurt us. I imagined they had sallied, and made the confusion I observed. I shall say no more about this; a particular account of it is wrote. I believe the like of it never was heard of. "

The destruction of St. Ninian's tower is attributed by most historians to the awkwardness of the Highlanders, in attempting to destroy their ammunition. "I am apt to think it was an accident, " observes Maxwell, "or, at least, the design of some very private person, for there was no warning given to any body to get out of the way. Nine or ten country people, and five of the Jacobite soldiers, perished from the explosion; and the Prince, over whose existence a special Providence appeared to have watched, was within being hurt when the explosion took place. "[169]

The Highland army was quartered on the first night of their march at Doune and Dumblain; and assembled the next day at Crieff. Here Charles Edward again reviewed them, and to his surprise found that they had mostly re-assembled, and that scarcely a thousand of the troops were wanting. The young Prince, who had reluctantly consented to the retreat upon the supposition that he had lost one half of his army, reproached Lord George Murray with having advised that step. Many were the censures heaped upon the General for his councils; and it must be acknowledged, that the caution apparent in his character was, in this instance, carried to an extreme. He excused himself on the plea of his opinion having been that of the whole army; but exonerated himself from any participation in the sudden departure, or, as he calls it, "the flight" from Stirling. At the council which was then called, heats and animosities rose to a height which had never before been witnessed, even among the vehement and discordant advisers of the Prince. After many fierce altercations, it was determined that Prince Charles should march to Inverness by the Highland road; and that Lord George Murray, with his horse, and the low country regiments, should proceed along the coast road, by Montrose and Aberdeen to the same place.

During the last few months the Marquis of Tullibardine had been stationary, employing himself in the fruitless endeavour to stimulate the tenantry and the neighbourhood to join the army of Charles Edward. After leaving Bannockburn he remained at Polmaise, a small village in Stirlingshire, until urged by Lord George to repair to Blair Castle, to garrison that place; for which purpose, according to his opinion, a body of fifty men would be sufficient. In his letters to his brother, Lord George recommends a degree of severity towards deserters which was not consonant with the mild temper of Tullibardine: "Those who have gone home without a special licence on furlough, must be exemplarily punished, either in their persons or effects, or in both; for when our all depends, lenity would be folly. " After urging the Marquis to send off the men to Blair by dozens, he adds, "If rewards and punishments do not, I know not what will. By the laws of God and man you have both in your power and your person: " thus alluding to the Marquis's position as a chief.

But these decisive measures were impracticable. "I was ordered by the Duke of Atholl" writes David Robertson from Blair, to his brother, an officer in Lord George's regiment, "to take up and imprison all deserters; but I might as well attempt to move a mountain, being left here without money, or men capable of being made officers. " Nor was the Marquis's power more effectual. The most sincere desire to comply with every wish or counsel of Lord George Murray's, actuated, indeed, this estimable man. He seems, from his letters, to have felt the most unbounded and affectionate admiration for his brother; a sentiment only inferior to his devotion to the Prince; yet we can perceive a covert allusion in some of his injunctions to those frequent disagreements with Charles, of which the Marquis was probably not ignorant. "Pray, take care of our young master's glory as well as your own, and the King's service, which ought to be dear to all honest men who are above selfish views. Excuse me, " adds the aged nobleman, whose anxieties and sufferings were soon to close in a prison, "for not writing with my own hand; since seeing you, excessive rheumatick pains has rendered it almost impossible. "

By Robertson of Strowan, a man noted for his eccentricities, a very gloomy view was taken of the proceedings of the generals and courtiers who surrounded Charles. He was ordered by the Prince to stay at home, and to stop all the deserters who came in his way. He obeyed the command; but obeyed with the observation, that "all were running to the devil, except the Duke of Atholl and the Laird of Strowan. " He hinted in his letters, that he could disclose much to the "Duke, " respecting his nearest relations, both as to their dislike to himself, and their disrespect to his Grace. The friendly intercourse between Lord George and his brother continued, nevertheless, unabated. The former on one occasion congratulates his brother on the valour of the "Atholl men, " at the battle of Falkirk. The encomium was answered by the Marquis's complaints of the sad change in the spirit and loyalty of the Clan since the defection of their "unnatural brother James" from the Stuart cause. Nothing but vexations and disappointments occurred to the Marquis on his return to Blair. His rents were refused by his tenants on account of their expenditure in the Prince's service, and the country around Perth was left exposed to the enemy. For some time entreaties from Lord George to his brother, that he would send men to replace those who were killed at Falkirk of the Atholl men, were met by excuses too well grounded in reason. All the "corners of the country" were searched by the Marquis's agent, to raise the men in an "amicable way, " but without avail. The exertions of poor Tullibardine, nevertheless, continued indefatigable, notwithstanding the truly Scottish complaints, sciatica and rheumatic pains. "I omit, " he writes, "nothing that lies in my power that can contribute towards the public service. God knows what dilatory and imposing evasions one has to struggle with amid a multitude of refractory people in these parts. " At length the sum of three hundred pounds was sent to him by Secretary Murray in order to maintain the recruits whom he had raised on his own estates.

Eventually the seeds of dissension were sown between Lord George Murray and his brother. Nor can we wonder, however we may grieve, at such an event. The aim of the one was personal glory, fame. The whole heart of the other was centred in the success of the cause. When he suspected that the intentions of that brother, of whom he was so proud, were less disinterested than his own, a mild, but earnest and mournful reproof was wrung from his kind and trusting heart. [170]

Until, however, the seat of war was transferred to the paternal home of Lord George Murray—whilst his immediate interests were spared—the Marquis of Tullibardine evinced the most sincere confidence in his intentions, and admiration for his talents. Afterwards, suspicions, which have been in a great measure dissipated by the testimony of brave and honourable men, might disturb the repose, but could not, eventually, sully the fame of Lord George Murray. In thus reverting to the domestic concerns of this celebrated man, the position of his lady and children naturally recur.

Lady George Murray had resided during the troubles of 1745 at Tullibardine, in the parish of Blackford, in Perthshire. The castle of Tullibardine had been fortified by a portion of the Earl of Mar's army in 1715: but was taken by the Earl of Argyle. Until after the close of the last insurrection it was inhabited by Lady George Murray; but when the fate of her husband was involved in the general wreck, the old building was suffered to fall to ruin. From this residence, such of Lady George Murray's letters to her husband as are preserved in the Atholl correspondence are dated. They are chiefly addressed to the Marquis of Tullibardine, and form the medium of correspondence between him and his brother. Here, too, she gave birth, after the battle of Falkirk, to a daughter named Katherine; and during the confinement which followed this event, her Ladyship's office as correspondent was fulfilled by her young daughter, who bore the name of Amelia. To the letter of this child, Lord Tullibardine replies with his accustomed courtesy and kindly feeling. "With extreme satisfaction I received, " he says, "a mighty well wrote letter from you, which could not but charm me with your endearing merit. I rejoice in being able to congratulate your mother and you on the glorious share my brother George has again had in the fresh victory which Providence has given the Prince Regent over his proud Hanoverian enemies! Dear child, I thank you kindly for enquiring after my health. " To these near, and, as it appears, cherished ties, Lord George was probably re-united during the march to Crieff. But whatever of domestic happiness he may have enjoyed, its duration was transient; and he passed on to a service full of the hardships of war, but in which he was doomed never more to possess the laurels of victory.

From Crieff, Lord George Murray marched to Perth, and thence by Montrose and Aberdeen to Inverness. During the inclemency of the winter many of the cavalry lost their horses; but the troopers being, as Sir Walter relates, "chiefly gentlemen, continued to adhere with fidelity to their ill-omened standards. "[171]

A storm of snow rendered the march from Aberdeen both dangerous and tedious. Lord George had above three hundred carriages of artillery to convey, although a great portion of the artillery was sunk in the river Tay, at Perth. In forming a junction at Inverness, the Prince had three objects in view—to reduce Fort-William and Fort-Augustus, on one side; on the other to disperse the army with which Lord Loudon had opposed him in the north; lastly, to keep possession of the east coast, from which quarter reinforcements and supplies were expected to arrive from France. It was, therefore, decided that Lord George Murray should continue along the eastern coast, in order to intercept Lord Loudon's army, in case it came that way. On the sixteenth of February he crossed the river Spey, and proceeded by Elgin, Forres, and Nairn, to Culloden, where he arrived the day before the castle of Inverness surrendered to Charles. Lord George Murray then gave the Prince an account of his march, of which even this hardy General speaks as of a journey of inconceivable trouble and fatigue. Here discussions took place, in which, as usual, the Prince differed in some important points from his Lieutenant-General. The plan which Lord George proposed was, to procure five thousand bolls of meal in Bamff, Murray, and Nairn, laying a tax in an equal manner on these several shires, and to send this supply to the Highlands; so that in case the Duke of Cumberland, who was now proceeding northwards, should follow them thither, they could have subsistence. To this scheme Charles objected; and the meal was lodged in Inverness. His confidence in his General, notwithstanding the incessant displays of his ability, was now wholly undermined. Charles's affairs were indeed rapidly declining; money, the principal sinew of war, was wanting. "His little stock might have held out a little longer, " observes Mr. Maxwell, "had it been well managed; but it is more than probable that his principal steward was a thief from the beginning. " The Secretary Murray, against whom this charge is levelled, was not, perhaps, more faithless when he appropriated to himself the funds of his unfortunate master, than when he planted in the breast of Charles, misgivings of his friends, and abused his influence to mislead a confiding nature. There was, however, no proof against Murray of Broughton of dishonesty, "but there were very strong presumptions; and his underlings, who suspected that their opportunity would not last long, made the best of it, and filled their pockets with the public money. "[172]

By the officers and soldiers at Culloden, Lord George was received with joy. They regretted his absence, and were pleased to say that had he been with them they should have "given a good account of Lord Loudon and his troops, whom they had been prevented from pursuing at Inverness. " Lord George soon found that these professions were sincere. The Prince was induced to send him to Dingwall, that he might assist the Earl of Cromartie in pursuing Lord Loudon, who had passed up to Tain. This scheme having proved impracticable, he returned to Inverness.

Meantime the county of Atholl suffered under the unparalleled cruelties of the English soldiery. The Duke of Cumberland had visited that interesting district; and it requires little more to be said, to comprehend that beauty was turned to desolation; that crimes hitherto unheard of among a British army reflected dishonour on the conquerors, and brought misery to the conquered. On the sixth of February, 1746, the Duke had arrived at Perth. His first orders were to seize the Duchess of Perth, the mother of the Duke, and the Viscountess Strathallan, and to carry them to a small, wretched prison in Edinburgh, where they remained nearly a year. The Duke of Cumberland was succeeded at Edinburgh by his brother-in-law, the Prince of Hesse, who had landed at Leith with five thousand infantry and five hundred huzzars in the pay of England. These were stationed in the capital, ready to swarm into the country to subdue its brave inhabitants.

Whilst Lord George Murray was still at Inverness, he heard that his cherished home, the territory of his proud forefathers, the scenes of his youth, were ravaged by a detachment of Cumberland's army. The houses of such gentlemen as had assisted Prince Charles were burned; and their families, after receiving every species of indignity that could palliate the guilt of a future revenge, and that could break honest hearts, were turned out to perish on the hills with cold and hunger. The very nature of Englishmen appears to have been changed during this most mournful, most disgraceful warfare; and never did the British army sink so low in morals, in humanity, as during the German yoke of a Prince whom one rejects as a countryman. [173]

Lord George was instantly ordered to go to Atholl. Little could he suspect the construction afterwards placed on his conduct, and the snare which was laid for him by his enemies, in the events of the next few weeks.

Lord George marched with unheard of dispatch towards Atholl. Already had the Duke of Cumberland placed at different parts, in that district, bands of the Argyleshire Campbells, to the amount of three hundred in number. A thousand more, it was reported, were coming from the same quarter; and it was Lord George's aim to intercept this reinforcement. He set off, followed by his brave "Atholl-men, " conducting his march through byeways across the mountains; and in one march, day and night, he traversed a tract of thirty miles. It was, however, impossible to transport cannon through these almost impassable solitudes; yet, with a force not exceeding seven hundred men, Lord George contrived to surprise the enemy at these posts. He entered Atholl in the early part of the night; his detachment then separated, and, dividing itself into small parties, each gentleman whose home had been invaded took the shortest road to his own house. The English soldiers were surprised in their sleep, and, according to the Chevalier Johnstone, lay murdered in their beds; but this is contradicted by many authorities. [174] These Highland gentlemen attacked, during that night, thirty of the posts in question, and all of them were carried. Few of the Government troops were put to the sword; about three hundred were taken prisoners, and between two and three hundred barricaded themselves in the Castle of Blair. [175]

The Marquis of Tullibardine had, it appears, been driven from that fortress some time previously. Misfortune was not new to one who had joined in the insurrection of 1715.

"As the late Rothiemurcus, [176] your father, " he writes to a friend, [177] in a letter to which he dared not even state his place of residence, "showed me particular friendship and kindness on just such an unfortunate occasion as the present, makes me hope you will have no less regard for me in taking care of some small concerns of mine; which consists in taking care of two of three of my servants and some baggage, which I send you, rather than it should fall into enemies' hands; so that if you cannot keep it, and get it sent me in time and place convenient, it may be of some use to yourself, whom I esteem on your family and father's account; though we have not had the occasion of a personal acquaintance, which I hope may yet agreeably happen, in whatever bad situation our affairs may at present appear; then I may agreeably be able to return you suitable thanks for such an obligation as will for ever oblige,

"Sir, "Your affectionate humble servant and cousin, "ATHOLL. "

14th March, 1746.

* * * * *

The Clan of Atholl was the largest that engaged in Prince Charles's service, and numbered nearly fifteen hundred men. Lord George now collected three hundred more of these vassals, and invested Blair Castle. One difficulty he had in the deficiency of cannon; he obtained, however, some field-pieces from Inverness, but his artillery was too light to make an impression on the walls. There was an alternative, which was, to reduce the castle by famine. Blair, as it happened, was defended by a stout and sturdy veteran, Sir Andrew Agnew, who was resolved only to yield upon extreme necessity his important charge. During the siege, Lord George wrote on the subject of the enterprise to his brother the Marquis of Tullibardine. The letter was answered in a manner which shows that some want of candour had been evinced towards the Marquis, who was regarded by all the Jacobites as the legitimate owner of Blair. The epistle breathes the tone of mournful resentment. "Since, contrary to the rules of right reason, you have been pleased to tell me a sham story about the expedition to Blair, " such are the expressions used by the Marquis of Tullibardine, "you may now do what the gentlemen of that country wish with the castle. "[178] With the true value of a high-born man for the memorials of his ancestors, the Marquis grieved most for the loss of his great-great-grandfather's grandfather's, and father's pictures. "They will be ane irreparable loss. " But every thing that could promote the public service was to be resigned cheerfully and willingly for that cause. Not only did he proffer the sacrifice of his castle, but he pointed out to his brother a gate which had formerly been a portcullis, leading into it. This was at that time half-built up, and boarded, with a hollow large enough to hold a horse at rack and manger; and the Marquis suggested that this place might be more easily penetrated than any other part of the wall, so as to make an entrance into the vaulted room called "the Servants' Hall. "

Whether or not Lord George decided to take advantage of this hint is unknown. The attack made upon the Castle of Blair was conducted by him in person, and was begun simultaneously with those headed by his followers upon the various posts at Blairfitty, Kinachie side, and several places near Blair. Upon the persons of the prisoners were found copies of their orders from the Duke of Cumberland, and these were signed by Colonel Campbell, and contained instructions to attack the rebels wherever they should meet them; and in case of resistance, it was the Duke's orders that *they should get no quarter*. [179] Stimulated by these intercepted documents, Lord George, early on the morning of the eighteenth of March, began the siege of Blair.

Many have been the accounts given, and various are the surmises upon the motives of Lord George in not reducing the castle; but in estimating the real difficulties of his undertaking, the testimony of a soldier and a contemporary must be taken in evidence.

Blair was defended by a man of no ordinary character, Sir Andrew Agnew, Lieutenant-Colonel of the Royal North British Fusiliers, who had been sent with a detachment from Perth by the route of Dunkeld, through the pass of Killicrankie, to take possession of the Castle.

When Sir Andrew first posted himself in Blair no apprehensions of a blockade were entertained; and no fear of a supply of provisions being cut off was suggested. The quantity of garrison provisions sent into it was therefore extremely small, as was also the store of ammunition. In regard to water, the garrison were in a better condition. A draw-well in the castle supplied them after the blockade: previously, the inhabitants had usually fetched the water they required from a neighbouring barn or brook, which formed itself into a pool in front of the house. [180]

Blair Castle was then an irregular and very high building, with walls of great thickness, having a great tower, called Cumming's Tower, projecting from the west end of the front of the house, which faces the north. This tower could be defended by musket shot from its windows.

Adjoining to the eastern gavel of the old house a new building had been begun, but had only been carried up a few feet at the time of the siege. Since the year 1745, great alterations have been made in this building, which has been lowered and modernized, and the Cumming's Tower wholly taken away.

It was between nine and ten in the morning when Lord George Murray appeared before Blair Castle, and planted his men so as to prevent the garrison from sallying out, or from getting in provisions. [181] The castle was soon so completely invested by the advanced guard of the Jacobites, that they fired from behind the nearest walls and enclosures at the picket guard of the besieged. Some horses were hurriedly taken into the Castle with a small quantity of provender; and in such haste, that one of these animals was put into the lower part of Cumming's Tower without forage or water.

There was a great entrance and staircase on the east side of the Castle; this was now barricaded, and a small guard placed near it;

the garrison, consisting of two hundred and seventy men, were then parcelled out into different chambers, with a charge not to fire until actually attacked. A sort of platform was laid over the new building of the Castle, and an ensign with a guard of twenty-five soldiers placed on this to defend that part from serving as a lodgement to the besiegers. There was also a guard placed over the draw-well, to prevent the water being drawn up except at a certain hour in the morning. Besides the garrison, there were within the Castle, about seven servants of the Duke of Atholl's; namely, a land steward, a female housekeeper, three maid servants, a gardener, and a gamekeeper.

Lord George Murray having established his quarters in the village of Blair, about a quarter of a mile from the north of the castle, soon sent down a summons to Sir Andrew Agnew, Bart. to surrender, intimating that "he should answer to the contrary at his peril. "

Now Sir Andrew was reputed to be a man of an outrageous temper; and the Highlanders, who could face the Duke of Cumberland's dragoons, shrank from encountering the sturdy, imperious old soldier. The only person, therefore, who could be prevailed upon to carry the summons, was a maid-servant from the inn at Blair, who being a comely Highland girl, and acquainted with some of the soldiers, conceived herself to be on so friendly a footing with them that she might encounter the risk. The summons was written on a very dirty piece of paper; and corresponded well with the appearance of the herald who conveyed it. Provided with this, the young woman set out; as she approached the Castle, she waived the summons over her head several times, and drawing near one of the windows on the basement story, made herself heard. She was received by the officers with boisterous mirth; they assured her that they should soon visit the village, and her master's house, again, and drive away the Highlanders. But, when entreated by the girl to take her into Sir Andrew's presence, they all at first refused; at last the summons was reluctantly conveyed to the commandant by a lieutenant more venturesome than the rest. This emissary soon, however, fled from the presence of the baronet, who broke out with the most vehement expressions of rage on reading the contents of the paper; uttered strong epithets against Lord George Murray, and threatened to shoot any messenger who might dare to convey any future communication.

The young girl returned to Blair. As she drew near the village, she perceived Lord George Murray, Lord Nairn, Clunie Macpherson and other officers standing in the churchyard of Blair; and observed that they were evidently diverted by her errand, and its result. [182]

From that time Lord George Murray made no attempt to hold any parley with the garrison, but continued to blockade the Castle. His men were even posted close up against the walls, wherever they could not be annoyed with the musketry; particularly at that part on which the scaffold guard was placed, where they stood, heaving up stones from time to time, and uttering their jokes against the veteran, Sir Andrew Agnew. [183]

"The cannon, " as Lord George Murray observes in his narrative, "were not only small, but bad. One of them seldom hit the Castle, though not half-musket shot from it. "

Various schemes were formed by Lord George during this siege, but many obstacles concurred to check them. It had indeed been proposed before Lord George left Inverness, to blow up Blair Castle; but not only had Lord George no orders to attempt that, but there seemed also to be a difficulty from the situation of the place.

It appeared at one time his intention, also, to have set the building on fire. "On the eighteenth, " writes Lord Elcho, "Lord George began to fire against the Castle with two four pounders; and as he had a furnace along with him, finding his bullets were too small to damage the walls, he endeavoured by firing red hot balls to set the house on fire, and several times set the roof on fire, but by the care of the besieged it was always extinguished. A constant fire of small arms was kept against the windows, and the besieged kept a close fire from the castle with their small arms. " "As the castle, " continues the same writer, "is situated upon rocky ground, there was no blowing it up; so the only chance Lord George had to get possession of it was to starve it, which he had some hopes of, as there were so many mouths in it. " From this opinion, the judgment of Lord George Murray, in some measure, differed. "It might, I believe, " he says, "have been entered by the old stables, under protection of which the wall could have been undermined, if I had been furnished with proper workmen. " But all his efforts, in both these schemes, proved ineffectual. The red hot balls lodging in the solid timbers of the roof, only charred, and did not ignite the beams; and falling down, were caught up in iron ladles brought out of the Duke of

Atholl's kitchen, and thrown into water. Disappointed in this attempt, Lord George removed his few field-pieces to a nearer position on the south side of the Castle, where, however, his firing produced no better effect than heretofore.

Never was there an officer more insensible to fear than the defender of Blair. Whilst Lord George was thus ineffectually battering the walls of the house, Sir Andrew Agnew looked out over the battlements; and seeing the little impression that was made on the walls, he exclaimed, "Hout! I daresay the man's mad, knocking down his own brother's house. "

Meantime the siege lasted nearly a fortnight, and the garrison were reduced to the greatest extremity for provisions. One hope, however, the commandant had, and that was of sallying forth, and escaping. The Castle of Menzies was then occupied by Colonel Webster, who was posted there in order to secure the passage of the river Tay; and, as an alternative to starvation, a scheme was suggested for stealing out from Blair in the night time, and marching through a mountainous part of country to join the king's troops at Castle Menzies.

Whilst this project was in contemplation, the brave garrison were threatened with a new danger. During the blockade, there was heard a noise of knocking, seemingly beneath the floor of the Castle, as if miners were at work in its deep vaults, to blow it up. All the inmates of Blair thought such must indeed be the case: for Lord George had now gained possession of a bowling-green near the Castle, and also of a house in which the bowls were kept: from this bowl-house a subterranean passage might easily have been dug to the very centre of the ground underneath the building, and a chamber or mine formed there for holding barrels of gunpowder, sufficient to complete the work of destruction. This scheme must have occurred to the mind of Lord George Murray, who was born at Blair, and well acquainted with its construction. His objections to pursue it appear, as has been stated, to have been perceived and controverted by the Marquis of Tullibardine. They arose, as he has himself declared, and as the English also appear to have considered, from his want of workmen to perform the attempt. The plan of undermining was not thought practicable; and the noise which so greatly alarmed the garrison was proved to be only the reverberation of strokes of an axe with which a soldier was cutting a block of wood which lay on the floor of one of the uppermost rooms. The most unfavourable suspicions were, however, eventually affixed to Lord George's neglect of this mode of attack. Whether such conduct proceeded, on his part, from an aversion to destroy the home of his youth, and his birthplace; whether he had still hopes of reducing Sir Andrew to capitulate; or whether, as it has been often vaguely asserted, a secret agreement existed between himself and James, Duke of Atholl, that the Castle should be saved, can only be determined by a far closer insight into motives than human power can obtain. We may accord to Lord George Murray, without a blemish on his fidelity, a pardonable reluctance to level to the dust the pride of his family; that every effort was made to subdue Blair, except the last, is evident from the testimony of all contemporary historians.

Meantime the garrison had one source of confidence in their extremity, on which sailors are more apt to reckon than landsmen. They trusted to the *luck* of their commandant. Never had the stout veteran who had fought, in 1706, at Ramilies, been either sick, or wounded. He had never been in any battle that the English did not win. Yet it was deemed prudent not to allow any means of aid to be neglected, in so pressing a danger as the state of the siege presented.

The Earl of Crawford was then supposed to be at Dunkeld, having the command both of the British troops and of a body of Hessians who had lately been marched from Edinburgh. It was resolved to send to that nobleman for aid. The Duke of Atholl's gardener, a man named Wilson, undertook that dangerous embassy; he was charged with a letter from Sir Andrew to the Earl, and was allowed to take his choice of any horse in the Castle. [184]

Before Sir Andrew and his starving garrison could gain intelligence of the fate of Wilson, or could have heard the result of his enterprise, a strange reverse in their affairs took place. On the morning of the first of April, not a single Highlander was to be seen by any of the guards on duty. All had vanished; and a visit from the young woman from the inn at Blair shortly followed their disappearance. From her, the garrison heard that Lord George had, in fear of the arrival of troops from Dunkeld, suddenly withdrawn with all his followers. The old Sir Andrew, nevertheless, fearful of some stratagem, would not allow his garrison to sally out: they were shut up until the following day, when the Earl of Crawford appeared before the castle, and relieved all fears. The officers and soldiers were then drawn out, with Sir Andrew at the head of it. "My Lord, " cried the old soldier, "I am very glad to see you; but, *by all that's good,* you are come too late, and we have nothing to give you to eat! " To which Lord Crawford answered courteously; and laughing, begged of Sir Andrew to partake of such provisions as he had brought with him. That day Sir Andrew and the Earl, and their officers, dined in the summer-house of the garden at Blair, in high spirits at the result of the siege.

The disappearance of Lord George Murray was soon explained; nor can the statement of those reasons which induced him to abandon the siege of Blair be given in a more satisfactory manner than as they were stated by Lord Elcho; to whom they must have appeared satisfactory, otherwise he would not have left so clear and decisive a testimony in favour of Lord George Murray's motives. It is worthy of remark, that Lord Elcho's statement agrees in every particular with that addressed some years afterwards by Lord George to Mr. Murray of Abercairney, and now preserved in the Jacobite Memoirs by Forbes. [185]

"On the twenty-fourth of March, the Hessians from Perth and Crieff moved to its relief. They encamped the first night at Nairn House, and next night at Dunkeld, and there was some firing betwixt them and a party of Lord George's across the river. Those that marched from Crieff encamped at Tay Bridge on the twenty-seventh. Upon this motion of the Hessians, Lord George sent an express to the Prince, to tell him that if he would send twelve hundred men, he would pitch upon an advantageous ground and fight them. The Prince sent him word he could not send him them in the way his army was then situated. On the thirty-first the Earl of Crawford marched with St. George's Dragoons, five hundred Hessians, and sixty Hussars, and encamped at Dawallie, four miles north of Dunkeld, and next day they advanced to Pittachrie. Both these days Lord George had several skirmishes with the hussars; but although he laid several snares for them, he never could catch but one of them, who was an officer and a Swede, who had his horse shot under him. Lord George used him very civilly, and sent him back with a letter of compliment which he wrote to the Prince of Hesse. On the first of April Lord George Murray drew his men up in battle opposite to Lord Crawford at Pittachrie, and then retreated before him, in order to draw him into the pass of Killicrankie; but Lord Crawford never moved, but sent for reinforcements to the Prince of Hesse. Lord George, upon hearing of the march of that reinforcement to sustain Lord Crawford, and that the body of Hessians from Lay Bridge were marching to Blair by Kinachin, quitted the country and marched his men to Strathspan, and from thence to Speyside. He himself went to Inverness, where he found his enemies had persuaded the Prince that he might have taken Blair Castle if he had had a mind, but that he had spared it because it was his brother's house; and in short they made the Prince believe, that in the letter he had wrote to the Prince of Hesse, he had engaged to betray him the first opportunity; and that by the Prince of Hesse and his brother's means, he was entirely reconciled to the government. What Mr. Murray had insinuated to the Prince about Lord George, on his first coming to Perth had made such an impression, that the Prince always believed it, notwithstanding Lord George's behaviour was such (especially in action) as to convince the whole army of the falsity of such accusations. However it opened his mind upon the matter of the Irish officers, so far as to make some of them promise to watch Lord George's motions, particularly in case of a battle, and they promised the Prince to shoot him, if they could find he intended to betray him."

From the following letter addressed by Lord George Murray to his brother the Marquis of Tullibardine, it is evident that he had had it in contemplation during some time, to abandon the siege of Blair, and that the sudden appearance of the body of Hessians six thousand strong, within a day's march of Blair, was not the only cause of his raising a siege which every one acknowledges must have terminated in favour of the besiegers within a few days.

"Blair, 29th of March, 1746.

"Dear Brother, [186]

"I received your letter of the 26th; I am sorry you seem to think I told you a sham story (as you express it) about our expedition here. I told you we were to endeavour to take possession of Castle Grant, and try to hinder that Clan taking party against us; this was done so far as in our power. I also told you if we could contrive to surprise any of the parties in this country we might attempt it; but that depended so much upon incidents, that my very hopes could not reach so far as we performed. Secrecy and expedition was our main point, once we resolved upon the thing, which was not till I met Clunie and Sheen in Badenoch. If the greatest fatigues, dangers, and hard duties deserve approbation, I think some thanks are due to us, and from none more than yourself; for my own part, I was once seventy hours without three of sleep; but we undergo all hardships for the good of common cause. You will ever find me, dear brother, your most affectionate brother and faithful servant,

"GEORGE MURRAY. "

"I am so ill supported with men, money, and every thing else, our people here have no pay, that after all our endeavours, I'm afraid we must abandon this country without the Castle. "

This letter brought the following characteristic reply. It is dated from Inverness, whither the Marquis had repaired. [187]

"Brother George.

"This evening I had yours of yesterday's date. As to any difference betwixt you and I, without prejudice to passed expedition and secrecy mentioned, at meeting it must be discussed the best way we can, since lately behaving according to dutiful sentiments, nobody is more satisfied than I am of your indefatigable activity for the public service. Had you sent me your letters to the Secretary, who I am very sorry to say is at Elgin dangerously ill, or any other of the Ministry to whom expresses were addressed, I should have directly endeavoured getting the most satisfactory answers could be sent your pressing reale demands, which are not well understood if much regarded by everybody here; I am informed by Mr. Hay and Cruben, who were just now with me, that all the men who were with you have been fully paid till Wednesday last; and that with some necessary foresight and pains, you might have had a good deal of provisions from below the Pass, whilst that expedient was practicable; since you might have naturally known that money cannot be soon sent from hence, but on an absolute necessity; you know that meal can be still brought you from Kiliwhimen. With that I wrote to you the twenty-sixth, in case the enemy could not be otherwise forced out of my house, I gave Sir Thomas Sheridan an account to be sent to you of a secret passage into it, which is here again transmitted, in case of making any advantageous use of it has been hitherto neglected; was it not hoped by this time you have near got the better of these obstinate intruders into the Castle, at any rate I should go myself and try if I could not usefully help towards reducing them to a speedy surrendering of such unfortified, though thick old walls as it is composed of. Pray continue your accustomed vigilance on such a valuable occasion as will render you dear to all honest men, as well as particularly giving me an opportunity of showing with what esteem I am, dear brother,

Your most affectionate brother,
And most humble servant. "
[No Signature.]

"Inverness, 30th of March, 1746. "

In addition to the testimony of Lord Elcho, that of Maxwell of Kirkconnel, has considerable weight in Lord George Murray's favour.

"He was censured, " observes this excellent writer, "by his enemies as being too tender of a family seat. [188] As I do not know the situation of this Castle, I cannot determine whether it was in his power to blow it up, or whether he had time to do it after he was informed of the march of the Hessians. But he has been so calumniated by the Secretary and his creatures, that nothing less than a direct proof ought to have any weight against him. In this case it is absurd to suspect him, because the family seat could never be in danger. If it was in his power to blow it up, he had only to acquaint the Governor when the mine was ready, and let him send one of his officers to view it; the Governor would certainly have prevented the effecting it and saved the Castle. "

"About the same time that the siege of Blair was abandoned, that of Fort William was also raised. It was found, indeed, difficult to make the Highlanders perform the regular duties of a siege; extremely brave in an attack, when allowed to fight in their own way, they were not possessed of that steady valour which is necessary to maintain a post; and it was not easy to keep them long in their quarters, or even at their posts, without action. "[189]

The loss of Blair, and the failure of the siege of Fort William, were followed by other misfortunes. Fatal mistakes in the vain endeavour to retrieve a sinking cause ensued. In the midst of his adversity, the young and gallant adventurer, for whom so much blood was shed, supported his spirits in a wonderful manner, and acted, with a heavy heart, the part of the gay and prosperous. He gave balls at Inverness, and even danced himself, which he had declined doing when in the midst of his prosperity at Edinburgh. Those who looked only on the surface of affairs were deceived by his appearance of happiness; but the well informed knew too well that the crisis which was to end the struggle was rapidly approaching. To complete the sad summary of disappointments and misfortunes, it was now ascertained that the expedition from Boulogne, and that from Dunkirk, with which the false-hearted French had so long amused the unfortunate Jacobites, were entirely and perfidiously relinquished.

Lord George Murray, meantime, was ordered to march to Inverness. He was now worn with fatigues, and by the protracted anxieties of his situation. Foreseeing, as he must have done, many of the dangers and difficulties of the contest; observing, on the one hand, his eldest brother, the Marquis of Tullibardine, the adherent of the Stuarts, proscribed, impoverished, a nominal proprietor of his patrimonial estates; on the other, beholding his second brother, the actual Duke of Atholl, cherished by Government, prosperous, honours showered down upon him; what impulses less strong than that of a generous, and fixed principle of fidelity could have maintained his exertions in a service so desperate as that in which he had engaged?

The great deficiency in Lord George Murray's character was the absence of hope; but, independent of that vital defect, his attributes as a soldier and a general cannot fail to excite admiration. His exertions were unparalleled; besides the marching and fatigue that others had to undergo, he had the vast responsibility of command. "Though others were relieved and took their turns, " he remarks, "I had none to relieve. " On first assuming the command, he received and despatched every express himself; and saw the guards and sentinels settled. In gaining intelligence he was indefatigable; and his discipline was such that the country suffered but little from the visitations of his well-governed forces. But the time was fast approaching when his great abilities, which never ceased to be acknowledged by the whole army, his fortitude, and personal valour were to be put to the severest test.

On the third of April, Lord George Murray joined Charles Edward at Inverness. On the eleventh intelligence was received that the Duke of Cumberland, who had been stationed for some time at Aberdeen, was marching towards Inverness. At first the intelligence of the Duke's approach was received with acclamations of joy; but the circumstances under which the battle of Culloden was eventually fought, and the fatigues and impediments by which it was prefaced, changed that sentiment into one of distrust and despondency. [190]

Upon receiving intelligence of the Duke's approach, expresses were sent in all directions in order to re-assemble the Jacobite forces. Those troops which had been at the siege of Fort William were on their march to Inverness; but Lord Cromartie and his detachment were still at a great distance; the Duke of Perth and Lord John Drummond were at Spey-side, with a considerable body of men and all the horse. These were ordered to retire as Cumberland's army approached. Unhappily, many of the Highlanders, it being now seed time, had slipped away to their homes, and it was, indeed, no easy task to allure them back. The influence of Lord George Murray over the forces continued, nevertheless, unabated. His mode of managing this fine, but rude people, was well adapted to his purpose, and proceeded from an intimate knowledge of their character. "Fear" he considered as necessary as "love. " "I was told, " he remarks, "that all the Highlanders were gentlemen, and never to be beaten, but I was well acquainted with their tempers. " Their chiefs even inflicted personal chastisement upon them, which they received without murmurs when conscious of an offence. But they would only receive correction from their own officers, and never would the chief of one Clan correct even the lowest soldier of another. "But I, " observes Lord George, "had as much authority over them all as each had amongst his own men; and I will venture to say that never an officer was more beloved of the whole, without exception, than I was. " At any time when there was a post of more danger than another, Lord George, possessing as he did this unbounded influence over the minds of his countrymen, found it more difficult to restrain those who were too forward, than in finding those who were willing to rush into peril.

On Sunday morning, the thirteenth of April, it became a matter of certainty among the Jacobite forces that the enemy had passed the Spey. On the following day, Lochiel joined the army; the Duke of Perth also returned, and the Prince and his forces assembled on an open moor, near Culloden. Many of the officers suggested that it would be desirable to retire to a stronger position than this exposed plain, until the army were all collected, but the baggage being at Inverness, this scheme was rejected. The experienced eye of Lord George Murray soon perceived that the ground which had been chosen was ill-adapted for the Highland mode of warfare, and he proposed that the other side of the water of Nairn should be reconnoitred. But objections were made to any change of position; and, situated as Lord George now was, distrusted by the Prince, and, perhaps, in some measure by others, since the failure at Blair, he was in no condition to contest so important a point. It was afterwards attempted to venture an attack by night. To this proposition not only the Prince, but Lord George and most of the other officers were at first favourable: but, in the evening, it being generally understood that there was no provision for the subsistence of the men the next day, a circumstance attributable to the negligence of the persons employed for the purpose at Inverness, a number of men dispersed in search of food. The forces being thus reduced, Lord George objected, in concert with others, to the projected night march; but Charles Edward, trusting to the bravery of his army, and being for fighting on all occasions, was determined on the attempt. "What he had seen them do, and the justice of his cause, made him too venturous. "[191] The attack was, therefore, agreed upon, and Lord George commanding the rear, after marching nearly six miles, found that it would be impossible to attack the enemy before day-break, and, therefore, gave it up, and returned to Culloden about five in the morning.

Fatigued and hungry, the army awaited the approach of the English forces. It was between ten and eleven in the morning when they drew up on the moor, and were placed in order of battle by O'Sullivan. Again Lord George observed to that officer, that the ground was unfavourable: the reply was, that the moor was so interspersed with moss and deep earth, that the enemy's horse and cannon could be of little service to them; and that it was therefore well selected. By this time the young and unfortunate Master of Lovat had joined the forces, but Lord Cromartie was still, by a fatal mistake, absent; and Macpherson, of Clunie, was at three or four miles distance, marching with all possible expedition towards Culloden. The stragglers and others were also collecting, so that, as Lord George conjectured, the army would have been increased by two or three thousand more men that night, or the next day. Stimulated by this reflection, he again looked wistfully to the position beyond the water, and considered that if they passed there, they would probably leave the moors to the enemy, and occupy a better post. But he was overruled.

* * * * *

"I shall say little, " writes Lord George Murray, in his journal, "of this battle, which was so fatal. " In a memoir, written by Colonel Ker, of Gradyne, an officer of distinguished military reputation, a minute and animated account is, however, given of all the incidents of the eventful fifteenth of April.

Charles Edward having with some difficulty procured some bread and whiskey at Culloden, reposed for a short time after marching all night. In the morning intelligence was brought him that the enemy were in sight. Whilst the army was forming, Colonel Ker was sent to reconnoitre the enemy. On returning, he informed the Prince and Lord George Murray, who was then with him, that the enemy were marching in three columns, with their cavalry on the left, so that they would form their line of battle in an instant. The Prince then ordered his men to draw up in two lines, and the few horse which he had were disposed in the rear towards the wings; the cannon was to be dispersed in the front; this was brought up with difficulty from the want of horses. The ground which had been occupied the day before was too distant for the army to reach; so that they were drawn up a mile to the westward with a stone enclosure which ran down to the water of Nairn, on the right of the first line.

The Highland soldiers, many of whom had been summoned from their sleep among the woods of Culloden, were aroused from among the bushes, and came drowsy, and half-exhausted to the field; yet they formed themselves into order of battle with wonderful dispatch. Unhappily no council of war was held upon the plain of Culloden in the hurry of that day. In addition to the confusion, and want of concert which this omission produced, was a still more injurious circumstance. The army, as has been related, was drawn up in two lines; Lord George commanded the first, which was composed of the Atholl brigade. This regiment was placed by Lord George on the right of the line: unfortunately, the Clan Macdonald, proud and fiery, claimed the precedence. They grounded their assertion of right to the usage of time immemorial; and to their having had it during the two previous battles. Lord George, on the other hand, uncompromising as usual, insisted that in those actions even, his Atholl men had the pre-eminence. The Prince, unable to decide, persuaded the chief of the Macdonalds to waive his claim; but the pride of the Scotch is never subdued; and whilst Macdonald yielded, their men were offended and disgusted with his compliance.

The Duke of Cumberland formed his line of battle at a great distance, and marched in battle order until he came within cannon shot, when he halted, and placed his artillery in different parts in the front. His army, to use a military phrase, outwinged that of Charles, both to the right and left, without his cavalry. [192]

It is not, as Lord George Murray observes, "an easy task to describe a battle. " Most officers are necessarily taken up with what is near them, and the confusion, noise, and agitation effectually impede observation. The commencement of the battle of Culloden was obscured by a thick fall of hail and snow, and on this occasion the tempestuous climate of Scotland favoured her enemies, for the Prince's army faced the wind, and encountered the snow-storm in their faces. It was expected that the Duke would begin the attack; and a party of his horse were sent during the interval to reconnoitre the Jacobite army. When they came within cannon shot, loud hurras were heard on both sides; and voices (soon for ever to be silenced) sent up to Heaven expressions of exultation and defiance. The young Chevalier, whilst awaiting that event, rode along the lines to encourage his men, placing himself in a post of danger, in which one of his servants was killed by his side. After some few minutes of solemn expectation, Lord George Murray, who commanded the right of the army, sent Colonel Ker to the Prince to know if he should begin the attack? an answer in the affirmative was returned. As the right was farther distant than the left, Colonel Ker went first to the Duke of Perth who commanded the left, and ordered him to begin; he then rode along the field until he came to the right line, where Lord George Murray received from him a similar command. The Prince then placed himself behind the centre of the army, having the whole of his forces under his eye, and thus being able to send orders on all exigencies.

The cannon of Prince Charles was first heard. It was returned with a firing from the enemy of grape shot, which did great execution.

The Highlanders, who were forbidden to move until the word of command was given, suffered that fire very impatiently. Some of them threw themselves flat on the ground, and a few gave way and ran off. [193] The artillery of the enemy was very well served; that of the Jacobites was managed by common soldiers, the cannoniers belonging to one battery being absent. The contest was in every way unequal; yet the brave insurgents, although ready to drop with fatigue, seemed to forget all their weariness and hunger when the enemy advanced.

At length, after some preliminary manoeuvres, the Prince sent orders to Lord George Murray to march up to the enemy. It seemed, indeed, high time to come to a close engagement; for the cannonading of the enemy, which was directed chiefly towards the place which the Prince occupied among the cavalry, was very destructive; yet still Lord George delayed the attack, judging, as it is supposed, that the adversaries were still at too great a distance, and that the strength of his men would be exhausted before they could reach them. There appears also to have been another reason for the delay; Lord George had, on his right, a farm-house, and some old enclosure walls, which the enemy now occupied; and he is conjectured to have been waiting until the Duke of Cumberland's army came up to these walls, which would prevent him being flanked by the dragoons, who were, he observed, mostly on the left. But the Duke did not advance. The Highlanders, who were impatient at the delay, called out loudly to be led on; and at last he gave the command to attack.

His orders were obeyed. As his line began to move, the enemy began a smart fire, which played chiefly upon the Atholl men, and was kept up by a detachment of Campbells, who were stationed behind the enclosure walls. It was the custom of the Highlanders to give a general discharge of their fire-arms, and then to rush, sword in hand, upon their foes: and the only chance of a victory for their party that day, was a general shock of their whole line at once; for the fury and valour of these northern warriors produced results almost incredible. Unhappily, several circumstances destroyed this advantage. The two armies were not exactly parallel to each other, the right of Prince Charles's being nearer to the foe than the left. The impetuosity of the Highlanders was such, that they broke their ranks before it was time to give their fire; their eagerness to come up with an enemy that had so greatly the advantage of them at such a distance, made them rush on with such violence, and in such a confusion, that their fire-arms were of little service. [194] This, it appears, was the disadvantage which Lord George had apprehended. But there was still another inconvenience: the wind, which had favoured the Jacobites at Falkirk, was now against them. They were buried in a cloud of smoke, and felt their enemies without seeing them. In spite of all these obstacles they went, sword in hand, and broke the first line of the enemy; but the second advancing, and firing on them, they gave way, leaving, says one who beheld the terrific scene, "many brave fellows on the spot. " The rout, which began on the right of the army, soon became general. The right line was, in fact, beaten before the centre could advance to support it: and the centre of the army gave way, whilst the Macdonalds, who were advancing on the left, seeing themselves abandoned on the right, and exposed to be flanked by enemies who had nothing to oppose them in front, retired also. [195]

Lord George Murray behaved with incomparable valour, as indeed did the whole of the line which he commanded, which was received by the enemy with bayonets. These were the more destructive, as the Highlanders would never be at the trouble, on a march, to carry targets. Yet the Duke's line of battle was broken in several places, and two pieces of cannon were taken. [196] The brave troops whom Lord George commanded marched up to the very point of the bayonets, which they could not see until they were upon them, on account of the smoke which was driven in their faces. As the first line of the English army was broken, and as others were brought up to their relief, some cannon, charged with cartouch shot from their second line, caused Lord George Murray's horse to start and plunge so much, that he thought the animal was wounded: he quitted his stirrups, and was thrown. "After thus being dismounted, I brought up, " writes Lord George, "two regiments of our second line, who gave them fire, but nothing could be done; all was lost. "[197] The only good effect of the reinforcement was to arrest for a while the pursuit of the cavalry, and thus to save many lives. The field of battle was soon abandoned to the fury of an enemy, whose brutal thirst for vengeance increased as the danger and opposition diminished. Some may consider that the day of Culloden was a day of disgrace to the Highlanders; but to them it was an event of honour, compared with the discredit which it brought upon their foes. To England was the disgrace. It was, at all events, even if we measure the standard of honour by the degree of military success, an inglorious victory. Independent of the inequality of numbers, was the inequality of circumstances; but greater, in many senses, on this occasion, were the conquered, than their conquerors.

The Prince, seeing his army entirely routed, was at length prevailed upon to retire. Most of his horse soldiers assembled round his person; and he rode leisurely, and in good order, for the enemy advanced very leisurely over the ground. "They made, " observes Maxwell, "no attack where there was any body of the Prince's men together, but contented themselves with sabering such unfortunate people as fell in their way, single and disarmed. " "As the Duke's corps, " Lord Elcho relates, "continued to pursue in order of battle, always firing their cannon and platoons in advancing, there were not so many people taken or killed as there would have been had they detached corps to pursue; but every body that fell into their hands got no quarter, except a few whom they reserved for public punishment. "

In the flight of the Prince's army, most of the left wing took the road to Inverness; the right wing crossed the water of Nairn, and went to Ruthven of Badenoch; the rest, to the number of five hundred, mostly officers, followed the Prince into Stratherick, where he had stopped about four miles from the field of Culloden. Of the Prince's conduct after the battle, a very painful impression is given by Lord Elcho. "As he had taken it into his head he had been betrayed, and particularly by Lord George Murray, he seemed very diffident of everybody except the Irish officers; and he appeared very anxious to know whether he had given them all higher commissions than they had at their arrival, on purpose that they might get them confirmed to them upon their return to France. He neither spoke to any of the Scots' officers present, nor inquired after any of the absent. Nor, indeed, at any of the preceding battles did he ever inquire after any of the wounded officers. He appeared very uneasy as long as the Scots were about him; and in a short time ordered them all to go to Ruthven of Badenoch, where he would send them orders; but before they had rode a mile, he sent Mr. Sheridan after them, to tell them that they might disperse, and everybody shift for himself the best way he could. Lord George Murray and Lord John Drummond repeated the same orders to all the body of the army that had assembled at Ruthven. The Prince kept with him some of Fitzjames's Horse, and went that night to a house in the head of Stratherick, where he met Lord Lovat and a great many other Scots' gentlemen, who advised him not to quit the country, but to stay and gather together his scattered forces. But he was so prejudiced against the Scots, that he was afraid they would give him up to make their peace with the Government; for some of the Irish were at pains to relate to him, in very strong terms, how the Scots had already sold his great-grandfather to the English: and, as he was naturally of a suspicious temper, it was not a difficult matter to persuade him of it. And he always believed it until the fidelity of the Highlanders shown to him during the long time he was hid in their country, convinced him and everybody else of the contrary. "[198]

This history of distrust and ingratitude is, however, to be contrasted with very different statements. When the Prince heard from Colonel Ker, after the battle, that Lord George Murray had been thrown from his horse, but was not wounded, Charles, in the presence of all the officers who were assembled around his person, desired Colonel Ker to find out Lord George, and to "take particular care of him. " Nor was there, among the whole number of those writers who witnessed the battle of Culloden, a dissentient voice with regard to the bravery of their Lieutenant-General and to the admirable disposition of his troops. Had he, like Lord Strathallan, sought and found his fate upon the field of battle, his memory would have been exalted into that of a hero.

Two days after the defeat, the Duke of Perth, the Marquis of Tullibardine, Lord George Murray, Lord Ogilvie, Lord Nairn, and several other chieftains and officers met at Ruthven in Badenoch, and discussed the events which had ended in the ruin of their cause. They were unanimous in concluding that the night attack, upon which many persons insisted as practicable, could not have been attempted. [199]

For some time after the battle, hopes were entertained of an effectual rallying of the forces. By a letter from one of the Prince's aides-de-camp, Alexander Macleod, to Clunie Macpherson, on the very day of the battle, it appears that his party soon hoped, or pretended to hope, "to pay Cumberland back in his own coin. " A review of the fragment of the army was projected at Fort-Augustus, on the seventeenth of April; and amends were promised to be made for the "ruffle at Culloden. "[200] "For God's sake, " wrote Mr. Macleod, "make haste to join us; and bring with you all the people that can possibly be got together. Take care in particular of Lumisden and Sheridan, as they carry with them the sinews of war. "

To this letter Lord George Murray added some lines, which prove how hopeless, at that moment, he considered any project of rallying; and, indeed, even before the epistle was dispatched to Clunie, the Prince had left Gorteleg, and taken refuge in "Clanranald's country."

Notwithstanding the Prince's flight, Lord George Murray, presuming that he could still make a stand, remained at Ruthven, where a force of between two and three thousand men was assembled. It was found, however, impossible, from the want of provisions, to keep such an army together; and, in a few days, a message from Charles, ordering his ill-fated adherents to disperse, decided their fate. At this epoch Lord George Murray addressed a letter to Charles, certainly not calculated to soothe the feelings of the unfortunate young man, nor to conciliate the bitter spirit which afterwards, during the lapse of years, never abated towards his former General. The letter began thus. [201]

"May it please your Royal Highness,

As no person in these Kingdoms ventured more frankly in the cause than myself, and as I had more at stake than almost all the others put together, I cannot but be very deeply affected with our late loss, and present situation; and I declare, that were your Royal Highness's person in safety, the loss of the cause, and the unfortunate and unhappy state of my countrymen is the only thing that grieves me; for I thank God I have resolution to bear my own family's ruin without a grudge. "

After this preface Lord George, in no softened terms, pointed out what he conceived to be the causes of the failure of the enterprise; — the imprudence of having set up the standard without aid from France; the deficiencies and blunders of Mr. O'Sullivan, whose business it was to reconnoitre the field of battle, but who had not so much as viewed it before the affair of Culloden. He next pointed out the negligence, if not treachery, of Mr. Hay, who had the charge of the provisions. To the disgraceful mismanagement of this important department might, indeed, the ruin of the army be traced. "For my own part, " added Lord George, "I never had any particular discussion with either of them; but I ever thought them incapable and unfit to serve in the stations they were placed in. "

After these too just remarks, Lord George formally resigned his commission into the Prince's hands. It had, it appears, been his intention to have done so after the failure at Blair; but he was dissuaded by his friends. "I hope your Royal Highness will now accept of my demission. What commands you may have for me in any other situation, please honour me with them. "

This letter was dated from Ruthven, two days after the battle of Culloden. The inference which has been drawn from it was, that Lord George did not contemplate the abandonment of the campaign. It appears to have been his opinion that the Highlanders could have made a summer campaign without any risk, marching, as they could, through places in which no regular troops could follow them. They could never starve as long as there were sheep and cattle in the country; and they might probably have carried on an offensive, instead of a defensive war. But Charles, disheartened, as men of over sanguine tempers usually are, in misfortune, to the last degree, resolved on escaping to France. He addressed a farewell letter to the Chiefs, and then commenced that long and perilous course of wanderings in which his character rose to heroism, and which presents one of the most interesting episodes in history of which our annals can boast.

Lord George Murray was long a fugitive from place to place in his native country, before he could find means to escape to the continent. In December (1746) he visited, in private, his friends in Edinburgh, and then embarking at Anstruther, in the Frith of Forth, he set sail for Holland. Whether he ever returned to his native country is doubtful, although it appears, from a letter among the Stuart papers, that he had it in contemplation, in order to bring over his wife and family.

His fate in a foreign land, however embittered by the ingratitude and hatred of Charles Edward, was cheered by the presence of his wife and children, with the exception of his eldest son, who was retained in Scotland, and educated under the auspices of James Duke of Atholl. His first movement after reaching Holland, was to repair to Rome, there to pay his respects to the Chevalier St. George, and to unfold to him the motives of his conduct in the foregoing campaign of 1745. The Chevalier, affectionately attached as he was to his eldest son, was aware of his defects, and sensible of the pernicious influence which was exercised over his mind by the enemies of Lord George Murray; James, who never appears in a more amiable light than in his correspondence, endeavoured to conciliate both parties. His letters to Charles Edward, treasured among the Stuart papers, display kindness and great good sense. His mediation in this instance was, however, wholly ineffectual. After the treacherous conduct of Murray of Broughton, the Prince began even to suspect that Lord George was concerned in the baseness of that individual. This notion was urgently combated by James; at the same time he recommended the Prince, not only as a matter of right, but of policy, to conciliate Lord George, who "owned that he had been wrong towards Charles, but insisted upon his zeal in the Prince's service. " "Persons, " adds the politic Chevalier, "like him may do both good and hurt; and it is prudent to manage them, and would manifestly be of prejudice could they be able to say their former services had been disregarded. " But James addressed himself to one who could never dissimulate. Whatever Charles's errors might be, they were not envenomed by any portion of cunning, and no motive of prudence could soften him towards one whom he unjustly disliked.

Lord George, who expected no favour from the English Government, was, nevertheless, anxious to be "near home. " He left Rome in May 1747, and after remaining some time at Bologna, proceeded to Paris. [202] Here Charles was playing that ill-judged and desperate game, which was better suited to a rash impostor, than to the acknowledged descendant of a long line of monarchs. Here he was rapidly effacing the remembrance of the brave and generous wanderer who trusted to the honesty of the Highlanders; who bore his misfortunes as if he had been born in that land of heroes.

The first idea of Charles, upon hearing of Lord George Murray's arrival in Paris, was to imprison him as a traitor. "I hope in God, " writes his father to the young Prince, "you will not think of getting Lord George secured after all I wrote to you about him, and will at least receive him civilly. " But no intercessions could nullify the indignation of Charles towards his former general.

It was far from Lord George Murray's intention, if we may believe the Chevalier St. George, again to embroil himself in public affairs, or even to remain in Paris. His intention was to live privately in Germany or Flanders, in the hope of being rejoined by his wife. Upon reaching Paris, he informed the Prince of his arrival; and proposed paying his respects to him at St. Omer, where Charles was then living. Late on the evening of the eleventh of July, 1747, a gentleman, who at first refused to give his name, but who afterwards announced himself as Mr. Stafford, called on Lord George to convey to him a message desiring him not to "go near" the Prince, and ordering him to leave Paris immediately. An answer was returned, signifying that the Prince's commands should be obeyed. Lord George left Paris, and he and the unfortunate young man whom he had served, met no more. It is possible that the irritation of Charles was aggravated by the recent intelligence of his brother's having become a cardinal: upon receiving the news of that event he shut himself up for some hours alone. The name of his brother was no longer to be uttered in his presence nor his health drunk at table. [203] Charles was at this time in the power of both the Kellys, who are described by one of his adherents as "false, ambitious, and sordidly avaricious. "

After visiting Poland, where he was received by Marshall Belriski as a relation, and where he endeavoured to negotiate the restitution of some crown jewels to James, as in right of the Chevalier's wife, the Princess Sobieski, Lord George settled at Cleves. He changed his name to that of De Valignie, and here he remained in obscurity with his family. "My wife, " he writes to the Chevalier St. George, "came here on the tenth of September, 1748, but was soon after seized with an intermitting fever, which has not yet left her. She begs leave to throw herself at your Majesty's feet. " In 1750, Lord George removed to Emmerick; here he wrote an account of his campaign, which he addressed to Mr. Hamilton of Bangour; from this, repeated extracts have been given in this memoir of his life. The kindness of James Stuart towards him continued unabated: he recommended him to the notice of the court of France; and consulted him as to the probable success of a future enterprise in Scotland. On such a project Lord George Murray expressed himself cautiously, yet somewhat encouragingly; and declared himself ready to shed the last drop of his blood in the cause. Happily his zeal was not again put to the test. Lord George appears, in his letters, to have cherished in his retirement at Emmerick, a lingering hope that at some future day the Stuarts might make another attempt. He was now in the decline of life, and yearning to behold again the country which he was destined to see no more. "How happily, " he writes to Mr. Edgar, [204] "should you and I be to sit over a bottle in Angus, or Perthshire, after a restoration, and talk over old services. May that soon happen! "

Meantime some members of Lord George's family suffered the severest distress. His uncle, Lord Nairn, had, it is true, escaped to France; but Lady Nairn and her daughter, Lady Clementina, were reduced to the utmost penury in Scotland. They remained in their native country, probably with the hope of saving the wreck of their fortunes, until all that the troops had spared was sold, and the money which accrued from the sale was exhausted. Such was the rapacity of the plunderers, that they took even Lady Nairn's watch and clothes. The Government, although in possession of her estate, never gave her one farthing for subsistence, but even made her pay a rent for the garden of one of Lord Nairn's own houses in which she lived. But this is only one instance of that catalogue of cruelties towards the Jacobites, which it would take volumes to detail.

In 1751, Lord George Murray visited Dresden, where, owing to the mediation of James Stuart, he was well received. His letters at this period refer frequently to the exertions which he made for Lord

Macleod, the son of Lord Cromartie: to this young man a company was given in Finland, in the Prussian service, and the Chevalier St. George furnished him with his accoutrements and equipage.

The eldest son of Lord George Murray remained, as we have seen, in Scotland; but the second was, through the favour of the Chevalier, recommended to the especial notice of the court of Prussia. The visit of Lord George to Dresden seems to have been chiefly designed to push the interests of this young man, who was introduced to the Count and Countess De Bruhl. The youth was to study the military science and exercises at Dresden, and at the same time to enjoy, in the house of the Pope's Nuncio, the advantage of seeing company, and of forming connections.

Having arranged these affairs, Lord George returned to Emmerick. His wife had left him for Scotland, in order to be confined there; and this event, attended by so much inconvenience, and prefaced by a voyage of twelve days, "put her, " as Lord George observed, "somewhat out of countenance, after twenty-three years' marriage. " Her return was delayed for some time. "I shall be pretty lonely this winter (1751), " writes Lord George to Mr. Edgar, "for my wife, who was brought to bed of a daughter the middle of September, recovered but very slowly, and now the season of the year is too far advanced for her to venture so long a voyage; besides, she has some thoughts that Lady Sinclair (his daughter) may come with her in the spring. " In his solitude, anxieties about his patrimonial property added to the sorrows of the exile. "I am told, "[205] he writes, "that the Duke of Atholl is desirous of selling the roialty of the Isle of Man to the London Government, for which, they say, he is offered fifteen thousand pounds sterling. Had it not been for my situation, I believe he could not have done it without my consent; but, I'm sorry to say it, and it is a truth, that he is full as much my enemy as any of that Government. He has sent my eldest son abroad, but, as I understand, with positive orders not to see nor correspond with me. All this is the more extraordinary that, thirty years ago, before he turned courtier, he seemed to have very different notions. Most people in Britain now regard neither probity nor any other virtue—all is selfish and vainal (venial). But how can I complean of such hard usage, when my royal master has met with what is a thousand times more cruel: he bears it like a Christian hero, and it would ill suit me to repine. I thank the Almighty I never did, and I think it my greatest honour and glory to suffer in so just and upright a cause. " Hope, however, of one day returning to Scotland, was not extinct. He thus continues: "Upon receipt of the note you sent me, I have gott the carabin, for which I return you many thanks. I expect to kill a wild bore with it; but I fain hope Providence may still order it that I may make use of it at home, and, if all succeeds to our wishes, how happy should I think myself to send you, when you returned to Angus, a good fatt stagg, shott in the forest of Atholl with your own gun. "

Until five years before his death, Lord George still cherished the hope that France would again find it her interest to support the claims of the Stuarts. He had always considered that the support of the French would be decisive of the success of the cause. "Had the ministers of the court of Versailles, ten years ago, been persuaded that the supporting of his Royal Highness the Prince, at the beginning of his attempt, in a proper manner with the best measures they could take for the interest of their master as well as that of the King, our gracious sovereign, I think I do not say too much if I affirm that his Royal Highness would not have failed of success. I had at that time opportunities of knowing the sentiments and way of thinking of most people in Great Britain. Many, very many, wished well to the cause. Great numbers would have looked on, and would have turned to the side that had success. But there is no recalling what is passed. I believe that in France they are convinced now of the error they were in at the time. If ever they resolve to espouse the cause of the royal family it must be in earnest, and their main view must be that. Then there would be no difficulty in adjusting limits in America. I have been much longer upon the subject than I intended. Perhaps zeal has led me too far. "

The period was now approaching when Lord George Murray was to close a life of vicissitude and turmoil. He died in 1760 at Medenblinck, in Holland, leaving three sons and two daughters. Upon the death of James Duke of Atholl in 1764, John, the eldest son of Lord George Murray, succeeded to the dukedom, and to the great possessions of the family. He married his first cousin, Charlotte, only daughter and heiress of his uncle, the Duke of Atholl; and in 1765 their Graces sold the sovereignty of the Isle of Man, upon the disposal of which Lord George Murray had expressed much solicitude, to the British Government. The present Duke of Atholl, who succeeded his father in 1830, is the grandson of John, third Duke of Atholl, and the great-grandson of Lord George Murray. The descendants of this justly celebrated man have, therefore, shared a happier fortune than those of many of the other attainted noblemen of his party.

The attainder was not, however, set aside in favour of the son of Lord George Murray without a petition to the King, upon which the House of Lords gave a favourable report, and the objection was overcome. [206] Besides his eldest son, Lord George left two others; James, of Strowan, in right of his mother; George, of Pitkeathly, who became Vice-Admiral of the White—and two daughters; Amelia, first married to Lord Sinclair, and afterwards to James Farquharson, of Inverness; and Charlotte, who died unmarried.

The mind of Lord George Murray was one of great original power, and less dependent upon those circumstances which usually affect the formation of character, than that of most men. He was determined and inflexible in opinions, yet cautious in action. That he was sincere and honourable there can now be little doubt. It was his consciousness of upright intentions which inspired him with contempt for the littleness of others; and with his love of superiority, his self-will and ambition, there was wrought a strong conviction of his own worth, as opposed to the hollowness of some of his party. Throughout all his letters, and in his journal, there is a strong evidence of his confidence in his own powers; of a self-sufficiency too lofty to be called vanity, but which sometimes descends to egotism. To his courage, his energy and perseverance, his military contemporaries have borne unanimous testimony. They seem entirely to have comprehended a character which the unfortunate Charles Edward could never appreciate. They felt the justness of his ascendancy, and discriminated between the bluntness of an ardent and honest mind, careless of ordinary forms, and the arrogance of an inferior capacity. As a soldier, indeed, the qualities of Lord George Murray rose to greatness: so enduring, and so fearless, so careless of danger to himself, yet so solicitous for others. As a general, some great defects may be pointed out in his composition, without detracting from his merits as a private individual.

Let us first turn to the bright side of the picture. In activity and exertion Lord George Murray has not been surpassed even by the more fortunate, although, perhaps, not greater commanders of modern times. He was indefatigable in business, and any one who desired access to him could see him at any hour, whether at meals or in bed. "On some occasions, " he remarks, "I have been waked six times a night, and had either orders to write, or letters to answer every time; for as I mostly commanded a separate body of the army, I had many details that, in a more regular army, would belong to different people. " Every order, even that which sent an officer to an out-post, was written by his own hand, and explained by him; every contingency that might occur in the execution was canvassed, and every objection that was suggested was answered by himself. The officers, therefore, confiding in their general, performed their duties with cheerfulness, and made their reports with exactness. There was no confusion, nor misapprehension, wherever Lord George presided. As a disciplinarian, he was pre-eminent; no army ever quitted a country with so little odium, nor left behind them such slight memorials of their march, as that of Charles Edward when it returned from Derby. The greatest excess that the Highlanders were known to commit was the seizing horses to carry their baggage, or to carry their sick; —and these it was Lord George's endeavour always to restore, even at a great inconvenience to the soldiers. Even with every precaution it was impossible wholly to restrain plundering, although the General undertook in person to control that evil. "How often, " he writes, "have I gone into houses on our marches to drive the men out of them, and drubbed them heartily? "

This able man possessed another great requisite as a commander. He thoroughly understood his materials, he was perfectly acquainted with the temper and disposition of his soldiers. It was the attribute which made Marlborough unconquerable; and, in an army chiefly of Highlanders, it was one of the greatest value. By this Lord George acquired over the members of every respective Clan as much influence as each Chief separately had. His corrections were well applied, and never lessened the confidence nor affections of the soldiery. From the highest to the lowest, the men and officers had a confidence in him, which induced them to apply to him for redress in grievances, and to consider him as an umpire in disputes.

But Lord George was not only a disciplinarian; in his own person, he set the example of a scrupulous honesty. "I never, " he writes in his explanation of his conduct, "took the least thing without paying the full value. I thought that I could not reasonably find fault with others in that, if I did not show them a good example. "

To the sick and wounded Lord George invariably paid the utmost attention; and, under his guidance, the Highlanders, heretofore so fierce towards each other in their contests, were remarkable for a degree of humanity which was disgracefully contrasted with the barbarity of their conquerors. Such were his general attributes in his military station. Whatever doubts may have existed in the mind of Charles Edward as to the fidelity of his General, are silenced by the long and hopeless exile of Lord George Murray, and by the continued friendship of the Chevalier St. George. No overtures, as in the case of the Earl of Mar, to the British Government, nor efforts on the part of his prosperous and favoured brother, the Duke of Atholl, have transpired to show that in saving Blair, there was a secret understanding that there should be a future reward, nor that any surmise of treachery had opened a door to reconciliation. Charles, be it remembered, was under that daily, hourly influence, which weakens the judgment, and exasperates the passions. His opinion of Lord George Murray must not be accepted as any evidence against one who had redeemed the inconsistencies of his youth by the great exertions of his manhood.

Some vital defects there were, nevertheless, in this General, of powerful intellect, and of earnest and honourable intentions. His character partook too largely of that quality which has raised his country as a nation in all other countries, prudence. For his peculiar situation he was far too cautious. Persevering and inflexible, he was destitute of hope. If it be true, that he entered into the undertaking with a conviction that the cause could never prosper, he was the last man that should have been the general of an army whose ardour, when not engaged in action, he invariably restrained. All contending opinions seem to hesitate and to falter when they relate to the retreat from Derby, the grand error of the enterprise; the fatal step, when the tide served, and the wind was propitious, and an opportunity never to be regained, was for ever lost.

In private society, Lord George Murray is reported to have been overbearing and hasty; his fine person, and handsome countenance were lessened in their agreeableness by a haughty deportment. He was simple, temperate, and self-denying in his habits. In his relations of life, he appears to have been respectable. His letters show him to have enjoyed, at least, the usual means of education offered to a soldier, who entered upon active service at sixteen, or to have improved his own acquirements. They are clear and explicit, and bear the impress of sincerity and good sense.

Distrusted as he was by Charles Edward, and misrepresented by others, we may accord to Lord George Murray the indulgence which he claims from posterity in these, the last words of his vindication: —

"Upon the whole, I shall conclude with saying, if I did not all the good I would, I am sure I did all I could. "

FOOTNOTES:

[1] Nisbet's Heraldry, part iii. p. 205.

[2] In the Life of the Marquis of Tullibardine, vol. i.

[3] See Nisbet's Heraldry.

[4] Nisbet's Heraldry, part iii. p. 206.

[5] See a MS. Account of the Highlands of Scotland, British Museum, King's Library.

[6] "Case of the Forfeited Estates, in a letter to a certain noble Lord. London, 1718. "

[7] Wodrow's Analecta, vol. iii. p. 232.

[8] See Appendix, No. 1. for a curious original letter from Mr. Spence; for this document I am indebted to my brother-in-law, Samuel Coltman, Esq. It was in the possession of his mother.

[9] "Genuine Memoirs of John Murray, Esq. London, 1746. "

[10] "Maxwell of Kirkconnel's Narrative, " p. 4.

[11] Life of James Murray, Esq.

[12] See Atholl Correspondence. Printed for the Abbotsford Club.

[13] Home, p. 31.

[14] Narrative, p. 1.

[15] Life of John Murray, Esq., p. 22.

[16] See Stuart Papers, in Dr. Brown's History of the Highlands.

[17] Life of J. Murray, Esq., p. 11.

[18] This disposition, observes a modern Historian, was inherited both by Charles Edward and his brother from their mother, the Princess Clementina, who devoted herself, during the years of their

infancy, to their welfare with unceasing care. —Histoire de Charles Edouard, par Amedée Pichot; tome première, p. 265.

[19] Life of Sir Robert Walpole, vol. ii. p. 490.

[20] Ibid. p. 492.

[21] Life of Sir Robert Walpole, vol. ii. p. 550.

[22] The Prince took off at the same time the interdict which had passed against any of Lord Orford's family appearing at his Court.

[23] Maxwell's Narrative, p. 13.

[24] See State Trials by Howell, vol. xviii. p. 661.

[25] Maxwell, p. 14.

[26] Memoirs of the Chevalier Johnstone, p. 19.

[27] Chevalier Johnstone's Memoirs. Translated from the French, p. 121.

[28] See Introduction to the Chevalier Johnstone's Memoirs.

[29] The Highlands of Scotland Described, MS. British Museum, 1748.

[30] See Forbes's Jacobite Memoirs, p. 30.

[31] One thousand is mentioned by the Chevalier Johnstone; two thousand, in other authorities. The Prince himself wrote to his father (Sept. 10th, from Perth), "I have got together 1300 men. " Forbes, note, p. 32.

[32] Johnstone's Memoirs, note, p. 11.

[33] Tales of a Grandfather, 3rd Series, vol. ii, p. 284.

[34] Forbes, p. 31.

[35] Lord Mahon.

[36] Maxwell, pp. 56, 57; also Tales of a Grandfather, 3rd Series, vol. ii. p. 285.

[37] I adopt this expression of Sir Walter Scott in the Tales of a Grandfather (vol. ii. 3rd Series, p. 205), which seems to imply some doubt on the subject.

[38] History of the Rebellion. Taken from the Scots Magazine, p. 36.

[39] Life of Murray of Broughton, p. 31.

[40] Maxwell's Narrative, p. 56.

[41] Forbes. Note, p. 32.

[42] Lord George Murray's Narrative. Forbes, p. 39.

[43] British Chronologist, vol. ii. p. 397.

[44] Forbes, p. 41.

[45] Forbes, p. 42.

[46] Henderson's History of the Rebellion, p. 88.

[47] Ibid.

[48] Henderson. Maxwell of Kirkconnel.

[49] Forbes, p. 43.

[50] Forbes, p. 46.

[51] Border Antiquities, by Sir Walter Scott. No. iv. vol. i.

[52] History of the Rebellion, from the Scots Magazine, p. 35.

[53] True Patriot, a weekly periodical, December 17, 1745.

[54] General Advertiser, 1745.

[55] Forbes, p. 47.

[56] Maxwell, p. 53.

[57] The True Patriot, December 10, 1745.

[58] Jacobite Correspondence, p. 3.

[59] Ibid. p. 41.

[60] Ibid. p. 30.

[61] Jacobite Correspondence, p. 48.

[62] Jacobite Correspondence, p. 67. Duke of Atholl to Lord George Murray.

[63] Jacobite Correspondence, p. 114.

[64] See Correspondence.

[65] Henderson's Hist. Rebellion, p. 129.

[66] Maxwell.

[67] Chambers.

[68] Home.

[69] Maxwell's Narrative, p. 61.

[70] Ibid.

[71] Chevalier Johnstone, p. 42.

[72] Chambers, Hist. Rebel. People's edition, p. 49.

[73] Chambers, p. 50.

[74] Lockhart Papers, vol. ii. p. 455.

[75] Jacobite Correspondence of the Atholl Family, p. 141.

[76] Chevalier Johnstone, p. 43.

[77] Border Antiquities, by Sir Walter Scott, p. 40; also Maxwell's Narrative, p. 63.

[78] Hutchinson's History of Cumberland.

[79] Lockhart Papers, vol. ii. p. 457.

[80] General Advertiser for 1745.

[81] Jacobite Memoirs, p. 49.

[82] Forbes's Jacobite Memoirs, p. 49.

[83] Forbes's Jacobite Memoirs, p. 50.

[84] Forbes, p. 51.

[85] Forbes, p. 52.

[86] Forbes, p. 53.

[87] See Lockhart, vol. ii. p. 456; also Lord Mahon, vol. iv. p. 428, note.

[88] Maxwell, p. 67.

[89] Maxwell says 4400 men. Two or three hundred were to be left in Carlisle, p. 68.

[90] Johnstone's Memoirs of the Rebellion, p. 45.

[91] Baines's History of Lancashire, II, 68.

[92] General Advertiser for 1745-46.

[93] Maxwell, page 68.

The following is a List of the Chevalier's officers and troops, taken from the History of the Rebellion, extracted from the Scots' Magazine for 1745 and 1746, p. 60. This List makes the amount of the forces considerably greater than the statement given elsewhere.

A LIST OF THE CHEVALIER'S OFFICERS AND TROOPS.

Regiments.	*Colonels.*	*Men.*
Lochyel	Cameron of Loch.	740
Appin	Stuart of Ardshiel	360
Atholl	Lord G. Murray	1000
Clanronald	Clan, of Clan., jun.	200
Keppoch	Macdonald of Keppoch	400
Glenco	Macdonald of Glenco	200
	Carried forward	2900

A LIST OF THE CHEVALIER'S OFFICERS AND TROOPS—*continued.*

Regiments.	*Colonels.*	*Men.*
	Brought forward	2900
Ogilvie	Lord Ogilvie	500
Glenbucket	Gordon of Glen.	427
Perth,	Duke of Perth (and Pitsligo'sfoot)	750
Robertson	Robertson of Strowan	200
Maclachan	Mac. of Maclachan	260
Glencarnick	Macgregor	300
Glengary	Macdonald of Glen., jun.	300
Nairn	Lord Nairn	200
Edinburgh	John Roy Stuart (and Lord Kelly's)	450
	In several small corps	1000
	Horse {Lord Elcho} {Lord Kilmarnock}	160

Lord Pitsligo's Horse	140
Total	7587

[94] "My grandfather, " says General Stuart, "always wore tartans; truis, and with the plaid thrown over the shoulder, when on horseback; and kilt, when on foot; and never any other clothes, except when in mourning. " App. XXII.

[95] Sketches of the Highlanders, by General Stuart of Garth. Vol. II. App. XXII. Also note.

[96] See the True Patriot, under the head Apocrypha, 1745.

[97] Stuart's Sketches, II. 76.

[98] Tales of a Grandfather, iii. 398.

[99] General Stuart's Sketches of the Highlanders, p. 67.

[100] State Trials, vol. xviii. p. 686.

[101] John Sobieski Stuart.

[102] Vestiarium Scoticum, p. 100, note. Edited by John Sobieski Stuart.

[103] These observations are all taken from the Notes to the Vestiarium Scoticum, a beautiful work, extremely interesting, as being written by the hand of a Stuart, and full of information.

[104] Maxwell, p. 70.

[105] Baines's History of Lancashire, iv. 69.

[106] Tales of a Grandfather, iii. p. 98.

[107] Maxwell, p. 71.

[108] Tales of a Grandfather.

[109] Baines's Lancashire, ii. p. 71; also iii. p. 254.

[110] Gentleman's Magazine, vol. xv. p. 644.

[111] I omit Horace Walpole's exact expression, which is more witty than proper.

[112] Sketches of the Highlanders, by General Stewart, vol. ii. p. 257; also Georgian Era, pp. 56, 57.

[113] Brown's Hist. of the Highlanders, vol. iii. p. 197.

[114] General Stewart, p. 233.

[115] Ibid. p. 246.

[116] Maxwell, p. 71.

[117] Chambers's Hist. of the Rebellion; Edition for the People, p. 54.

[118] Glover's Hist. of Derbyshire, vol. i. p. 32. There is, in Ashbourn church, an exquisite monument, sculptured by Banks, and supposed to have given the notion of the figures in Lichfield Cathedral to Chantry. A young girl, the only child of her parents, Sir Brook and Lady Boothby, reposes on a cushion, not at rest, but in the uneasy posture of suffering. On the tablet beneath are these words: "I was not in safety, neither had I rest, and the trouble came. " To which were added; "The unfortunate parents ventured their all on the frail bark, and the wreck was total. "—A history and an admonition.

[119] Maxwell, p. 72.

[120] Extract from the Derby Mercury. Glover's Hist. of Derbyshire, vol. ii. p. 1 to 420.

[121] Glover, vol. ii. pt. 415; from Hutton's Derby.

[122] Glover, vol. ii. pt. 1. p. 240.

[123] Glover, vol. ii. pt. i. p. 421. From the Derby Mercury, the first number of which was issued March 23, 1732, by Mr. Samuel Drewry, Market-place. Appendix to Glover's Hist., 616.

[124] Probably the house wherein Lord George Murray was lodged, belonged to a member of the Heathcote family, of Stoncliffe Hall, Darley Dale, Derbyshire.

[125] Tales of a Grandfather, iii. p. 103.

[126] Maxwell, p. 73.

[127] Lord George Murray's Narrative, Forbes, p. 55 and 56.

[128] Maxwell of Kirkconnell, p. 74.

[129] Chevalier Johnstone, p. 51.

[130] Ibid. p. 52.

[131] Chambers, p. 56, and Lord Elcho's MS.

[132] Maxwell, p. 75.

[133] Maxwell, p. 75 76.

[134] Maxwell, p. 76.

[135] Chevalier Johnstone, p. 157.

[136] Lord Mahon's History of England, vol. iii. p. 445.

[137] General Stewart's Sketches, vol. ii. p. 263.

[138] Lord Mahon, vol. iii. p. 446.

[139] Tales of a Grandfather, vol. iii. p. 107.

[140] Jacobite Memoirs, p. 57.

[141] Such is the account of a writer in the Derby Mercury, see Glover's History of Derby; but this statement is at variance with Lord George Murray's Journal.

[142] The Grandmother of the Author.

[143] Tradition.

[144] Glover, vol. ii. pt. i. p. 422.

[145] Lord Elcho's MS.

[146] Glover, vol. ii. pt. i. p. 422.

[147] Maxwell, p. 80.

[148] This account is taken from Maxwell's narrative, p. 84 and 85; and from the Chevalier Johnstone's Memoirs, p. 60 and 61.

[149] Jacobite Mem. p. 71.

[150] The Hussars, under the command of Lord Pitsligo, had gone off to Penrith.

[151] Jacobite Mem. p. 72.

[152] Note to General Stewart's Sketches, vol. i. p. 58.

[153] Maxwell.

[154] Jacobite Mem. p. 62.

[155] Maxwell, p. 88.

[156] Tales of a Grandfather, vol. iii. p. 125.

[157] Jacobite Mem. p. 74.

[158] Johnstone, p. 75.

[159] This statement tends somewhat to disprove the assertion that Roman Catholic priests occupied the pulpits at Derby, made in the papers of the time. See p. 136

[160] Maxwell.

[161] Johnstone, p. 82.

[162] Maxwell p. 103.

[163] Lord Murray's Narrative, Forbes, p. 88.

[164] General Stuart, I., p. 78.

[165] Forbes; note, p. 94.

[166] Chambers's Hist. of the Rebellion, p. 70.

[167] Tales of a Grandfather, iii. 166.

[168] Forbes, p. 100. Maxwell, p. 115. See, also, for the references to the last eight pages, Lord Mahon, Henderson, Chambers, and Home.

[169] Scots' Magazine, p. 138.

[170] Atholl Correspondence, p. 163. *et passim*.

[171] Tales of a Grandfather, vol. iii. p. 176.

[172] Maxwell, p. 131; also Forbes, p. 193.

[173] Lord George Murray's Journal. Forbes, p. 166. Johnstone's Memoirs, p. 116. Maxwell, p. 133.

[174] According to Lord Elcho's account (MS.), ten or twelve only were killed, and the rest taken prisoners.

[175] Forbes' Johnstone.

[176] Grant of Rothiemurcus.

[177] Atholl Correspondence, p. 211.

[178] See vol. i.—Life of the Marquis of Tullibardine.

[179] Lord Elcho's MS.

[180] See a very curious account of the Siege of Blair Castle, written by a subaltern officer in the King's Service. Scots' Magazine for 1808.

[181] Forbes, p. 108.

[182] Scots' Magazine, p. 33.

[183] Ibid.

[184] There was one horse which seemed endowed with supernatural strength, for when, eventually, the Castle was relieved, the horse, which had been shut up without forage, was found, after eight or ten days of abstinence, alive, and "wildly staggering about" in its confinement. It was afterwards sent as a present by Captain Wentworth, to whom it belonged, to his sister in England.

[185] See Forbes, p. 108, 109.

[186] Jacobite Correspondence, p. 217.

[187] Jacobite Correspondence, p. 218.

[188] Maxwell, p. 13.

[189] Maxwell, p. 134.

[190] These circumstances will be fully detailed in the Life of the Duke of Perth.

[191] Maxwell.

[192] Colonel Ker's Narrative, Forbes, p. 140 and 141.

[193] Lord Elcho's MS.

[194] Maxwell, p. 153.

[195] Lord Elcho's MS.

[196] Colonel Ker's Narrative, p. 142.

[197] Lord G. Murray's Account, Forbes, p. 124.

[198] Lord Elcho's MS.

[199] Lockhart, vol. ii. p. 533.

[200] Atholl Correspondence, p. 221.

[201] Brown's History of the Highlands, pt. v. p. 261. ; from the Stuart Papers.

[202] See Stuart Papers. Brown, *passim*.

[203] Stuart Papers; from Dr. Brown.

[204] Secretary to the Chevalier St. George.

[205] Stuart Papers. Appendix. Brown, p. 95.

[206] Chambers. Ed. for the People, p. 141.

JAMES DRUMMOND, STYLED DUKE OF PERTH.

In a history of the House of Drummond, compiled in the year 1681, by Lord Strathallan, the author thus addresses his relative, James, Earl of Perth, on the subject of their common ancestry:

"Take heire a view of youre noble and renowned ancestors, of whose blood you are descended in a right and uninterrupted male line; as also of so many of the consanguinities and ancient affinities of youre family in the infancy thereof, as the penury of our oldest records and the credit of our best traditions has happily preserved from the grave of oblivion. The splendor of your fame, " he adds, "needs no commendation, more than the sune does to a candle; and even a little of the truth from me may be obnoxious to the slander of flattery, or partiality, by reason of my interest in it. Therefore I'll say the less; only this is generally known for a truth, that justice, loyaltie, and prudence, which have been but incident virtues and qualities in others, are all three as inherent ornaments, and hereditary in yours."[207]

Such praise far exceeds in value the mere homage to ancient lineage. With these noble qualities, the race of Drummond combined the courage to defend their rights, and the magnanimity to protect the feeble. This last characteristic is beautifully described in the following words:

"For justice, as a poor stranger, often thrust out of doors from great houses, where grandeur and utility are commonly the idolls that's worshipped, —*quid non mortalia pectora cogis?* —has always found sanctuary in yours, which has ever been ane encouragement to the good, a terror to the bad, and free from the oppression of either. "

To this magnanimous spirit were added loyalty to the sovereign, and prudence in the management of private affairs; a virtue of no small price, for it rendered the House of Drummond independent of Court favour, and gave to its prosperity a solid basis. "The chiefs of this family lived, " says their historian, "handsomely, like themselves; and still improved or preserved their fortunes since the first founder."

The origin of this race is, perhaps, as interesting as that of any of the Scottish nobility, and has the additional merit of being well ascertained.

After the death of Edward the Confessor, the next claimant to the Crown, Edgar Atheling, alarmed for his safety after the Norman Conquest, took shipping with his mother Agatha, and with his two sisters, Margaret and Christiana, intended to escape to Hungary; but owing to a violent storm, or, as the noble historian of the Drummonds well expresses it, "through Divine Providence, " he was driven upon the Scottish coast, and forced to land upon the north side of the Firth of Forth. He took shelter in a little harbour west of the Queen's Ferry, ever since called St. Margaret's Hook, from Edgar's sister Margaret, who, for the "rare perfectiones of her body and mind, " was afterwards chosen by Malcolm Canmore, to the great satisfaction of the nation, for his Queen. Margaret was therefore married to the Scottish monarch at Dunfermline in the year 1066.

This alliance was not the only advantage derived by the young and exiled English King from his accidental landing in Scotland. Penetrated with gratitude for former services conferred upon himself by Edward the Confessor, Malcolm supported the cause of Edgar, and received and bestowed upon his adherents lands and offices, in token of kindness to his royal guest. Hence some of the most potent families in the kingdom had their origin.

Amongst the train of Edgar Atheling at Dunfermline was an Hungarian, eminent for his faithful services, but especially for his skilful and successful conduct of the vessel in which the fugitives had sailed from England. He was highly esteemed by the grateful Queen Margaret, who recommended him to the King; and, for his reward, lands, offices, and a coat of arms suitable to his quality, were conferred on him, together with the name of Drummond.

It was about this period that surnames were first introduced, and that patronymicks were found insufficient to designate heroes. Since the new designations were often derived from some office, as well as the possession of lands and peculiar attributes, the Hungarian obtained his name in consequence of his nautical skill; Dromont, or Dromond, being, in different nations, the name of a ship, whence the commander was called Dromount, or Dromoner.

The first lands bestowed upon the Hungarian were situated in Dumbartonshire, and in the jurisdiction of the Lennox; a county full of rivers, lochs, and mountains, "emblematically expressed, " says Lord Strathallan, "in the coats of arms then given to him, wherein hunting, waters, hounds, inhabitants wild and naked, are represented. " To these gifts was added the office of Thane, Seneschal, or Stuart Heritable of Lennox, —names all meaning the same thing, but altering with the times. [208]

The Hungarian, whose Christian name is conjectured to have been Maurice, was then naturalized a Scot; and all the parts of his coat-armour were contrived to indicate his adventures, his name, office, and nation. He died in an encounter near Alnwick Castle, fighting valiantly, in order to avenge the surprise of that place by William Rufus, in 1093.

The records of the family of Drummond were for several generations defective after the death of Maurice; but there exists no doubt but that he was the founder of a family once so prosperous, and afterwards so unfortunate. The name of Maurice was preserved, according to the Scottish custom of naming the eldest son after his father, for many succeeding generations.

The family continued to increase in importance, and to enjoy the favour of royalty; and the marriage of the beautiful Annabella Drummond to Robert the Third, King of Scotland, produced an alliance between the House of Drummond and the royal families of Austria and Burgundy. In 1487 James the Third ennobled the race by making John Drummond, the twelfth chief in succession, a Lord of Parliament. As the annals of the race are reviewed, many instances of valour, wisdom, and unchangeable probity arise; whilst some events, which have the features of romance, diversify the chronicle. Among these is the story of the fair Margaret Drummond, who has been celebrated by several of our best historians.

Between Margaret and James the Fourth of Scotland an attachment existed. They were cousins; and a pretext was made by the nobles and council, on that account, to prevent a marriage which they alleged to be within the degrees of consanguinity permitted by the Canon law: nevertheless, under promise of a marriage, Margaret consented to live with her royal lover, and the result of that connexion was a daughter. This happened when James was only in his sixteenth year, and whilst he was Duke of Rothsay; yet the monarch was so much touched in conscience by the engagement, or betrothal, between him and the young lady, that he remained unmarried until the age of thirty, about a year after the death of Margaret Drummond.

That event, it was surmised, was caused by poison; the common tradition being that a potion was provided for Margaret at breakfast, in order to free the King from his bonds, that he might "match with England. " "But it so happened, " says the narrative, [209] "that she called two of her sisters, then with her in Drummond, to accompany her that morning, to wit, Lilias, Lady Fleming, and a younger, Sybilla, a maid; whereby it fell out all the three were destroyed with the force of the poyson. They ly burried in a curious vault covered with three faire blue marble stones, joyned closs together, about the middle of the queir of the cathedral church of Dumblane; for about this time the burial-place for the familie of Drummond at Innerpeffrie was not yet built. The monument which containes the ashes of these three ladyes stands entire to this day, and confirms the credit of this sad storie. "

The daughter of Margaret Drummond, Lady Margaret Stuart, was well provided for by the King; and was married, in the year 1497, to Lord Gordon, the eldest son of the Earl of Huntley, "a gallant and handsome youth. " From this union four noble families are descended; the Gordons, Earls of Huntley; the Countess of Sutherland; the Countess of Atholl, who was the mother of Lady Lovat; and Lady Saltoun. James the Fourth testified his regret for the death of his beloved Margaret, and his solicitude for her soul's benefit, in a manner characteristic of his age and character. In the Treasurer's accounts for February 1502-3, there occurs this entry, "Item, to the priests that sing in Dumblane for Margaret Drummond, their quarter fee, five pounds: " and this item, occurring regularly during the reign of James the Fourth, "Paid to two priests who were appointed to sing masses for Margaret in the cathedral of Dumblane, where she was buried, " marks his remembrance of his betrothed wife.

One of the greatest ornaments of the ancient House of Drummond was William Drummond, a descendant of the Drummonds of Carnock, son of Sir John Drummond of Hawthornden, and author of the "History of the Five James's, " Kings of Scotland. [210] The friend of Drayton, and of Ben Jonson, this man of rare virtues presents one of the brightest examples of that class to which he belonged, the

Scottish country-gentleman. True-hearted, like the rest of his race, Drummond was never called forth from a retirement over which virtue and letters cast their charms, except by the commotions of his country. His grief at the death of Charles the First, whom he survived only one year, is said to have shortened his days.

In 1605, the title of Earl of Perth was added to the other honours of the family of Drummond, [211] who derived a still further accession of honour and repute by the probity and firmness of its members in the great Rebellion. Like most of the other Scottish families of rank, they suffered great losses, and fell into embarrassed circumstances on account of heavy fines exacted by Oliver Cromwell. The house, Castle Drummond, was garrisoned by the Protector's troops, and the estates were ravaged and ruined. Yet the valiant and true-hearted descendants of those who had been thus punished for their allegiance, were ready again to adopt the same cause, and to adhere to the same principles that had guided their forefathers.

In the person of James Drummond, fourth Earl of Perth, who succeeded his father the third Earl, in 1675, several high honours were centred. He was made, by Charles the Second, Justice-General, and afterwards Lord High Chancellor of Scotland. He continued to be a favourite with James the Second; and in 1688, when James fled from England, the Earl of Perth, endeavouring to follow him, was thrown into prison, first at Kirkaldy, and afterwards at Stirling, until the privy council, upon his giving security for five thousand pounds, permitted him to follow his royal master. From James, the Earl received the title of Duke, which his successors adopted, and which was given to them by the Jacobite party, of which we find repeated instances in the letters of Lord Mar. His son, Lord Drummond, succeeded to all the inconveniences which attend the partisans of the unfortunate. Returning from France, in 1695, he was obliged to give security for his good conduct, in a large sum. In consequence of the assassination plot, the vigilance of Government was increased, and, in 1696, he was committed to Edinburgh Castle. During the reign of William, a system of exaction was carried on with respect to this family.

"In a word, " says the author of Lochiell's Memoirs, himself a Drummond, speaking of James Lord Drummond, "that noble lord was miserably harassed all this reign. He represented a family which had always been a blessing to the country where it resided; and he himself was possessed of so many amiable qualities, that he was too generally beloved not to be suspected by such zealous ministers. He was humble, magnificent, and generous; and had a certain elevation and greatness of soul that gave an air of dignity and grandeur to all his words and actions. He had a person well-turned, graceful and genteel, and was besides the most polite and best bred lord of his age. His affability, humanity, and goodness gained upon all with whom he conversed; and as he had many friends, so it was not known that he had any personal enemies. He had too much sincerity and honour for the times. The crafty and designing are always apt to cover their vices under the mask of the most noble and sublime virtues; and it is natural enough for great souls to believe that every person of figure truly is what he ought to be, and that a person of true honour thinks it even criminal to suspect that any he is conversing with is capable of debasing[212] the dignity of his nature so low as to be guilty of such vile and ignoble practices. None could be freer of these, or indeed of all other vices, than the noble person I speak of. The fixed and unalterable principles of justice and integrity, which always made the rules of his conduct, were transmitted to him with his blood, and are virtues inherent and hereditary in the constitution of that noble family. "[213]

Lord Drummond was afterwards engaged in the insurrection of 1715: he was attainted, but escaped to France, and, dying in 1730, left the inheritance of estates which he had saved by a timely precaution, and the empty title of Duke of Perth, [214] to his son James Drummond, the unfortunate subject of this memoir.

Such was the character borne by the father of James, Duke of Perth. This ill-fated adherent of the Stuarts was born on the eleventh of May 1713; and three months afterwards, on the twenty-eighth of August, his father deemed it expedient to execute a deed conveying the family estates to him, by which means the property, at that time, escaped forfeiture. Like many other young men under similar circumstances, this young nobleman was educated at the Scottish College of Douay, consistently with the principles of his family, who were at that time Roman Catholics.

In his twenty-first year, the young Duke of Perth came over to Scotland, and devoted himself, in the absence of his father, to the management of his estate. It is probable that his own inclinations might have led him to prefer the occupations of an elegant leisure to the turmoils of contention; but, be that as it may, it was not reserved for the head of the House of Drummond to rest contentedly in his own halls.

The nearest kinsmen of the young nobleman were active partisans of the Chevalier St. George. His brother, Lord John Drummond who had been confirmed in all his devotion to the cause by his education at Douay, had entered the service of the King of France, and had raised a regiment called the Royal Scots, of which he was the Colonel. He was destined to take an active share in the events to which all were at this time looking forward, some with dread, others with impatience. But his influence was less likely to be permanent over his brother, than that of the Duke's mother, whose wishes were all deeply engaged in behalf of James Stuart.

This lady, styled Duchess of Perth, was the daughter of George first Duke of Gordon, and of Lady Elizabeth Howard, Duchess of Gordon, who, in 1711, had astonished the Faculty of Advocates at Edinburgh by sending them a silver medal with the head of the Chevalier engraved upon it. The Duchess of Perth inherited her mother's determined character and political principles; for her adherence to which she eventually suffered, together with other ladies of rank, by imprisonment.

These ties were strong inducements to the young Duke of Perth to take an active part in the affair of 1745, and it is said to have been chiefly on his mother's persuasions that he took his first step. But there was another individual, whose good-faith to the cause had been proved by exertion and suffering; this was the brave William, Viscount Strathallan, who possessed higher qualities than those of personal valour and loyalty. "His character as a good Christian, " writes Bishop Forbes, "setting aside his other personal qualities and rank in the world, as it did endear him to all his acquaintances, so did it make his death universally regretted. "[215]

Lord Strathallan was the eldest surviving son of Sir John Drummond of Macheany, whom he had succeeded in his estates; and, in 1711, became Viscount Strathallan, Lord Madertie, and Lord Drummond of Cromlix, in consequence of the death of his cousin. [216] He had engaged in the rebellion of 1715, and had been taken prisoner, as well as his brother, Mr. Thomas Drummond, at the battle of Sheriff Muir; but no proceedings had been instituted against him. His escape on that occasion, as well as the part which his kinsman, the

Earl of Perth, took on that eventful day, are thus alluded to in an old ballad entitled the Battle of the Sheriff Muir.

"To the tune of the 'Horseman's Sport.'

"Lord Perth stood the storm; Seaforth, and lukewarm
Kilsyth, and Strathallan, not sla', man,
And Hamilton fled—the man was not bred,
For he had no fancy to fa', man.
So we ran, and they ran; and they ran, and we ran;
And we ran, and they ran awa', man."[217]

Lord Strathallan joined the standard of Prince Charles in 1745, and afterwards acted an important part in the events of that period. He was not only himself a zealous supporter of the Stuarts, but was aided in no common degree by his wife, the eldest daughter of the Baroness Nairn and of Lord William Murray, —in his schemes and exertions. Lady Strathallan inherited from her mother, a woman of undoubted spirit and energy, the determination to act, and the fortitude to sustain the consequences of her exertions. But there was still another individual, not to specify various members of the same family, whose aid was most important to the cause of the Jacobites.

This was Andrew Drummond, one of the family of Macheany, and uncle of Lord Strathallan. He was the founder of the banking-house of Drummond at Charing Cross, which was formed, as it has been surmised, for the express purpose of facilitating supplies to the partisans of the Chevalier. This spirited member of the family remained unchanged in his principles during the course of a life protracted until the age of eighty-one. His part in the great events of the day was well known, and meanly avenged by Sir Robert Walpole, who, in the course of the insurrection, caused a run upon the bank. The concern, backed by its powerful connections, stood its ground; but the banker forgave not the minister. When the tumults of 1745 were at an end, Mr. Drummond so far yielded to the dictates of prudence as to go to court: he was received by George the Second, to whom he paid his obeisance. But when the minister, anxious to conciliate his stern and formidable foe, advanced to offer him his hand, Mr. Drummond turned round, folded his hands behind his back, and walked away. "It was my duty, " he said afterwards, "to pay my respects to his Majesty, but I am not obliged to shake hands with his minister! "

On the young James Drummond Duke of Perth, as chief of the House of Drummond, the eyes of the Jacobites were turned, with expectations which were, to the utmost of the young nobleman's power, fulfilled. It was by his mother's desire that he had been educated in France, where he was confirmed in the principles of the Romish faith. He possessed, indeed, some acquirements, and displayed certain qualities calculated to inspire hope in those who depended upon his exertions that he would prove a valuable adherent to the cause. Naturally courageous, his military turn had been improved by a knowledge of the theory of war: his disposition united great vivacity to the endearing qualities of benevolence and liberality; he had the every-day virtues of good-nature, mildness, and courtesy. His pursuits were creditable to a nobleman. He was skilled in mathematics, an elegant draughtsman, a scholar in various languages, a general lover of literature, and a patron of the liberal arts. Nor was a fondness for horse-racing, in which he indulged, and in which his horses frequently bore away the prize, likely to render him unpopular in the eyes of his countrymen. But there were some serious drawbacks to the utility of the young nobleman as a public man.

His health, in the first place, was precarious. When a child, a barrel had been rolled over him, and a bruise was received in his lungs, to the effects of which his friends attributed a weakness and oppression from which he usually suffered at bed-time; when "he usually, " as a contemporary relates, "took a little boiled bread and milk, or some such gentle food. "[218] This was an inauspicious commencement of an active and anxious career. It was afterwards discovered, that with all his acquirements and accomplishments, and with his natural gallantry, the Duke was no practical soldier.

In obtaining an influence over the minds of his countrymen, the young Duke possessed one great advantage. He was descended from a House noted for the highest principles of honour. [219]

"To give the reader an undeniable proof of the generous maxims of that House, " says the author of Lochiell's memoirs, "it will be proper to notice, that, by the laws of Scotland, no person succeeding to an estate is, in a legal sense, vested in the property until he serves himself heir to the person from whom he derives his title. The heir often took the advantage of this when the creditors were negligent, and passing by his father, and perhaps his grandfather, served heir to him who was last infefted; for unless they were actually seised of the estate according to the forms of law, they were no more than simple possessors, and could not encumber the land with any deed or debts; whereby the heir got clear of all that intervened betwixt himself and the person whom he represented by his service. This was an unjustifiable practice, which the diligence of creditors might always have prevented; and which is now wholly prevented by an act of parliament obliging every one possessing an estate to pay the debts of his predecessors, as well as his own, whether representing them by a service or not.

"But the House of Perth was always so firmly attached to honour and justice, that there are no less than fifteen retours, descending lineally from father to son, extant among their records.

"Now a retour is a writ returned from the Court of Attorney, testifying the service of every succeeding heir; and is therefore an unexceptionable evidence of paying his predecessor's debts, and of performing his obligations and deeds. Such has been, and still is, the uniform practice of the truly noble Lords of the House of Montrose and, perhaps, some others of the ancient nobility have followed the same course, which will not only entail a blessing upon their family and posterity, but will likewise be a perpetual memorial of their integrity, honour, and antiquity. "

The young Duke of Perth fully maintained this high character of honour and liberal dealings, and as a landholder and a chief, he would, had he been spared, have proved himself a valuable member of society. He was, relates an historian, a father to the poor; —and the interval of ten years between his return to Scotland and the Rebellion was engaged in establishing manufactures for the employment of his tenantry, and in acts of beneficence. Unhappily, it was not long before political combinations diverted the attention which was so well bestowed in the improvement of his country.

In the beginning of the year 1740, seven persons of distinction signed the association, engaging themselves to take arms, and to venture their lives and fortunes for the Stuarts. Among these was the Duke of Perth. This association was committed to Drummond of Bochaldy, who, besides, carried with him a list of those chiefs and chieftains who, the subscribers thought, were willing to join them, should a body of troops land from France. This list contained so great a number of names, that Murray of Broughton, in his evidence at the trial of Lord Lovat, said he considered it to be "a general list of the

Highlands; " a palpable refutation of the reasoning of those who have represented the Jacobite insurrection as a partial and factious movement.

The Duke of Perth had now irrevocably pledged himself to engage in the cause, which required a very different character of mind to that which he seems to have possessed. Like the unfortunate Lord Derwentwater, he was calculated to adorn a smooth and prosperous course; but not to contend with fiery spirits, nor to act in concert with overbearing tempers. Averse to interference, and retiring in his disposition, the Duke was conceived, by those who mistook arrogance for talent, to have been possessed of only limited abilities. The friend or relative who composed the epitaph to his memory inscribed on the Duke's tomb at Antwerp, has borne testimony to the strength of his understanding. All have coincided in commending the honour and faith which procured him the respect of all parties, and the chivalric bravery which won him the affection of the soldiery.

It is a melancholy task to trace the career of one so high-minded, so gentle, and so formed to adorn the peaceful tenour of a country life, through scenes of turmoil, disaster, and dismay; and, during the continuance of arduous exertions, to recall the slow and certain progress of a fatal disease, which progressed during hardships too severe for the delicate frame of this amiable young man to sustain without danger.

The younger brother of the Duke, Lord John Drummond, was constituted of different materials. Courteous, honourable, and high-minded, like his brother, he added to those attributes of the gentleman a strong capacity for military affairs, to which he had applied himself from his earliest youth. Intrepid and resolute, the roughness of the soldier was softened in this fine martial character by an elegance and ease of manner which sprang from a kind and gentle temper. The energy of Lord John Drummond's mind was shown by the enlistment of the Scottish Legion, under the protection of Louis the Fifteenth. In him the soldiers always knew that they had a sure, and firm friend: like his brother, when on the conquering side, clemency and humanity were never, even in the heat of victory, forgotten by the young general. Individuals like these lamented and unfortunate brothers give a mournful interest to the history of the Jacobites.

The Duke of Perth was one of the most sanguine of those who desired to see Charles Edward land on the coast of Scotland. Of the representations which induced the Prince to take that step, and especially of the part taken in the affair by the well-known Murray of Broughton, various accounts have been given. From Mr. Home we learn, that Mr. Murray used every argument in his power to deter the Prince from invading Scotland without a regular force to support him. This account was doubtless the version which the Secretary himself gave of his part in the business. The statement of Lord Elcho differs greatly from that of Mr. Home. [220]

"Mr. Murray, " says Lord Elcho, "in the beginning of the year 1745, sent one young Glengarry to the Prince with a state of his affairs in Scotland, in which it is believed he represented everybody that had ever spoke warmly of the Stuart family, as people that would join him if he came. "[221] After Mr. Murray's own visit to France, he had an interview with all the members of the Association, and there detailed to them the conference he had had with the Prince. The Duke of Perth was the only person who did not, in that council, expressly declare against the Prince's coming to Scotland without assistance from France.

The battle of Fontenoy, on the eleventh of May 1745, in which the British army was cut to pieces, encouraged, nevertheless, the ardent spirit of Charles to proceed in his enterprise. The number of regular troops in Scotland he well knew, was at that time inconsiderable; and he had, as he conceived, from the representations of Murray, no other opponents than the British army. He was, probably, wholly ignorant of the powerful enemies who afterwards co-operated against him in the south-western parts of Scotland. [222]

The Duke of Perth had already, in the beginning of the year, received, as well as others, his commission. He was appointed General of the forces in the north of Scotland, and was therefore one of the most important personages for Government to seize. The Duke was at that time at Drummond Castle, a place only exceeded in beauty and splendour, in the Highlands, by Dunkeld and Blair. The aspect of this commanding edifice is one which recalls the association of ancient power and princely wealth. Beneath its walls is an expanse of a magnificent and varied country, combining all those features which characterize lands long held in peace by opulent and liberal possessors. "Noble avenues, profuse woods, " thus speaks one of unerring accuracy, "a waste of lawn and pasture, an unrestrained scope, everything bespeaks the carelessness of liberality and extensive possessions; while the ancient castle, its earliest part belonging to the year 1500, stamps on it that air of high and distant opulence which adds so deep a moral interest to the rural features of baronial Britain. "[223]

From the castle it was now attempted to make the Duke of Perth a prisoner; but since it would have been impossible to detain a Chief, prisoner in his own halls, and among his own retainers, a stratagem, peculiarly revolting to the Highland code of honour, was adopted to ensnare the young nobleman.

Two Highland officers, Sir Patrick Murray and Mr. Campbell of Inverary, were employed in this transaction, and a warrant was given to them to apprehend the Duke of Perth. This they knew to be impossible without a large force; they therefore condescended to lower the character of Scotchmen, by violating the first principles which regulate the intercourse of gentlemen. They were base enough to abuse the hospitality of the kind and ready host who had often welcomed them to Drummond Castle.

One day, these gentlemen sent the Duke word that they should dine with him; he returned, in answer, that he should be proud to see them. On the twenty-sixth of July, 1745, they went, and were entertained at dinner with the liberal courtesy which always shone forth under that roof. One of the Duke's footmen, meantime, having espied an armed force about the house, called his Grace to the door of the room, and begged him to take care of himself. This caution was even repeated more than once; but the Duke, trusting that others were like himself, only smiled, and said he did not think that any gentleman "could be guilty of so dirty an action. " But he found that he was mistaken. After dinner, when the officers had drunk a little, they took courage to inform the Duke of their errand; and, to confirm their statement, one of them drew the warrant out of his pocket. The Duke behaved with great presence of mind; he received their summons calmly, but begged permission to retire to a closet in the room where they were sitting, to get himself ready. This was assented to: the Duke went into the closet, in which, however, there was a door; he opened it and, slipping down a flight of stairs, escaped to a wood adjacent to his Castle. This wood was already surrounded by an armed force, and he was obliged to crawl on his hands and feet to avoid being observed by the sentinels. In such a situation he was hindered and wounded by briers and thorns, and at last was obliged to hide himself in a dry ditch from his pursuers. They were, indeed, misled by the servants at the Castle, who, upon their inquiring for the fugitive, declared that he had gone away on horseback. The officers however on their return to Crieff, where they were quartered, passed so near the place where he lay, that he heard what they were saying. When all the soldiers were out of sight, he sprang up; and seeing a countryman with a pony, having no bridle, but only a halter about its neck, he begged to have the use of it, and his request was granted. After this, he first rode to the house of Mr. Murray of Abercairney, and afterwards to that of Mr. Drummond of Logie. Here he was saved by one of those presentiments of evil which one can neither explain nor deny. In the dead of night he was awakened by his host, who begged the Duke to take refuge elsewhere; for fears, which he could not account for, haunted his mind. The fugitive arose from his bed, and set off elsewhere. Shortly afterwards the house was invaded by a party of armed men, who came to search for him, but retired disappointed. His next meeting with his faithless guest, Sir Patrick Murray, was on the field of Gladsmuir, when the treacherous officer was made prisoner. The Duke then took his revenge with characteristic good-humour; for, after saluting the captured officer, he said smilingly, "Sir Patie, I am to dine with *you* to-day. "[224]

After his escape from Logie, the Duke of Perth crossed over to Angus, incognito, and, attended only by one servant, rode through the north country without molestation, and arrived at the camp of Prince Charles. Here he met the afterwards celebrated Roy Stuart, then a captain of Grenadiers in Lord John Drummond's' regiment. That officer had embarked at Helvoetsluys for Harwich, where he had scarcely arrived before the ship in which he had sailed was searched by authority of a Government warrant.

Charles Edward was at this time at Castle Mingry, whence accounts had travelled to the capital of his arrival and projected hostilities. It was long before his intentions were even believed; and, when believed, they were treated at first with contempt. The Duke of Argyll, who was then at Roseneath, had an intercepted letter of the Prince's put into his hands, addressed to Sir Alexander Macdonald, together with a copy of one to the Laird of Macleod. The Duke hastened to Edinburgh, and laid these papers before Mr. Craigie the advocate. "What a strange chimera, " said Craigie, laughing, "is it to suppose a young man with seven persons capable of overturning a throne! " "His landing with seven persons only, " replied Argyll gravely, "is a circumstance the more to be feared. "[225]

Sir John Cope, nevertheless, long delayed obeying the orders of Government to march northwards, although great pains were taken by some of the Whig party to magnify the danger, and to add to the terrors of the foe. Reports were even stated, in the presence of the magistrates, of a camp in Ardnamirchan, which was a large Scots mile in circumference, —of several ships of war hovering near the coast, —of cannon of an enormous size; whilst the young Chevalier was described as one of the strongest men in Christendom. All agreed that the invader had chosen the period of his enterprise judiciously. Scotland contained but few forces, and those were newly levied men, sufficient in number merely to garrison the forts and to overawe smugglers.

Never was a country less prepared to receive an invasion, [226] and General Cope's blunders soon encouraged the hopes of the Jacobites, until they were elated beyond measure. The sanguine Charles Edward pledged the General's health in a glass of brandy: "Here's a health to Mr. Cope! " he cried, in the presence of his forces; "and, if all the Usurper's generals follow his example, I shall soon be at St. James's. " The toast was given by the private soldiers, to whom whiskey was distributed to drink it. Well furnished with artillery, of which the insurgents were destitute, General Cope might have obtained an easy victory, or at any rate have dispersed the Jacobite army. Happy would it have been for Scotland, had the rebellion thus been extinguished, before the brave had sunk in civil strife, or loyal hearts been broken in the silent agony of imprisonment! Many acts of heroism, numberless traits of fortitude, would indeed have been lost to the mournful admiration of posterity; but the vigorous hand, which crushes a hopeless struggle in its outset, is ever, in effect, the hand of mercy.

From this time the Duke of Perth shared in the short-lived triumph of his Prince. He marched with the army to Dunkeld, where, supping in the house of James, Duke of Atholl, who retired at their approach, the unfortunate Charles Edward forced a gaiety which he was said, at that time, not to feel; asked for Scottish dishes; and, having picked up a few words of Gaelic, pledged the Highland officers in that tongue. The Duke of Perth attended in the triumphant entrance into Perth on the fourth of September. This was the first town of consequence that Charles Edward had visited; and his appearance, mounted on a fine horse presented to him by Major Macdonell, and dressed in a superb suit of tartan trimmed with gold, produced a great impression upon the assembled multitude, who greeted him with loud acclamations. He was conducted in triumph to the house of Viscount Stormont, the eldest brother of the celebrated Earl of Mansfield. Lord Stormont, though friendly to the cause, was not disposed to risk his life and property for the Stuarts. He withdrew from the dangerous honour of entertaining the Prince, yet left his family to receive him with all loyalty, and the Chevalier took up his abode at Lord Stormont's. It was an antique house with a wooden front, which stood on the spot now occupied by the Perth Union Bank, near the bottom of the High-street. [227] The evening was closed by a ball given by the Prince to the ladies of the town. The Prince, probably wearied by the day's proceedings, danced only one dance, and then withdrew. His bed, it is said, was prepared by the fair hands of Lord Stormont's sister.

On the following day a different scene took place, for all was not compliment that Charles encountered in the loyal town of Perth. Mass having been celebrated publicly, Charles was as publicly rebuked by a minister of the Kirk, who reminded him of his father's failure in the last Rebellion, which he attributed to his adherence to Popery, to "which he had sacrificed his crown. " "I prefer, " replied the young Chevalier boldly, "a heavenly crown to an earthly one!"[228]

The Duke of Perth had summoned many of his tenants to meet him at Blair, where he required them to bring all the rent due, under pain of punishment; and he now ordered them also to carry arms to the extent of their power. He is said to have insisted upon his privilege as Chief, with a degree of rigour which, when his power was exerted to force his tenants into a course of certain peril, cannot be justified. Unhappily, the practice was of too frequent occurrence among some of the chieftains to permit us entirely to dismiss it as a calumny. The amiable Lord Derwentwater, the brave Lord Southesk, as has been remarked elsewhere, and proved by letters and contemporary statements, were not free from a similar charge. The following anecdote is so little in accordance with the forbearance assigned to the Duke of Perth both by enemies and friends, that it must, however, be read with distrust. It is related by James Macpherson: [229] speaking of the compulsory measures adopted, he says, "To this oppression of the Duke of Perth's likewise several submitted (such are the terrors of arbitrary power). Three however resisted, declaring that besides the inconvenience which the neglect of their affairs would subject them to, and the danger of the undertaking, it was against their conscience to assist the cause of Popery against the true religion of their country; to which one of them had the boldness to add, he was sorry to see his Grace embarked in such a cause. Upon this, the Duke, flying into a rage, snatched up a pistol which lay in his tent, and immediately shot the poor man through the head. After which the other two made their escape from him, and one from the camp, the other being pursued and killed by one of the rebels, who was witness to the whole transaction. "

Whilst the army remained at Perth, a singular incident occurred, which seems to prove that the subsequent surrender of Edinburgh was by no means unexpected by Prince Charles. [230]

One evening, when Macpherson was on duty as one of the Prince's guards, a person came to the camp, and was by his desire conducted to the presence of the Chevalier. A long conference ensued, at which the Duke of Perth and the Marquis of Tullibardine were present. Soon after the departure of this stranger, it was rumoured that Edinburgh was to be betrayed to the Jacobites, and that they were to take possession in a few days. There must, therefore, have been some secret communication.

In the memorable events which followed this rumour, the Duke of Perth continually shared. He rode by the side of Charles Edward when the gallant adventurer, leaving Perth on the eleventh of September, crossed the Firth at the Frew, and passed so near the walls of Stirling, that the balls fired upon him and his forces from the castle fell within twenty yards of the Prince. He proceeded on the march, commenced by the Chevalier with the sum of only one guinea in his pocket, until they arrived at Gray's Hill, a place two miles west of Edinburgh. Here deputies from the town arrived to treat with Charles. "I do not treat with subjects, " was the Chevalier's reply; whilst the Duke of Perth added, "The King's declaration, and the Prince's manifesto, are such as every subject ought to accept with joy. "

Meantime, a company of volunteers under the command of Captain Drummond, a gentleman of very different political sentiments to those of the majority of this name, had assembled in the College yard, when, after being addressed by their gallant leader, they proffered their services to aid the dragoons stationed in the city, under the command of General Guest, in repelling the Jacobites. On Sunday, the fire-bell sounding in the time of Divine service, emptied all the churches; and the people, rushing into the streets, beheld the volunteers drawn up in the Lawn Market, awaiting the arrival of the dragoons, with whom they were prepared to march out of the town to repel the rebels. But this gallant resolution was not put into execution; and a force of two thousand strong, not half of the soldiery having fire-locks, was suffered to force their way into a town garrisoned by two thousand seven hundred soldiers, all well supplied with arms and ammunition.

That Edinburgh was surrendered by the treachery of its Provost, seems beyond all doubt. Archibald Stewart, who held that office at this critical moment, gave many indications of perfidy or cowardice, which have been duly related, although with little comment, by historians. Notwithstanding that the approach of the insurgents had been by measured paces, and that they had advanced so leisurely as to spend some hours lying on the bank of a rivulet near Linlithgow, no preparations for defence had been made, although it was the wish of many of the inhabitants to resist the Jacobite army. It had been found that all the calms, or moulds for bullets, had been bought up; ladies having gone to the shops where they were made, to purchase them. When the danger became proximate, the Provost merely remarked, that, if the enemy wished to enter, he did not know how they could be prevented. He viewed the fortifications, it is true, and rummaged up some grenades that had lain in a chest since 1715. But the most suspicious incident occurred during a meeting of the Town Council, when a Highland spy, having a letter in his hand, was apprehended, and brought before the assembly. The letter was given to the Provost, who hurried it into his pocket, and in great haste broke up the assembly. [231] In all the deliberations for the defence of the city, it was perceived that Mr. Provost Stewart was a dead-weight upon any measures of vigour; and nothing could have been done to preserve Edinburgh from surrendering, unless he had been absolutely bound in chains. Yet this unworthy magistrate, so faithless to his trust, so discreditable an instrument of the Jacobite cause, was afterwards acquitted, after a trial of four days, by the Lords Justiciary.

The progress of that cause now appeared such as to promise success to the future exertions of its partisans. On the seventeenth of September, the Prince received the news that Edinburgh was taken, and a stand of one thousand arms seized; a circumstance which added greatly to the joy of the insurgents, who stood in need of arms. "When the army came near town, " writes Lord Elcho, "it was met by vast multitudes of people, who by their repeated shouts and huzzas expressed a great deal of joy to see the Prince. When they came into the suburbs, the crowd was prodigious, and all wishing the Prince prosperity; in short, nobody doubted but that he would be joined by ten thousand men at Edinburgh, if he could arm them. The army took the road to Duddingston: Lord Strathallan marching first, at the head of the horse; the Prince next, on horseback, with the Duke of Perth on his right, and Lord Elcho on his left; then Lord George Murray, on foot, at the head of the column of infantry. From Duddingston, the army entered the King's Park, by a breach made in the wall. Lord George halted some time in the park, but afterwards marched the foot to Duddingston; and the Prince continued on horseback, always followed by the crowd, who were happy if they could touch his boots, or his horse furniture. In the steepest part of the road going down to the Abbey, he was obliged to alight and walk; but the mob, out of curiosity, and some out of fondness, to touch him or kiss his hand, were like to throw him down: so, as soon as he was down the hill, he mounted his horse and rode through St. Anne's Yard into Holyrood House, amidst the cries of six thousand people, who filled the air with their acclamations of joy. He dismounted in the inner court, and went up stairs into the gallery; and from thence into the Duke of Hamilton's apartments, which he occupied all the time he was at Edinburgh. The crowd continued all night in the outer court of the Abbey, and huzzaed every time the Prince appeared at the window. He was joined, upon his entering the Abbey, by the Earl of Kelly, Lord Balmerino, Mr. Hepburn of Keith, Mr. Lockhart younger of Carnwath, Mr. Graham younger of Airth, Mr. Rollo younger of Powhouse, Mr. Stirling of Craigbarnet, Mr. Hamilton of Bangor, Sir David Murray, and several other gentlemen of distinction: but not one of the mob, who were so fond of seeing him, were asked to enlist in his service; and, when he marched to fight Cope, he had not one of them in his army. "[232]

The Prince, who was thus received with acclamations into the home of his forefathers, was at this time in the bloom of youth, being in the twenty-fifth year of his age. Neither the agitation produced by the events of that critical day on his sensitive temper, nor the fatigue of the previous march to a young soldier, could diminish the grace of his deportment, nor hide the natural majesty of his carriage. "The figure and presence of Charles Stuart, " even Home remarks, "were not ill-suited to his lofty pretensions. " He was in height about five feet ten inches, of a slender form; his features were aquiline; his complexion, though ruddy from the Highland air, was naturally fair. He had the pointed chin, and small mouth in proportion to his other features, of Charles the First. The colour of his eyes has been variously described; being, according to some, "large rolling brown eyes, " whilst in many of his portraits he is depicted as having full blue eyes. [233] The hair of Charles Stuart was concealed under a "pale peruke; " but, is said to have been red, or, according to most of his portraits, of a sandy hue. As he rode, with extreme grace, upon a fine bay gelding presented to him by the Duke of Perth, the bystanders remarked that an "irregular smile, " as one of them has expressed it, lighted up, by fits, a countenance which told but too plainly every emotion of the heart. An anxious, watchful look was, at times, directed to those around and near him; and, in particular, rested on the face of Lord Elcho, who, though a gallant officer, the Prince may perhaps have too well conjectured, was not, even at that early period, a sincere and firm adherent. To the Duke of Perth, on the contrary, the ill-fated young Chevalier showed a marked respect, and sat for some moments on horseback in St. Anne's Yard, whilst the Duke, like "an intelligent farmer, informed him of the different nature and produce of the different parcels of ground. "[234] Dressed, as he was, in the Highland garb, —a blue sash wrought with gold coming over his shoulder, a green velvet bonnet with a gold lace round it on his head, a white cockade, —the cross of St. Andrew on his breast, his hand resting on a silver-hilted sword, and a pair of pistols on his saddle; —associated in the minds of all around him with the remembrance of Scotland in her independence, and of Scottish monarchs in their greatness, the enthusiasm which was inspired in a slow, but ardent people cannot be a matter of surprise. Long did the remembrance of that day continue to be cherished, in mingled pride and sorrow! It is true, the opinions of men differed according to their secret bias. The Jacobites, who looked on the young Prince, compared him to Robert the Bruce, to whom he bore, they fancied, a resemblance. The Whigs beheld in him the gentleman of fashion, but not the hero and the conqueror. All parties seem to have remarked the dejection and languor of his manner as he prepared to enter the palace of Holyrood.

It was, indeed, impossible, from the deportment of Charles on his first introduction into Scotland, or from his conduct whilst his affairs prospered, to comprehend the strength of his determination, or to calculate upon his power of endurance. In prosperity he was, it is true, brave, courteous, often amiable, often generous, but sometimes betraying the petulance and obstinacy which historians have been fond of considering as hereditary propensities in the heroic young man, but which are the common attributes of the inexperienced and the spoiled. In adversity he was meek, grateful, magnanimous; capable of forgetting his own unparalleled sufferings, in considering those of others; never breathing an accent of revenge; rising above fortune. He resembled Charles the Second more in his hatred of shedding blood, than in his vices, which were in the young Chevalier the effect of circumstances, rather than of a depraved nature. He had the fortitude of Charles the First: in truth, and right intention he exceeded both of these his ancestors; and in this, as in other respects, he showed more of the Scottish character, more of the true sense of Highland honour, than any of his immediate predecessors in the Stuart line. Naturally gay, though variable; quick and shrewd, rather than deep or strong in intellect; easily to be flattered, too easily led by some, too wilful in resisting the counsels of others, —as a Prince, as the head of a Court, he soon won upon the affections of the people who beheld him; but there were vital defects mingled with his great and good qualities, which well verified the saying of the Whigs, "that he would prove neither a hero nor a conqueror. "

As the Prince walked along the piazza close to the apartment of the Duke of Hamilton, a gentleman stepped out of the crowd, and, drawing his sword, raised his arm aloft, and walked up stairs before Charles Edward. The remarkable person who thus signalized his loyalty was James Hepburn of Keith, a gentleman of learning and intelligence, whose Jacobitism was of a more enlightened description than that of the party with whom he thus identified himself. Since the insurrection of 1715, in which, when a very young man, he had been engaged, Mr. Hepburn had become a professed Jacobite. Yet he disclaimed the hereditary, indefeasible right of Kings, and condemned the measures of James the Second. Cherishing even these opinions, he had nevertheless kept himself during twenty years ready to take up arms for Charles Edward, from a hatred to the Union between England and Scotland, a measure which he deemed injurious and humiliating to his country. Idolized by the Jacobites, beloved by some of the Whigs, a "model of ancient simplicity, manliness and honour, "[235] the accession of Hepburn to the Jacobite cause was lamented by those who esteemed him, and who saw in his notions of the independence of Scotland only a visionary speculation.

The entrance of Prince Charles had taken place early in the day: soon after noon he was proclaimed Regent at the ancient Cross of Edinburgh, and his father's manifesto was read in the same place. Six heralds in their robes, with a trumpet, came to the Cross, which was surrounded by the brave Camerons in three ranks. The streets and windows were crowded to excess; whilst David Beato, a writing-master in Edinburgh, read the papers to the heralds. The beautiful Mrs. Murray of Broughton sat on horseback with a drawn sword in her hand beside the Cross, her dress decorated with the white ribbon which was the token of adherence to the House of Stuart. Whilst these events took place, a spectator in the crowd, viewing clearly that all was the show of power, without the substantial capacity to perpetuate it, resolved to write the history of what, he foresaw, would be a short-lived though perhaps fierce contest. He was not mistaken. This individual was Alexander Henderson.

The following account is given by Lord Elcho of the Chevalier's court during the short time that he inhabited Holyrood House. [236]

"The Prince lived in Edinburgh, from the twenty-second of September to the thirty-first of October, with great splendour and magnificence; —had every morning a numerous court of his officers. After he had held a council, he dined with his principal officers in public, where there was always a crowd of all sorts of people to see him dine. After dinner he rode out, attended by his life-guards, and reviewed his army; where there were always a great number of spectators, in coaches and on horseback. After the review he came to the Abbey, where he received the ladies of fashion that came to his drawing-room. Then he supped in public; and generally there was music at supper, and a ball afterwards. Before he left Edinburgh, he despatched Sir James Stewart to manage his affairs in the country and solicit succours. "

This remarkable scene was soon followed by the battle of Preston Pans. The memorable words of Charles Edward before the victory, "I have flung away the scabbard! " were followed by a total rout of the King's troops. The Duke of Perth was appointed Lieutenant-general of the forces. After the engagement which ensued, when the heat of the contest was over, he distinguished himself in a manner in which every brave and loyal man would wish to imitate his example, —by saving the lives of the combatants. His tenantry, commanded by Lord Nairn, were among the most eager of the combatants on that day. When the defeat of the King's troops was manifest, a terrible carnage ensued. Some of the conquered threw down their arms, and begged for quarter, which was refused them; others, who fled into the enclosures, were murdered; and all who were overtaken were cut in the most cruel manner by broad-swords and Lochaber axes.

The kind-hearted Duke of Perth, seeing this slaughter, made a signal to Cameron of Lochiel to stop the impetuosity of his men; and sent his aid-de-camp, or, as he was then called, his gentleman, for that purpose. No sooner had the Duke done this, than he sprang himself upon a fleet bay mare, a racer, which had won the King's plate at Leith some years before; and, taking a Major of the King's troops along with him, "shot like an arrow through the field, " and saved numbers: as also did his gentleman, Mr. Stuart. [237]

But these efforts were insufficient to prevent a cruel and terrible destruction of some of the bravest and best of the British officers. In the battle of Preston Pans fell the famous Colonel Gardiner. His fate was, it is said, envied by General Cope, who, witnessing the destruction of his army, wished to have died on the field.

Whilst the Highlanders were carried away to the house of Colonel Gardiner, close by, the young Chevalier stood by the road-side, having sent to Edinburgh by the advice of the Duke of Perth for surgeons. At this moment, Henderson, that spectator of the proclamation who had resolved to write a history of the war, having slept at Musselburgh, only at two miles' distance, the night before, stepped forward to take a survey of the field. "It was one scene of horror, capable, " writes this historian, [238] "of softening the hardest heart, being strewed not so much with the dead as with the wounded: the broken guns, halberts, pikes, and canteens showing the work of the day. In the midst of this distressing spectacle, an act of mercy shone forth, like a light from Heaven. " "Major Bowles, " continues Henderson, "of Hamilton's Dragoons, being dismounted, the enemy fell upon and wounded him in eleven different places; and just as some inhuman wretch was fetching a stroke, which perhaps would have proved mortal, Mr. Stuart threw up his sword and awarded the blow. "

From Preston Pans Charles Edward rode to Pinkie House, a seat of the Marquis of Tweedale. In the elation of victory, a consideration which can alone excuse the disregard of the sufferings of others which the foregoing narrative states, the Prince is said to have left the bulk of the wounded upon the field until the next day, when they were brought in carts to the infirmary of Edinburgh. The neighbourhood was afterwards scattered over with the wounded who recovered, and who begged throughout the country, where they met with kindness and humanity from all, except from the Adventurers, as they were called. Such is the testimony of one who has not failed to bear witness to acts of humanity where they really existed; and it would be unfair to suppress the statements of contemporaries on either side of the question. At the same time, this account is wholly at variance with the deep sorrow afterwards betrayed by Charles when he spoke of the sufferings of the Scottish people on his account; nor is it consistent with the sensibility and humanity evinced, as the same historian avows, by the Duke of Perth. [239]

Upon the return of Prince Charles to Edinburgh, in order to carry on affairs with every appearance of royalty, he appointed a council, who met every day at Holyrood House at ten o'clock for the despatch of business. The members of this council were the two Lieutenants-general, the Duke of Perth, and Lord George Murray, who had been appointed in conjunction with the former; Secretary Murray; Sullivan, Quarter-master-general; Lord Pitsligo, Lord Elcho, Sir Thomas Sheridan, and all the Highland chiefs.

The fine characteristics, and powerful mind of Lord George Murray, and the prominent part which he took in the insurrection, demand a long and separate account. Among the rest of this ill-starred council, the principal members in point of rank, if not of influence, were Alexander, Lord Forbes of Pitsligo, who, after the battle of Preston, joined the Prince's standard with a troop of a hundred horse. The character of this nobleman gave his example a great influence among all who knew him, and who respected the ardent piety, bordering upon fanaticism, which characterized his religious sentiments, and the heartfelt earnestness of his political opinions. Early in life this venerable man had sworn allegiance to William the Third, and taken his seat in Parliament; he became, however, an opponent to the Union, and, from the period of that measure, his course was a decided system of calm and steady adherence to Jacobite principles. He engaged in the rebellion of 1715, yet by the forbearance of Government was permitted to retain his title and estate. He now again embarked in the same adventurous cause, leaving the study of moral philosophy, on which he had written several essays, and the security of a private career, for the sake of conscience. No hope of gain, no inducement of ambition, lured this adherent of Charles

Edward to the standard of the Stuarts. Aged, and so infirm that he was compelled by his bodily weakness to accept the generous proposal of Charles Edward to travel on all the marches in the Prince's carriage, whilst the Chevalier walked at the head of his army, Lord Pitsligo again came forward at what he conceived to be the dictates of duty. His example drew many others into the undertaking. Of course, his subsequent history closed in the usual melancholy manner: his life was, it is true, spared; but his estates were forfeited, and his title extinguished. He died at Auchiries, in Aberdeenshire.

David, Lord Elcho, who held also a place in the council, and who was colonel of the first troop of Horseguards, was the son of James, fourth Earl of Wemyss, and of Janet the daughter of Colonel Francis Charteris of Amisfield, whose immense property was afterwards vested in the Wemyss family. Lord Elcho was at this time only twenty-four years of age, and therefore his appointment to the colonelcy of the horse was a signal compliment to his abilities. Of his personal character much may be gleaned from his unpublished narrative, written in a dry, caustic, and uninspiring style; and penned by one who seems to have desired to do justice, but whose personal dislike to the young Chevalier over-masters his inclination to the cause. Notwithstanding a plain disapproval of many measures, and a marked conviction of the wilfulness of his young leader, Lord Elcho was true to the cause which he had adopted. His account of the manner in which the council of the Regent, as he was styled, was conducted, is so characteristic, not only of those to whom he refers, but of his own mind, that I shall give it in the unvarnished phraseology in which he composed it. [240]

"The Prince in his council used always first to declare what he was for, and then he asked everybody's opinion in their turn. There was one-third of the council whose principles were, that Kings and Princes can never either act, or think wrong; so, in consequence, they always confirmed whatever the Prince said. The other two-thirds, who thought that Kings and Princes thought sometimes like other men, and were not altogether infallible, and that this Prince was no more so than others, begged leave to differ from him, when they could give sufficient reasons for their difference of opinion, which very often was no hard matter to do; for as the Prince and his old governor, Sir Thomas Sheridan, were altogether ignorant of the ways and customs in Great Britain, and both much for the doctrine of absolute monarchy, they would very often, had they not been prevented, have fallen into blunders which might have hurt the cause. The Prince could not bear to hear anybody differ in sentiment from him, and took a dislike to everybody that did; for he had a notion of commanding this army, as any general does a body of mercenaries, and so let them know only what he pleased, and they obey without inquiring further about the matter. This might have done better had his favourites been people of the country; but they were Irish, and had nothing at stake. The Scotch, who ought to be supposed to give the best advice they were capable of giving, thought they had a little right to know, and be consulted in what was for the good of the cause in which they had so much concern; and, if it had not been for their insisting strongly upon it, the Prince, when he found that his sentiments were not always approved of, would have abolished his council long ere he did. There was a very good paper sent one day by a gentleman in Edinburgh, to be perused by this council. The Prince, when he heard it read, said that it was below his dignity to enter into such a reasoning with subjects, and ordered the paper to be laid aside. The paper afterwards was printed under the title of the Prince's Declaration to the People of England, and is esteemed the best manifesto published in those times; for the ones that were printed at Rome and Paris were reckoned not well calculated for the present age. "

Before the Prince had left Edinburgh, intrigues had begun to distract his councils. "An ill-timed emulation, " remarks an eye-witness of the rebellion, "soon crept in, and bred great dissension and animosities: the council was insensibly divided into factions, and came to be of little use, when measures were approved of, or condemned, not for themselves, but for the sake of their author. "[241] Unhappily, the Duke of Perth, amiable, but inexperienced and unsuspecting, confided in one whose machinations, guided by an unbounded love of rule, eventually accelerated the ruin of the cause.

The very name of Murray of Broughton recalls with a shudder the remembrance of selfish ambition and treachery. This unprincipled man, private secretary to Charles Edward, had a remarkable influence over the young Chevalier's mind; an influence acquired during a long and intimate acquaintance abroad. "He was, " observes Mr. Maxwell, "the only personal acquaintance the Prince found in Scotland. " To a desire of having the sole government of the Prince's council he "sacrificed what chance there was of a restoration, although upon that all his hopes were built. " The expedition to Scotland and England was, according to the same authority, the entire suggestion of Murray; and the credit of that success which had hitherto attended the attempt, was now solely attributed to the secretary's advice. "The Duke of Perth, " adds the same writer, "judging of Murray's heart by his own, entertained the highest opinion of his integrity, went readily into all his schemes, and confirmed the Prince in the esteem he had already conceived for Murray. "

The man whom Murray most dreaded as a rival was Lord George Murray, the coadjutor with the Duke of Perth in the command of the army; and it soon became no difficult task, not only to persuade Prince Charles, who knew but little personally of Lord George, that that impetuous but honest man was a traitor, but also to inspire the amiable Duke of Perth with suspicions foreign to his generous nature. Few of the calm spectators of the struggle were very sanguine as to its result; but the moderate hopes which they dared to entertain were all dashed to the ground by the unbridled love of sway which the secretary indulged, and which filled him with a base and bitter enmity towards men of talent and influence. Too truly is the effect of his representations told in these few and simple words, written by one who was devotedly attached to the misled, confiding Charles, upon whose ignorance of the world Murray condescended to practise. [242]

"All those gentlemen that joined the Prince after Murray, were made known under the character he thought fit to give them; and all employments about the Prince's person, and many in the army, were of his nomination. These he filled with such as he had reason to think would never thwart his measures, but be content to be his tools and creatures without aspiring higher. Thus, some places of the greatest trust were given to little insignificant fellows; while there were abundance of gentlemen of figure and merit that had no employment at all, and who might have been of great use, had they been properly employed. Those that Murray had thus placed, seconded his little dirty views: it was their interest, too, to keep their betters at a distance from the Prince's person and acquaintance. These were some of the disadvantages the Prince laboured under during this whole expedition. "

As soon as the expedition into England was decided, a gentleman was dispatched to France to hasten the assistance expected from that quarter. The first intention of the insurgents was to march to Newcastle, and give battle to General Wade; then to proceed, if the

Prince proved victorious, by the eastern coast to England, in order to favour the expected landing of the French upon that side. This scheme was overruled by Lord George Murray, with what success history has declared. It was natural, when all was lost, for those who wished well to the cause, to retrace their steps, and to desire that any measures had been adopted, rather than those which had proved so disastrous: but this is the common feeling of regret, and cannot be relied on as the sober dictate of judgment.

On his departure from Edinburgh, the young Chevalier was followed by the good will of many who had viewed his arrival with regret. The people, says Maxwell of Kirkconnel, "were affected with the dangers they apprehended he might be exposed to, and doubtful whether they ever should see him again. "[243] "Everybody was mightily taken, " adds the same writer, "with the Prince's figure and personal behaviour. There was but one voice about them. " What was still more important, the short duration of military rule exercised by Charles Edward had been so conducted as to create no disgust. The guard of the city had been entrusted to Cameron of Lochiel, the younger; and under his firm and judicious controul, the persons and effects of the citizens, had been as secure as in time of peace. "The people had the pleasure of seeing the whole apparatus of war, without feeling the effects of it. "[244] Day after day some new and graceful instance of the humanity and kindness of the young Chevalier's disposition had transpired. At this period of his life there was a degree of magnanimity in the sentiments of one, of whose principles despair, and the desertion of his friends afterwards made such a wreck. The following trait of this ill-fated young man is too beautiful—it reflects too much credit, through him, upon the party of whom he was the head—to be omitted; more especially as the narrative from which it is taken is not in the hands of general readers.

"But what gave people the highest idea of him was, the negative he gave to a thing that very nearly concerned his interest, and upon which the success of his enterprise perhaps depended. It was proposed to send one of the prisoners to London, to demand of that court a cartel for the exchange of prisoners taken and to be taken during this war, and to intimate that a refusal would be looked upon as a resolution on their part to give no quarter. It was visible a cartel would be of great advantage to the Prince's affairs: his friends would be more ready to declare for him, if they had nothing to fear but the chance of war in the field; and, if the Court of London refused to settle a cartel, the Prince was authorised to treat his prisoners in the same manner that the Elector of Hanover was determined to treat such of the Prince's friends as might fall into his hands. It was urged, a few examples would compel the Court of London to comply. It was to be presumed that the officers of the English army would make a point of it. They had never engaged in the service, but upon such terms as are in use among all civilized nations, and it would be no stain on their honour to lay down their commissions if these terms were not observed; and, that, owing to the obstinacy of their own Prince. Though this scheme was plausible, and represented as very important, the Prince could never be brought into it; it was below him to make empty threats, and he would never put such as those into execution; he would never, in cold blood, take away lives which he had saved in heat of action at peril of his own. "[245]

On the thirty-first of October, the Prince set out from Holyrood House in the evening, amid a crowd of people assembled to bid him farewell. On the following day he joined one column of his army at Dalkeith. The army marched in two columns, by different roads, to Carlisle: that which the Prince commanded, and which was conducted by Lord George Murray, was composed of the Guards, and the Clans; Charles Edward marched on foot at the head of the Highlanders, and the Guards led the van. The other column went by Peebles and Moffat, having with them the artillery and heavy baggage. It was composed of the Atholl brigade, the Duke of Perth's regiment, Lord Ogilvie, of Glenbucket, and Roy Stuart's regiment. The greater part of the horse was commanded by the Duke of Perth. A week afterwards these two columns were re-united, and the troops were quartered in villages to the west of Carlisle.

On the thirteenth of October the town of Carlisle was invested by the Duke of Perth and Lord George Murray, with the horse and Lowland regiments. The conduct of the Duke of Perth, during the siege of five days which ensued, has been a subject of eulogy for every writer who has undertaken to relate the affairs of the period. The siege was attempted in the face of many difficulties, the Prince having no battering cannon; so that, if the town had been well defended, it would have been found impossible to reduce it: still, being a place of great strength, and the key to England, he resolved to make the attempt.

It was in this undertaking that the Duke of Perth reaped the benefit of his scientific knowledge of the art of war, and that he showed a degree of skill as well as of military ardour, which would, had his life been spared, have rendered him an excellent general. The castle of Carlisle, built upon the east angle of the fortifications, was of course the object of his attack. On Tuesday, the thirteenth of October, after his return from Brampton, where the Prince remained with the Clans to cover the siege, the Duke began his operations. His officers had forced four carpenters to go along with them in order to assist in erecting the batteries. In short, all ablebodied men were seized on by the insurgents, and those who had horses and ladders were constrained to carry them to the siege of Carlisle.

The Duke then "broke ground, " to use a military expression, about three hundred yards from the citadel, at the Spring Garden; and encountered the fire of the cannon from the town, approaching so near that the garrison even threw grenadoes at them. On Wednesday, the trenches were opened, and were conducted by Mr. Grant, chief engineer, whose skill was greatly commended. On Friday morning, batteries were erected within forty fathoms of the walls. During all this time the cannon and small arms from the castle played furiously, but with so little destruction to the besiegers, that only two men were killed.

The weather was so intensely cold, that even the Highlanders could scarcely sustain its inclemency; yet the Duke of Perth and the Marquis of Tullibardine, the one delicate in constitution, the other broken and in advancing age, worked at the trenches like any common labourer, in their shirts. On the Friday, when the cannon began to play, and the scaling-ladders were brought out for an assault, a white flag was hung out, and the city offered to surrender. An express was sent to the Chevalier at Brampton; whose answer was, "that he would not do things by halves, " and that the city had no reason to expect terms, unless the castle surrendered also. That event took place, in consequence, immediately; and the capitulation was signed by the Duke of Perth, and by Colonel Durand, who had been sent from London to defend Carlisle. In the afternoon of the same day, the Duke of Perth entered the town, and took possession in the name of James the Third, whose manifesto was read; the mayor and aldermen attending the Duke, the sword and mace being carried before them.

The Duke of Perth won many of those who were enemies to Charles Edward, over to his cause, by the humanity and civility with which he treated the conquered citizens, over whom he had the chief command until Charles arrived. But even the important advantage thus gained could not still the animosities which had been kindled in the breasts of those who ought to have laid aside all private considerations for the good of their common undertaking. Hitherto Lord George Murray and the Duke of Perth had had separate commands, and had not interfered with each other until the siege of Carlisle. Here the Duke had acted as the chief in command; he had directed the attack, signed the capitulation, and given orders in the town until the Prince arrived. This was a precedent for the whole campaign, and it ill-suited the fiery temper of Lord George Murray to brook it tamely. There was, indeed, much to be said in favour of Lord George's alleged wrongs, in this preference of one so young and inexperienced as the Duke of Perth. In the first place, Lord George was an older Lieutenant-General than his rival; nor could it be agreeable to his Lordship to serve under a man so much his inferior in age and experience. "Lord George, " observes Mr. Maxwell, "thought himself the fittest man to be at the head of the army; nor was he the only person that thought so. Had it been left to the gentlemen of the army to choose a general, Lord George would have carried it by vast odds against the Duke of Perth. " But there was still another pretext, which was insisted upon as a reason less offensive to the Duke of Perth, whose gentle and noble qualities had much endeared him even to those who did not wish to see him chief in command; this was his religious persuasion. It was argued that, at that time in England, Roman Catholics were excluded from all employments, civil and military, by laws anterior to the Revolution; it was contended that these laws, whether just or not, ought to be complied with until they were repealed; and that a defiance of these laws would confirm all that had been heard of old from the press and from the pulpit, of the Prince's designs to subvert both Church and State: neither could it be alleged in excuse for the young Prince, that a superiority of genius or of experience had won this distinction, in opposition to custom, for the Duke of Perth.

Whilst these murmurs distracted the camp, immediately after the surrender of Carlisle, Lord George Murray resigned his commission of Lieutenant-General, and informed the Prince that thenceforth he would serve as a volunteer. Upon this step, Mr. Maxwell, who seems to have known intimately the merits of the case, makes the following temperate and beautiful reflection. [246] "It would be rash in me to pretend to determine whether ambition, or zeal for the Prince's service, determined Lord George to take this step; or, if both had a share in it, which was predominant: it belongs to the Searcher of hearts to judge of an action which might have proceeded from very different motives. "

Under these circumstances, violent discussions took place in the army; and the result was, the wise resolution on the part of a certain officer, not improbably Mr. Maxwell himself, to represent the consequences of these altercations to the Duke of Perth. The undertaking was one of delicacy and difficulty; but the individual who undertook it had not miscalculated the true gentlemanly humility, the real dignity and disinterestedness, of the gallant man to whom he addressed himself. The narrative goes on as follows:

"A gentleman who had been witness to such conversation, and dreaded nothing so much as dissension in a cause which could never succeed but by unanimity, resolved to speak to the Duke of Perth upon this ungrateful subject. He had observed that those that were loudest in their complaints were least inclined to give themselves any trouble in finding out a remedy. "

"The Duke, who at this time was happy, but not elevated, upon his success, reasoned very coolly on the matter. He could never be convinced that it was unreasonable that he should have the principal command; but when it was represented to him, that since that opinion prevailed, whether well or ill founded, the Prince's affairs might equally suffer, he took his resolution in a moment; said he never had anything in view but the Prince's interest, and would cheerfully sacrifice everything to it. And he was as good as his word; for he took the first opportunity of acquainting the Prince with the complaints that were against him, insisted upon being allowed to give up his command, and to serve henceforth at the head of his regiment. "

After his resignation, the Duke of Perth sank gracefully into the duties of the post assigned to him. But his ardour in the cause was unsubdued; and he was frequently known, during the march from Carlisle to Derby, to ride down three horses a day when information of the enemy was to be procured.

The short sojourn of the Prince at Derby, and the inglorious retreat, have been detailed by the various biographers and historians of that period; but, amongst the various accounts which have been given, that which is contained in a letter from Derby has not hitherto been presented to the reader, except in a collection rarely to be met with, and now but little known. [247]

On Wednesday, the 4th of December (1745), two of the insurgents entered the town, inquired for the magistrates, and demanded billets for nine thousand men, and more. A short time afterwards the vanguard broke into the town, consisting of about thirty men, clothed in blue faced with gold, and scarlet waistcoats with gold lace; and, being "likely men, " they made a good appearance. They were drawn up in the market-place, and remained there two hours; at the same time the bells were rung, and bonfires were lighted, in order to do away with the impression that the Chevalier's vanguard had been received disrespectfully. About three o'clock Lord Elcho, on horseback, arrived at the head of the Life-guards, about one hundred and fifty men, the flower of the army, who rode gallantly into the town, dressed like the vanguard, making a very fine display. The Guards were followed by the main body of the army, who marched in tolerable order, two or three abreast, with eight standards, mostly having white flags and a red cross; the bag-pipers playing as they entered. Whilst they were in the market-place, they caused the Chevalier to be proclaimed King, and then asked for the magistrates. These functionaries appeared without their gowns of office, having cautiously sent them out of the town; a circumstance which was with some difficulty excused by the insurgents.

In the dusk of the evening Charles Edward arrived: he walked on foot, attended by many of his men, who followed him to Exeter House, where the Prince remained until his retreat northwards. Here he had guards placed all round the house, and here he maintained the semblance of a Court, in the very heart of that country which he so longed to enter.

The temporary abode of Charles Edward still remains in perfect repair, and much in the same state, with the exception of change of furniture, as when he held levees there. Exeter House at that time belonged to Brownlow, Earl of Exeter, whose connexion with the town of Derby was owing to his marriage with a lady of that city. The house stands back from Full Street, and is situated within a small triangular court. An air of repose, notwithstanding the noise of a busy and important town, characterizes this interesting dwelling. It is devoid of pretension; its gables and chimneys proclaim the Elizabethan period. A wide staircase, rising from a small hall, leads to a square, oak-panelled drawing-room, the presence-chamber in the days of the ill-fated Charles. On either side are chambers, retaining, as far as the walls are concerned, much of the character of former days, but furnished recently. One of these served the Prince as a sleeping-room; the rest were occupied by his officers of state, and by such of his retinue as could be accommodated in a house of moderate size. The tenement contains many small rooms and closets, well adapted, had there been need, for concealment and escape.

The back of Exeter House is picturesque in the extreme. The character of the building is here more distinctly ancient; and its architecture is uniform, though simple. Beyond the steps by which you descend from a spacious dining-room, is a long lawn, enclosed between high walls, and extending to the brink of the river Derwent. A tradition prevails in Derby, that, after the retreat, one of the Highland officers who had been left behind, hearing of the approach of the Duke of Cumberland's army, escaped through this garden, and, plunging into the river, swam down its quiet waters for a considerable distance, until he gained a part of the opposite shore where he thought he might land without detection. Another more interesting association connects the spot with the poet Dr. Darwin, who is said to have planted some willows which grow on the opposite side of the river to Exeter House.

Here Charles remained for some days. The Dukes of Atholl and Perth, and the other noblemen who commanded regiments, together with Lady Ogilvie and Mrs. Murray of Broughton, were lodged in the best gentlemen's houses. Every house was tolerably well filled; but the Highlanders continued pouring in till ten or eleven o'clock, until the burgesses of Derby began to think they "should never have seen the last of them. " "At their coming in, " says the writer of the letter referred to, "they were generally treated with bread, cheese, beer and ale, while all hands were aloft getting supper ready. After supper, being weary with their long march, they went to rest, most upon straw-beds, some in beds. " On Friday morning, only two days after the minds of the inhabitants had been agitated by the arrival of the Jacobites, they heard the drums beat to arms, and the bag-pipers playing about the town. It was supposed that this was a summons to a march to Loughborough, on the way to London; but a very different resolution had been adopted.

The Prince's council had, the very morning before, met to advise their inexperienced leader as to the steps which he might deem it advisable to take. The memorable decision to return to the north was not arrived at without a painful scene, such as those who felt deeply the situation of the Chevalier could never forget. The sentiments with which the ardent young man listened to the proposal are thus detailed by Mr. Maxwell. The statement at once exonerates the Prince of two faults with which his memory has been taxed, those of cowardice and obstinacy. To a coward the great risk of advancing would have appeared in strong colours. An obstinate man would never have yielded to the arguments which were proffered. The description which Maxwell gives of the Prince's flatterers is such as too fatally applies to the generality of those who have not the courage to be sincere. [248]

"The Prince, naturally bold and enterprising, and hitherto successful in everything, was shocked with the mention of a retreat. Since he set out from Edinburgh, he had never a thought but of going on, and fighting everything he found in his way to London. He had the highest idea of the bravery of his own men, and a despicable opinion of his enemies: he had hitherto had reason for both, and was confirmed in these notions by some of those who were nearest his person. These sycophants, more intent upon securing his favour than promoting his interest, were eternally saying whatever they thought would please, and never hazarded a disagreeable truth. "[249]

The Duke of Perth coincided, on this occasion, with Charles in wishing to advance; or, to use the words of Lord George Murray, "the Duke of Perth was for it, since his Royal Highness was. "[250] It now seems to be admitted that the judgment of the strong mind of Lord George Murray was less sound in this instance than the opinion of those who were more guided by feeling than by reflection, less cautious than the sagacious General, less willing and less able to balance the arguments on either side. [251]

"There are not a few, " remarks Mr. Maxwell, "who still think the Prince would have carried his point had he gone on from Derby. They built much upon the confusion there was at London, and the panic which prevailed among the Elector's troops at this juncture. It is impossible to decide with any degree of certainty whether he would or would not have succeeded; that depended upon the disposition of the Army, and of the City of London, ready to declare for the Prince. "

Never had the soldiery been in greater spirits than during their stay at Derby; but the deepest dejection prevailed, when, in spite of some manoeuvres to deceive them, they found themselves on the road to Ashbourn. The despair and disgust of the Prince were as painful to behold, as they were natural. He had played for the highest stake, and lost it. Yet one there was who could look on the drooping figure of the disconsolate young man as he followed the van of the army, and attribute to ill-humour the dejection of that ardent and generous mind. The following is an extract from Lord Elcho's narrative.

"Doncaster. —The Prince, who had marched all the way to Derby on foot at the head of a column of infantry, now mounted on horseback, and rode generally after the van of the army, and appeared to be out of humour. Upon the army marching out of Derby, Mr. Morgan, an English gentleman, came up to Mr. Vaughan, who was riding in the Life-guards, and after saluting him said, 'D—— me, Vaughan, they are going to Scotland! ' Mr. Vaughan replied, 'Wherever they go, I am determined, now I have joined them, to go along with them. ' Upon which Mr. Morgan said with an oath, 'I had rather be *hanged* than go to Scotland to *starve*. ' Mr. Morgan *was hanged* in 1746; and Mr. Vaughan is an officer in Spain. "[252]

In six days afterwards the Jacobite army arrived at Preston, and from this place, where the Prince halted, he sent the Duke of Perth to Scotland to summon his friends from Perth to join him, in order to renew the attack upon England. The Prince was resolved to retire only until he met that reinforcement, and then to march to London, be the consequence what it would. [253] But this scheme, so dearly cherished by Charles, was impracticable. The Duke of Perth, taking with him an escort of seventy or eighty horse, set out for Kendal. He was assailed as he passed through that place by a mob, which he dispersed by firing on them, and resumed his march; but near Penrith he was attacked by a far more formidable force in a band of militia both horse and foot, greatly superior in numbers to his troops, and was obliged to retire to Kendal. On the fifteenth he rejoined the Prince's army, after this fruitless attempt. The retreat of the Prince's army, managed as it was with consummate skill by Lord George Murray, continued without any division of the forces until they had passed the river Esk. There the army separated; and the Duke of Perth commanding one column of the army took the eastern line to Scotland, while Charles marched to Annan in Dumfrieshire.

The siege of Stirling is the next event of note in which we find the Duke of Perth engaged. He here acted again as Lieutenant-General, and commanded the siege. Here, too, the valour and fidelity of two other members of his family were again proved. Lord John Drummond, who had landed in Scotland while the Jacobites were at Derby, with the French brigade, was slightly wounded in the battle of Falkirk. He had the honour of being near the Prince in the centre of the battle with his grenadiers; and it was on his artillery and engineers that the Chevalier chiefly depended for success in reducing Stirling. Lord Strathallan had also assembled his men, and joined the army.

While the Prince's army were flushed with the victory of Falkirk, the alternative of again marching to London, or of continuing the siege of Stirling, was discussed. The last-mentioned plan was unhappily adopted; and the Duke of Perth called upon General Blakeney to surrender. The answer was, that the General had always hitherto been regarded as a man of honour, and that he would always behave himself as such, and would hold out the place as long as it was tenable. Upon this, fresh works were erected; and Monsieur Mirabel, the chief engineer, gave it as his opinion that the castle would be reduced in a few days. The unfortunate result of that ill-advised siege, and the consequent retreat of the Prince from Stirling, have been, with every appearance of reason, as much blamed as the retreat from Derby. It was a fatal resolution, and one which was not adopted by the Prince without sincere reluctance, and not until after a strong representation, signed at Falkirk by Lord George Murray and by all the Clans, begging that his Royal Highness would consent to retreat, had been presented to him. The great desertion that had taken place since the battle was adduced as a reason for this movement; and the siege of Stirling, it was also urged, must necessarily be raised, on account of the inclemency of the weather, which the soldiers could hardly bear in their trenches, and the impaired state of the artillery. [254]

The winter was passed in a plan of operations, for which the generalship of Prince Charles, or rather the able judgment of Lord George Murray, has been eulogized. Making the neighbourhood of Inverness the centre, from which he could direct all the operations of his various generals, the Prince employed his army of eight thousand men extensively and usefully. The siege of Fort William was carried on by Brigadier Stapleton; Lord George Murray had invested Blair Castle; Lord John Drummond was making head against General Bland; the Duke of Perth was in pursuit of Lord Loudon. This portion of the operations was attended with so much difficulty and danger, that Charles must have entertained a high opinion of him to whom it was entrusted.

Lord Cromartie had been already sent to disperse, if possible, Lord Loudon's little army; but that skilful and estimable nobleman had successfully eluded his adversary, who found it impossible either to entice him into an action, or to force him out of the country. Lord Loudon had taken up his quarters at Dornoch, on the frith which divides Rosshire from Sutherland. Here he was secure, as Lord Cromartie had no boats. It was therefore deemed necessary to have two detachments; one to guard the passage of the frith, the other to go by the head of it. This was a matter of some difficulty, for the Prince had at that time hardly as many men at Inverness as were necessary to guard his person. It was, however, essential to attack Lord Loudon, whose army cut off all communication with Caithness, whence the Prince expected provisions and men. In this dilemma an expedient had been thought of some time previously, and preparations had been made for it; but the execution was extremely dangerous. Mr. Maxwell gives the following account of it: [255]

"All the fishing-boats that could be got on the coast of Moray had been brought to Findhorn; the difficulty was, to cross the frith of Moray unperceived by the English ships that were continually cruizing there: if the design was suspected, it could not succeed. Two or three North-country gentlemen, that were employed in this affair, had conducted it with great secrecy and expedition. All was ready at Findhorn when the orders came from Inverness to make the attempt, and the enemy had no suspicion. Moir of Stoneywood set out with this little fleet in the beginning of the night, got safe across the frith of Moray, and arrived in the morning at Tain, where the Duke of Perth, whom the Prince had sent to command this expedition, was ready. The men were embarked with great despatch, and by means of a thick fog, which happened very opportunely, got over to Sutherland without being perceived. The Duke of Perth marched directly to the enemies' quarters, and, after some disappointments, owing to his being the dupe of his good nature and politeness, succeeded in dispersing Lord Loudon's army: and this era, in the opinion of Mr. Maxwell, is the finest part of the Prince's expedition." Henceforth, all was dismay and disaster.

The affairs of Charles Edward had now begun visibly to decline, for money, the sinews of the war, was not to be had; and the military chest, plundered, as it has been stated, by villains who robbed the

Prince by false musters, was exhausted. The hopes of the Chevalier were in the lowest state, when the intelligence reached Inverness that the Duke of Cumberland was advancing from Aberdeen to attack his forces. Upon receiving these tidings, the Prince sent messengers far and wide to call in his scattered troops, expecting that he should be strong enough to venture a battle.

The Duke of Perth, who at that time commanded all the troops that were to the eastward of Inverness, was planted near the river Spey. When the enemy approached, he retired to Elgin. On the same day, the twelfth of April 1746, the Duke of Cumberland passed the Spey, and encamped within three or four miles of Elgin.

This retreat of the Duke of Perth has been severely condemned. It appears, however, that he, and Lord John Drummond who was with him, could not muster two thousand five hundred men. The river, which was very low, was fordable in many places; so much so, that the enemy might march a battalion in front. The Duke had no artillery, whilst the enemy had a very good train. There was no possibility of sending reinforcements from Inverness; above all, says Mr. Maxwell, "nothing was to be risked that might dishearten the common soldiers on the eve of a general and decisive action. "

But the same candid and experienced soldier acknowledges that the Duke of Perth remained too long at Nairn, whither he retired, and where the Duke of Cumberland advanced within a mile of the town, and followed the retiring army of Perth for a mile or two, though to no purpose, the foot-soldiers being protected by Fitzjames's Horse. The delay at Nairn has, it is true, been excused, on the grounds of a command from Prince Charles to the Duke of Perth and his brother not to retire too hastily before Cumberland, but to keep as near to him as was consistent with their safety. This message "put them on their mettle, and well-nigh occasioned their destruction. " The Duke of Perth continued to retreat, until he halted somewhat short of Culloden, where the Prince arrived that evening, and took up his quarters at Culloden House. [256]

The following day was the fifteenth of April, the anniversary of that on which the Duke of Cumberland, the disgrace of his family, the hard-hearted conqueror of a brave and humane foe, first saw the light. It was expected that he would choose his birth-day for the combat, but the fatal engagement of Culloden was deferred until the following morning.

The battle of Culloden was prefaced by a general sentiment of despair among those who shared its perils.

"This, " says Mr. Maxwell, [257] referring to the morning of the engagement, "was the first time the Prince, ever thought his affairs desperate. He saw his little army much reduced, and half-dead with hunger and fatigue, and found himself under a necessity of fighting in that miserable condition, for he would not think of a retreat; which he had never yielded to but with the greatest reluctance, and which, on this occasion, he imagined would disperse the few men he had, and put an inglorious end to his expedition. He resolved to wait for the enemy, be the event what it would; and he did not wait long, for he had been but a few hours at Culloden, when his scouts brought him word that the enemy was within two miles, advancing towards the moor, where the Prince had drawn up his army the day before. The men were scattered among the woods of Culloden, the greatest part fast asleep. As soon as the alarm was given, the officers ran about on all sides to rouse them, if I may use the expression, among the bushes; and some went to Inverness, to bring back such of the men as hunger had driven there. Notwithstanding the pains taken by the officers to assemble the men, there were several hundreds absent from the battle, though within a mile of it: some were quite exhausted, and not able to crawl; and others asleep in coverts that had not been beat up. However, in less time than one could have imagined, the best part of the army was assembled, and formed on the moor, where it had been drawn up the day before. Every corps knew its post, and went straight without waiting for fresh orders; the order of battle was as follows: the army was drawn up in two lines; the first was composed of the Atholl brigade, which had the right; the Camerons, Stuarts of Appin, Frazers, Macintoshes, Farquharsons, Chisholms, Perths, Roy Stuart's regiment, and the Macdonalds, who had the left. "

The Highlanders, though faint with fatigue and want of sleep, forgot all their hardships at the approach of an enemy; and, as a shout was sent up from the Duke of Cumberland's army, they returned it with the spirit of a valiant and undaunted people.

The order of battle was as follows: the right wing was commanded by Lord George Murray, and the left by the Duke of Perth; the centre of the first line by Lord John Drummond, and the centre of the second by Brigadier Stapleton. There were five cannon on the right, and four on the left of the army. [258]

The Duke of Perth had therefore, from his important command, the privilege of spending the short period of existence, which, as the event proved, Providence allotted to him, in the service of a Prince whom he loved; whilst he had the good fortune to escape that responsibility which fell to the lot of his rival, Lord George Murray. The influence which that nobleman had acquired over the council of war had enabled him far to eclipse the Duke of Perth in importance; but it was the fate of Lord George Murray to pay a heavy penalty for that distinction.

But not only did the amiable and high-minded Duke of Perth calmly surrender to one, who was esteemed a better leader than himself, the post of honour; but he endeavoured to reconcile to the indignity put upon them the fierce spirit of the Macdonalds, who were obliged to cede their accustomed place on the right to the Atholl men. "If, " said the Duke, "you fight with your usual bravery, you will make the left wing a right wing; in which case I shall ever afterwards assume the honourable surname of Macdonald. "[259] The Duke's standard was borne, on this occasion, by the Laird of Comrie, whose descendant still shows the claymore which his ancestors brandished; whilst the Duke exclaimed aloud, "Claymore! "[260] Happy would it have been for Charles, had a similar spirit purified the motives of all those on whom he was fated to depend!

The battle was soon ended! Half-an-hour of slaughter and despair terminated the final struggle of the Stuarts for the throne of Britain! During that fearful though brief[261] space, one thousand of the Jacobites were killed; no quarter being given on either side. Exhausted by fatigue and want of food, the brave Highlanders fell thick as autumn leaves upon the blood-stained moor, near Culloden House. About two hundred only on the King's side perished in the encounter. During the whole battle, taking into account the previous cannonading, the Jacobites lost, as the prisoners afterwards stated, four thousand men. But it was not until after the fury of the fight ceased, that the true horrors of war really began. These may be said to consist, not in the ardour of a strife in which the passions, madly engaged, have no check, nor stay; but in the cold, vindictive, brutal, and remorseless after-deeds, which stamp for ever the miseries of a conflict upon the broken hearts of the survivors.

"Exceeding few, " says Mr. Maxwell, "were made prisoners in the field of battle, which was such a scene of horror and inhumanity as is rarely to be met with among civilized nations. Every circumstance concurs to heighten the enormity of the cruelties exercised on this occasion; the shortness of the action, the cheapness of the victory, and, above all, the moderation the Prince had shown during his prosperity, —the leniency, and even tenderness, with which he had always treated his enemies. But that which was done on the field of Culloden was but a prelude to a long series of massacres committed in cold blood, which I shall have occasion to mention afterwards."[262]

The Chevalier, leaving that part of the field upon which bodies in layers of three or four deep were lying, rode along the moor in the direction of Fort Augustus, where he passed the river of Nairn. He halted, and held a conference with Sir Thomas Sheridan, Sullivan, and Hay; and, having taken his resolution, he sent young Sullivan to the gentlemen who had followed him, and who were now pretty numerous. Sheridan at first pretended to conduct them to the place where the Prince was to re-assemble his army; but, having ridden half a mile towards Ruthven, he there stopped, and dismissed them all in the Prince's name, telling them it was the Prince's "pleasure that they should shift for themselves. "

This abrupt and impolitic, not to say ungracious and unsoldier-like proceeding, has been justified by the necessity of the moment. There were no magazines in the Highlands, in which an unusual scarcity prevailed. The Lowlanders, more especially, must have starved in a country that had not the means of supporting its own inhabitants, and of which they knew neither the roads nor the language. It is, however, but too probable, that various suspicions, which were afterwards dispelled, of the fidelity of the Scots, induced Charles to throw himself into the hands of his Irish attendants at this critical juncture. [263]

The Duke of Perth, with his brother Lord John Drummond, and Lord George Murray, with the Atholl men, and almost all the Low-country men who had been in the Jacobite army, retired to Ruthven, where they remained a short time with two or three thousand men, but without a day's subsistence. The leaders of this band finding it impossible to keep the men together, and receiving no orders from the Prince, came to a resolution of separating. They took a melancholy farewell of each other, brothers and companions in arms, and many of them united by ties of relationship. The chieftains dispersed to seek places of shelter, to escape the pursuit of Cumberland's "bloodhounds: " the men went to their homes.

Such is the statement of Maxwell of Kirkconnel, relative to the Duke of Perth: according to another account, the course which the Duke pursued was the following: —

He is said to have been wounded in the back and hands in the battle, and to have fled with great precipitancy from the field of battle. He obtained, it is supposed, that shelter which, even under the most dangerous and disastrous circumstances, was rarely refused to the poor Jacobites. The exact spot of his retreat has never been ascertained; yet persons living have been heard to say, that in the houses of their grandfathers or ancestors, the Duke of Perth took refuge, until the vigilance of pursuit had abated. The obscurity into which this and other subjects connected with 1745 have fallen, may be accounted for by the apathy which, at the beginning of the present century existed concerning all subjects connected with the ill-starred enterprise of the Stuarts; and the loss of much interesting information, which the curiosity of modern times would endeavour in vain to resuscitate, has been the result.

Tradition, however, often a sure guide, and seldom, at all events, wholly erroneous, has preserved some trace of the unfortunate wanderer's adventures after all was at an end. As it might be expected, and as common report in the neighbourhood of Drummond Castle states, the Duke returned to the protection of his own people. To them, and to his stately home, he was fondly attached, notwithstanding his foreign education. On first going from Perth to join the insurrection, as he lost sight of his Castle, he turned round, and as if anticipating all the consequences of that step, exclaimed, 'O! my bonny Drummond Castle, and my bonny lands! '

The personal appearance of the Duke was well known over all the country, for he was universally beloved, and was in the practice of riding at the head of his tenantry and friends, called in that neighbourhood 'his guards, ' to Michaelmas Market at Crieff, the greatest fair in those parts; where thousands assembled to buy and sell cattle and horses. He was therefore afterwards easily recognised, although in disguise.

"Sometime after the battle of Culloden, " as the same authority relates, [264] "the Duke returned to Drummond Castle, where his mother usually resided; and lived there very privately, skulking about the woods and in disguise; he was repeatedly seen in a female dress, barefooted, and bare-headed. Once a party came to search the castle unexpectedly; he instantly got into a wall press or closet, or recess of some sort, where a woman shut him in, and standing before it, remained motionless till they left that room, to carry on the search, when he got out at a window and gained the retreats in the woods. After he had withdrawn from Scotland, and settled in the north of England, he occasionally visited Strathearn. "

In one of these visits he called, disguised as an old travelling soldier, at Drummond Castle, and desired the housekeeper to show him the rooms of the mansion. She was humming the song of "the Duke of Perth's Lament, " and having learnt the name of the song he desired her to sing it no more. When he got into his own apartment he cried out, "This is the Duke's own room; " when, lifting his arm to lay hold of one of the pictures, she observed he was in tears, and perceived better dress under his disguise, which convinced her he was the Duke himself. [265]

For some time the Duke continued these wanderings, stopping now and then to gaze upon his Castle, the sight of which affected him to tears. "It was now, " says the writer of the case of Thomas Drummond, "that for obvious reasons, to elude discovery, the report of his death on shipboard or otherwise, would be propagated by his friends and encouraged by himself. " It is stated upon the same evidence, that instead of sailing to France, as it has been generally believed, the Duke fled to England; that he was conveyed on board a ship and landed at South Shields, a few miles only distant from Biddick, a small sequestered village, chiefly inhabited at that time by banditti, who set all authority at defiance. Biddick is situated near the river Wear, a few miles from Sunderland; it was, at that time, both from situation and from the character of its inhabitants, a likely place for one flying from the power of the law to find a shelter; it was, indeed, a common retreat for the unfortunate and the criminal. That the Duke of Perth actually took refuge there for some time, is an assertion which has gained credence from the following reasons: —

In the first place: "In the History, Directory, and Gazette of the counties of Northumberland and Durham, and the town and counties of Newcastle-upon-Tyne, by William Parson and William White, two volumes, 1827-28, the following passage occurs relating to Biddick, in the parish of Houghton-le-Spring: —

"It was here that the unfortunate James Drummond, commonly called Duke of Perth, took sanctuary after the rebellion of 1745-6, under the protection of Nicholas Lambton, Esq., of South Biddick, where he died, and was buried at Pain-Shaw. "

In the case of Thomas Drummond, (on whom I shall hereafter make some comments,) letters stated to be from Lord John Drummond are referred to, and quoted in part. These are said to have been addressed by Lord John Drummond from Boulogne, to the Duke at Houghton-le-Spring. The passage quoted runs thus: "I think you had better come to France, and you would be out of danger; as I find you are living in obscurity at Houghton-le-Spring. I doubt that it is a dangerous place; you say it is reported that you died on your passage. I hope and trust you will still live in obscurity. " These expressions, which it must be owned have very much the air of being coined for the purpose, would certainly, were the supposed letters authenticated, establish the fact of the Duke's retreat to Houghton-le-Spring.

Upon the doubtful nature of the intelligence, which was alone gleaned by the friends and relatives of the Duke of Perth, a superstructure of romance, as it certainly appears to be, was reared. The Duke was never, as it was believed, married; and in 1784 the estates were restored to his kinsman, the Honourable John Drummond, who was created Baron Perth, and who died in 1800, leaving the estates, with the honour of chieftainship, to his daughter Clementina Sarah, now Lady Willoughby D'Eresby.

In 1831, a claimant to the honours and estates appeared in Thomas Drummond, who declared himself to be the grandson of James Duke of Perth; according to his account, the Duke of Perth on reaching Biddick, took up his abode with a man named John Armstrong, a collier or pitman. The occupation of this man was, it was stated, an inducement for this choice on the part of the Duke, as in case of pursuit, the abyss at a coal-pit might afford a secure retreat; since no one would dare to enter a coal-pit without the permission of the owners.

The Duke, it is stated in the case of Thomas Drummond, commenced soon after his arrival at Biddick, the employment of a shoemaker, in order to lull suspicion; he lost money by his endeavours, and soon relinquished his new trade. He is said to have become, in the course of time, much attached to the daughter of his host, John Armstrong, and to have married her at the parish church of Houghton-le-Spring, in 1749. He resided with his wife's family until his first child was born, when he removed to the boat-house, a dwelling with the use and privilege of a ferry-boat attached to it, and belonging to Nicholas Lambton, Esq. of Biddick; who, knowing the rank and misfortunes of the Duke, bestowed it on him from compassion. Here he lived, and with the aid of a small huckster's shop on the premises, supported a family, which in process of time, amounted to six or seven children; two of whom, Mrs. Atkinson and Mrs. Peters, aged women, but still in full possession of their intellect, have given their testimony to the identity of this shoemaker and huckster to the Duke of Perth. [266]

The papers, letters, documents and writings, a favourite diamond ring, and a ducal patent of nobility, were, however, "all lost in the great flood of the river Wear in 1771; " and the Duke is said to have deeply lamented this misfortune. It is not, however, very likely that he would have carried his ducal patent with him in his flight; and had he afterwards sent for it from Drummond Castle, some of his family must have been apprised of his existence.

It is stated, however, but only on hearsay, that thirteen years after the year 1745, the Duke visited his forfeited Castle of Drummond, disguised as an old beggar, and dressed up in a light coloured wig. This rumour rests chiefly upon the evidence of the Rev. Dr. Malcolm, LLD., who, in 1808, published a Genealogical Memoir of the ancient and noble House of Drummond; and who declared, on being applied to by the family of Thomas Drummond, that he had been told by Mrs. Sommers, the daughter-in-law of Patrick Drummond, Esq., of Drummondernock, the intimate friend of the Duke of Perth, that the Duke survived the events of the battle of Culloden a long time, and years afterwards, visited his estates, and was recognised by many of his "trusty tenants. "[267] A similar report was, at the same time, very prevalent at Strathearn; and it has been positively affirmed, that a visit was received by Mr. Græme, at Garnock, from the Duke of Perth, long after he was believed to be dead. At this time, it is indeed wholly impossible to verify, or even satisfactorily to refute such statements; but the existence of a report in Scotland, that the Duke did not perish at sea, may be received as an undoubted fact. [268] In 1831, when the case of Thomas Drummond was first agitated, Mrs. Atkinson and Mrs. Elizabeth Peters, the supposed daughters of James Duke of Perth, were both alive, and on their evidence much of the stability of the case depended. The claimant, Thomas Drummond, who is stated to have been the eldest son of James, son of James Duke of Perth, was born in 1792, and was living in 1831 at Houghton-le-Spring, in the occupation of a pitman. Much doubt is thrown upon the whole of the case, which was not followed up, by the length of time which elapsed before any claim was made on the part of this supposed descendant of the Duke of Perth. The act for the restoration of the forfeited estates was not passed, indeed, until two years after the death (as it is stated) of the Duke of Perth, that is, in 1784; yet one would suppose that he would have carefully instructed his son in the proper manner to assert his rights in case of such an event. That son lived to a mature age, married and died, yet made no effort to recover what were said to be his just rights. [269]

Such is the statement of those who seek to establish the belief that the Duke of Perth lived to a good old age, married, had children, and left heirs to his title and estates. On the other hand, it is certain that it was generally considered certain, at the time of the insurrection, that the Duke died on his voyage to France; and it was even alluded to by one of the counsel at the trials of Lord Kilmarnock and Lord Balmerino in August 1746, when the name of the Duke of Perth being mentioned, "who, " said the Speaker, "I see by the papers, is dead. " But it *is* certainly *remarkable,* that neither Maxwell of Kirkconnel, nor Lord Elcho, the one in his narrative which has been printed, the other in his manuscript memoir, mention the death of the Duke of Perth on the voyage, which, as they both state, they shared with him. So important and interesting a circumstance would not, one may suppose, have occurred without their alluding to it. "All the gentlemen, " Lord Elcho relates, "who crossed to Nantes, proceeded to Paris after their disembarkation; "[270] but he enters into no further particulars of their destination. His silence, and that of Maxwell of Kirkconnel, regarding the Duke of Perth's death, seems, if it really took place, to have been inexplicable.

All doubt, but that the story of the unfortunate Duke's death was really true, appears however to be set at rest by the epitaph which some friendly or kindred hand has inscribed on a tomb in the chapel of the English Nuns at Antwerp, commemorating the virtues and the fate of the Duke, and of his brother Lord John Drummond. This monumental tribute would hardly have been inscribed without some degree of certainty that the remains of the Duke were indeed interred there.

M. S.[271]

Fratrum Illustriss, Jac. et Joan. Ducum de Perth,
Antiquiss. Nobiliss. Familiæ de Drummond apud Scotos,

Principum.
Jacobus, ad studia humaniora proclivior,
Literis excultus,
Artium bonarum et liberalium fautor eximius;
In commune consulens,
Semper in otio civis dignissimus.
Mirâ morum suavitate, et animi fortitudine ornatus,
Intaminatâ fide splendebat humani generis amicus.
In pace clarus, in bello clarior;
Appulso enim Carolo P. in Scotiam,
Gladio in causâ gentis Stuartorum rearrepto,
Veterorum curâ posthabitâ,
Gloriæ et virtuti unice prospiciens,
Alacri vultu labores belli spectabat;
Pericula omnia minima ducebat:
In prælio strenuus, in victoriâ clemens, heros egregius.
Copiis Caroli tandem dissipatis,
Patriâ, amicis, re domi amplissimâ,
Cunctis præter mentem recti consciam, fortiter desertis,
In Galliam tendens, solum natale fugit.
Verum assiduis laboribus et patriæ malis gravibus oppressus,
In mari magno,
Die natale revertente, ob. 13 Maii, 1746; æt. 33.
Et reliquiæ, ventis adversis, terrâ sacratâ interclusæ,
In undis sepultæ.
Joannes, ingenio felici martiali imbutus,
A primâ adolescentiâ, militiæ artibus operam dedit.
Fortis, intrepidus, propositi tenax,
Mansuetudine generosâ, et facilitate morum, militis asperitate lenitâ.
Legioni Scoticæ regali, ab ipsomet conscriptæ,
A Rege Christianiss. Lud. XV. præpositus.
Flagrante bello civili in Britanniâ,
Auxilis Gallorum duxit;
Et post conflictum infaustum Cullodinensem,
In eadem navi cum fratre profugus.
In Flandriâ, sub Imperatore Com. de Saxe, multùm meruit:
Subjectis semper præsidium,
Belli calamitatum (agnoscite Britanni!) insigne levamen.

Ad summos Martis dignitates gradatim assurgens,
Gloriæ nobilis metæ appetens,
In medio cursu, improvisa lethi vi raptus,
28 Septemb. A.D. 1747, Æt. 33.
In Angl. monach. Sacello Antwerpiæ jacet

The preceding narrative is given to the reader without any further comment, except upon the general improbability of the story. It might not appear impossible that the Duke may have taken refuge in the then wild county of Durham for a time, but that two credible historians, Maxwell of Kirkconnel, and Lord Elcho, assert positively that he sailed for Nantes in a vessel which went by the north-west coast of Ireland; Lord Elcho and Maxwell being themselves on board, seems decisive of the entire failure of the case before quoted. It seems also wholly incredible, that the Duke of Perth, whose rank was still acknowledged in France, and whose early education in that country must have familiarised him with its habits, should have remained contentedly during the whole of his life, associating with persons of the lowest grade, in an obscure village in Durham.

At the time of the Duke of Perth's death in 1747, one brother, Lord John Drummond, was living. This brave man, whose virtues and whose fate are recorded in the epitaph, survived his amiable and accomplished brother only one year, and died suddenly of a fever, after serving under Marshal Saxe at the siege of Bergen-op-Zoom. His services in the insurrection of 1745 were considerable; like his brother, he escaped to France after the contest was concluded. He died unmarried; and two sisters, the Lady Mary, and the Lady Henrietta Drummond, died also unmarried. The mother of James Duke of Perth long survived him, living until 1773. It is said in the case of Thomas Drummond, that she never forgave her son for what she considered his lukewarmness in the cause of the Stuarts, and refused to have any intercourse with him after the failure of the rebellion; but those who thus write, must have formed a very erroneous conception of the Duke's conduct: if he might not escape such a charge, who could deserve the praise of zeal, sincerity, and disinterestedness?

The duchess was one of the most strenuous supporters of the Stuarts, and suffered for her loyalty to them by an imprisonment in Edinburgh Castle. She was committed to prison on the eleventh of February, 1746, and liberated on bail on the seventeenth.

On the forfeiture of the Drummond estates she retired to Stobhall, where she remained until her death, at the advanced age of ninety. She was considered a woman of great spirit, energy, and ability, and is supposed to have influenced her son in his political opinions and actions.

Some idea may be formed of the painful circumstances which follow the forfeiture of estates from the following passage, extracted from the introduction to the letters of James Earl of Perth, Chancellor of Scotland in the time of James the Second, and lately printed for the Camden Society. [272]

"When a considerable portion of the Drummond estates were restored to the heir (no poor boon, though dilapidated, lopped, and impoverished,) he found upon them four settlements of cottages, in which the soldiery had been located after the battle of Culloden, to keep down the *rebels*. There were thirty near Drummond Castle, another division at Cullander, a third at Balibeg, and a fourth at Stobhall. Demolition might satisfy the abhorrence of the latter three, but what could reconcile him to the outrage under his very eyes, as he looked from his chamber or castle terrace? It was intolerable, and that every trace might be obliterated, he caused an embankment to be made, and carried a lake-like sheet of water over the very chimney tops of the military dwellings. There is now the beautiful lake, gleaming with fish, and haunted by the wild birds of the Highlands; and we believe the deepest diver of them all, could not observe one stone upon another of the cabins which held the ruthless military oppressors left by the Duke of Cumberland a century ago. "

The usual accounts of the Duke's movements after the battle of Culloden, state, however, that about a month subsequent to that event, when the fugitive Charles Stuart, in the commencement of his wanderings, landed by accident upon the little isle of Errifort, on the east side of Lewis, he saw, from the summit of a hill which he had climbed, two frigates sailing northwards. The Chevalier in vain endeavoured to persuade the boatmen who had brought him from Lewis, to go out and reconnoitre these ships. His companions judged these vessels to be English; the Prince alone guessed them to be French. He was right. They were two frigates from Nantes, which had been sent with money, arms, and ammunition to succour Charles, and were now returning to France. On board one of them was the Duke of Perth, Lord Elcho, Lord John Drummond, old Lochiel, Sir Thomas Sheridan and his nephew Mr. Hay, Maxwell of

Kirkconnel, and Mr. Lockhart of Carnwath, and several Low-country gentlemen, who had been wandering about in these remote parts when the frigates were setting out on their return, [273] and finding that the Prince was gone, and that nothing was to be done for his service, had determined to escape. On the tenth of June these frigates reached Nantes: Lord Elcho affirms that "all arrived safe at Nantes; " one only is said never to have gained that shore. Worn out by fatigues too severe, and, perhaps, the progress of disease being aided by sorrow, the Duke of Perth is generally stated to have died on ship-board on his passage. His malady is understood to have been consumption.

Another celebrated member of this distinguished family, Lord Strathallan, was not spared to witness the total ruin of all his hopes. He fell at the battle of Culloden. The impression among his descendants is, that, seeing the defeat certain, he rushed into the thick of the battle, determined to perish. In 1746 Lord Strathallan's name was included in the Bill of Attainder then passed; but, in 1824, one of the most graceful acts of George the Fourth, whose sentiments of compassion for the Stuarts and their adherents do credit to his memory, was the restoration of the present Viscount Strathallan to the peerage by the title of the sixth Viscount.

It is with regret that we take leave, amid the discordant scenes of an historical narrative, of one whose high purposes and blameless career are the best tribute to virtue, the noblest ornament of the party which he espoused. Modest, yet courageous; moderate, though in the ardour of youth; devout, without bigotry; and capable of every self-sacrifice for the good of others, on the memory of the young Duke of Perth not a shadow rests to attract the attention of the harsh to defects of intention, unjustly attributed to the leader of the Jacobite insurrection.

FOOTNOTES:

[207] Genealogy of the Most Noble and Ancient House of Drummond. By a Freind to Vertue and the Family. —Unpublished.

[208] The office of Thane or Seneschal was, to be the *Giusticiare* or guardian of that country; to lead the men up to the war, according to the roll or list made out; and to be collector for the Athbane of the kingdom for the King's rents in that district. The Athbane was the highest officer in the kingdom—Chief Minister, Treasurer, Steward.

The Thanes were next to the Athbanes, and were the first that King Malcolm advanced to the new title of Earls. —See Lord Strathallan's Genealogy of the House of Drummond.

[209] Genealogy of the House of Drummond, 139.

[210] Amongst his other literary efforts, Drummond of Hawthornden left a MS "Historie of the Family of Perth. "

[211] Lady Willoughby D'Eresby is heiress to the estate of Perth, and representative in the female line of the Earldom of Perth in Scotland and of the Dukedom in France. At the same time that the Dukedom of Perth was created, the last Earl's brother was created Duke de Melfort. His descendants are, therefore, the male representatives of the Earldom of Perth, and George Drummond Perth de Melfort in France is now claiming the title. (Letter from Viscount Strathallan, to whose courtesy I am indebted for this information.)

[212] "Reducing. "—Editor

[213] Memoirs of Sir Ewen Cameron of Lochiell.

[214] The title of Duke was afterwards assumed by the young chief of the House of Drummond, and was given to him by the Jacobites generally; but, in consequence of his father's attainder, and the forfeiture of his title, he was, in the eye of the law, simply a commoner. Hence he is described by Home as "James Drummond, commonly called Duke of Perth, his father having been so created by James the Second at St. Germains. " The right of the Duke to this dignity was at that time, and it still is, recognised in France. Without entering into the merits of the question of right, and to prevent confusion, it is therefore expedient to designate this Jacobite nobleman by the name usually assigned to him in his own time.

[215] Forbes's Jacobite Memoirs, p. 296.

[216] Wood's Peerage.

[217] Curious Collection of Scottish Songs; Aberdeen, 1821.

[218] Henderson, History of the Rebellion of '45, p. 19. 1753

[219] Memoirs of Lochiell, p. 30.

[220] History of the Rebellion, p. 35.

[221] Lord Elcho's Narrative, MS.

[222] See the History of the Rebellion, by Rae; and the Cochrane Correspondence.

[223] Maculloch's Highlands.

[224] Forbes's Jacobite Memoirs, p. 17.

[225] Henderson, p. 30.

[226] Henderson, p. 30.

[227] Chambers' History of the Rebellion; Edit. for the People; p. 19.

[228] "History of the Present Rebellion in Scotland, 1745. From the relation of Mr. James Macpherson, who was first in the service of the Rebels. "

In contradiction to this statement, to which Macpherson adds, that the Chevalier attended Mass daily, the testimony of one of the daily papers (the Caledonian Mercury) may be given, as inserted by Mr. Chambers in his very interesting History of the Rebellion of 1745. The Prince visited an Episcopal chapel; the name of the clergyman, Armstrong, and the text, Isaiah xiv. 12, are specified. It was the first Protestant place of worship that the Prince had ever attended. Hist. of the Rebellion, p. 21.

[229] History of the Present Rebellion, p. 19. —It is remarkable that two Histories of the two rebellions were composed by men who had changed sides. That of 1715 by Patten, who was rewarded for his disclosures, as King's evidence, by a pension. What reward was bestowed on Mr. James Macpherson does not yet appear.

[230] History of the Present Rebellion, p. 26.

[231] Notes and Observations taken from MSS. in the possession of A. Macdonald, Esq., Register Office, Edinburgh.

[232] Lord Elcho's MS.

[233] In Exeter House, Derby, there is a portrait of Prince Charles, painted by Wright of Derby, in which the eyes are hazel. That in the Earl of Newburgh's possession, at Hassop, has blue eyes.

[234] Henderson, p. 51. Home, p. 100.

[235] Home, 101. Alexander Henderson.

[236] Lord Elcho's Narrative, MS.

[237] Henderson, p. 84.

[238] Henderson, p. 88.

[239] Henderson differs in this account from Home. "Charles, " says the latter, "remained on the field of battle till mid-day, giving orders for the relief of the wounded of both armies, for the disposal of his prisoners, and preserving, both from temper and from judgment, every appearance of moderation and humanity, " p. 122.

[240] Lord Elcho's MS.

[241] Maxwell of Kirkconnel's Narrative, p. 55.

[242] Maxwell of Kirkconnel's Narrative, p. 57.

[243] Maxwell's Narrative, p. 59.

[244] Maxwell's Narrative, p. 46.

[245] Maxwell of Kirkconnel's Narrative, p. 48.

[246] Maxwell, p. 65.

[247] History of the Rebellion of 1745 and 1746. Extracted from the Scots' Magazine, p. 99.

[248] Maxwell's Narrative, p. 74.

[249] Maxwell, p. 76.

[250] Jacobite Memoirs.

[251] Lord Mahon is decidedly of this opinion. See Vol. iv. Hist. of England, respecting the Jacobites.

[252] Lord Elcho's MS.
[253] Maxwell, p. 80.

[254] Maxwell, p. 112.

[255] P. 129.

[256] Maxwell, p. 140.

[257] P. 147.

[258] Chambers.

[259] Lord Elcho's Narrative.

[260] The estate of Comrie is now in the possession of Sir David Dundas, and the descendant of its former owner, and the Duke's standard-bearer is reduced to be the landlord of the village inn. See Letters of James Duke of Perth, Chancellor of Scotland. Printed for the Camden Society, and edited by Wm. Jerdan, Esq.

[261] The battle, according to the newspapers of the day, lasted about half an hour.

[262] Maxwell, p. 154.

[263] See Lord Elcho's MS. Narrative; which, however, since it is written in a bitter spirit, and varies in many details and in most opinions from Maxwell's, I am not disposed wholly to trust.

[264] The traditionary accounts have been collected, in the case of Thos. Drummond, a claimant of the honours and estates of the Earldom of Perth. Newcastle upon Tyne, 1831. I do not vouch for the truth of these anecdotes, but they have an air of probability.

[265] Case of Thomas Drummond, p. 18.

[266] See case of Thomas Drummond, p. 26.

[267] Case, p. 34. Dr. Malcolm had in his book made a different statement; but had contemplated re-publishing his work, with corrections, among which the existence (after 1747) of James Drummond, was to be asserted.

[268] For this information, and also for a copy of the case of Thomas Drummond, I am indebted to the kindness of W. E. Aytoun, Esq.

[269] In 1816, another appeal, and a fresh claim to the Drummond estates, and to the Earldom of Perth, were brought forward by the descendant of John Drummond, the great-uncle of James, Duke of Perth. The said John Drummond was raised to the dignity of the English peerage in 1685, by James the Second, by the title of Viscount Melfort; in 1686 he was raised to the dignity of Earl of Melfort; and afterwards, following the monarch to St. Germains, was created Duke of Melfort.

The great-grandson of the Duke of Melfort was a Roman Catholic priest, who officiated some years back at the chapel in Moorfields; he was living in 1831 in France, at a very advanced age.

The pamphlet in which, in 1816, he asserted his claim, and which was laid before the House of Lords, was professedly written "by an unfortunate nobleman; " with the appeal of Charles Edward (Drummond), Duke of Melfort, heir male, and chief representative of the House of Drummond of Perth, submitted to the United Kingdom of Great Britain, &c., 8vo., London, 1816.

[270] Lord Elcho's MS.

[271] For the copies of these epitaphs I am indebted to Robert Chambers, Esq. This is that gentleman's account of the inscriptions:—

"The within is a correct copy of the inscription, as entered in Bishop Forbes's MS., vol. 9, dated on title page, 1761. The entry of inscriptions is immediately subsequent to a copied letter or memorandum of May, 1764, and antecedent to one of November, 1765.

"Fama perennis, lauru porrecta, vetat mori
Principes immaculatis Proavum honoribus dignos.

Hoc Elogium,
D.D.D.
T.D. L.L.D.

"N. B.—The above is engraven, all in capitals, on the tomb at Antwerp, with the coat armorial of the family on the top of the inscription. "

The following is the English translation of the originals in Latin, copied from the papers of Bishop Forbes: —

Sacred to the Memory
of
the most illustrious brothers, James and John,
Dukes of Perth,
Chiefs of the House of Drummond,
a very ancient and noble family in Scotland.
James,
the more disposed of the two to the study of Belles Lettres,
excelled in Literature;
was eminent as a favourer of the Fine
and Liberal arts.
Providing for the common good,
he was always a most worthy citizen in peace.
Characterized by the sweetness of his manners,
and distinguished by the strength of his mind,
He ever shone with unstained faith as a friend of mankind.
Great in peace, he was still greater in war,
For when Prince Charles landed in Scotland,
He drew his sword in the cause of the House of Stuart,
Put all other cares aside,
And uniformly looking forward to glory and worth,
He ever gazed with a cheerful countenance on the toils of war:
He was utterly regardless of all danger,
Without want of energy in battle, he was merciful in victory,
Indeed a man of rare occurrence;
At length when the forces of Charles were wasted away,
His native land, his friends, and a very ample estate,
Were all, when weighed in estimation with a mind conscious of
right,
Bravely deserted:
Turning his steps towards France, he fled his
Native country.

Oppressed by the troubles of his lot, and the
Heavy misfortunes of his country,
He died on the great ocean,
On the 13th of May, in the thirty-third year of his age;
And his remains, precluded from consecrated ground by adverse winds,
Were given to the deep.
John,
Imbued with a happy turn of mind for military affairs,
From early youth applied himself to the military art.
Brave, intrepid, and firm in purpose,
He was ennobled by gentleness, and softened the asperity of the soldier
by the ease of his manners.
He was placed over the Royal Scotch Legion,
Enlisted by himself,
By the most Christian King,
Louis XV.
Whilst the Civil War was raging in Britain
He led the French Auxiliary Forces,
And after the unfortunate battle of Culloden,
Was a fugitive in the same ship as his brother.
In Flanders, under the General Count Saxe,
He served a long time,
Ever a defence to those under his command,
A remarkable comforter (Learn, O Britons!) in the calamities of war;
Gradually rising to the highest dignities of war,
And seeking to attain the goal of noble glory,
He was carried away by sudden death in the midst of his course,
28th September, A.D. 1747. Aged 33.

[272] Edited by W. Jerdan, Esq., M.R. S.L., 1845.

[273] Maxwell, p. 166.

FLORA MACDONALD.

The character of this celebrated woman, heroic, yet gentle, was formed in the privacy of the strictest Highland seclusion. She was born in the island of South Uist, in 1720: she was the daughter of Macdonald of Milton. The Clan of her family was that of Macdonald of Clanranald; the Chief of which is called in Gaelic, Mack-ire-Allein, and in English, the captain of Clan Ranald. The estate of this Chief, which is held principally from the Crown, is situated in Moidart and Arisaig on the continent of Scotland, and in the islands of Uist, Benbecula, and Rum. His vassals, capable of military service, amounted in 1745 to five hundred. [274]

The Hebrides were at that time regarded in the more civilized parts of Europe somewhat in the same light as the Arctic regions are now considered by the inhabitants of England, and other polished nations: "When I was at Ferney in 1764, " Boswell relates, "I mentioned our design (of going to the Hebrides) to Voltaire. He looked at me as if I had talked of going to the North Pole, and said, 'You do not insist on my accompanying you! ' 'No, sir. ' 'Then I am very willing you should go. '" In this remote, and, in the circles of London, almost unknown region, Flora Macdonald was born and educated.

The death of her father, Macdonald of Milton, when she was only a year old, made an important change in the destiny of the little Highland girl. Her mother married again, and became the wife of Macdonald of Armadale in Skye. Flora was, therefore, removed from the island of South Uist to an island which was nearer to the means of acquiring information than her native place.

It was a popular error of the times, more especially among the English Whigs, to regard the Highlanders of every grade, as an ignorant, barbarous race. So far as the lowest classes were concerned, this imputation might be well-founded, though certainly not so well as it has much longer been in the same classes in England. Previously to the reign of George the Third many of the peasantry could not read, and many could not understand what they read in English. There were few books in Gaelic, and the defect was only partially supplied by the instruction of bards and seneachies. But, among the middle and higher classes, education was generally diffused. The excellent grammar-schools in Inverness, Fortrose, and

Dunkeld sent out men well-informed, excellent classical scholars, and these from among that order which in England is the most illiterate—the gentlemen-farmers. The Universities gave them even a greater extent of advantages. When the Hessian troops were quartered in Atholl, the commanding officers, who were accomplished gentlemen, found a ready communication in Latin at every inn. Upon the Colonel of the Hessian cavalry halting at Dunkeld, he was addressed by the innkeeper in Latin. This class of innkeepers has wholly, unhappily, disappeared in the Highlands. [275]

But it was in the island of Skye that classical learning was the most general, and there an extraordinary degree of intelligence and acquirement prevailed among the landed gentry. "I believe, " observes General Stewart, "it is rather unique for the gentry of a remote corner to learn Latin, merely to talk to each other; yet so it was in Skye. " The acquisition of this branch of learning was not, indeed, expensive. Latin was taught for two shillings and sixpence the quarter, and English and writing for one shilling. Indeed it is scarcely more now. The people seldom quitted their insular homes, except when on service; and, to the silence of their wild secluded scenes, the romance of poetry and the composition of song gave a relief and a charm.

The education of Flora Macdonald received probably little aid from the classical teacher; but her mind was formed, not among the rude and uncultured, but among those who appreciated letters; and the influence of such an advantage in elevating and strengthening the character must be taken into account in forming a due estimation of her heroic qualities. Thus situated, Flora passed her life in obscurity, until, at the age of twenty-four, the events which succeeded the battle of Culloden brought those energies, which had been nurtured in retirement, into active exertion. Indeed, until about a year before she engaged in that enterprise which has rendered her name so celebrated, she had never quitted the islands of South Uist and Skye; she had, at that time, passed about nine months in the family of Macdonald of Largoe in Argyleshire, and this was the only change of scene, or of sphere, which she had ever witnessed. [276]

Her step-father was an enemy to the cause which, from her earliest years, her heart espoused. A company of militia had been formed to assist the British Government by Sir Alexander Macdonald, the chieftain of one division of the clan, and in this regiment Macdonald of Armadale held a commission as captain, at the time when the Duke of Cumberland was "making inquisition for blood" throughout the western Highlands. But the prepossessions of Flora were unalienably engaged in favour of the exiled Stuarts; and they were not, perhaps, the less likely to glow from being necessarily suppressed. Her disposition, notwithstanding all her subsequent display of courage, was extremely mild; and her manners corresponded to her temper. Her complexion was fair; and her figure, though small, well-proportioned. In more advanced life Boswell, who with Dr. Johnson visited her, characterized her person and deportment as "genteel. " There was nothing unfeminine, either in her form or in her manners, to detract from the charm of her great natural vivacity, or give a tone of hardness to her strong good sense, calm judgment, and power of decision. Her voice was sweet and low; the harsher accents of the Scottish tongue were not to be detected in her discourse; and she spoke, as Bishop Forbes relates, "English (or rather Scots) easily, and not at all through the Erse tone. " In all the varied circumstances of her life, she manifested a perfect modesty and propriety of behaviour, coupled with that noble simplicity of character which led her to regard with surprise the tributes which were afterwards paid to her conduct, and to express her conviction that far too much value was placed upon what she deemed merely an act of common humanity.

In Skye, the "Isle of Mist" of the poet, she could hear imperfect intelligence of the wanderings of the Jacobite leaders. She was connected by kindred with some under whose roof the Prince had taken refuge.

The first movement which the Prince made after taking leave of Lord Lovat at Gortuleg, was to repair first to Fort Augustus, and then to Invergarie near Fort Augustus. Here he took leave of those followers who had attended him as he quitted the field of Culloden; and retained only Mr. O'Sullivan, Captain O'Neil, Captain Alan Macdonald, and one Burke, a servant. It was not until he had remained a whole day at Fort Augustus that the Prince could be persuaded that all hopes of his troops rejoining him were at an end. On Friday, the eighteenth of April, he went to Lochnargaig, where he stayed one night with Dr. Cameron of Glenkearn; and on the following day he proceeded to Oban, which is situated on a corner of Clanranald's estate. He was, therefore, under the protection of a kinsman of Flora Macdonald. He pursued his journey on the next day to the country of Arisaig, and rested at a small village called

Glenbeisdale, whence he proceeded to Boradale, the place at which he had first landed in beginning the enterprise which was now terminated.

It had been the opinion of Clanranald, one of the Prince's most faithful adherents, that he ought not to leave the mainland, but to take shelter in different small huts, which should be built for his accommodation; whilst Clanranald should take a trip to the Isles, and look out for a vessel to convey the unfortunate wanderer into France. By the influence of Mr. O'Sullivan this counsel was overruled; and Clanranald, finding that Charles was determined to sail for Long Island, provided an eight-oared boat, which belonged to Alexander Macdonald of Boradale; and, having provided it with rowers and other requisites for the voyage, the party set sail from Lochnanuagh for the Isle of Uist on the twenty-fourth of April. They assumed false names: the Prince was called Mr. Sinclair; Mr. O'Sullivan was old Sinclair, his father; Captain Alan Macdonald, a relation of Clanranald, became Mr. Graham. [277] Donald Macleod the pilot, and about six men, rowers, also accompanied the Prince, but did not change their names; a clergyman of the Church of Rome attended the party. The design which Charles Edward had formed, was to reach the Long Island, under which name are comprehended those Western Islands which run in a straight line from north to south, and are at a short distance from each other. From some part of the Long Island Charles hoped to procure a vessel in which he could escape to France, or at any rate to Orkney, and thence to Norway or Sweden. At this time a proclamation, offering a reward of thirty thousand pounds for his apprehension, had been issued by the British Government.

The Prince set sail on the evening of the twenty-sixth of April, embarking at Boradale, on the very spot where he had landed, with just sufficient daylight to get clear of Loch Luagh; for, as the coast had been guarded by English ships ever since his arrival in Scotland, it was not safe to go beyond the mouth of the Loch in open day. Before the voyage was commenced, the Prince was warned by his faithful pilot that there would be a storm that night. "I see it coming! " But Charles Edward, anxious to leave the main land, where parties were dispersed in pursuit of him, was determined to trust his fate to the winds. The party, therefore, entered the boat, the Prince seating himself at the feet of the pilot. There was also another Macleod in the boat; this was Murdoch, the son of the pilot, a boy of fifteen years of age. The character of this youth was of no common order. When he had heard of the battle of Culloden, he had provided himself with a claymore, a dirk, and a pistol; and had run off from school to take his chance in the field. After the defeat he found means to trace out the road which the Prince had taken, and to follow him step by step; "and this was the way, " related Donald Macleod, "that I met wi' my poor boy. "

Another person who was in the boat, and who afterwards made a conspicuous figure in that romance of real life, was Ned Bourke, or Burke. This man had belonged to a most valuable class, the chairmen of Edinburgh, whose honesty is proverbial; their activity and civility almost incredible to English notions. Bourke was not, as his name seemed to imply, an Irishman; but a native of North Uist. He had been a servant to Mr. Alexander Macleod, one of Charles Edward's aides-de-camp; and was the man who had led the Prince off the field of battle, and guided him all the way to Boradale: for Ned Bourke knew Scotland, and indeed a great portion of England, well, having been servant to several gentlemen. In this, his most important service, the honest man did not disgrace his ancient and honourable calling as a chairman. "Excellent things" were spoken of him to Donald Macleod, who seems to have made some demur as to his Irish name, and to have objected to taking him on board.

Thus guided, and thus guarded, Charles Edward might fear the winds and waves; but treachery was not to be dreaded. Not far had the men rowed before a violent storm arose; such as even Donald had not, from his own account, ever been "trysted with before, " though he had all his life been a seafaring man. The Prince was now as impatient to return to the land as he had been to quit it; "for, " he said, "I would rather face cannons and muskets than be in such a storm as this! " But Donald was firm in proceeding on the voyage: "Since we are here, " he replied, "we have nothing for it, but, under God, to set out to sea directly. " He refused to steer for the rock, which runs three miles along the side of the loch; observing, "Is it not as good for us to be drowned in clear water, as to be dashed to pieces on a rock, and drowned also? "

A solemn silence followed this decisive reply. Every one expected instant destruction. The night was pitch-dark; and there was no light in the boat. They dreaded being landed on some part of the island of Skye, where the militia were in arms to prevent the Prince's escape. But, to use the words of the pilot, "As God would have it, " that danger was not encountered. By daybreak the party discovered that they were close to Rushness, in the island of Benbecula, having run according to the pilot's account, thirty-two leagues in eight hours. During this perilous voyage the spirits of Charles never sank; he encouraged every one around him, working himself at the oars: "he was, " says Mr. Maxwell, "the only one that seemed void of concern."

Such were the circumstances under which Charles Edward landed in the Long Island; —the event which brought him into communication with Flora Macdonald. She was at that time calmly engaged in the usual duties of her station; but the spirit so prevalent in the Highlands was not extinguished in the Western Islands, either by the dread of the English militia, or by the defeat of the Prince. All the Jacobites of that period, to adopt the language of President Forbes, "how prudent soever, became mad; all doubtful people became Jacobites; and all bankrupts became heroes, and talked of nothing but hereditary right and victory. And what was more grievous to men of gallantry, and, if you believe me, more mischievous to the public, all the fine ladies, if you except one or two, became passionately fond of the young adventurer, and used all their arts for him in the most intemperate manner. "[278] It was not, however, an idle, romantic fancy, but a fixed sentiment of duty, acting upon a kindly heart, which originated the enthusiasm of Flora.

Whilst the Prince was traversing the Long Island in poverty and danger, a desolate wanderer wanting the common necessaries of life, but still patient and cheerful ever hoping once more to assemble his faithful Highlanders, —living at one time four days in a desert island, then putting to sea pursued by ships, —Flora Macdonald had accidentally quitted her usual residence at Armadale in Skye, for the purpose of visiting her step-brother at Milton.

During her abode at Milton, Captain O'Neil, who was loitering about the country for the purpose of gaining intelligence for Charles Edward, formed an acquaintance with this young lady, and, it is said, paid his addresses to her. More than two months had now elapsed since Charles first trusted his hopes to the chance of finding a vessel on the coast of the Long Island, to take him to France. During that period his fortunes had assumed a far more threatening aspect than at any previous time. Friends had proved faithless; Murray of Broughton, whom the Prince then still regarded as one of the "firmest, honestest men in the world, " had shown to others his real motives, and the deep selfishness, cowardice, and rapacity, of his heart. In his utmost need, when the Prince was in want of food, that wretched man had, in reply to a message from Charles asking money, answered that he had none; having *only* sixty louis-d'ors for himself, which were not worth sending. What was perhaps of more immediate moment was, that, whilst the friends of the young Chevalier had diminished, the number of his foes around him had increased. Fifteen ships of war were to be seen near the coasts of the Long Island, thus most effectually destroying all hopes of a French vessel being able to cruize near the shore. To complete his misfortunes, the Duke of Cumberland, upon learning that his unfortunate kinsman had sheltered himself in the Western Islands, had sent Captain Caroline Scott, an officer as infamous as Hawley and Lockhart, to scour the Long Island.

Such were the circumstances of Charles towards the latter end of June 1746. He was then coursing along the shores of the Long Island, until, pursued by French ships, he was obliged to land, happily for himself, on the island of Benbecula, between the North and South Uist. Providence seemed to have conducted him to that wild and bleak shore. Scarcely had he reached it, than a storm arose, and drove his pursuers off the coast. Here the Prince and his starving companions were overjoyed to find a number of crabs, or, as the Scottish pilot termed them, *partans*; a boon to the famished wanderers. From a hut, about two miles from the shore, Charles removed, first to the house of Lady Clanranald; and afterwards, by the advice of Clanranald, he went to South Uist, and took up his abode near the hill of Coradale in the centre of the island, that being thought the most secure retreat. Here Charles remained until again driven from this hut by the approach of Captain Scott, with a detachment of five hundred men, who advanced close to the place where he was concealed. The unfortunate Prince then determined upon a last and painful effort to save those who had braved hitherto the severities of their lot for his sake. He parted with all his followers except O'Neil. Donald Macleod shed tears on bidding him farewell. Macleod was taken prisoner a few days afterwards in Benbecula, by Lieutenant Allan Macdonald, of Knock, in Slate, in the island of Skye. He was put on board the Furnace, [279] and brought down to the cabin before General Campbell, who examined him minutely. The General asked him "if he had been along with the Pretender? " "Yes, " said Donald, "I was along with that young gentleman, and I winna deny it. " "Do you know, " said the General, "what money was upon the gentleman's head? no less a sum than four thousand pounds sterling, which would have made you and your family happy for ever. " "What then, " said Donald, "what could I have gotten by it? I could not have enjoyed it for two days, conscience would have gotten the better of me; and although I could have got England and Scotland for my Prince, I would not have allowed a hair of his head to be hurt. "[280]

After this separation, the Prince, accompanied by O'Neil, again returned to traverse the mountainous districts of South Uist. He walked in the direction of Benbecula, and about midnight entered a shealing, or hut, which belonged to Angus Macdonald, the brother of his future deliverer. The interview which shortly took place between them, was not, as it may readily be conceived, unpremeditated. [281] Repeatedly, before the meeting, had O'Neil asked Flora whether she would like to see the Prince? She answered with emotion that she would. She had even expressed an earnest desire to see him; and had said, if she could be of any use in aiding him to escape from his enemies, she would do it.

O'Neil had had various opportunities of studying the real character of Flora Macdonald. He must have had an extraordinary notion of her energy when he first proposed to her, whilst they met in Clanranald's house, to take the Prince with her to Skye, dressed up in woman's clothes. This proposition appeared to Flora so "fantastical and dangerous, " that she positively declined it. "A Macdonald, a Macleod, a Campbell militia were, " she observed, "in South Uist in quest of the Prince: a guard was posted at every ferry; every boat was seized; no person could leave Long Island without a passport; and the channel between Uist and Skye was covered with ships of war. " Such was her resolution whilst she discussed the subject with O'Neil at the house of her kinsman, Clanranald. Nor does that sense of the dangers of her undertaking lessen the heroism of the enterprise. But her woman's heart, however timid it might be at Clanranald's castle, was touched, when she beheld the Prince; and compassion, from which spring the noblest resolves, inspired her to exertion.

As the Prince, attended by O'Neil, drew near to the hut belonging to Angus Macdonald, the latter quitted Charles, and went aside, with a design to inform himself whether the independent companies of militia were to pass that way, or not, on the following day, as he had been informed. Such, at least, was his pretext; but he had an appointment with Flora Macdonald, who was awaiting him near the hut. To his question, she answered that "they would not pass until the day after. " Then O'Neil ventured to tell the young lady that he had brought a friend to see her. She inquired in some agitation "if it was the Prince? " He replied that it was, and he instantly brought her into the shealing. The kind heart of Flora was afflicted at the sight. Charles was exhausted with fatigue and misery; he had become thin and weak, and his health was greatly affected by the hardships which he had undergone. He and O'Neil had lost indeed the means of personal comfort; they had but two shirts with them, and every article of wearing apparel was worn out. To a feeble mind, the depressed state of Prince Charles's affairs, his broken-down aspect, and the dangers which surrounded him, would have inspired reluctance to serve one so desolate. These circumstances, however, only softened the resistance which Flora had at first made to the scheme suggested for his escape, and renewed her desire to aid him.

After her first introduction, the discourse for some time turned upon his dangerous situation; the best remedy for which was, as both the Prince and O'Neil hinted, for Flora to convey him in disguise to Skye, where her mother lived. This seemed the more feasible, from the situation which her father-in-law held, and which would enable him to give a pass for herself and her servant.

The Prince assented to the expediency of the proposal, which originated with O'Neil, and immediately asked Flora if she would undertake to carry the plan into effect. Flora answered with great respect and loyalty, but declined, saying that "Sir Alexander Macdonald, who commanded the militia in Skye, was too much her friend for her to be the instrument of his ruin. " O'Neil endeavoured to combat this opinion, representing that Sir Alexander was not then in the country, and could not therefore be implicated: he added, that she might easily convey the Prince to her mother's, at Armadale, as she lived close by the waterside. O'Neil also told her of the honour and immortal fame which would redound from so glorious an action; and the Prince assured her that he should always retain a deep sense of "so conspicuous a service. " The firmness of Flora had resisted the arguments of O'Neil; but it was overcome by these few words from the Prince. She consented to let O'Neil know on the following day at what time every arrangement would be made for the plan which had been proposed, and she left the Prince and his adherent to shelter themselves in the mountains of Coradale. [282]

On leaving the shealing, Flora at first returned to Milton; but, having fully made up her mind to undertake the enterprise, she set out for

Ormaclade, the seat of Clanranald, on Saturday the twenty-first of June. Her journey was not without perilous adventures. On passing a ford, she was taken prisoner by one of the militia, on account of not having a passport. She inquired by whom they were commanded; and, finding that her step-father was their captain, she refused to give an answer to the questions put to her until she saw him. She was made a prisoner for that night; her captivity being shared by her servant Neil Mac Kechan, a clansman, who was the father of Marshal Macdonald, Duke of Tarentum. In the morning, Hugh Macdonald of Armadale, the step-father of Flora, arrived, and liberated her; granting a passport for herself, her servant, and for another woman whom she styled Betty Burke, a good spinster, whom Armadale in the innocency of his heart recommended to his wife at Armadale, as she had much lint to spin. His letter has been preserved; and there is every reason to believe, that, when writing it, Armadale was wholly unconscious of the design of Flora. [283]

The letter of Armadale to his wife ran as follows: —"I have sent your daughter from this country lest she should be frightened with the troops lying here. She has got one Betty Burke, an Irish girl, who, as she tells me, is a good spinner. If her spinning pleases you, you may keep her till she spins all your lint: or, if you have any wool to spin, you may employ her. I have sent Mac Kechan along with your daughter and Betty Burke, to take care of them. I am, your dutiful husband,

"HUGH MACDONALD. " "June 22nd, 1746. "

*****

It was late in the afternoon of the Sunday on which Flora had obtained her passport, before she could communicate with her friends in the mountains; about four o'clock, however, they received a message telling them that *all was well*. The Prince and his companion, therefore, determined immediately to join their protectress.

Upon being set at liberty, Flora went immediately to Ormaclade, where she had, in Lady Clanranald, an enthusiastic assistant. She remained at Ormaclade for several days, making arrangements for the complete disguise of the Prince.

The Prince and O'Neil had only waited for the arrival of Flora's messenger to set out and meet their heroic friend; but the trusty individual who had brought them the tidings that *all was well*, informed them that they could not pass either of the fords which separated South Uist from Benbecula, as they were guarded by militia. In this extremity the Prince knew not how he should ever reach the place appointed for his meeting with Flora, which was Rossinish, in Benbecula, from which spot she was to conduct him to Skye. An inhabitant of South Uist, seeing his perplexity, offered him a boat: the proffered aid was accepted; and Charles, with O'Neil, was landed on a promontory which the pilot of the boat assured the Prince was the island of Benbecula. Charles therefore dismissed the boatmen, with orders to meet him on the opposite side of the island; and began his journey. He had not gone far when he found himself surrounded with water, and perceived that the pilot had made a mistake. Neither Charles nor his companions had ever before been in this part of Benbecula. They looked around them on the desolate prospect, and perceived that they were on a peninsula, perfectly desert, and which at high-water was separated from Benbecula. At first Charles hoped, that, when the tide was out, some passage might be discovered; but the waves retired and no passage appeared. The Prince was not disheartened; for his courage, never justly questioned, had gained its best allies, patience and fortitude, during the adversities of the last few months. He supported the fainting spirits of his companions; and, to encourage them to search for a passage, said that he knew of one, although he was in fact as ignorant as they were. At length he discovered a passage, and the party reached a little hut, which they were assured was in Benbecula. [284] He marched on, exhausted as he was, to Rossinish, and arrived there at midnight, but found not the deliverer they expected; on the contrary, he learned that they were within fifty miles of the enemy. Hungry as they were, having eaten nothing all day, the Prince and his fainting companions were obliged to retreat four miles. Captain O'Neil was then sent to Ormaclade, to inquire why Flora had not been true to her appointment. She told him that she now considered that North Uist would be a safer place of refuge than Skye, and that she had engaged a cousin of hers to receive him there. O'Neil remained at Ormaclade, and sent a boy to inform the Prince, who was now only at eight miles' distance, of this proposal; but that scheme was soon abandoned, the gentleman to whom Flora referred refusing to receive the Prince. In this dilemma, Charles was informed that his enemies had quitted Rossinish, and he therefore hastened to that place. His safe arrival there was, indeed, almost miraculous.

Near him was a guard of fifty men; the island was full of militia; and the secret of his being in it was known to many a poor cotter. But, in these vicissitudes of his eventful and unhappy life, the Prince was thrown among a faithful and honourable people, in whose bosoms the conviction was planted, that to betray him would bring down a curse upon themselves and their posterity.

On arriving at Rossinish, Captain O'Neil was again dispatched to Flora to express the disappointment of Charles on not seeing her, and to beg her to join him. She promised faithfully to do so on the following day; and she kept her word. Having hired a six-oared boat to convey her to Skye, and appointed it to be at a certain part of the coast, she set out for Rossinish: accompanied by Lady Clanranald, whose participation in the cause was shortly afterwards punished by imprisonment; —by a Mrs. Macdonald, and by Mac Kechan, her servant. They entered a hut, where they found this unfortunate descendant of an ill-fated race preparing his own dinner. It consisted of the heart, liver, and kidneys of a sheep, which he was turning upon a wooden spit. The compassion of the ladies was roused by this sight; but Charles, as he bade them welcome to the humble repast, moralized on his fate. He observed, that all *kings* would be benefited by such an ordeal as that which he had endured. His philosophy was seasoned by the hope of attaining what he ever desired, —the hereditary monarchy which he believed to be his birthright. He observed, that the wretched to-day, may be happy to-morrow. At the dinner, Flora Macdonald sat on the right-hand of the Prince, and Lady Clanranald on the left.

After the meal was ended, Charles was requested by Flora to assume the female apparel which Lady Clanranald had brought. It was, of course, very homely, and consisted of a flowered linen gown, a light-coloured quilted petticoat, and a mantle of clean camlet, made after the Irish fashion, with a hood. Their dangers, as he put on his dress, did not check the merriment of the party; and many jokes were passed upon the costume of Betty Burke. A small shallop was lying near the shore, and Flora proposed that they should remove near to the place whence they were to embark, for her fears had been excited by a message which arrived from Ormaclade, acquainting Lady Clanranald that a party of soldiers, under the infamous Captain Fergusson, had arrived at her house, and had taken up their quarters there. Lady Clanranald hastened home, where she managed to deceive and perplex both General Campbell, who had lately arrived in Benbecula, and Captain Fergusson.

And now another trial was at hand: —it was necessary for Captain O'Neil and the Prince to separate. The Irishman would fain have remained with Charles, but Flora was firm, as well as kind; her opinion on this point was decided; and O'Neil was obliged to yield. This point was not gained without much difficulty, for Charles even remonstrated. O'Neil took his leave, and made his way, through a country traversed by troops, to South Uist, where O'Sullivan had been left. "I could now, " writes Captain O'Neil in his journal, when he relates his departure from the Prince, "only recommend him to God and his good fortune. " This kind-hearted man was afterwards taken prisoner by Captain Fergusson, who had him stripped and threatened not only with the rack, but also with being whipped by his hangman, because he would not disclose where the Prince was. These cruelties were opposed, however, by a junior officer, who, coming out with a drawn sword, threatened Fergusson with a beating, and saved O'Neil from the punishment which was to have been the requital of his fidelity.

When all were gone, except Flora, the Prince, and Mac Kechan, the party proceeded to the sea-shore, where they arrived wet and wearied, and passed the night upon a rock. They made a fire to warm themselves, and endeavoured still to maintain hope and cheerfulness. How picturesque and singular must have been the group, thus awaiting the moment which should perhaps only conduct them to fresh perils! As they reclined among the heath which grew on the rock, four wherries, filled with armed men, caused the little party to extinguish their fire, and to hide themselves in the heather. The wherries, which made at first for the shore, sailed by to the southward, within a gun-shot of the spot where Charles Edward and Flora were concealed. At eight o'clock in the evening of Saturday, the twenty-eighth of June 1746, the Prince and she set sail from Benbecula for Skye.

The evening on which they quitted the shores which had been to them such scenes of peril was clear; but, not long after they had embarked, the sea became rough, and the weather stormy. Prince Charles resolved never to despond, sang songs to prevent the spirits of the company from flagging, and talked gaily and hopefully of the future. Exhausted by her previous exertions, Flora sank into a sleep; and Charles carefully watched her slumbers, being afraid lest the voices of the boatmen should arouse her, or, in the dark, that any of the men should step upon her. She awoke in a surprise at some little bustle in the boat, and asked hastily "What was the matter? " What must have been her emotions at that moment!

The next day, Sunday, was one of anxiety. The boatmen had lost their track, and had no compass; the wind had changed, it was then calm. They made, however, towards Waternish, in the west of Skye; but they found the place possessed by militia, and three boats were visible near the shore. A man on board one of the boats fired at them; on which they made away as fast as they could; for, in addition to that danger, several ships of war were now in sight. The Prince and his friends took shelter, therefore, in a cleft of a rock on the shore, and there remained to rest the men, who had been up all night, and to prepare their provisions for dinner. The party then resumed their voyage: fortunately it was calm, for otherwise, in any distress of weather, they must have been overtaken and have perished, for an alarm had already been given of the appearance of a strange boat, and the militia were upon the watch; the promised reward set upon Charles having excited all the vigilance of his enemies. At length, after rowing some time, they landed at Kilbride in Troternish, in Skye, about twelve miles to the north of Waternish. But several parties of militia were in the neighbourhood. Flora now quitted the boat, and went with Neil Mac Kechan to Mugstat, the residence of Sir Alexander Macdonald: here she desired one of the servants to apprise Lady Macdonald of her arrival. The lady was not unprepared to receive her, for a kinswoman had gone a short time before to tell her of the enterprise in which Flora had engaged.

Lady Margaret was well disposed to give the cause every assistance in her power. She was the daughter of the celebrated Susanna, Countess of Eglintoune, and of Alexander, ninth Earl of Eglintoune, who was supposed, while ostensibly supporting the family on the throne, to be a secret friend of the Stuarts. [285] Lady Margaret was one of seven sisters, famed for their loveliness, and for the "Eglintoune air, " a term applied to that family as a tribute to the lofty grace of their deportment. "It was a goodly sight, " observes Mr. Chambers, "a century ago, to see the long processions of sedans containing Lady Eglintoune and her daughters devolve from the Close, [286] and proceed to the Assembly Rooms in the West Bow, where there was usually a considerable crowd of plebeian admirers congregated, to behold their lofty and graceful figures step from the chairs on the pavement. " Lady Margaret was greatly beloved in Skye. When she rode through the island, the people ran before her, and took the stones off the road, lest her horse should stumble. Her husband was also very popular. Such was the hospitality of Mugstat, that every week a hogshead of claret was drunk at his table. [287]

Lady Margaret had now been married six years to Sir Alexander Macdonald of Macdonald. She was the mother of three sons, two of whom were eminently distinguished. The first, Sir James Macdonald, was a young man of singular accomplishments, and the friend of Lord Lyttleton; he was endowed "with great talents for business, great propriety of behaviour, great politeness of manners. " To these acquirements he added those amiable qualities, which, united to great erudition, procured him the title of the "Marcellus of the Western Isles. " His early death was regarded as a general calamity; his tomb was honoured by an inscription composed by Lyttleton. When Dr. Johnson visited the isle of Skye, this young man, who died at Rome in the twenty-fifth year of his age, was still mentioned with tears. His brother, Sir Alexander, the English-bred chieftain, but ill-supplied his loss. He was no Highlander. "Were I in your place, sir, " said Johnson to the young chieftain, "in seven years I would make this an independent island. I would roast oxen whole, and hang out a flag as a signal to the Macdonalds to come and get beef and whiskey. " Sir Alexander, of whom Johnson had heard heavy complaints of rents racked, and the islanders driven to emigration, bore with politeness the rough assaults of the Doctor: he nevertheless started difficulties. "Nay, sir, " rejoined Johnson, "if you are born to object, I have done with you, sir. I would have a magazine of arms. " "They would rust, " was the meek reply. "Let there be men to clean them, " cried the Doctor, "your ancestors did not use to let their arms rust! " Such was Lady Margaret's second son. The third, and youngest son of Lady Margaret, revived, however, all the fondly remembered virtues of Sir James. Some persons may still recall the benignant appearance of the late venerable Sir Archibald Macdonald, Lord Chief Baron of the Court of Exchequer in England: there are many who must recollect his virtues and acquirements with respect.

The character of Lady Margaret was not that of her second son; but of a spirited generous woman. She was not one who would allow the arms of her ancestors "to rust. " Before the Prince's arrival, her energies had been employed in contriving the fittest route for him to take after leaving Mugstat, for she was as enthusiastic an adherent of Charles Edward as any of her female relations. Whilst he was in North Uist, he had sent Lady Margaret a letter, enclosed, by Hugh Macdonald of Balishair, to his brother Donald Roy Macdonald, with orders to deliver it to Lady Margaret alone; and, in case of attack while at sea, to sink it, by tying it to a stone. This letter revealed the secret of the Prince's intention to quit the Long Island: it informed Lady Margaret that Charles wanted almost all necessary habiliments; and desired that some shirts and blankets might be provided for him; the Prince having hitherto slept only in his plaid, a custom which he retained almost constantly during his wanderings. Balishair's letter had also unfolded a plan at that time in contemplation, that Charles should take refuge on the small grass-island called Fladdanuach, belonging to Sir Alexander Macdonald, and having only one tenant upon it. Thither Lady Margaret was to send Donald Roy Macdonald with the articles to be in readiness for the Prince.

Lady Margaret had instantly complied with these injunctions. Eventually the notion of making Fladdanuach the retreat of Charles was given up; but the zealous Lady Margaret had made the most careful preparations for that scheme, and it was not from any negligence on her part that it was abandoned. The packet sent by Balishair contained, however, another valuable paper. This was a letter written in Prince Charles's own hand, chiefly one of compliment, and full of gratitude to Lady Margaret for sending him newspapers, which had been delivered to him through Macdonald of Balishair.

This precious letter had, some time before Flora had arrived at Mugstat, been delivered to Lady Margaret. When she received it, she rose from her seat, and kissing it said, alluding to a precaution which had been recommended, "I will never burn it; I will preserve it for the sake of him who wrote it to me. Although King George's forces should come to the house, I shall find means to secure it. " Afterwards, however, her house being searched by the dreaded Fergusson, she considered it necessary for Charles's safety to burn it; although, as it proved, there was no search whatsoever for papers.

Lady Margaret had been aided in her efforts and plans by a zealous kinsman, Captain Roy Macdonald, who had been wounded at the battle of Culloden. This person was still under medical care, and was living in the house of a surgeon named Maclean, at Troternish. When Charles landed at Skye, Roy Macdonald, wounded as he was, had sailed to Fladdanuach, at Lady Margaret's bidding, with clothes and money, and had returned just in time to witness her perplexity at the Prince's unexpected arrival.

Upon that event being made known by Flora Macdonald to Lady Margaret, she sent a message to Captain Roy Macdonald, entreating him to come to her immediately. He complied, and found Lady Margaret walking in the garden of Mugstat, talking very earnestly to Alexander Macdonald of Kingsburgh, a gentleman of the neighbourhood, who acted as factor, or chamberlain, to Sir Alexander. As Roy Macdonald approached, Lady Margaret exclaimed, holding up her hands, "Oh, Donald Roy, we are ruined for ever! " It was then imparted to him that the Prince was within a quarter of a mile from Mugstat, in woman's clothes; that Lieutenant Macleod, who was employed to guard that part of Skye, and three or four of his militia-men, were about the house; a number of others being not far distant: what was still more alarming, Flora Macdonald and the Lieutenant were at that time conversing together in the dining-room.

A consultation immediately ensued as to the plan the most proper to ensure Charles Edward's safety. Donald Roy Macdonald declared, that, whatever they should agree upon, "He would undertake (God willing) to accomplish at the risk of his life. " Kingsburgh was first called upon to give his opinion. He proposed that the Prince should sail by the point of Troternish to Raasay, because it would be impossible for him to remain in Skye with safety. This plan was, however, opposed by Lady Margaret, who said, that, if the Prince was to sail for Raasay, it were better that he should remain at Mugstat all night. In short, no scheme appeared practicable; and the consultation was frequently broken off in despair, and renewed only to start fresh difficulties. At last Donald Roy said, "What do you think, Kingsburgh, if the Prince should run the risk of making his way over to Portree by land? " Kingsburgh, notwithstanding that he was full of apprehension, thought that the plan might be tried, although the distance from Mugstat to Portree was fourteen long Highland miles. At first it was decided that Donald Roy should be the bearer of this scheme to the Prince; but it was afterwards argued, that, since the Prince must make "a monstrous figure" in woman's clothes, there might be some suspicion excited by Donald Roy's talking to so singular a stranger. It was therefore determined that no one except Flora Macdonald should be entrusted with the perilous task of taking messages to Charles at his station on the shore. Lady Margaret in the course of this conversation expressed "that she was in great difficulties. " It was impossible that she could apply to any of the Clan for assistance. The general belief was, that Sir Alexander Macdonald was unfriendly to the Prince, and that no greater favour could be shown by the chief than seizing the royal fugitive. This increased the danger of Charles's remaining in Skye, and threw her entirely upon the good offices of Kingsburgh and Roy Donald.

During this conference Flora Macdonald was keeping up what she afterwards described to Bishop Forbes as "a close chit-chat" with Lieutenant Macleod, who put to her questions which she answered as "she thought fit. " Lady Margaret, meantime, could not forbear going in and out in great anxiety; a circumstance which Flora observed, and which could not but add to her embarrassment; nevertheless, this extraordinary young woman maintained the utmost composure. She even dined in company with the Lieutenant without betraying her perplexity in a single instance: never was the value of that admirable quality, presence of mind, more forcibly seen than in this instance. It had been the office of the Lieutenant to examine every boat that had landed, and to investigate into the motives and destination of every passenger. How the boat which had conveyed the Prince to Skye escaped search has not been explained. At all events, Flora completely baffled every inquiry; and perhaps no one could do so better than a Scottish woman. The ordinary caution in reply, observable in Highland females, is very striking. The Prince was awaiting his fate all this time upon the rock at the shore, not above a gun-shot from the foot of the garden. The faithful and anxious servant Mac Kechan went to him repeatedly, but without molestation; and Macdonald of Kingsburgh, who could not controul his anxiety to see Charles Edward, providing himself with a bottle of wine and some bread, also repaired to him. The Prince was then sitting upon the shore, having startled a flock of sheep, the running of which first attracted Kingsburgh to the place where he was planted.

Charles had removed to a more distant spot than that which he had at first selected, for he had been apprised by Neil Mac Kechan of Kingsburgh's intended visit, and conducted by that faithful servant to the back of a certain hill, where he was requested to wait until Kingsburgh should reach him. It was also announced to Charles by Neil, that he was to go to Portree, resting by the way at the house of Kingsburgh, who was a staunch Jacobite.

When Kingsburgh drew near to the place where Charles awaited him, he saw the Prince approaching him with a short thick cudgel (not a very feminine appendage) in his hand. "Are you, " cried Charles, "Mr. Macdonald of Kingsburgh? " "Yes, sir, " replied

Kingsburgh. "Then, " said Charles, "all is well; come let us be going. " Macdonald, however, first begged the Prince to partake of some refreshment, which he did; the top of a rock serving for a table. This being done, they proceeded on their journey; Kingsburgh telling his fellow-traveller with no less admiration than joy, "that he could recollect no cause either of business or duty for his being at Mugstat that day. " "I'll tell you the cause, " said the Prince; "Providence sent you hither to take care of me. "

They were now interrupted by some country-people coming from the kirk. These sociable rustics were disposed to favour the Prince and his companion with their conversation. Kingsburgh could think of no other way of getting rid of them than saying, "Eh, sirs! cannot ye let alone talking o' your worldly affairs on the sabbath? and have patience till another day? " The poor people took the pious hint and moved off. [288]

For some time after the Prince had set out, Flora remained at Mugstat, where Lady Margaret, who could only speak to her in presence of the officer, pressed her much to stay, and feigned a great anxiety to retain her for a few days, telling her that she had promised to do so the first time that she came that way. But Flora excused herself, saying that she wanted to be at home in these troublesome times, and also to see her mother. She was at length suffered to depart, accompanied by Mrs. Macdonald of Kirkibost, the lady who had apprised Lady Margaret of her visit, but who was not in the secret of the Prince's disguise. This lady's maid and man servant, and Mac Kechan completed the party. Lady Margaret during the whole of this agitating affair never saw the Prince "in any shape."[289]

Flora and her companions soon overtook the Prince and Kingsburgh. They found the curiosity of her companion somewhat inconvenient, for Mrs. Macdonald was very anxious to see the "strange woman's" face; but it was always turned away from her inquisitive gaze. Yet Mrs. Macdonald made her observations nevertheless. "She never, " she said, "had seen before such an impudent-looking woman—and she must either be an Irish woman, or a man in woman's clothes! " Flora, who had the happy and rare art of not saying too much, replied that "she was an Irishwoman, for she had seen her before. " The maid who attended Mrs. Macdonald took notice of the supposed Irish woman's awkward way of managing her petticoats, and remarked what long strides she took in walking. In particular, in wading a rivulet, the Prince lifted up his troublesome garments so high, that Mac Kechan called out to him "for God's sake to take care, or he would discover himself. " Charles laughed heartily, and thanked him for his cautions: he much feared that they would be neglected. Flora began to be apprehensive of the loquacious and observant mistress and maid. She, as well as Mrs. Macdonald, was now on horseback, and she proposed that the ladies should go on a little faster, and leave those on foot to take their time. There was another object in this arrangement: the country was traversed by parties of militia, and it was necessary for the Prince and Kingsburgh to diverge by a cross-road over the hills to the place of their destination. They went therefore by by-paths, south-south-east, to Kingsburgh's house, which they reached at midnight; Flora having arrived there a short time before. She had parted with her other companions on the road.

During this journey of seven long miles, which were performed in a drenching rain, there was no slight risk, owing to the very singular demeanour of the Prince, and to the awkwardness with which he performed his part. Betty Burke was regarded by the gazing passers-by as a very strange woman. When the country-people greeted him with an obeisance, he returned it with a bow instead of a curtsey; and in all his gestures he forgot the woman, and retained the man. After the remonstrance upon holding his skirts too high, he let them fall down into the streams which often intersected his path. "Your enemies, sir, " remarked Kingsburgh, "call you a Pretender, but you are the worst at your trade that I ever saw. " "Why, " replied Charles laughing, "they do me perhaps as much injustice in this as in other respects. I have all my life despised assumed characters, and am the worst dissembler in the world. "

Lady Kingsburgh, not expecting her husband that night, had retired to rest; and her house was not at this time in the best possible condition for receiving visitors. Kingsburgh, however, introduced Charles into the hall, and sent a servant up-stairs to desire Lady Kingsburgh to rise and dress herself. But the lady was not disposed to comply with her husband's commands that night. She sent a message to beg that he and his guests would help themselves to whatsoever they found in the house, and excuse her absence. As soon as she had despatched this answer, her daughter, a child of seven years of age, ran into the room, and told her, with much astonishment, that her father had brought home the most odd *"ill-shaken-up wife"* that she had ever seen, and had conducted her into the hall. Kingsburgh now made his appearance, and entreated his wife to come down-stairs, her presence being absolutely requisite. [290] Lady Kingsburgh was now really aroused. She could not help suspecting that her husband had taken into his house some of those proscribed and wretched fugitives who were skulking about the country. She could well imagine the distress of many of the Jacobites, for a paper had been, for some weeks, read in the kirks, forbidding all persons to give any sort of sustenance to a rebel, under pain of being deprived of it themselves. [291]

She now dressed herself, sending her little girl into the hall to fetch her keys. The child went down-stairs, but returned, saying that she could not go into the hall, the "strange woman" was walking backwards and forwards in so frightful a manner. Lady Kingsburgh therefore went herself, but stopped short at the door on seeing the stranger, whose aspect seems to have been unusually gaunt and unwomanly. Her husband, however, bade her go in for her keys, and at last she found courage to enter.

As she walked into the hall, Charles arose from his seat and advanced to meet her. According to the custom of the day, which applied both to ladies and gentlemen, he offered her the compliment of a salute. Lady Kingsburgh felt the roughness of no woman's cheek against her own. Alarmed at the discovery, she nearly fainted; she spoke not, neither did the stranger. She went hastily towards Kingsburgh, and told him her suspicions. No reproaches were uttered on her part for the introduction, which had evidently some risk connected with it; she merely asked, "Does this strange woman know anything about the Prince? " Her husband, taking her hand, replied, "My dear, this is the Prince himself. " "The Prince! " returned Lady Kingsburgh; "then we shall all be hanged! " "We can die but once, " answered Kingsburgh; "could we die in a better cause? We are only doing an act of humanity. "

He then desired her to send in supper. "Let us have eggs, butter, cheese, or whatever can be procured in the shortest time. " The lady remonstrated. "Eggs, butter, and cheese for a Prince! " "he will never look at such a supper. " "Ah, my dear, " returned Kingsburgh, "you little know how this poor Prince has fared of late. Our supper will be a banquet to him. Besides, any formal preparation would excite suspicion. Make haste, and come to supper yourself. " Lady Kingsburgh had now a new source of alarm. "*I* come to supper! " she cried; "I do not know how to behave before a Prince. " She was reassured by her husband, who told her that there was no difficulty in behaving before *this* Prince, who was so easy and obliging.

The party, who had undergone such a day's journey, sat up nearly till dawn, and became merry over their supper. Never was there a more joyous or inspiring guest at a feast than the unfortunate Charles. He was now in the house of a trusted adherent; and his spirits, which had been unaltered even in huts and caverns, gladdened all present. His favourite toast, was "To the Black Eye! " by which, as his pilot to the Long Island, Donald Macleod, relates, he meant the second daughter of France; "and I never heard him, " said Donald, "name any particular health but that alone. When he spoke of that lady, which he did frequently, he appeared to be more than ordinarily well-pleased. "[292]

The Prince ate heartily, and drank a bumper of brandy to the health of his host and hostess. When the ladies had retired, he took out a little black piece of tobacco-pipe which had been his consolation in all his wanderings, and began to smoke. Like most persons who have recourse to a similar practice, Prince Charles framed an excuse for it on the plea of health, telling Kingsburgh, that he had found it essential, in order to cure the tooth-ache, from which he had suffered much. His pipe had obtained the name, among his companions, of the "*cutty*".

A small china punch-bowl was then produced by the host, and was twice replenished with the very popular beverage called toddy, of which the Prince expressed his unqualified approbation. Conversation, thus aided and exhilarated, flowed freely; and the charm of Charles's gay courtesy was long remembered by his Highland landlord, who thus, at the risk of all that was dear to him, welcomed the unfortunate wanderer to his home. Morning dawned before either the Prince or Kingsburgh talked of retiring. At last Kingsburgh became anxious. He knew that it was necessary for Charles to proceed to Portree early the next day; and he earnestly desired that the Prince should have some rest. He refused to fill the bowl again, and began to urge his Highness to retire. Charles eagerly pressed for another supply of usquebaugh and warm water. In the contention, the bowl, which Kingsburgh had brought from Mugstat for the Prince to drink the wine out of on the shore, was broken. This ended the altercation, and Charles retired to rest.

The next day was far advanced before the Prince, after his conviviality of the preceding evening, was aroused; and the watchful Flora in vain sent Kingsburgh into his chamber to persuade him to rise. Kingsburgh had not the heart to awaken the fugitive from a repose which he so rarely enjoyed, and, on finding him in a profound sleep, retired. At last, one o'clock had struck, and the Prince was summoned to begin another journey. Kingsburgh, inquiring if he had had a good night, was answered that he had never enjoyed a better one in his life. "I had almost forgotten, " said Charles, "what a good bed was. " He then prepared to set out. He was first to go to Portree; his destination being, ultimately, the island of Raasay. The choice of this place as a retreat originated in the ancient league which subsisted between the families of Macdonald and of Raasay. Whenever the head of either family died, his sword was given to the head of the other. The chief of Raasay had joined the Highland army, but had saved his estate by conveying it to his son, young Macleod. Sir Alexander Macdonald, on that occasion, had thus addressed his neighbour and ally: "Don't be afraid, Raasay; I'll use my interest to keep you safe; and, if your estate should be taken, I'll buy it for the family. And he would have done it. "[293]

On quitting Kingsburgh, the Prince was determined to cast off his disguise. Kingsburgh was favourable to the change, but Flora would not consent to it: it was necessary, she thought, that the wanderer should leave the house in the same dress as he had entered it; so that, if inquiry were made, the servants would not be able to describe his appearance. He, therefore, once more figured in the habiliments of Betty Burke; and the only change, which was at the suggestion of Kingsburgh, was in the article of shoes; those in which he had walked being now worn out; a new pair was therefore supplied by Kingsburgh. When the exchange was made, Kingsburgh hung up the old shoes in a corner of his room, observing, that they might still do him some service. Charles inquired, "How? " "Why, " replied Kingsburgh, "when you are at St. James's, I shall hold up these shoes before you, and thus remind you of your night's entertainment and protection under my roof. " Charles, with a smile, desired him to be as "good as his word. " These precious deposits, never being required to appear at St. James's, were, after old Kingsburgh's death, cut into pieces, and kept as relics by the Jacobite ladies, and even by the grave but enthusiastic Bishop Forbes. [294]

It had been decided that Flora Macdonald should proceed on horseback to Portree by a different road, and should meet the Prince there. She therefore took a temporary leave of Charles; and Kingsburgh accompanied him to a wood not far from his house. When the Prince had departed, Lady Kingsburgh went up-stairs, and folded up the sheets in which he had slept, declaring that they should never be washed nor used till her death, when they should be made into her winding-sheet. She was afterwards induced to divide this valuable memorial with Flora Macdonald.

Mac Kechan, and a little herd-boy by way of a guide, alone accompanied the Prince, as he set out upon a laborious walk of fourteen miles towards Portree. It would have excited much suspicion, had any more important persons attended him. At an appointed place Charles threw off his female attire, and again "grasped the claymore. " His clothes were concealed in a bush until they could be carried to Kingsburgh's house, where they were burnt upon the alarm of a search on the part of the military. The gown only was retained, by the express desire of Kingsburgh's daughter. [295] The Prince now once more wore the Highland dress, which had been furnished him by Kingsburgh.

Meantime, Captain Roy Macdonald had gone to seek the young Macleod of Raasay, or, as he was called, Rona, whose very brother-in-law, Archibald Macqueen, was then in search for the Prince in South Uist. Young Macleod, though at first indisposed to confide the place where his father had taken refuge to Roy Macdonald, ended eventually by expressing, both on his own part and on that of his father, the strongest desire to serve the Prince, especially in his distress. "Then, " said Roy Macdonald, "I expect the Prince this night at Portree; and as there is no boat on this side fit to carry him over to Raasay, you must do your best, Rona, to get one for the purpose to ferry the Prince over to Raasay, for thither he means to set out from Portree. " Rona undertook this service, but was unwilling to leave Portree until he should see the Prince; for he had not been "out" in the last campaign. But, being repeatedly urged by Roy Macdonald, he at last embarked in a crazy old boat which filled perpetually with water, and could only with assistance be made to convey passengers from Portree to Raasay, a distance nearly of five miles. Before young Raasay embarked, Roy Macdonald had received a note from Kingsburgh, importing that Flora Macdonald was so fatigued that she could not go to Portree so soon as she had intended; and ordering the captain to provide a boat to ferry her about to Strath, because it would be easier to her "to make it out" by sea than overland. Captain Roy Macdonald took the hint, and judged exactly for whom the boat thus carefully alluded to was to be provided. On Monday the thirtieth of June, young Raasay, and his brothers Murdoch Macleod and Malcolm Macleod, arrived after a short, but perilous voyage within a mile of Portree. Malcolm went to the shore, leaving Rona in the boat. As he walked from the beach, he saw three persons approaching. It is said, that at Raasay nine months of the year are rainy. This June evening was one of the rainy periods; and Malcolm Macleod could not, through the darkness, discover who these three persons were. The place of meeting agreed upon was a small public-house near the shore, about half a mile from the port of Portree; to this house Malcolm Macleod sent to Captain Roy Macdonald, desiring him to come out and speak to a friend. Roy Macdonald complied with the summons, taking with him a half mutchkin stoup full of whiskey. Macleod then informed him that Rona and his brother Murdoch were on the shore with a boat, which, with much difficulty and danger they had brought from Raasay to convey the Prince to that island; he begged that they would not delay, as it was raining very heavily.

Donald Roy Macdonald then told Malcolm that the three persons whom he had seen going towards the public-house were the Prince, Mac Kechan, and the herd-boy. Of their approach he had been apprized by the energetic Flora, who had arrived at Portree some hours previously.

Donald Roy Macdonald, who is described as being the model of "a perfect Highland gentleman, " shared the enthusiasm of Flora. Although still lame from the wound in his foot, he had, during the course of that evening, looked out incessantly for the Prince, but was unable to see him. He had not, however, been long in the public-house, before the voice of the herd-boy calling for the landlord, and desiring to know if one Donald Roy Macdonald were there, drew his attention. He stepped out, and was told by the boy that there was a gentleman, a little above the house, who desired to speak to him. The captain sent the boy away, and immediately went to the spot where the Prince stood. Charles embraced him, putting his head first over one shoulder, and then over the other; and telling Donald to use no ceremony, for that it was impossible to know who might be observing them. When Donald expressed his regret at the darkness of the night, Charles said, "I am more sorry that *our lady*" (so he called Flora Macdonald) "should be so abused with the rain. "

After they entered the house, a curious scene took place. "The Prince, " relates Donald Roy, [296] "no sooner entered the house than he asked if a dram could be got there, the rain pouring down from his clothes; he having on plaid, without breeches, trews, or even philibeg. Before he sat down, he got his dram; and then the company desired him to shift, and put on a dry shirt, Captain Roy Macdonald giving him his philibeg. The Prince refused to shift, as Miss Flora Macdonald was in the room; but the captain and Neil Mac Kechan told him, it was not time to stand upon ceremonies, and prevailed upon him to put on a dry shirt. By this time they had brought some meat into the room, (the Prince having called for it before he would think of shifting,) which consisted of butter, cheese, bread, and roasted fish. "

The Prince was so hungry and exhausted, after a walk from Kingsburgh to Portree, "seven good Highland miles, " that he began to eat before he put on his coat. The supply of food which he had brought with him consisted of a cold hen, a bottle of brandy, and a lump of sugar in one of his pockets: these, with the addition of a bottle of whiskey procured at Portree, constituted his store of provisions until he reached Raasay. On seeing the Prince eat heartily, whilst only in his shirt and philibeg, Captain Donald Macdonald could not forbear smiling. "Sir, " he observed, "I believe that is the English fashion, " "What fashion do you mean? " asked the Prince. "They say, " replied Donald, "that the English, when they eat heartily, throw off their clothes. " "They are right, " answered Charles, "lest anything should incommode their hands when they are at work. " The Prince then asked, if any drink could be had. He was told that he could have nothing but whiskey or water, for no such thing as beer or ale was to be had in the isle of Skye. Then Charles asked if he could have some milk, but was informed that there was none in the house. The only beverage which seemed attainable was water, of which there was a supply in what Captain Donald Macdonald called an "ugly cog, " which the landlord of the house used for throwing water out of his boat. This vessel though coarse, was clean. "The captain, " relates Donald Roy, "had been taking a drink out of the cog, and he reached it to the Prince, [297] who took it out of his hand, and, after looking at the cog, he stared the captain in the face, who upon this made up to him (the landlord being in the room), and whispered him softly in the ear to drink out of it without any ceremony; for though the cog looked ill, yet it was clean; and, if he should show any nicety, it might raise a suspicion about him in the landlord's mind. The Prince said, 'You are right, ' and took a hearty draught of water out of the rough cog, and then he put on his coat. "

During all this scene, Captain Roy Macdonald could scarcely disguise his anxiety that the Prince should leave Portree. But Charles was reluctant to relinquish shelter and society; the rain was still heavily pouring down, and the night on which the unfortunate wanderer was again to trust his fate to strangers was very dark. In vain, therefore, did Macdonald, when the landlord had left the room, represent to Charles, that this, being a public-house, was frequented by all "sorts of folks, " and that some curiosity would be excited by his appearance. There was, indeed, no rest for the proscribed fugitive. Charles then asked for tobacco, that he might smoke a pipe "before he went off. " Macdonald answered, that there was no tobacco, except that which was very coarse; only "roll tobacco. " But Charles persisted in having it, saying "that it would serve his horn very well. " The landlord therefore was ordered to bring in a quarter of a pound, which he did in scales, at four-pence halfpenny. The Prince gave a sixpence, but the landlord was desired by Captain Macdonald to bring in the change. Charles smiled at Donald Roy's exactness, and said he would not be at the trouble to pick up the halfpence; but Donald Roy persuaded him to do so, saying, that in his Highness's present situation he would find "bawbees very useful to him. "

A bottle of whiskey having been dispatched between the Prince, Donald Roy Macdonald, and Neil Mac Kechan, and the pipe being finished, Charles reluctantly began to talk of his departure. He had learned to rely upon the fidelity of the brave Clan, one young and gentle daughter of which had protected him from South Uist, and brought him through a country swarming with militia to Portree. He was unwilling to be separated from Donald Roy, and entreated him in a low voice to accompany him. But Donald begged him to remember that it was not in his power to be useful to him, considering the open wound in his left foot; that he should only prove a burden to him, for it would be out of his power to skulk from place to place; and indeed it would be necessary for him to ride on horseback, so that any of the parties of militia who were ranging about would be sure to descry him at a distance, and that would be ruin to the chance of escape. Charles then said, that "he had always found himself safe in the hands of a Macdonald, and that, as long as he could have a Macdonald with him, he still should think himself safe. " Again and again he urged this point. It was affecting to see how confidingly this ill-fated young man, noble in his nature, leaned upon those whom he had learned to trust. It is melancholy to reflect that a temper so kindly should ever have been worked up, and irritated almost to madness, by those intrigues and misrepresentations which eventually, combining with the wreck of his other moral qualities, alienated him from all who really loved him.

"The Prince, " as Donald relates, "could not think of parting with him at all. " This was the first time that Charles had entrusted himself, without a single familiar friend or attendant, to strangers. "Are you, " he said, again addressing Donald, "afraid to go with me? So long as *I* have, you shall not want. " Again Captain Macdonald referred to his crippled foot: "he behoved to see, " he said, "that his going would only expose the Prince to new dangers, of which he had already too many to contend with. " In the course of the conversation he took occasion to tell the Prince, since he had honoured the Macdonalds with his regard, that, although Sir Alexander Macdonald and his followers did not join his standard, they wished him well. "I am sensible enough of all that, " was the reply of Charles. Donald also inquired whether the Prince was well provided with money; as in case of need, Lady Margaret Macdonald would supply his wants. But Charles, after expressing his gratitude to Lady Margaret, declined her aid, as he believed that he had sufficient to carry him to the mainland.

This painful and memorable scene came at last to a conclusion. After being repeatedly urged by Donald to depart, Charles bade Mac Kechan farewell. He then turned to Flora Macdonald: "I believe, madam, " he said, "that I owe you a crown of borrowed money. " She answered, in her literal and simple manner, "It was only half-a-crown. " This sum the Prince paid her. He then saluted her, and said: "Notwithstanding all that has happened, I hope, madam, we shall meet in St. James's yet. " In this calm, and, apparently laconic manner, he bade Flora adieu. But, though fate did not permit Charles to testify his gratitude at St. James's, he is said never to have mentioned without a deep sense of his obligations the name of his young protectress. In her loyal and simple heart a sense of duty, enthusiastic reverence, and fond regret dwelt, whilst that heart continued to beat; and, through the vicissitudes of her after-life, the service which she had rendered to the Prince recurred like a ray of sunshine upon a destiny almost continually clouded and darkened by calamity.

Flora was left alone at Portree, attended still by Mac Kechan, who afterwards escaped, rejoined the Prince, and went to France with him. Mac Kechan was a man of good education, and was conjectured by Bishop Forbes to have been the author of the "Alexis, or the Young Adventurer, " a romance embodying the principal incidents of Charles Edward's life; but of this there is no proof.

Meanwhile the Prince proceeded to the shore. He tied the bottle of whiskey, bought of the landlord, to his belt on one side, and the brandy, the cold hen, and the four shirts on the other. As he went, he saw the landlord of the public-house looking out of a window after him; on which he changed his road. He met young Raasay and his brothers at the appointed place; and it was there agreed, that in a few days Donald Macdonald should follow the Prince to Raasay. At his departure the Prince took out the lump of sugar from his pocket, and said, "Pray give this to *our lady*, for I fear she will get no sugar where she is going. " The captain refused however to accept of that which seems to have been considered as a great delicacy. Charles then enjoined Captain Macdonald to secrecy as to his destination. "Tell nobody—no, not *our lady*—where I am going; for it is right that my course should not be known. "[298] They then parted; and at daybreak, July the first, 1746, Charles sailed for Raasay. Captain Macdonald then returned to Portree, where he slept a great portion of the next day. Here he was closely questioned by the landlord, who said, that he had a great notion that the gentleman who had supped at his house was the Prince, for he had something noble about him. Probably the imprudent liberality of Charles, and his carelessness about money, may have added to the impression which his lofty air and fascinating manners generally produced. On the fourth of July, Charles, after various adventures in the island of Raasay, escaped to the mountains. This event was announced by a letter sent mysteriously by Murdoch Macleod to Roy Macdonald, and delivered to him in the darkness of night. It had neither address on it, nor place, nor date; but was written by Charles.

"Sir,

"I have parted as I intended. Make my compliments to all to whom I have given trouble. I am, sir, your humble servant,

"JAMES HERMION. "

This letter was burned by Roy Macdonald, though with great reluctance, on the day when he subsequently learned that Flora Macdonald had been made a prisoner.

Flora, after parting from the Prince, went to Armadale to her mother, after a very fatiguing journey across the country. Her emotions on separating from Charles have been expressed in a poem entitled "The Lament of Flora Macdonald, " beginning thus:

"Far o'er the hills of the heather so green,
  And down by the Corrie that skips in the sea,
The bonny young Flora sat weeping her love—
  The dew on her plaid, and the tear in her e'e.
She looked at a boat with the breezes that swung,
And ay as it lessened she sighed and she sung,
  'Farewell to the lad I shall ne'er see again!
Farewell to my hero, the gallant and young!
  Farewell to the lad I shall ne'er see again,'"[299]

During eight or ten days Flora remained in her house at Armadale without imparting to any one, even to her mother, the events of the last week. To make her mother a participator in that affair would indeed have been no act of kindness, at a time when the merest suspicion of being a Jacobite was regarded as a crime.

At the expiration of ten days Flora received a message from a person of her own name, Donald Macdonald of Castletown, in Skye, about four miles from Armadale, to bid her come to his house in order to meet there the commanding officer of an independent company, one Macleod of Taliskar, who had ordered Macdonald to surrender. Flora, a little suspicious of what might happen, thought proper to consult with her friends as to what step she should take. They unanimously agreed that she ought not to go; but "go she would. " Then they consulted together what she should say in case of an investigation. But Flora had made up her mind as to the answers she should give. She set out to meet her fate. She probably expected that she should be released after a short examination; for she knew not then through what channel the part which she had taken in the Prince's escape had transpired. The fact was, that the boatmen who had brought her with Charles from Skye had on their return communicated to Captain Fergusson every particular of the Prince's appearance, and had even described the gown which he had worn.

Flora afterwards remembered, that at Mugstat Lady Margaret had warned her that this would be the case, and had pointed out to her the indiscretion of allowing these men to go back to North Uist.

As she went on the road to Castleton, Flora met her father-in-law, Macdonald of Armadale, who was returning home; and shortly afterwards she was apprehended by Captain Macleod of Taliskar, with a party of soldiers, who were going to seek for her at her mother's house. She was not suffered to take leave of her mother, nor of her other friends; but was carried on board the Furnace, a sloop of war, commanded by Captain John Fergusson, and which lay near Raasay. Happily for Flora, General Campbell was on board, and by his orders she was treated with the utmost respect. At her first examination she merely acknowledged, that, on leaving Uist, she had been solicited by "a great lusty woman" to give her a passage, as she was a soldier's wife. Her request, Flora said, was granted; and the woman, upon being landed in Skye, had walked away, and Flora had seen nothing more of the stranger.

But upon finding that she was mildly treated, and on hearing that the boatmen had related every circumstance of her voyage, she confessed the whole truth to General Campbell.

The vessel was bound for Leith. About three weeks after she had been apprehended, as the ship cruized about, it approached the shore of Armadale. Here Flora was permitted to land, in order to bid adieu to her parents. She was sent ashore under a guard of two officers and a party of soldiers, and was forbidden to say anything in Erse, or anything at all except in presence of the officers. Here she stayed two hours, and then returned to the ship. With what emotions she left the island of Skye and found herself carried as a prisoner to Leith, it is not perhaps in these tranquil days easy to conceive.

After her apprehension, her father-in-law, Armadale, to use the phrase of some of the unfortunate Jacobites, "began a-skulking; " a report having gone about that he had given a pass to his daughter, although aware that she was travelling with "the Pretender" disguised in woman's clothes. There was also another source of suspicion against him, which was his having the Prince's pistols in his keeping. These were given him by Macdonald of Milton, the brother of Flora; they had been received either from Charles himself, or from O'Sullivan or O'Neil; but still they furnished a proof of some communication between Charles Edward and Armadale. Another sufferer was Donald Roy Macdonald. Among not the least energetic of those who aided the escape of Charles Edward from the Long Island, was Donald Roy Macdonald. A model of the true Highland gentleman in deportment, handsome in person, his conduct fully bore out his character. To this warm-hearted disinterested young man the Prince quickly attached himself. Crippled as he was, he was obliged also to "go a-skulking. " He concealed himself in three different caves, where by turns he made his abode for eight weeks, wrapping himself up in his plaid, and making his bed of the heather; his subsistence he owed to the care of Lady Margaret Macdonald, who brought him food, though at the risk of her own safety. It is consolatory to find heroic friendship, or compassionate interest, enlivening the melancholy annals of civil contentions, of revenge and treachery.

The sufferings of Captain Macdonald during his concealment, although alleviated by Lady Margaret's care, were nevertheless considerable. During the months of July and August, which he passed in the caves, the midges and flies annoyed his frame, sensitive from the still open wound, and drove him for coolness into the recesses of the caverns. It was necessary to be very careful in stepping out, lest the country-people should discover his retreat. Late at night, or very early in the morning, he crept out to supply his bottle with water from some neighbouring *burn* or rivulet. At last, the act of indemnity set him free. Until the month of November 1746, his wound, exasperated by constant exertion, was very troublesome. His misery was solaced by the care and skill of a friendly surgeon, who sent Donald Roy dressings by a proper hand, even while he remained in the cave, and at last the wound healed. In an account of the Prince's escape, written by Donald at the request of Bishop Forbes, he says, "He (Donald Roy) now walks as cleverly as ever, without any the smallest pain or halt; and made his last journey from Skye to Edinburgh in twelve days on foot, and, as he came along, visited several friends and acquaintances. "[300]

One cannot help rejoicing that Lady Margaret Macdonald escaped all inconvenience, except suspicion. The conduct of her husband, Sir Alexander, had been prudent. During the progress of the insurrection he had written to Keppoch, after the retreat from Stirling: —"Seeing I look upon your affairs as in a desperate state, I will not join you: but then, I assure you, I will as little rise against you. " Of Sir Alexander's followers, a force amounting to five hundred men, only two had joined the Prince; these were James

Macdonald of the isle of Hisker, [301] and Captain Donald Roy Macdonald. [302] The estates of Sir Alexander, therefore, remained uninjured, and his family continued to enjoy them.

The chief sufferers from the visit of Prince Charles to their house were Macdonald of Kingsburgh and his wife.

Upon hearing of the Prince's escape, Captain Fergusson went first to Mugstat; where gaining no intelligence, he proceeded to Kingsburgh. He there examined every person with the utmost exactness, and inquired into every particular of the accommodation afforded to one whom he styled "the Pretender. " "Whom you mean by *the Pretender*, I do not pretend to guess! " was the reply of Mrs. Macdonald of Kingsburgh.

Kingsburgh was made prisoner, and was sent to Fort Augustus on parole without any guard, by General Campbell's order. But the clemency shown by Campbell ceased when Kingsburgh reached Fort Augustus. He was thrown into a dungeon, was plundered of everything, and loaded with irons. Sir Everard Faulkner, who was employed to examine him, reminded him how fine an opportunity he had lost of "making himself and his family for ever. " "Had I gold and silver piled heap upon heap to the bulk of yon huge mountain, " was the noble reply, "that mass could not afford me half the satisfaction I find in my own breast from doing what I have done! " Whilst he was confined at Fort Augustus, an officer of distinction came to him, and asked him if he should know the Prince's head if he saw it. "I should know the head very well if it were on the shoulders, " was the answer. "But if it were not on the shoulders? " said the officer. "In that case I will not pretend to know anything about it, " returned Kingsburgh. His discrimination was not put to the test.

Kingsburgh was removed to Edinburgh castle under a strong guard of Kingston's Light-horse. He was at first put into a room with several other gentlemen, but was afterwards removed into solitary confinement, and not allowed to speak to any one, except to the officer on guard, and the keeper, who acted as his servant. In this place he remained for a year, when by the act of grace he was set at liberty on the fourth of July 1747; "having thus, " as an author has observed, "got a whole year's safe lodging for affording that of one night! "[303]

Before her farewell to her friends in Armadale, Flora Macdonald had exchanged the vessel which Captain Fergusson commanded, for one commanded by Commodore Smith, a gentleman capable of estimating her character. At Armadale, she procured a change of clothes, and took as her personal attendant an honest girl, named Kate Macdonald, who could speak nothing but Gaelic. This girl offered herself as a servant, finding that Flora could get no one else to attend her in her calamity.

Among her companions in trouble, she found, on returning to the ship, Captain O'Neil, who had persuaded her to undertake the enterprise which had produced her present imprisonment. This gentleman had also, when he urged her good offices, proffered his hand in marriage, in order that her reputation might not suffer by her adventure by "flood and field. " When Flora saw him on board the vessel, she went up to him, and slapping him on the cheek, said, "To that black face I owe all my misfortune! " O'Neil however answered, "that, instead of being her misfortune, it was her highest honour, and it would yet redound more to her credit, if she did not pretend to be ashamed of what she had done. "[304] She was confined for a short time in Dunstaffnage castle. This now ruinous fortress, once a royal residence, is situated near the mouth of Loch Etive, a short distance from Oban, in Argyleshire; it stands upon a rocky promontory which juts out into the lake, which is one of the most secluded and solemn scenes that nature, in all the grandeur of those regions, presents. [305] Near the castle is a convenient building, which is now, as probably it was in 1745, inhabited by the factors of the Duke of Argyle, who is the hereditary keeper of Dunstaffnage castle, under the Crown. It was probably in this house that Flora was lodged. The castle is on three of its sides little else than a shell; but the fourth is in tolerable repair. The entrance to this sequestered and solemn abode is from the sea, by a staircase; probably in old times a drawbridge, which fell from a staircase. The ancient grandeur of Dunstaffnage, long used as one of the earliest residences of the Scottish kings; famed also as the place from which the stone of Dunstaffnage, sometimes called the Stone of Scone, on which they were crowned, was brought; had long passed away before Flora tenanted its chambers. But the associations which it presented were not likely to dim the ardour of her loyalty to the last of that race who had once held their sway over the proud castle of Dunstaffnage; nor would the roofless chapel, of exquisite architectural beauty, near Dunstaffnage, where many of the Scottish kings repose, be an object devoid of deep and mournful interest to one who had lately beheld a singular instance of the mutability of all human grandeur. Two letters, which show the mode of Flora Macdonald's introduction to the keeper of the castle, Neil Campbell, have been preserved. [306] One of them is as follows:

"Horse-Shoe Bay, Aug. 1746.

"Dear Sir,

"I must desire the favour of you to forward my letters by an express to Inverary; and, if any are left with you, let them be sent by the bearer. I shall stay here with Commodore Smith till Sunday morning. If you can't come, I beg to know if you have any men now in garrison at your house, and how many? Make my compliments to your lady, and tell her I am obliged to desire the favour of her for some days to receive a very pretty young rebel. Her zeal, and the persuasion of those who ought to have given her better advice, has drawn her into a most unhappy scrape by assisting the young Pretender to make his escape. I need say nothing further till we meet; only assure you that I am, dear sir, your sincere friend and humble servant,

"JOHN CAMPBELL. "

"I suppose you have heard of Miss Flora Macdonald. "

Early in September the ship arrived in Leith Roads, and remained there until November. By this time the fame of this obscure Highland girl had reached the well-wishers to Prince Charles in Edinburgh, and many crowded to see her. Among these was the Rev. Robert Forbes, who happened at that time to be Episcopal minister of the port. At this period the Episcopal Church of Scotland consisted of a few scattered congregations, under the spiritual guidance of a reduced number of titular bishops. The Church was, however, deeply attached to the Stuarts; and the pious and enthusiastic man who now visited Flora in her adversity, was among the most zealous of the adherents to that ill-fated cause. He had himself known calamity, having been apprehended at St. Ninian's in the preceding year, 1745, and imprisoned until the following May. This circumstance, which had prevented him from taking any active part in the commotions, preserved Mr. Forbes in safety; and his exertions, which were directed to the purpose of collecting, from such of the insurgents as fell in his way, narratives of their several parts in the events of 1745, have been very effective. Through his efforts a valuable collection of authentic memoirs, from which extracts have been published within these last few years, have added a new light, and consequently a new charm, to the narrative of Prince Charles's adventures, and to the biography of his followers.

Mr. Forbes, at the time when he visited Flora, was residing in the house of Lady Bruce of Kinross, within the walls of Cromwell's citadel at Leith. It was one part of Mr. Forbes's plan, in the pursuit of which he contemplated forming an accurate history of the whole insurrection, to visit the State prisoners as they were either carried to London, or passed on their return to the Highlands. Most of his collection was therefore formed at the close of the last campaign, when the recollections of the unfortunate actors in the affair were vivid and accurate. Among other minor occupations was the acquisition of relics of Charles Edward, whom the worthy divine almost idolized. "Perhaps, " says Mr. Chambers, [307] "the most curious and characteristic part of the work is a series of relics which are found attached to the inside of the boards of certain volumes. In one I find a slip of thick blue silk cloth, of a texture like sarcenet, beneath which is written, 'The above is a piece of the Prince's garter. ' Below this is a small square piece of printed linen, the figures being in lilac on a white ground, with the following inscription: 'The above is a piece of the identical gown which the Prince wore for five or six days, when he was obliged to disguise himself in a female dress, under the name of Betty Burke. A *swatch* of the said gown was sent from Mrs. Macdonald of Kingsburgh, ' Then follows a slip of tape, with the following note: 'The following is a piece of that identical apron-string which the Prince wore about him when in a female dress. The above bit I received out of Miss Flora Macdonald's own hands, upon Thursday, November 5, 1747. '"

In 1762, this reverend enthusiast was chosen by the presbyteries of Caithness and Orkney as their bishop, and was consecrated at Cupar in Fife in the same year. He was the last bishop whose charge was limited only to those two districts.

Mr. Forbes was accompanied in his visits to Flora Macdonald, while at Leith, by Lady Bruce, Lady Mary Cochrane, Mrs. Clerk, and many other ladies; who made valuable presents of clothes to the heroine, and who listened to her narrative, as she delivered it to Mr. Forbes, with many expressions of sympathy and applause. When she related that part of her voyage from Uist in which the Prince watched over her whilst asleep, some of these fair Jacobites cried out, "O, madam! what a happy creature you are, to have that dear Prince to watch over you in your sleep. " "I could, " cried Mrs. Mary Clerk, "wipe your shoes with pleasure, and think it my honour to do so, when I reflect that you had the Prince for your handmaid! " Perhaps not the worst gift sent to Flora, during her stay at Leith, was a thimble and needles, with white thread of different sorts, from Lady Bruce. This act of friendship Flora felt as much as any that she received, for she had suffered as much from the state of idleness during her being in custody, as from any other privation. [308]

Her time thus passed away almost cheerfully. Her gentle, prudent, and placid deportment won upon the esteem of those who were least friendly to her opinions. The officers who were appointed to guard her, although they could not permit her to set her foot on shore, were pleased at the attention which she received from visitors. Commodore Smith behaved to her with fatherly regard. Whilst she was in Leith Roads, in the Eltham, he presented her with a handsome riding-suit, in plain mounting, and some fine linen for riding-shirts. He gave her advice how to act in her difficult and perilous situation, and even allowed the officers to go ashore to seek for good company for their prisoner; although persons who merely came from curiosity were denied access. Captain Knowles of the Bridgewater, also in the Leith Roads, was most courteous and considerate to the amiable prisoner. When her friends visited her, she was allowed to ask for such refreshments for them as she thought proper; as if she had been at her own fireside. Easy, modest, and winning, in the midst of all her anxiety for her friends, and in the uncertainty of her own fate, she was cheerful; yet a subdued and modest gravity gave an interest to her unpretending character. When solicited to join in the amusement of dancing, she refused, alleging that her "dancing-days were over; and that, at all events, she could not dance until she should be assured of the Prince's safety, and until she had the happiness of seeing him again. "

At length, carrying with her the good wishes of all who had conversed with her, Flora left the harbour of Leith. After being conveyed from place to place, she was put on board the Royal Sovereign on the twenty-seventh of November, the vessel then lying at the Nore, and conveyed to London. Here she was kept a prisoner under circumstances of great mitigation, for she was lodged in a private house. In this situation she continued for a year; when the Act of indemnity, passed in 1747, set her at liberty. She was then discharged, without a single question being addressed to her on the subject of her conduct. After being released, —at the instigation, according to a tradition in her family, of Frederic Prince of Wales, —she was domesticated in the family of the Dowager Lady Primrose, an ardent Jacobite, who afterwards, in 1750, was courageous enough to receive the young Chevalier during a visit of five days, which were employed by Charles in the vain endeavour to form another scheme of invasion. The abode of Lady Primrose was the resort of the fashionable world; and crowds of the higher classes hastened to pay their tribute to the heroine of the day. It may be readily conjectured, how singular an impression the quiet, simple manners of Flora must have made upon the excited minds of those who looked, perhaps, for high pretensions, —for the presence of an amazon, and the expressions of an heroine of romance. The compliments which were offered to Flora, excited in her mind nothing but the most unequivocal surprise that so simple an act should produce so extraordinary a sensation. She is stated to have been presented to Frederic Prince of Wales, and to have received from him the highest compliment to her fidelity and heroism. When, in explanation of her conduct, Flora Macdonald said that she would perform the same act of humanity to any person who might be similarly situated, the Prince remarked, "You would, I hope, madam, do the same, were the same event to happen over again. " The grace and courtesy of this speech may partly be attributed to the amiable traits which profligate habits had not wholly obliterated in the Prince; partly to his avowed opposition to his royal father, and the bad terms on which he stood with his brother. It must still be acknowledged, that Frederic displayed no ordinary degree of good-feeling in this interview with Flora. His son George the Third, and his grandson George the Fourth, both did credit to themselves by sentiments equally generous towards their ill-fated and royal kinsman.

After this intoxicating scene, presenting in their most brilliant colours, to the eye of one who had never visited either Edinburgh or London, the fascinations of the higher classes of society, Flora returned to Skye. She left the metropolis unchanged in her early affections, unaltered in the simplicity of her manners. The country, presenting so lately the miserable spectacle of civil war, was now calmed into a mournful tranquillity, as she passed through it on her journey to Skye; but in the Highlands, and more especially in the Western Isles, the love and loyalty which had of old been devoted to the Stuarts were unaltered. It was, indeed, long before they were obliterated; and, for years after the fatal 1745, the name of Charles Edward was uttered with tears. Nor is this sentiment of respect even now extinct; nor will it, perhaps, ever be wholly annihilated.

The journey from London to Skye was performed by Flora in a postchaise, and her expenses were defrayed by Lady Primrose. Her companion was, by her own choice, Malcolm Macleod of Raasay, who had met the Prince at Portree, and had completed the work begun by Flora. He too had been imprisoned, but had regained his liberty. "So, " afterwards Malcolm related to his friends, with a triumphant air, "I went to London to be hanged, and returned in a postchaise with Miss Flora Macdonald! " They visited Dr. Burton, another released prisoner, at York. Here Malcolm was asked by that gentleman what was his opinion of Prince Charles. "He is the most cautious man not to be a coward, and the bravest not to be rash, that I ever saw, " was the reply.

In 1750, Flora Macdonald was married to her cousin Alexander Macdonald the younger of Kingsburgh, who appears to have been worthy of his distinguished wife. In person, young Kingsburgh had completely the figure of a gallant Highlander, the graceful mien and manly looks which a certain popular Scots' song has attributed to that character. "When receiving Dr. Johnson in after-years, Kingsburgh appeared in true Highland costume, with his plaid thrown about him, a large blue bonnet with a knot of black ribbon like a cockade, a brown short coat of a kind of duffil, a tartan waistcoat with gold buttons and gold button-holes, a bluish philibeg, and tartan hose. He had jet hair tied behind; and was a large stately man, with a steady sensible countenance. "[309] Such was the man to whom, after a short eventful period of peril and vicissitude, it was the lot of Flora Macdonald to be united. Kingsburgh is also declared by Boswell to have had one virtue of his country in perfection—that of hospitality; and, in this, to have far surpassed the son of Lady Margaret Macdonald, Sir Alexander Macdonald of Armadale, an English-bred chieftain, at whose house Dr. Johnson and his friend "had small company, and could not boast of their cheer. " That gentleman, "an Eton-bred scholar, " had few sympathies with the poor tenants by whom he was surrounded. So true is Dr. Johnson's remark, "that the Highland chiefs should not be allowed to go farther south than Aberdeen. "

In her union with young Kingsburgh Flora enjoyed a source of satisfaction not to be estimated lightly. She became the daughter-in-law of a man whose virtues were remembered with the deepest respect in Skye. [310] When in 1773 Dr. Johnson and Boswell visited the island, they found Flora and her husband living in apparent prosperity in the dwelling wherein Charles Edward had been so hospitably entertained. Kingsburgh the younger, as the head of the house, received the Doctor at his door, and with respectful attention supported him into the house. A comfortable parlour with a good fire was appropriated to the guests, and the "dram" went round. Presently supper was served, and then Flora made her appearance. "To see Dr. Samuel Johnson, the great champion of the English Tories, salute Miss Flora Macdonald in the isle of Skye, was, " as Boswell observes, "a striking sight. " In their notions Flora and the Doctor were in many respects congenial; and Dr. Johnson not only had imbibed a high opinion of Flora, but found that opinion confirmed on acquaintance.

Conversation flowed freely. Flora told him that during a recent visit to the main land she had heard that Mr. Boswell was coming to Skye; and that Mr. Johnson, a young English *"buck, "* was coming with him. Dr. Johnson was highly entertained with this fancy. He retired however early to rest, and reposed on the very bed on which Charles Edward had slept so long and so soundly on his way from Mugstat to Portree. The room was decorated with a great variety of maps and prints; among others was Hogarth's head of Wilkes grinning, with the cap of Liberty on a pole by him. Boswell appears, as far as we can guess from his expressions, to have shared the apartment. "To see Dr. Samuel Johnson, " remarks Boswell, "lying on that bed in the isle of Skye, in the house of Miss Flora Macdonald, again struck me with such a group of ideas as it is not easy for words to express. " Upon Boswell giving vent to this burst of rapture, Dr. Johnson smiled and said, "I have had no ambitious thoughts in it. " He afterwards remarked that he would have given a great deal rather than not have lain in that bed. [311]

On quitting the house, Dr. Johnson and his friend were rowed by Kingsburgh, across one of the lochs which flow in upon all the coasts of Skye, to a place called Grishinish; and here the Highland host bade his guests adieu. All seemed smiling and prosperous; but even at this time Kingsburgh was embarrassed in his affairs, and contemplated going to America.

That scheme was eventually accomplished. During the passion for emigration which prevailed in the Highlands, Kingsburgh removed to North Carolina, where he purchased an estate. Scarcely had he settled upon his property before the American war broke out. Like most of the Jacobites who were in America at that time, he sided with the British Government. He even took up arms in the cause, and became captain of a regiment called the North Carolina Highlanders. Many singular adventures occurred both to him and to Flora in the course of the contest. At length they returned to Skye, but not together; she sailed first. In the voyage home, her ship encountered a French ship of war. An action ensued. Whilst the ladies among the passengers were below, Flora stayed on deck, and encouraged the sailors with her voice and manner. She was thrown down in the confusion, and broke her arm. With her wonted vivacity she afterwards observed, that she had risked her life both for the House of Stuart and for that of Brunswick, but had got very little for her pains. Her husband remained in America for some time after she returned to Scotland, but joined her at last.

Flora had a numerous family of sons and daughters. Charles, her eldest son, was a captain in the Queen's Rangers. He was worthy of bearing his mother's name. As his kinsman, the late Lord Macdonald, saw his remains lowered into the grave, he remarked, "There lies the most finished gentleman of my family and name! " Alexander, the second son, also in the King's service, was lost at sea. Ranald, the third, was a captain of Marines. He was remarkable for his elegant person, and estimable for his high professional reputation. James, the fourth son, served in Tarlton's British Legion, and was a brave officer. The late Lieutenant-Colonel John Macdonald, in Exeter, long survived his brothers. This officer was introduced to King George the Fourth, who observed, on his presentation, to those around him, "This gentleman is the son of a lady to whom my family (thus designating the Stuarts) owe a great obligation. " Of two daughters, one, Mrs. Macleod of Lochbuy, died not many years ago.

The following letters refer to the family who have been thus enumerated. [312]

FROM MRS. MACDONALD TO MRS. MACKENZIE OF DELVIN, BY DUNKELL.

"Dunvegan, twenty-fourth July, 1780

"Dear Madam,

"I arrived at Inverness the third day after parting with you, in good health and without any accidents, which I always dread; my young 'squire continued always very obliging and attentive to me. I stayed at Inverness for three days. I had the good-luck to meet with a female companion from that to Skye. I was the fourth day, with great difficulty, at Raasay, for my hands being so pained with the riding.

"I arrived here a few days ago with my young daughter, who promises to be a stout Highland dairg, quite overgrown of her age. Nanny and her small family are well: her husband was not sailed the last accounts she had from him.

"I have the pleasure to inform you, upon my arrival here, that I had two letters from my husband; the latter dated tenth May. He was then in very good health, and informs me that my son Charles has got the command of a troop of horse in Lord Cathcart's regiment. But alas! I have heard nothing since I left you about my son Sandy, [313] which you may be sure gives me great uneasiness; but still hope for the best.

"By public and private news, I hope we will soon have peace re-established, to our great satisfaction: which, as it's a thing long expected and wished for, will be for the utility of the whole nation; especially to poor me, that has my all engaged, —fond to hear news, and yet afraid to get it.

"I wait here till a favourable opportunity for the Long Island shall offer itself. —As I am upon all occasions under the greatest obligations to you, would you get a letter from my son Johny sooner than I would get one from him, you would very much oblige me by dropping me a few lines communicating to me the most material part of his letter.

"I hope you and the ladies of your family will always accept of my kindest respects; and I ever am, with esteem, dear madam, your affectionate, humble servant,

"FLORA MACDONALD.

"Please direct to me, to Mrs. Macdonald, late of Kingsborrow, South Uist, by Dunvegan. "

Two years, it seems, elapsed, and the summer of 1782 arrived, and the fate of Alexander Macdonald was still unknown; yet the mother's heart still clung to hope, as it proved by the following letter. No murmurs escape from one who seems to have sustained unrepiningly the sorrows which reach the heart most truly; the wreck of fortune, not for ourselves, but for our children, and the terrors of suspense. One source of consolation she possessed: her surviving sons were brave, honourable, and respected. But "Sandy" never returned.

MRS. MACKENZIE OF DELVINE, BY DUNKELL.

"Milton, third of July, 1782.

"Dear Madam,

"I received your agreeable favour a fortnight ago, and am happy to find that your health is not worse than when I left you. I return you my sincere thanks for your being so mindful of me as to send me the agreeable news about Johny's arrival, which relieved me from a great deal of distress, as that was the first accounts I had of him since he sailed. I think, poor man! he has been very lucky, for getting into bread so soon after landing. I had a letter from John, which, I suppose, came by the same conveyance with yours. I am told by others that it will be in his power now to show his talents, as being in the engineer department. He speaks feelingly of the advantages he got in his youth, and the good example showed him, which I hope will keep him from doing anything that is either sinful or shameful. [314]

"I received a letter from Captain Macdonald, my husband, dated from Halifax, the twelfth of November '82; he was then recovering his health, but had been very tender for some time before. My son Charles is captain in the British Legion, and James a lieutenant in the same: they are both in New York. Ranald is captain of Marines, and was with Rodney at the taking of St. Eustatia. As for my son Sandy, who was a-missing, I had accounts of his being carried to Lisbon, but nothing certain, which I look upon the whole as a hearsay; but the kindness of Providence is still to be looked upon, as I have no reason to complain, as God has been pleased to spare his father and the rest. I am now at my brother's house, on my way to Skye, to attend my daughter, who is to lie-in in August; they are all in health at present.

As for my health at present, it's tolerable, considering my anxious mind and distress of times.

"It gives me a great deal of pleasure to hear such good accounts of young Mr. M'Kinnie: [315] no doubt he has a great debt to pay, who represents his worthy and amiable uncle. I hope you will be so good as remember me to your female companions. I do not despair of the pleasure of seeing you once more, if peace was restored; and I am, dear madam, with respect and esteem, your affectionate friend,

"FLORA MACDONALD. "

Flora died in 1790, having attained the age of seventy. Her corpse was interred, wrapt in the sheet on which Charles Edward had lain at Kingsburgh, and which she had carried with her to America, intending that, wherever she should be entombed, it should serve as her winding-sheet.

The life and character of Flora Macdonald exemplify how true it is, that, in the performance of daily duties, and in domestic life, the loftiest qualities of woman may be formed; for the hourly practice of self-controul, the exercise of judgment, the acquisition of fortitude, tend to the perfection of those virtues which ennobled her career. In all her trials she acted a woman's part. Her spirit was fortified by a strength that was ever gentle. She was raised by circumstances above a private sphere; when these ceased to actuate her, she returned cheerfully to what many might deem obscurity, but which she gladdened by a kind and cheerful temper. No vain-glory, no egotism, vulgarized her one great effort. The simplicity of her character was inherent and unextinguishable; and the deep interest which was attached to her character was never lessened by any display. Her enthusiasm for the Stuart cause ceased only with her life. When any person thoughtlessly, or cruelly, applied the term "Pretender" to the Prince whom she reverenced, her anger for a moment was aroused. But contention ill accorded with the truly feminine, yet noble and well-principled, mind of Flora Macdonald. Upon the error or truth of that belief in hereditary and indefeasible right which she entertained, it is of little moment, in estimating her virtues, to pass an opinion. Perhaps we may venture to conclude with Dr. Johnson, "that being in rebellion, from a notion of another's right, is not connected with depravity; and that we had this proof of it, that all mankind applaud the pardoning of rebels, which they would not do in the case of murderers and robbers. "

FOOTNOTES:

[274] General Stewart's Sketches of the Highlanders, vol. ii. p. 5. App.

[275] See General Stewart's Sketches.

[276] Chambers. Note, p. 106.

[277] Lockhart's Memoirs, vol. ii. p. 540.

[278] Stewart, vol. i. p. 105.

[279] Brown's Highlands, p. 284.

[280] Donald Macleod's Narrative, in Bishop Forbes's collection.

[281] Home, App. p. 45.

[282] O'Neil's Narrative.

[283] Brown's History of the Highlands, p. 285, note, vol. iii.

[284] Maxwell of Kirkconnel, p. 178.

[285] Chambers' Traditions of Edinburgh, p. 255.

[286] Eglintoune House was situated on the west side of the old Stamp-office Close, High Street. It is now occupied by a vintner. —Chambers' Traditions, p. 256.

[287] Boswell, p. 320.

[288] A Genuine Account of the Prince's escape. —Scots' Magazine for 1749.

[289] Captain Roy Macdonald's Narrative. Forbes, p. 419.

[290] Chambers. Edit. for the People, p. 101.

[291] Note in Scots' Magazine for 1749; from a MS. by Colonel Macalister.

[292] Donald Macleod's Narrative. Forbes, p. 391.

[293] Boswell's Journey to the Hebrides, p. 207.

[294] Chambers, p. 102, and note.

[295] It was, (be it known, for the gratification of those curious in such matters,) "sprigged with blue. "

[296] Jacobite Memoirs, p. 448.

[297] Forbes, p. 449.

[298] Forbes, p. 413.

[299] Curious Tracts in the British Museum, vol. iv. Scotland.

[300] Jacobite Memoirs, p. 447.

[301] A small isle about eight miles to the westward of South Uist.

[302] Forbes. Narrative of Captain Donald Macdonald.

[303] Scots' Magazine for 1749.

[304] Note in Chambers' Memoirs of the Rebellion.

[305] Preface to the Jacobite Memoirs by Mr. Robert Chambers, to whom the public owe so much on this and other subjects.

[306] Brown's Hist. of the Highlands, vol. iii. p. 309.

[307] Preface to Jacobite Memoirs, xi.

[308] Chambers, p. 106. Taken from the Lyon in Mourning, MSS.

[309] Boswell's Tour to the Hebrides.

[310] Dr. Johnson's Tour to the Hebrides, p. 319.

[311] Dr. Johnson's Tour to the Hebrides, p. 217.

[312] From the Collection of Charles Kirkpatrick Sharpe, Esq. They were printed, on the occasion of the Queen's visit to Scotland, in the Edinburgh Advertiser for 1844.

[313] So named, in compliment to Sir Alexander Macdonald of Slate, or rather to his wife, Lady Margaret, the friend of Flora Macdonald.

[314] This alludes to the attention paid him when young, and under the care of Mr. Mackenzie, by that gentleman and his family.

[315] The late Sir Alexander Muir Mackenzie of Delvine, Bart.

WILLIAM BOYD, EARL OF KILMARNOCK.

The unfortunate nobleman who is the subject of this Memoir, could boast of as long line of ancestors as most families in Europe. Among his forefathers were men eminent for loyalty, and distinguished for bravery, and of honour as untainted as their blood; but when William, fourth Earl of Kilmarnock, succeeded to his title, there was little except this high ancestry to elate him with pride, or to raise him above dependence upon circumstances.

The Earl of Kilmarnock derived his title from a royal borough of the same name, in the shire of Cunningham in Ayrshire; and, in former times when the chieftainship was in repute in that part of Scotland, that branch of the family of Boyd, or Boyde, from whom the Earl was descended, claimed to be chiefs.

The greatness of the Boyd family commenced with Simon, the brother of Walter, first High Steward of Scotland, and founder of the Monastery of Paisley, in 1160. Robert, the son of Simon, is designated in the foundation church of that monastery, as nephew of Walter, High Steward; and is distinguished on account of his fair complexion, by the word Boyt, or Boyd, [316] from the Celtic Boidh, signifying fair, or yellow. "He was, " says Nisbet, "doubtless, predecessor to the Lords Boyd, and Earls of Kilmarnock. "[317]

The family of Boyd continued to flourish until, in the fifteenth century, it was ennobled by James the Third, who owed to one of its members, Sir Alexander Boyd of Duncow, esteemed to be a mirror of chivalry, an inculcation into the military exercises, which were deemed, in those days, essential to the education of royalty. But the sunshine of kingly favour was not enjoyed by the Boyds without some alloy. Robert Boyd of Kilmarnock, who was raised to the peerage, under the title of Lord Boyd, and whose eldest son was created Earl of Arran, experienced various vicissitudes. He died in England, in exile; and his brother, Sir Alexander, perished in 1469, on a scaffold, erected on the Castle Hill of Edinburgh. The fortunes of the family were, however, restored in the person of Thomas, Earl of Arran, who married the eldest sister of King James the Third. The beautiful island of Arran was given as the dower of this lady: and her husband, who is said in the Paston Letters to have been a "light, clever, and well-spoken, fair archer; devoutest, most perfect, and truest to his lady, of Knights, " enjoyed a short gleam of royal favour. His vicissitudes, however, befel him whilst on an embassy in Denmark, his enemies undermined him at home: he was driven to wander in foreign countries, and died at Antwerp, where a magnificent monument was erected to his memory, by Charles the Bold, Duke of Burgundy. His title was attainted, but his property was restored to his son; and in 1655, the title of Earl of Kilmarnock was added to that of Lord Boyd, which alone seems to have been retained by the family during the intervening generations.

During the reign of Charles the First, his descendants were considered to be steady Royalists; but, notwithstanding their claiming descent from the Stuarts, the views and principles of the family in the troublous period of the Revolution of 1688, underwent a total change. William, the third Earl of Kilmarnock, and the father of the unhappy adherent of Charles Edward, took the oaths of allegiance to the reigning family, and supported the Treaty of Union; joining at first the party entitled the *Squâdrone volante*; but eventually deserting them for the Whigs. When the Insurrection of 1715 broke out, this nobleman plainly manifested that the notions which had actuated his ancestor to join the association at Cumberland in favour of Charles the First, were no longer deemed valid by him. The superiority of the Burgh of Kilmarnock having been granted in 1672 to his ancestors, the Earl summoned the inhabitants of the Burgh to assemble, and to arm themselves in support of Government. At the general meeting of the fencible corps at Cunningham, Lord Kilmarnock appeared, followed by five hundred of his men, well armed, and so admirably trained, that they made the best figure on that occasion among the forces collected. [318] In compliance with orders which he received from the Duke of Argyll, Lord Kilmarnock marched with his volunteers to garrison the houses of Drummakil, Cardross, and Gastartan, in order to prevent the rebels from crossing the Forth. Unhappily for the fortunes of his family, the Earl died two years afterwards: and in the year 1717, his son, then a boy of fourteen years of age, succeeded to his title.

The mother of the young nobleman still survived: she was the Lady Eupheme, daughter of William, eleventh Earl of Ross; and one child only, the Earl of Kilmarnock, had been the issue of her marriage.

The youth, whose fate afterwards extorted pity from the most prejudiced spectators of his fate, was educated in the principles of the Scottish Church. These, as the chaplain who attended Lord Kilmarnock in the last days of his existence observes, are far from "having the least tendency to sedition, " and a very different bias was apparent in the conduct of the Presbyterian ministers during the whole course of the insurrections of 1745. The young nobleman appears to have imbibed, with this persuasion, a sincere conviction of those incontrovertible, and all-important truths of Christianity which, happily, the contentions of sect cannot nullify, nor the passions of mankind assail. "He always believed, " such is his own declaration, "in the great truths of God's Being and Providence, and in a future state of rewards and punishments for virtue and vice. " He had never, he declared at that solemn moment when nothing appeared to him of consequence save truth, "been involved in the fashionable scepticism of the times. " As he grew up, a character more amiable than energetic, and dispositions more calculated to inspire love than to insure respect, manifested themselves in the young nobleman. He was singularly handsome, being tall and slender, and possessing what was termed by an eyewitness of his trial, "an extreme fine person; " he was mild, and well-bred, humble, and conscientious. It is true, that in his hours of penitence he recalled, with anguish, "a careless and dissolute life, " by which, as he affirmed, he reduced himself to great and perplexing difficulties; he repented for his "love of vanity and addictedness to impurity and sensual pleasure, " which had "brought pollution and guilt upon his soul, and debased his reason, and, for a time, suspended the exercise of his social affections, which were, by nature, strong in him, and, in particular, the love of his country. " Such was his own account of that youth, which, deprived of the guidance of a father, with high rank and great personal attractions to endanger it, was passed, according to his own confession, in dissipation and folly. It appears, nevertheless, that he was greatly respected by his neighbours and tenantry, who were not, perhaps, disposed to judge very severely the errors of a young and popular man.

When only eleven years of age, Lord Kilmarnock, then Lord Boyd, had appeared in arms for Government with his father; on which occasion he conducted himself so gracefully as to attract the admiration of all beholders. [319] His early prepossessions, granting that they may have accorded with those of his father, were, however, soon dissipated when he allied himself with a family who had been conspicuous in the Jacobite cause. This was the house of Livingstone, Earl of Linlithgow and Calendar; George, the fourth Earl, having, in 1715, been engaged in the insurrection under Lord Mar, had been attainted, and his estate of one thousand two hundred and ninety-six pounds yearly forfeited to the Crown. Nor has this forfeiture ever been reversed; and the present representative of the family, Sir Thomas Livingstone, of Westquarter and Bedlormie, remains, notwithstanding an appeal in 1784 before Lord Kenyon, then Attorney-General, a commoner. [320]

Lady Anne Livingstone, who was the object of the young Lord Kilmarnock's choice, is reported to have been a woman of great beauty, and, from her exertions in her husband's behalf, appears to have possessed a fine, determined spirit. Although her father's title was not restored, she had sufficient interest, in 1721, to obtain from the English Government a lease of the forfeited estates for fifty-nine years, at the rent of eight hundred and seventy-two pounds, twelve shillings per annum. [321] This was, no doubt, a source of considerable pecuniary benefit to her, and also of assistance, very greatly required by Lord Kilmarnock, who was in impoverished circumstances. Honours, indeed, centered in him, but were productive of no real benefit. By the grandmother of his wife, the Lady Margaret Hay, sole surviving daughter of Charles the twelfth Earl of Errol, he had a claim to that Earldom, which, coupling with its dignity that of the hereditary High Constable of Scotland, descended in the female line, and after the death of a brother in infancy, constituted the Lady Anne Livingstone a Countess of Errol in her own right. Thus, Lord Kilmarnock had, to borrow Horace Walpole's expression, "four earldoms in him, " Kilmarnock, Errol, Linlithgow, and Calendar; and yet he is said to have been so poor, as "often to have wanted a dinner. " But to this mode of expression we must not entirely trust for accuracy. With the inheritance of the Earldoms of Errol, and of Linlithgow, and Calendar, there came a stock of old Jacobite principles; Lord Linlithgow had, indeed, suffered what was perhaps worse than death for his adherence to James Stuart. The Earl of Errol, the grandfather of Lady Kilmarnock, had led a more prudent course. Still he was a hearty Jacobite, and though, as Lockhart declares, he did not at first make a "great outward appearance, " yet he was much trusted by the party; his family had always been favourable to the Stuarts, and he was, also, generally considered to cherish similar sentiments. [322] He had, nevertheless, taken the oaths to Government in 1705; yet on the alarm of an invasion in 1708, he was deemed so dangerous a person that he was sent as a prisoner to Edinburgh Castle, where he died.

The love suit of Lord Kilmarnock was not likely, under his impoverished circumstances, to prosper uninterruptedly. When he succeeded to his estate he had found it much encumbered, and a considerable portion of the old inheritance alienated. Lord Kilmarnock's disposition was not formed for economy; he was generous even to profusion, and, as we have seen had not escaped the temptations incident to his age. His addresses to the Lady Anne Livingstone are said to have been prompted by his necessities; her fortune was deemed considerable; and her family, well knowing the state of the Earl's affairs, regarded his proposals of marriage unfavourably. But the young nobleman during the course of his courtship, and in opposing these objections, formed an interest in the heart of the young lady. He was, indeed, a man born to charm the imagination of the romantic, if not at that period of his youth, to rivet affection by esteem. In his boyhood, although he made some degree of progress in classical attainments, and even in philosophy and mathematics, thus proving that natural ability was not wanting, he was far more successful in attaining mere accomplishments, which add a powerful charm to comeliness and symmetry than in mastering more solid studies. He became an adept in fencing, in riding, in drawing, and also in music; and acquired the distinctive and comprehensive designation, of being "a polite gentleman. "[323]

Disgusted with the cold discussions on settlements and rent rolls, and disregarding maternal cautions, Lady Anne soon followed the dictates of her own heart. She married the young and handsome nobleman without her mother's consent, and a tardy sanction to the union was wrung from Lady Livingstone only when it was too late to withhold her approval.

The marriage was not, it was said by those who were disposed to scandalize the Earl of Kilmarnock, productive of happiness. The young Countess was possessed, indeed, of beauty, wit, and good sense: but her husband, if we may accredit the memoirs of his life, gave her much cause to complain of his conduct. They lived, however, as the same doubtful authority states, "if not happily, at least civilly together. " Such is the statement of a contemporary writer; it must, however, be adopted with just as much allowance as we give to similar reports raised by party writers in the present day: and it will be shown[324] not to accord with the dying declarations of Lord Kilmarnock. "I leave behind, " he wrote to his agent, "in Lady Kilmarnock, what is dearest to me. "[325] Subsequently to his marriage, Lord Kilmarnock's necessities and the additional burden of a family induced him to apply to the English Government for a pension, founded, as it is probable, on his father's services to Government in 1715. But this statement, and the conditions upon which the bounty was given are left in obscurity. "Whether, " says the anonymous biographer of Lord Kilmarnock, "my Lord Kilmarnock's pension was a ministerial bribe, or a royal bounty, is a question I cannot determine with any certainty; but I have reason to suspect the former, since few pensions, granted by a certain administration, that of Sir Robert Walpole, deserved the latter. " The same writer truly observes, that little or no dependance is to be placed on that loyalty which wants the support of bribes and pensions. "The practice, " he adds, "is too general, and a defection of this kind of men may be fatal to the state. "[326] The pension, as it appears from Horace Walpole's letters, was taken from Lord Kilmarnock by Lord Wilmington. "Lord Kilmarnock, " he writes to Sir Horace Mann, "is a Presbyterian, with four earldoms in view, but so poor since Lord Wilmington's stopping a pension that my father had given him, that he often wanted a dinner. "[327]

In the last days of his existence the Earl, indeed, acknowledged that the state of his affairs was, in part, the reason of his defection from Government. He attributed it, (though, it must be stated, under the pressing arguments of a minister of religion who considered what he termed "rebellion" as the most heinous sin,) to the great and pressing difficulties into which he had brought himself, by extravagance and dissipation: and declared, according to the account of his spiritual guide, that the "exigency of his affairs was very pressing at the time of the rebellion; and that, besides the general hope he had of mending his fortune by the success of it, he was also tempted by another prospect, of retrieving his circumstances if he followed the Pretender's standard. "[328]

Until the commencement of the insurrection of 1745, Lord Kilmarnock enjoyed the possession of Dean Castle, a very ancient edifice, situated about half a mile north east of the town of Kilmarnock, in Ayrshire. "It is, " says Grose in his Antiquities of Scotland, "at a small distance from the main road leading from Kilmarnock to Stewarton, and consists of a large vaulted square tower, which seems to have been built about the beginning of the fifteenth century: this is surrounded by a court and other buildings more modern. "[329] Such is the description of Dean Castle before the year 1735; when, to add to Lord Kilmarnock's other necessities, it was partially destroyed by fire, leaving only a ruin which he was too much impoverished even to restore to its former habitable state. In the "great square tower, " referred to by Grose, and of which a view is preserved in his work on Scotland, the Boyd family had dwelt in the days of their greatness, when one of their race was created Earl of Arran. In that tower had the Earl imprisoned his royal wife, the Lady Margaret, sister of James the Third, who was divorced from him, pleading, as some say, a prior contract with the Lord Hamilton, to whom she was afterwards united, taking to him the Isle of Arran as her dower.

It does not appear that the Earl of Kilmarnock was originally in the confidence of the Jacobite party: and their designs were not only matured, but far in full operation before he took an open or active part in the Stuart cause. It happened, however, that when Charles Edward resided at Holyrood, the Countess of Kilmarnock was living in Edinburgh. Her beauty, and the gaiety of her manners, attracted the admiration of the young Prince, who bestowed no small portion of attention on the fascinating daughter of one of his father's adherents. Lady Kilmarnock was as much attached to pleasure as the young and beautiful usually are: she delighted in public diversions, and led the way to all parties of amusement. Her ambition, no less than her early prepossessions conspired, it is said, to make her a Jacobite; and she hoped, by the favour of Charles Edward, to obtain the restoration of her father's title. Her entreaties to the Earl of Kilmarnock to join the standard of the Prince were stimulated, therefore, by a double motive; and, indeed, to a generous and romantic mind, there required neither the inducements of ambition, nor of gratified vanity, to espouse that part which seemed most natural to the Scotch. After the battle of Preston Pans, Lady Kilmarnock's persuasions took effect: her husband presented himself to the young Chevalier, who received him with every mark of esteem and distinction, declared him a member of the privy council, raised him to the rank of a general, and appointed him colonel of his guards. [330]

Another occurrence is, however, stated to have had a considerable influence in forming the Earl's decision.

During the course of the conflict, he met, at Linlithgow, that incomparable man, and excellent officer, Colonel Gardiner. This individual, whose character forms so fine a relief to the party-spirited and debased condition of the British army in the time of George the Second, was a native of Linlithgowshire, having been born at Carriden, in the year of the Revolution, 1688. His life commencing in that important era, had been one of events. He had first entered the Dutch service; then had served in Marlborough's army at Ramilies. Until this incident of his life, the young soldier, then only nineteen, had run a course of dissolute pleasure, and had obtained, from the frankness and gaiety of his disposition, the name of the *happy rake*. Being in the Forlorn hope, he was wounded, and left in a state hovering between life and death, on the field, and in state of partial insensibility, from which he was aroused at times to perfect consciousness.

The ball which had struck Gardiner, had entered his mouth; and without breaking a single tooth, or touching the forepart of his tongue, had passed through his neck, coming out above an inch and a half on the left side of the vertebræ. He was abandoned by Marlborough's troops, who, according to their custom, left the wounded to their fate, while they pursued their advantages against the French.

In this state, the first serious emotions of gratitude, the first convictions of a peculiar Providence suggested themselves to the mind of the young officer: and although they did not, for some years, produce an absolute amendment of life, they laid the foundation of his future conversion, and of that exemplary piety and purity which extorted admiration even in a dissolute age. After being present at every battle that Marlborough had fought in Flanders, Colonel Gardiner had signalized his courage in the Insurrection of 1715; and in 1745 he was again ordered to the north to meet the Jacobite forces near Edinburgh. [331]

It was during this, his last campaign, when broken by ill health and premature age, for this brave and good man despaired of the restoration of peace to his country, that he supped in company with Lord Kilmarnock, at Linlithgow. Colonel Gardiner's prognostications had long been most gloomy. "I have heard him say, " declared Dr. Doddridge, "many years before the Scottish Insurrection, that a few thousands might have a fair chance for marching from Edinburgh to London, uncontrolled, and throw the whole kingdom into an astonishment. " This opinion was derived from his knowledge of the defenceless state of the country, and the general prevailing disaffection. And the pious, but somewhat distrustful views of Gardiner led him to assign yet more solemn reasons for his anticipations of evil. "For my own part, though I fear nothing for myself, my apprehensions for the public are very gloomy, considering the deplorable prevalency of almost all kinds of wickedness among us; the natural consequences of the contempt of the Gospel. I am daily offering up my prayers to God for this sinful land of ours, over which His judgments seem to be gathering; and my strength is sometimes so exhausted with those strong cries and tears, which I pour out before God upon this occasion, that I am hardly able to stand when I arise from my knees. "[332]

Imbued with these convictions, Colonel Gardiner, when he was retreating at Linlithgow with the troops under his command, spoke unguardedly to Lord Kilmarnock of the prospects of the English army, and thus confirmed the wavering inclination of that ill-fated nobleman to follow Charles Edward. [333] The decisive step was not, it appears, taken until after the battle of Preston Pans, in which Colonel Gardiner, who had a mournful presentiment of the event of that engagement, fell, after a deportment truly worthy of the British soldier, and of the Christian. This brave officer, after having received two wounds, fought on, his feeble frame animated by the almost supernatural force of strong determination. As he headed a party of foot who had lost their leader, and cried out, "Fire on, my lads, fear nothing; " his right-arm was cut down by a Highlander who advanced with a scythe, fastened to a pole. He was dragged from his horse; and the work of butchery was completed by another Highlander, who struck him on the head with a broadsword: Gardiner had only power to say to his servant, "Take care of yourself. " The faithful creature hastened to an adjoining mill for a cart to convey his master to a place of safety. It was not until two hours had elapsed, that he was able to return. The mangled body, all stripped and plundered, was, even then, still breathing; and the agony of that gallant spirit was protracted until the next day, when he expired in the house of the minister of Tranent.

This digression, introducing as it does, one of the *real* heroes of this mournful period, may be pardoned.

According to the evidence on his trial, Lord Kilmarnock first joined the standard of Charles Edward on the "banks of the river which divides England from Scotland; "[334] but Maxwell of Kirkconnel mentions that the Earl marched from Edinburgh on the thirty-first of October, 1745, at the head of a little squadron of horse grenadiers, with whom were some Perthshire gentlemen, who, in the absence of their own commander, were placed under the conduct of Lord Kilmarnock. [335] After this decisive step, Lord Kilmarnock continued to follow Charles during the whole of that ill-fated campaign, which ended in the battle of Culloden. During the various events of that disastrous undertaking, his character, like that of many other commanders in the Chevalier's army, suffered from imputations of cruelty. That this vice was not accordant with his general disposition of mind, the minister who attended him on his death-bed sufficiently attests. "For myself, " declares Mr. Foster, "I must do this unhappy criminal the justice to own, that he *never* appeared, during the course of my attendance upon him, to be of any other than a soft, benevolent disposition. His behaviour was always mild and temperate. I could discern no resentment, no disturbance or agitation in him. "[336] So gentle a character is not the growth of a day; and if ever Lord Kilmarnock were betrayed into actions of violence, it must have been under circumstances of a peculiar nature.

Among other charges which were specified against him, was a participation in the blowing up of the church of St. Ninian's, in the retreat from Stirling. But when, in the retirement of his prison chamber, the unfortunate nobleman reviewed his conduct, and confessed the errors of his life, he fully and satisfactorily cleared himself from the heinous imputation implied in this work of destruction. When the army of Charles were retiring from Stirling he was confined to his bed ill of a fever. The first intimation that he had of the blowing up of the tower of St. Ninian's was the noise, of which he never could obtain a clear account. By the insurgents it was represented as accidental: "this can I certainly say, as to myself, that I had no knowledge before hand, nor any concurrence in a designed act of cruelty. " Such was Lord Kilmarnock's declaration to Mr. Foster.

Another instance of barbarity also laid to the charge of the Earl was, his alleged treatment of certain prisoners of war who were intrusted to his care in the church of Inverness. He was accused of stripping these unfortunate persons of their clothes. Upon this point he admitted that an order to deprive the prisoners of their garments for the use of the Highlanders was issued by Charles Edward: that the warrant for executing this order was sent to him. He did not, as he declared, enter the church in person, but committed the office of execution to an inferior officer. The prisoners, as might be expected, refused to submit to this indignity; upon which a second order was issued, and their clothes were taken from them. The well-timed remonstrance of Boyer, Marquis D'Eguilles, who had been sent by the court of France in the character of Ambassador to Charles Edward, arrested, however, the act of cruelty, which not even extreme necessity can excuse. This nobleman had arrived some time previously at Montrose, bringing in the ship in which he sailed, arms and a small sum of money, [337] and his influence, which was exerted in behalf of the captives, was happily considerable. He represented to the Earl of Kilmarnock, that the rules of war did not authorise the outrage which was contemplated. Lord Kilmarnock, convinced by his remarks, repaired to Charles Edward, leaving heaps of the clothes lying in the streets of Inverness, with sentinels standing to guard them. By the arguments which he addressed to the Prince, these garments were restored to their unfortunate owners; and a great stain on the memory both of Charles and of his adherent was thus partially effaced.

Of such a nature were those imputations which were charged upon Lord Kilmarnock; but they appear to have met with only a transient credence; whilst a general impression of his gentleness, and a prevailing regret for his fate endured as long as the memory of the dire contest, and of its tragical termination, dwelt in the recollection of those who witnessed those mournful times.

After the battle of Culloden, the prisoners were immediately set free. The Duke of Cumberland, as he entered Inverness, taking his road amid the carcasses of the dead strewed in the way, called for the keys of the prisons, and with his own hands released the captives there, and, clapping them on the shoulders as they came down stairs, exclaimed, "brother soldiers, you are free. "[338] Unfortunately his compassion was of a party nature, and was only aroused for his own adherents.

At Culloden, fatal to so many brave men, Lord Kilmarnock was spared only to taste much more deeply of the pangs of death than if he had met it in battle. His fate had, indeed, been anticipated by the superstitious; and it was considered a rash instance of hardihood in the unfortunate nobleman to resist an omen which, about a year before the rebellion had broken out, is said to have happened in his house.

One day, as the maid who attended usually upon Lady Kilmarnock was inspecting some linen in an upper room of Dean Castle, the door of the apartment suddenly opened of its own accord, and the view of a bloody head, resembling that of Lord Kilmarnock, was presented to the affrighted woman. As she gazed in horror, the head rolled near her. She endeavoured in vain to repel it with her foot. She became powerless, but she was still able to scream; her shrieks brought Lord Kilmarnock and his Countess to the chamber. The apparition had vanished; but she related succinctly the story "which, at that time, " says the historian who repeats it, [339] "Lord Kilmarnock too much ridiculed, though it could have been wished that he had been forewarned by the omen. Such was the superstition of the times, in which ignorance and credulity found such ready supporters. "

At Culloden, this ill-fated nobleman occupied a post not far from the Prince, in the rear of whom was a line of reserve, consisting of three columns, the first of which, on the left, was commanded by Lord Kilmarnock; the centre column by Lord Lewis Gordon and Glenbucket; and the right by the justly-celebrated Roy Stewart. In the opposite ranks, an ensign in the royal regiment, was his son, Lord Boyd. During the confusion of the fight, when half-blinded by the smoke, the unhappy Lord Kilmarnock, as if fated to fulfil the omen, mistook a party of English Dragoons for FitzJames's Horse, and was accordingly taken prisoner. He was led along the lines of the British infantry. The vaunted beauty of his countenance, and the matchless graces of which so much has been said, were now obliterated by the disorder of his person, and his humiliating position. His hat had been lost in the conflict, and his long hair fell about his face. The soldiers as he was led along stood in mute compassion at this sight. Among those who thus looked upon this unfortunate man was his son, Lord Boyd, who was constrained to witness, without attempting to alleviate, the distress of that moment. When the Earl passed the place where his son stood, the youth, unable to bear that his father should be thus exposed bareheaded to the storm which played upon the scene of carnage, stepped out of the ranks and taking his own hat from his head, placed it on that of his father. It was the work of an instant, and not a syllable escaped the lips of the agitated young man. [340]

Lord Kilmarnock was carried from the moor, which already, to use the words of an eyewitness among the Government troops, "was covered with blood; the men, what with killing the enemy, dabbling their feet in the blood, and splashing it about one another, looked like so many butchers. "[341] Never, did even their enemies declare, was a field of battle bestrewn with a finer, perhaps with a nobler race. "Every body allowed, " writes one of Cumberland's officers, "that men of a larger size, larger limbs, and better proportioned, could not be found. " The flower of their unhappy country;

hundreds of these had not yet been blessed with the repose of death, but were left to languish in agony until the next day, when they were butchered by the orders of Cumberland. One of them, John Alexander Fraser, in the Master of Lovat's regiment, was rescued by Lord Boyd from destruction. A soldier had struck him with the butt of his musket, intending, according to the orders given, to beat out his brains. The poor wretch, his nose and cheek-bone broken, and one of his eyes pierced, still breathed when this young nobleman passed him. He observed the poor creature, and ordered his servants to carry him to a neighbouring kiln, where, in time, his wounds were cured. "He lived, " observes Mr. Chambers, "many years afterwards, a dismal memorial of the cruelties of Culloden. "[342]

According to one account, Lord Kilmarnock owed his escape from the field of battle with his life to the brave and generous Lord Ancrum, who delivered him to the Duke of Cumberland; and the same narrative adds, that the Duke issued orders that no one should mention the Earl's imprisonment to his son, but considerately imparted the intelligence to the young man himself. It is only fair to mention this redeeming trait in a man who had so many awful, and almost inexpiable sins to answer for at the last day, when not our professions of kindness, but our acts of mercy or of wrong will be placed before a solemn and final account.

After his surrender at Culloden, the Earl of Kilmarnock was conveyed to London. That metropolis, in some of its most attractive features, was well known to him: he had frequently resided there for several months during the year, and had associated with the friends of government who were near the court. He was now to view it under a very different aspect; and during the period which elapsed between his surrender and his trial, he had ample time to weigh the respective value of that society which had formerly so much delighted him, and in which, it is said he "had affected to talk freely of religion; " and of those great truths which were now his only source of support.

Whatever may have been his early errors, the remaining days of Lord Kilmarnock were characterized by gentleness to those who were placed in authority over him; forbearance to those who slandered him, and submission to God. Unable to conquer a natural intense love of life, he assumed no pretended intrepidity: [343] yet manifested a still greater concern for his character, than for his fate. Society in general, as well as the annalists of the times, mourned for him, and with him; and many who beheld his doom, would have sacrificed much of their own personal safety to avert the close of that tragic scene. But these were not times when the generous might venture to interfere with security. [344]

Two noblemen, differing greatly in character from Lord Kilmarnock, shared his imprisonment: Arthur, sixth Earl of Balmerinoch, or, as it is usually spelled Balmerino, (pronounced Balmérino), and George, Earl of Cromartie.

Of these individuals, Lord Balmerino, although an uncultured soldier, has excited by far the greatest interest. He was descended, like most of his associates from an ancient family. It was of German origin, [345] first known in Scotland in the reign of Robert Bruce, to whose sister, a German Knight, sirnamed Elphingston, or Elphinstone, was married. Such was the esteem in which Robert Bruce held his foreign brother-in-law, that he gave him lands in Midlothian, which still bear the name of Elphinstone. [346] Hence was he called Elphinstone of that Ilk—a mode of expression employed in Scotland to prevent the repetition of the same name. In process of time certain estates which a descendant of the German Knight acquired at Arthbeg, in Stirlingshire, were also endowed with that surname; and, during several centuries, the martial and hardy race to whom those lands belonged continued in the same sphere, that of private gentlemen, chiefs of the House of Elphinstone. They were remarkable, in successive generations, for that bold and manly character which eventually distinguished their ill-fated descendant, Arthur Balmerino, and which, in time, extorted applause from the most prejudiced politicians of the opposite party. Alexander Elphinstone, in the reign of David the Second, might have emulated the supposed deeds of Guy Earl of Warwick; he rivalled him in gigantic figure, in immense strength, and knightly prowess. His disposition was not only martial, but chivalric; for, conscious of extraordinary power, "he was more able, " says a writer of the last century, "to overlook an affront, than men less capable of resenting it. " His son, inferior in bodily strength, equalled him in military exploits, which distinguished indeed a succession of the Elphinstones of that Ilk. [347] At Flodden, John Elphinstone, who was created a Lord of Parliament by James the Fourth, was killed by the side of his royal master, and being not unlike to that monarch in face and figure, his body was carried to Berwick by the English, who mistook it for that of the King. [348] In the reign of James the Sixth, James, the second son of the third Lord Elphinstone, was created a

Baron by the name and title of Lord Balmerino. He rose to high honours in the State; but the first disgrace that befell the family occurred in this reign. This was the marriage of John, the second Lord Balmerino, to Jane Ker, sister of the infamous Ker, Earl of Somerset, and favourite of James the Sixth, who, for his sake, denounced a curse on his posterity, which seems, says the writer before quoted, "to have followed them and the nation ever since. "

Like most of the noble families in Scotland, the house of Balmerino became impoverished during the civil wars; and when the father of Arthur Elphinstone succeeded to his title, he found his estates wofully diminished. He was, however, one of those men who were capable, by ability and prudence, of redeeming the fortunes of his family. Circumstances were, indeed, adverse to the prosperity of any whose loyalty to the Stuarts was suspected. Lord Balmerino was prudent, but he was sincere. He was "a man of excellent parts, improved by reading, being, perhaps, one of the very best lawyers in the kingdom, and very expert in the Scottish constitution; he reasoned much and pertinently in Parliament, and testifying, on all occasions, an unshaken loyalty to his Prince, and zealous affection to his country, he gained the esteem and love of all good men. "

Such was the father, of whom this noble character was drawn, to whom Arthur, Lord Balmerino, owed his being. Such was the man whom it would have been the wiser policy of the British Ministry to have conciliated, on the accession of George the First, but whose son they drove into an act of imprudence by their distrust and injustice.

The first wife of John, fourth Lord Balmerino, was the daughter of Hugh, Earl of Eglintoun, and, consequently, she was connected with some of the most strenuous supporters of the Stuart cause in the kingdom of Scotland. By her he had two sons, Hugh, who was killed in 1708, at the siege of Lisle, and James, who was educated to the profession of the law. Upon the death of this lady, Lord Balmerino married Anne, daughter of Ross, the last Archbishop of St. Andrews, and by her had two sons: Arthur, who became eventually Lord Balmerino, and Alexander, who died in 1733, unmarried; and a daughter, Anne, who died also unmarried. The subject of this memoir may, therefore, be deemed the last of the House of Balmerino. [349]

Arthur Elphinstone was born in the year 1688. He had, until late in life, no expectation of succeeding to the title of his father after the death of Hugh, there being still an elder brother, James. The characteristics of all this branch of the Elphinstone family appear almost invariably to have been those of honour and justice, and James resembled his father in the integrity of his principles. The following character is drawn of him by a contemporary writer: "He was rather a solid pleader than a refined orator; but he understood the law so well, and preserved the chastity of his character so tenderly, by avoiding being concerned in any scandalous actions, that he was listened to with great attention by the bench, at a time when it was filled by the most eminent lawyers that ever appeared in Scotland. "

The abilities of this able and conscientious man soon raised him to the bench, where he discharged his duties with that high and nice sense of integrity which can only be described by the word honour. He never mixed party-spirit with his judgments: he lent himself to no ministerial purposes. The dignity of the judge was preserved in his manly and courageous character: and such was his application to business, that his court was thronged with practitioners when those of other judges were nearly deserted.

Arthur, his younger brother, possessed not his application, but displayed much, nevertheless, of the natural ability of his family. "He was not much acquainted with books; and though he was rich in repartee, yet he never affected to reason. " Such is the remark of a contemporary writer. Yet who might not envy the clear, undisturbed intellect which showed him, in a moment of peculiar temptation, the value of plain dealing, and the inestimable price of a good conscience?

Some members of a family seem fated to suffer for the others. Arthur Elphinstone was educated in the principles which brought him to the scaffold: they were those of his father and brother, who were both fortunate enough to preserve them in their own breasts, and yet not to encounter trouble on that account. And, during the reign of Queen Anne the family appear to have been deemed so well affected, as to procure them promotion, not only in civil but military service. When very young, Arthur Elphinstone obtained the command of a company of foot in Lord Shannon's regiment, on the accession of George the First. His real opinions were, however, manifested by his resignation of his commission; and by his joining the standard of Lord Mar, under whom he commanded a company, and served in the battle of Sherriff Muir. By throwing up his commission, he escaped being punished as a deserter, and was allowed to retire to the Continent. According to some accounts, he went first to Denmark; by others it is said, that he entered at once into the French service. He remained, at all events, twenty years in exile from his family; but in 1733, an event occurred, which greatly increased the natural desire which his father, declining in strength, had long cherished of again beholding his son. Alexander Elphinstone, the younger brother of Arthur, died at Leith, two years before the Insurrection broke out. This young man had had the misfortune in 1730, to fight a duel, shortly after which his adversary, Lieutenant Swift, had died of his wounds. The combat took place on the Links of Leith; the affair was notorious, and Alexander had been threatened with a prosecution, which was not, however, put into execution.

This painful circumstance, coupled with Alexander Elphinstone's death, may have naturally added to the wish which Lord Balmerino entertained, to rescue his exiled son from the sentence of outlawry under which he stood, and to restore him again to his home. Probably the desire of perpetuating honours which had been gained by legitimate exertions, may have been contemplated by the aged nobleman when he revolved in his mind how he could compass the safe return of his younger, and surviving son, to Scotland. James, the heir to the title, great as was the lustre which his abilities and integrity shed upon it, was not likely to perpetuate more honours, having no children by his wife Elizabeth Carnegie, daughter of David, fourth Earl of Northesk.

It is one of the innumerable instances of human short-sightedness, that the very recall of Arthur Elphinstone to Scotland was the cause of the extinction of family honours, and of that line in which they rested. According to some accounts, he remained abroad until the general Act of Indemnity, from which he was not excepted, took effect: [350] but by others it is stated, that his father, having made a strong application to Government, obtained a free pardon for his son. If such were the case, there seems a degree of ingratitude in again joining the enemies of Government, which one can scarcely reconcile with the generous character of this brave man.

He was in Switzerland when he received a summons to return to his native country. His conduct upon the arrival of this intelligence was honest and candid towards him, to whom, according to his notions, he owed allegiance. He wrote to the Chevalier (St. George) and laid open the circumstances of the case before him; stating that he should not accept the proffered pardon without his permission. James answered this explanation with his own hand; and not only gave Arthur Elphinstone permission to return to Scotland, but informed him that he had ordered his banker at Paris to pay his travelling expenses. Thus authorized, Arthur returned home, welcomed by his aged father with a satisfaction which happily was not destined to be alloyed by any adverse circumstances during the lifetime of the venerable nobleman.

Thus was this ill-fated man restored to that land which probably, although long severed from its glens and mountains, he had not ceased to love. He was now of middle age, being in his forty-fifth year; but his disposition, in spite of his long residence among foreigners, was still thoroughly Scotch. He was as undaunted by danger as any of his valiant ancestors had been, consequently he had no need to have recourse to guile; in short, falsehood would have been impossible to that frank nature. He was blunt in speech, but endowed with the kindest heart that ever throbbed in the dungeons of that grim fortress in which his manly career was closed. He had not, however, the prudence which is characteristic of his countrymen: and which, once well understood, is as distinct from selfishness and craft as their martial vehemence has generally been from cruelty. A service in foreign campaigns had not lessened his ideas of honour; which were perhaps more truly cherished among military men on the Continent, than at that period in England. Few British troops, for example, ever proved themselves more worthy of the name of soldiers than the Hessians who served in Scotland in 1745. To the fine and soldierly attributes of Lord Balmerino, to an intrepidity almost amounting to indifference, to a warm and generous heart, were united that ready and careless humour which accord so well with the loftier qualities of the mind, and certainly rather enhance, than detract from the charm of graver attributes of character.

In appearance, Lord Balmerino was strongly contrasted with the fellow-sufferer with whom his name is indelibly associated. "His person, " writes a contemporary, "was very plain, his shape clumsy, but his make strong: and he had no marks of the polite gentleman about him. He was illiterate in respect of his birth; but rather from a total want of application to letters, than want of ability. "[351] His manners are said to have been natural, if not courtly; his countenance only inferior in its ungainliness to that of Lovat, but, expressing, we may suppose, a very different temper of mind, harsh as were its features, it captivated, as well as that of the handsome Kilmarnock, female regard. [352]

According to some statements, Lord Balmerino married in 1711, before the first Insurrection; [353] but no distinct allusion to a connection of so early a period is to be found in the authenticated narratives of his life. It was not, it seems evident, until after his return from Switzerland, that he married Margaret, daughter of Captain Chalmers—"the pretty Peggy, " who was at once his solace and his sorrow when in the Tower of London. In 1736, the father, whom he had returned to cheer in his decline, died at his house in Leith, and was buried at the family seat at Restalrig in Leith. His son James, succeeded to the title. [354]

When the intelligence arrived, that Charles Edward had landed in Scotland, Arthur Elphinstone hastened to the standard of the Prince. On the thirty-first of October, 1745, he marched from Edinburgh, on the expedition to England, having the command of a troop of horse, not complete, in number about forty. [355] His military talents were well known, for he had distinguished himself in several campaigns in Flanders. [356] But, as he took into the field only his menial servants, no very important posts were entrusted to him; and his career appears not to have been signalized by any remarkable military exploits. In short, it may be truly said of him as of Dr. Donne by Izaak Walton, that "nothing in his life became him like the leaving it. "

After joining the insurgent army, Lord Balmerino engaged in all the various movements of that enterprise. After the siege of Carlisle he entered that city at the head of his troop, with pipes playing, and colours flying, having been at twelve miles' distance when the town was taken; he then proceeded in the fatal expedition to Derby, and returned a second time to Carlisle, preceding in his march the main body of the army towards Scotland. He was present at the battle of Falkirk, but did not engage in it: some of the cavalry having been kept as a *corps de reserve* in that engagement. His participation in that day's victory was, however, afterwards imputed to him as an act of rebellion, although he was merely drawn up in a field near the field of battle, in company with Lord Kilmarnock and Lord Pitsligo. The body which he commanded, went by the name of Arthur Elphinstone's Life Guards. [357]

A few weeks before the battle of Culloden, the elder brother of Arthur Elphinstone, James Lord Balmerino, died, leaving the title which he had enjoyed for so short a period, to the brother, who was then engaged in so perilous a course. This accession of honour brought with it little increase of fortune, but rather the responsibility of succeeding to encumbered estates. Of these most had, indeed, passed into other families. To the first Lord Balmerino charters of numerous lands and baronies had been given; Barntoun, Barrie, Balumby, Innerpeffer, Balgregie, Balmerino, Dingwall, &c., were among his possessions. In 1605, the barony of Restalrig, in South Leith, was sold to Lord Balmerino by the noted and profligate Robert Logan, Baron of Restalrig, to whose family that now valuable property, including the grounds lying near the river, had belonged, until the days of the Queen Regent, Mary. This estate, on which Lord Balmerino's father resided, appears to have been almost the only vestige of the former opulence of this branch of the Elphinstone family. [358] His embarrassed circumstances are deemed by some writers to have had a considerable share in deciding Lord Balmerino to join in a contest in which he had so little to lose; but it appeared, in the hour of trial, that his principles of allegiance to the Stuarts had been unaltered since the days of his youth, and that they were alone sufficient to account for the part which he adopted. At the battle of Culloden Lord Balmerino was made prisoner by the Grants, to whom, as one of the witnesses on his trial affirmed, he surrendered himself. He was conveyed to Castle Grant, and from thence to London, to the same dreary fortress in which Lord Kilmarnock was likewise immured. The fate of these two unfortunate men, hitherto but little dependant on each other, was henceforth associated, until the existence of both was closed on the scaffold.

George, the third Earl of Cromartie, was the only one of their fellow-prisoners who was arraigned and tried with Kilmarnock and Balmerino. He had taken even a more decided part in the insurrection than Balmerino, having raised four hundred of his clan, who were with him in the battle of Falkirk. His son, the young Lord Macleod, was also in the Jacobite army, and both father and son were surprised at Dunrobin, by a party of the Earl of Sutherland's militia, on the fifteenth of April, and taken prisoners. Lord Cromartie had, as well as Lords Kilmarnock and Balmerino, strong ties to life, strong claims upon his reason to have withheld him from a hazardous participation in a cause of peril. He had been married more than twenty years to Isabel, daughter of Sir William Gordon, and had by her a numerous family. For this nobleman, a powerful interest was afterwards successfully exerted.

These three noblemen were brought to London early in June. They were shortly afterwards followed by about eight hundred companions in misfortune. Of these, who arrived in the Thames on the twenty-first of June, about two hundred were left at Tilbury Fort; while six hundred were deposited in the various prisons of the metropolis. From henceforth scenes of distress, and even of horror, were daily presented to the prisoners. The Marquis of Tullibardine expired soon after his arrival at the Tower; Lord Macleod, with happier fate, rejoined his father; Mr. Murray of Broughton, who was treated with a distinction, at that time, unexplicable, was also lodged in the same fortress. Those who were led to expect the severest measures, might envy the calm departure of the good old Marquis of Tullibardine; but all hearts bled when the gallant Colonel Townley, a Roman Catholic gentleman of distinction, was dragged on a sledge, along with other prisoners, to Kennington, his arms pinioned; insulted by a brutal multitude, and there hanged. The horrid barbarities of this sentence being fulfilled on his body, which was still breathing, the hangman preparing to take out the heart and bowels, struck it several times on the chest, before life (and perhaps consciousness) was wholly extinct.

Day after day, the awful tragedies were repeated, exceeding any similar displays of power since the days of the Tudors. Each of these *martyrs*, as the voice of their own party pronounced them, in their last moments declared, that "they died in a just cause—that they did not repent of what they had done—that they doubted not their deaths would be avenged. " When, after nine executions had taken place in one morning, the heart of the last sufferer was thrown into the fire, a savage shout from the infuriated multitude followed the words "God save King George! " The unfortunate man who had just perished was a young gentleman, named Dawson, a graduate of St. John's College, Cambridge. He had for some time been engaged to a young lady of good family, and great interest had been made to procure his pardon. The lovers were sanguine in their expectations, and the day of his release was to have been that of their marriage.

When all hope was at an end, the young lady, not deterred by the remonstrances of her kindred, resolved upon following Mr. Dawson to the place of execution. Her intention was at length acceded to: she drove in a hackney-coach after the sledges, accompanied by a relative, and by one female friend. As the shout of brutal joy succeeded the silence of the solemn scene, the words "My love, —I follow thee, —I follow thee! " burst from the lips of the broken-hearted girl. She fell on the neck of her companion, and, whilst she uttered these words, "Sweet Jesus! —receive our souls together! " expired. [359] Recitals of these domestic tragedies, proofs of the unrelenting spirit of government, tended to break the firmness of some of those who survived.

Lord Cromartie sank into dejection; Kilmarnock's fine and gentle nature was gradually purified for heaven. Balmerino rose to heroism.

The prisons were crowded with captives; the noblemen alone were committed to the Tower; even two of the Scottish chiefs were sent to Newgate; the officers were committed to the new gaol, Southwark; the common men to the Marshalsea. Meantime, strong and prompt measures were determined upon by Government.

Bills of indictment for high treason were found against Lord Kilmarnock, the Earl of Cromartie, and the Lord Balmerino, by the grand jury of the county of Surrey: a writ of certiorari was issued for removing the indictments into the House of Peers, on the twenty-sixth of June, and their trial was appointed to take place on the twenty-eighth of July following. Westminster Hall was accordingly prepared for the trials, and a high steward appointed in the person of the justly celebrated Lord Hardwicke.

On the petition of Lord Kilmarnock, Mr. George Ross was engaged as his solicitor, with permission to have free access to him at all times. On the appointed day the trials commenced. Westminster Hall was fitted up with unprecedented magnificence; and tickets were issued by the Lord Chamberlain to the Peers, to give access to their friends. At eight o'clock in the morning, the Judges in their robes, with the Garter-King-at-Arms, the Usher of the Black Rod, and the Serjeant-at-Arms waited on the Lord High Steward at his house in Ormond Street: Garter in his coat of the king's arms, and Black Rod, having the white staff attended them. After a short interval the procession to Westminster Hall began: Lord Hardwicke, designated during the term of the trial as "his Grace, " came forth to his coach, his train borne, and followed by the chief judges and judges. His coach was preceded by his Grace's twenty gentlemen, uncovered, in five coaches two and two; by the Serjeant-at-Arms, and the Black

Rod. The heralds occupied the back seats of his Grace's coach; the judges in their coaches followed. As the procession entered the Palace-yard, the soldiers rested their muskets and the drums beat, as to the Royal Family.

Meantime, the Peers in their robes were assembled; the Lord High Steward having passed to the House, through the Painted Chamber, prayers were read; and the peers were called over by Garter-King-at-Arms. The Lord Steward, followed first by his four gentlemen attendants, two and two; and afterwards by the clerks of the House of Lords, and the clerks of the Crown; by the Peers, and the Peers' sons, proceeded to Westminster Hall, the Lord Steward being alone uncovered, and his train borne by a page.

Proclamation for silence having been made by the Lord Steward's serjeant-at-arms, the commission was read, the lords standing up, uncovered. Then his Grace, making obeisance to the lords, reseated himself; and Garter, and the Black Rod, with their reverences, jointly presented the white staff, on their knees, to his Grace. Thus fully invested with his office, the Lord Steward took his staff in his hand and descended from the woolsack to a chair prepared for him on an ascent before the throne.

The three lords had been brought during this time from the Tower. The Earl of Kilmarnock was conveyed in Lord Cornwallis's coach, attended by General Williamson, Deputy Governor of the Tower; the Earl of Cromartie, in General Williamson's coach, attended by Captain Marshal; and Lord Balmerino in the third coach, attended by Mr. Fowler, Gentleman Gaoler, who had the axe covered by his side. A strong body of soldiers escorted these carriages.

The three lords being conducted into the Hall, proclamation was made by the Serjeant-at-Arms that the Lieutenant of the Tower should bring his prisoners to the bar, the proclamation being made in this form: —"Oyez, oyez, oyez, Lieutenant of the Tower of London, bring forward your prisoners, William Earl of Kilmarnock, George Earl of Cromartie, and Arthur Lord Balmerino, together with the copies of their respective commitments, pursuant to the order of the House of Lords. "

Then the lords were led to the bar of the House by the Lieutenant-Governor, the axe being carried before them with its edge turned from them. The prisoners, when they approached the bar, made three reverences, and fell upon their knees. Then said the Lord High Steward your "lordships may arise; " upon which the three lords arose and bowed to his Grace the High Steward, and to the House, which compliment was returned by the Lord High Steward, and by the Peers.

Thus began the trial; "the greatest, and the most melancholy scene, " wrote Horace Walpole to Sir Horace Mann, "that I ever saw. As it was the most interesting sight, it was the most solemn and fine; a coronation is but a puppet show, and all the splendour of it idle; but this sight at once feasted one's eyes, and engaged one's passions; "—a signal avowal for one whom a long continuance in the world's business, and, perhaps, worse, its pleasures, had hardened. A hundred and thirty-nine lords were present, making a noble sight on their benches, and assisting at a ceremony which is said to have been conducted with the most awful solemnity and decency throughout, with one or two exceptions. [360]

The Lord Chancellor Hardwicke, who presided on this occasion, has been justly deemed one of the brightest ornaments of the woolsack. The son of an attorney at Dover, as Philip Yorke, he had risen to the highest offices of the law, by his immense acquirements, and his incomparable powers of illustration and arrangement. By his marriage with a niece of the celebrated Lord Somers, he strengthened his political interest, which, however, it required few adventitious circumstances to secure. Three great men have expressed their admiration of Lord Hardwicke almost in similar terms: Lord Mansfield, Burke, and Wilkes. "When his lordship pronounced his decrees, wisdom herself might be supposed to speak. "[361] In manner, he was usually considered to be dignified, impressive, and unruffled; and his intentions were allowed to be as pure and elevated, as his views were patriotic.

On this eventful day, since we cannot reject the testimony of an eye-witness of discernment, we must believe that party spirit, which had usually so little influence over his sense of justice, swayed the prepossessions of Lord Hardwicke. At all events, it affected his treatment of the unhappy men to whom he displayed a petulance wholly derogatory to his character as a judge, and discreditable to his feelings as a man. "Instead of keeping up the humane dignity of the law of England, whose character is to point out any favour to the criminal, he crossed them, and almost scolded at any offer they made towards defence. " Such is the remark of Horace Walpole. [362]

Comely in person, and possessing a fine voice, Lord Hardwicke had every opportunity, on this occasion, of a graceful display of dignity and courtesy; yet his deportment, usually so calm and lofty, was obsequious, "curiously searching for occasion to bow to the minister, and, consequently, applying to the other ministers, in a manner, for their orders; —not even ready at the ceremonial. " Notwithstanding, Lord Hardwicke, on his death-bed, could with confidence declare "that he had never wronged any man. " The unhappy Jacobites seem, indeed, to have been considered exceptions to all the common rules of clemency. None of the Royal Family were present at the trial, from a proper regard for the feelings of the prisoners, and also, perhaps, from a nice sense of the peculiarity of their own condition.

After the warrants to the Lieutenant of the Tower were read, the Lord High Steward addressed the prisoners, telling them that although their crimes were of the most heinous nature, they were still open to such defences as circumstances, and the rules of law and justice would allow. The indictments for high treason were then read: to these, Lords Kilmarnock and Cromartie pleaded guilty; but when the question was put to Lord Balmerino, he demanded boldly, but respectfully to be heard, objecting to two clauses in the indictment, in which he was styled "Arthur Lord Balmerino, of the town of Carlisle, " and also charging him with being at the taking of Carlisle, when he could prove "that he was not within twelve miles of it. " Not insisting upon these objections, and the question being again put to him, he then pleaded, 'not guilty. ' Lord Kilmarnock and Lord Cromartie were removed from the bar, and the trial of Balmerino began. It was prefaced by addresses from Sir Richard Loyd, king's counsel, and from Mr. Serjeant Skinner, who made, what was justly considered by H. Walpole, "the most absurd speech imaginable, " calling "Rebellion, surely the sin of witchcraft, " and applying to the Duke of Cumberland the unfortunate appellation of "Scipio. "[363] The Attorney General followed, and witnesses were afterwards examined, who fully proved, though accused by Balmerino of some inconsistencies, his acts of adherence to the Chevalier; his being present in towns where James Stuart was proclaimed King; his wearing the regimentals of Prince Charles's body guards; his marching into Carlisle at the head of his troops, with a white cockade in his cap; his presence at the battle of Falkirk, in a field with Lords Kilmarnock and Pitsligo, who were at the head of a corps of reserve. Six witnesses were examined, but there was no cross-examination, except such as Balmerino himself attempted. The witnesses were chiefly men who had served in the same cause for which the brave Balmerino was soon to suffer. After they had delivered their testimony, the "old hero, " as he was well styled, shook hands cordially with them. In one or two instances, as far as can be judged by the answers, the evidence seems to have been given with reluctance. Lord Balmerino being asked if he had any thing to offer in his defence, he observed that none of the witnesses had agreed upon the same day as that which was named in the indictment for being at Carlisle; and objected to the indictment, that he was not at the taking of Carlisle as therein specified. His objections were taken into consideration; the Lords retired to their chamber, and there consulted the judges whether it be necessary that an overt act of high treason should be proved to have been committed on the particular day named in the indictment.

The answer being in the negative, every hope of acquittal was annihilated for Balmerino. He gave up every further defence, and apologised with his usual blunt courtesy for giving their Lordships so much trouble: he said that his objections had been the result of advice given by Mr. Ross, his solicitor, who had laid the case before counsel. The question was then put by the Lord High Steward, standing up, uncovered, to the Lords, beginning with the youngest peer, Lord Herbert of Cherbury; "whether Arthur Lord Balmerino were guilty of high treason, or not guilty? " An unanimous reply was uttered by all those who were present; "guilty upon my honour. " Lord Balmerino, who had retired while the question was put, was then brought back to the bar to hear the decision of the Lords. It was received with the intrepidity which had, all throughout the trial, characterised the soldier and the man. During the intervals of form, his natural playfulness and humour appeared, and the kindness of his disposition was manifested. A little boy being in the course of the trial near him, but not tall enough to see, he took him up, made room for the child, and placed him near himself. The axe inspired him with no associations of fear. He played upon it, while talking, with his fingers, and some one coming up to listen to what he was saying, he held it up like a fan between his face and that of the gentleman-gaoler, to the great amusement of all beholders. And this carelessness of the emblem of death was but a prelude to the calmness with which he met his fate. "All he troubled himself about, " as a writer of the time observed, "was to end as he begun, and to let his sun set with as *full* and *fair* a light as it was possible. "[364] During the time that the Lords were withdrawn, the Solicitor-General Murray, and brother of Murray of Broughton, addressed Balmerino, asking him "how he could give the Lords so much trouble, " when he had been told by his solicitor that the plea could be of no use to him? The defection and perfidy of Murray of Broughton were now generally known; and the officious insolence of his inquiry was both revolting and indiscreet. Balmerino asked who this person was, and being told, exclaimed, "Oh! Mr. Murray, I am extremely glad to see you. I have been with several of your relations, the poor lady, your mother, was of great use to us at Perth. "[365] An admirable and well-merited rebuke. He afterwards declared humorously that one of his reasons for not pleading guilty was, "that so many fine ladies might not be disappointed of their show. "

Besides the interest which at such a moment the grave dignity of Kilmarnock, contrasted with the lofty indifference of Balmerino, might excite, there was some diversion among the Peers, owing to the eccentricity of several of their body. Of these, one, Lord Windsor, affectedly said when asked for his vote, "I am sorry I must say, *guilty upon my honour*. " Another nobleman, Lord Stamford, refused to answer to the name of Henry, having been christened Harry. "What a great way of thinking, " remarks Horace Walpole, "on such an occasion. " Lord Foley withdrew, as being a well-wisher to poor Balmerino; Lord Stair on the plea of kindred—"uncle, " as Horace Walpole sneeringly remarks, to his great-grandfather; and the Earl of Moray on account of his relationship to Balmerino, his mother, Jane Elphinstone, being sister to that nobleman. [366]

But the greatest source of amusement to all who were present was the celebrated Audrey, or to speak in more polite phrase, Ethelreda, Lady Townshend, the wife of Charles, third Viscount Townshend, and the mother of the celebrated wit, Charles Townshend. Lady Townshend was renowned for her epigrams, to which, perhaps, in this case, her being separated from her husband gave additional point. When she heard her husband vote, "*guilty upon my honour*, " she remarked, "I always knew *my* Lord was *guilty*, but I never knew that he would own it upon his *honour*. " Her sarcastic humour was often exhibited at the expense of friend or foe. When some one related that Whitfield had recanted, "No, madam, " she replied, "he has only *canted*. " And when Lord Bath ventured to complain to this audacious leader of fashion, that he had a pain in his side, she cried out, "Oh! that cannot be, you have *no side*. "

A touch of feminine feeling softened the harshness of the professed wit, always a dangerous, and scarcely ever a pleasing character in woman. As Lady Townshend gazed on the prisoners at the bar, and saw the elegant and melancholy aspect of Lord Kilmarnock, the heart that was not wholly seared by a worldly career is said to have been deeply and seriously touched by the graces of that incomparable person, and the mournful dignity of his manner. Perhaps, opposition to her husband, whose grandfather was Minister to George the First, and whose mother was a Walpole, gave the additional luxury of partisanship; that passion which lasted even some weeks after the scene was closed; and when the fashionable world were left to enjoy, undisturbed by any fears of any future rebellion, all the dangerous attractions of the dissolute Court.

The first day's proceedings being at an end, the prisoners were remanded to the Tower. On the following morning the proceedings were resumed, and the Lords having assembled in the Painted Chamber, took their places in Westminster Hall. The three lords were then again brought to the bar, again kneeled down, again were bidden to arise. The Attorney-General having prayed for judgment upon the prisoners, they were desired by the Lord High Steward to say "why judgment of death should not be passed against them according to law. "

The reply of Lord Kilmarnock is described as having been a "very fine speech, delivered in a very fine voice; " his behaviour during the whole of the trial, a "most just mixture between dignity and submission. " Such is the avowal of one who could not be supposed very favourable to the party; but whose better feelings were, for once, called into play during this remarkable scene. [367]

The address of Lord Kilmarnock, however beautiful and touching in expression, will not, however, satisfy those who look for consistency in the most solemn moments of this chequered state of trial; but in perusing the summary of it, let it be remembered that he was a father; the father of those who had already suffered deeply for his adherence to Charles Edward; that he was the husband of a lady who, whatever may have been their differences, was at that awful hour still fondly beloved; that he dreaded penury for his children, an apprehension which those who remembered the fate of the Jacobites of 1715 might well recall; a dread, aggravated by his rank; a dread, the bitterness of which is indescribable; the temptations it offers unspeakably great. These considerations, far stronger than the fear of death, actuated Lord Kilmarnock. He arose, and a deep silence was procured, whilst he offered no justification of his conduct, "which had been, " he said, "of too heinous a nature to be vindicated, and which any endeavour to excuse would rather aggravate than diminish. " He declared himself ready to submit to the sentence which he was conscious that he had deserved. "Covered with confusion and grief, I throw myself at his Majesty's feet. "

He then appealed to the uniform honour of his life, previous to the insurrection, in evidence of his principles. "My sphere of action, indeed, was narrow; but as much as I could do in that sphere, it is well known, I have always exerted myself to the utmost in every part of his Majesty's service I had an opportunity to act in, from my first appearance in the world, to the time I was drawn into the crime, for which I now appeal before your Lordships. "

He referred to his conduct during the civil contest; to his endeavours to avert needless injury to his opponents; to his care of the prisoners, a plea which he yet allowed to be no atonement for the "blood he had been accessary to the spilling of. Neither, " he said, "do I plead it as such, as at all in defence of my crime. "

"I have a son, my lords, " he proceeded, "who has the honour to carry his Majesty's commission; whose behaviour, I believe, will sufficiently evince, that he has been educated in the firmest revolution principles, and brought up with the warmest attachment to his Majesty's interests, and the highest zeal for his most sacred person.

"It was my chief care to instruct him in these principles from his earliest youth, and to confirm him, as he grew up, in the justice and necessity of them to the good and welfare of the nation. And, I thank God, I have succeeded; —for his father's example did not shake his loyalty; the ties of nature yielded to those of duty; he adhered to the principles of his family, and nobly exposed his life at the battle of Culloden, in defence of his King and the liberties of Great Britain, in which I, his unfortunate father, was in arms to destroy. "

Lord Kilmarnock next alluded to the services of his father in 1715, when his zeal and activity in the service of Government had caused his death: "I had then, " he added, "the honour to serve under him. "

Lord Kilmarnock proceeded to explain his own circumstances at the time of the insurrection: he declared that he was not one of those dangerous persons who could raise a number of men when they will, and command them on any enterprise they will: "my interests,

" he said, "lie on the south side of the Forth, in the well inhabited, and well affected counties of Kilmarnock and Falkirk, in the shires of Ayr and Stirling. " His influence he declared to be very small.

This portion of his appeal was ill-advised; for it seems to have been the policy of Government to have selected as objects of royal mercy those who had most in their power, not the feeble and impoverished members of the Jacobite party. It has been shown what favour would have been manifested to the chief of the powerful clan Cameron, had he deigned to receive it: and the event proved, that not the decayed branches, but the vigorous shoots were spared. Lord Cromartie, who had taken a far more signal part in the insurrection than either Kilmarnock or Balmerino, and whose resources were considerable, was eventually pardoned, probably with the hope of conciliating a numerous clan.

After appealing to his surrender in extenuation of his sentence, and beseeching the intercession of the Lords with his Majesty, Lord Kilmarnock concluded—"It is by Britons only that I pray to be recommended to a British monarch. But if justice allow not of mercy, my lords, I will lay down my life with patience and resignation; my last breath shall be employed in the most fervent prayers for the preservation and prosperity of his Majesty, and to beg his forgiveness, and the forgiveness of my country. " He concluded, amid the tears and commiseration of a great majority of those who heard his address.

The Earl of Cromartie was then called upon to speak in arrest of judgment. His defence is said to have been a masterly piece of eloquence. It ended with a pathetic appeal, which fell powerless on those who heard him. [368]

"But, after all, if my safety shall be found inconsistent with that of the public, and nothing but my blood be thought necessary to atone for my unhappy crimes; if the sacrifice of my life, my fortune, and family, are judged indispensable for stopping the loud demands of public justice; if, notwithstanding all the allegations that can be urged in my favour, the bitter cup is not to pass from me, not mine, but thy will, O God, be done. "[369]

Balmerino then arose to answer the accustomed question. He produced a paper, which was read for him at the bar, by the clerk of the court. It was a plea which had been sent by the House of Lords that morning to the prisoners, and which, it was hoped, would save all of these unfortunate men. It contained an objection to the indictments, stating that the act for regulating the trials of rebels, and empowering his Majesty to remove such as are taken in arms from one county to another, where they might be tried by the common courts of peers, did not take effect till after the facts, implying treason, had been committed by the prisoners. [370] The two Earls had not made use of this plea, but Lord Balmerino availed himself of it, and demanded counsel on it. Upon the treatment which he then encountered, the following remark is made by one who viewed the scene, and whose commiseration for the Jacobites forms one of the few amiable traits of his character. [371]

"The High Steward, " relates Horace Walpole, "almost in a passion, told him, that when he had been offered counsel, he did not accept it; —but do think on the ridicule of sending them the plea, and then denying them counsel on it. "[372] A discussion among the Lords then took place; and the Duke of Newcastle, who, as the same writer truly remarks, "never lost an opportunity of being absurd, " took it up as a ministerial point "in defence of his creature, the Chancellor. " Lord Granville, however, moved, according to order, to return to the Chamber of Parliament, where the Duke of Bedford and many others spoke warmly for their "having counsel, " and that privilege was granted. "I said *their*, " observes Walpole, "because the plea would have saved them all, and affected nine rebels who had been hanged that very morning. "

The Lords having returned to the Hall, and the prisoners being again called to the bar, Lord Balmerino was desired to choose his counsel. He named Mr. Forester, and Mr. Wilbraham, the latter being a very able lawyer in the House of Commons. Lord Hardwicke is said to have remarked privately, that Wilbraham, he was sure, "would as soon be hanged as plead such a cause. " But he was mistaken: the conclusion of the trial was again deferred until the following day, Friday, August the first, when Mr. Wilbraham, accompanied by Mr. Forester, appeared in court as counsel for the prisoners. Previously, however, to the proceedings of the last day, Lord Balmerino was informed that his only hope was ill-founded; the plea was deemed invalid by the counsel; and the straw which had, with the kindest and most laudable intentions, been thrown on the stream to arrest his fate, was insufficient to save him. He bore this disappointment with that fortitude which has raised the character of his countrymen: when he appeared on that last day, in Westminster Hall, with his brother prisoners, he submitted, in the following brief and simple words, to his destiny. "As your lordships have been pleased to allow me counsel, I have advised with them; and my counsel tell me, there is nothing in that paper which I delivered in on Wednesday last, that will be of any use to me; so I will not give your lordships any more trouble. "

When again asked, according to the usual form, as well as the other prisoners, whether he had anything more to say in arrest of judgment, Lord Balmerino replied; "No, my Lords, I only desire to be heard for a moment. " Expressing his regret that he should have taken up so much of their lordships' time, he assured them that the plea had not been put in to gain time, but because he had believed there was something in the objection that would do him good. He afterwards added these few words, which one might have wished unsaid: "My lords, I acknowledge my crime, and I beg your lordships will intercede with his Majesty for me. "

The Serjeant-at-Arms was then distinctly heard proclaiming silence; and the Lord High Steward delivered what Horace Walpole has termed, "his very long, and very poor speech, with only one or two good passages in it. " On this, there may be, doubtless, contending opinions. Those who looked upon the prisoners, and saw men in the full vigour of life, condemned to death, for acting upon acknowledged, though misapplied principles, could scarcely listen to that protracted harangue with an unbiassed judgment. The tenour of the Lord High Steward's address had, throughout, one marked feature; it presented no hope of mercy; it left no apology nor plea upon which the unhappy prisoners might expect it. It amplified every view of their crime, and pointed out, in strong and able language, its effect upon every relation of society.

In conclusion, Lord Hardwicke said, "I will add no more: it has been his Majesty's justice to bring your lordships to a legal trial; and it has been his wisdom to show, that as a small part of his national forces was sufficient to subdue the rebel army in the field, so the ordinary course of his law is strong enough to bring even their chiefs to justice.

"What remains for me, is a very painful, though a very necessary part. It is to pronounce that sentence which the law has provided for crimes of this magnitude—a sentence full of horror! Such as the wisdom of our ancestors has ordained, as one guard about the sacred person of the king, and as a fence about this excellent constitution, to be a terror to evil doers, and a security to them that do well. "

And then was heard, thrilling every tender heart with horror, the sentence of hanging, first to be put into execution, and followed by decapitation. The horrible particularities were added—"*of being hanged by the neck, —but not till you are dead—for you must be cut down alive;* "—the rest of this sentence, since it has long ago been suffered to fall into oblivion, may, for the sake of our English feelings, rest there. By those to whom it was addressed, it was heard in the full conviction that it might be carried out on them: since that very morning, nine prisoners of gentle birth had suffered the extreme penalties of that barbarous law. [373]

Of the calm manner in which his doom was heard by one of the state prisoners, Horace Walpole has left the following striking anecdote:

"Old Balmerino keeps up his spirits to the same pitch of gaiety: in the cell at Westminster, he showed Lord Kilmarnock how he must lay his head; bid him not wince, lest the strokes should cut his head or his shoulders; and advised him to bite his lips. As they were to return, he begged they might have another bottle together, as they should never meet any more till—he pointed to his neck. At getting into his coach, he said to the gaoler, 'Take care, or you will break my shins with this d— —d axe. '"[374]

The English populace could not forbear delighting in the composure of Balmerino, who, on returning from Westminster Hall after his sentence, could stop the coach in which he was about to be conducted to the Tower to buy gooseberries; or, as he expressed it in his national phrase, *honey-blobs*. [375]

That night, not contented with saying publicly at his levee, that Lord Kilmarnock had proposed murdering the English prisoners, the Duke of Cumberland proposed giving his mistress a ball; but the notion was abandoned, lest it should have been regarded as an insult to the prisoners, and *not* because a particle of highminded regret for the sufferers could ever enter that hard and depraved heart. Too well did the citizens of London understand the Duke of Cumberland's merits, when, it being proposed to present him with the freedom of some company, one of the aldermen cried aloud, "Then let it be of the Butchers'! "[376]

The commission was dissolved in the usual forms: "all manner of persons here present were desired to depart in the fear of God, and of our sovereign Lord the King. " The white staff of office was broken by the Lord High Steward; the Lords adjourned to the Chamber of Parliament; the prisoners returned to the Tower. [377]

Three weeks elapsed, after the trial, before the execution of Lord Kilmarnock and Lord Balmerino. During that interval, hope sometimes visited the prisoners in their cells, great intercession being made for them by persons of the highest rank. But it was in vain, for the counsels of the Duke of Cumberland influenced the heart of his royal father, who it is generally believed, would otherwise have been disposed to compassion. During this interval, the sorrows of the prisoners were aggravated by frequent rumours that their beloved Prince was taken; but he was safe among his Highlanders, and defied the power even of an armed force to surprise him in his singular and various retreats.

The Earl of Cromartie was the only one of the three prisoners to whom royal mercy was extended. This nobleman had been considered, before the Insurrection, as the only branch of the Mackenzies who could be relied upon. He had been backward in joining the Jacobite army, and had never shared the confidence of Charles Edward. He had been disgusted with the preference shown to Murray and to Sullivan, to the prejudice of more powerful adherents of the cause: and it was reported, had rather surrendered himself to the Earl of Sutherland's followers, than resisted when they apprehended him. [378]

Amiable in private life, affable in manner, and exempt from the pride of a Highland chieftain, this nobleman had been beloved by his neighbours of inferior rank; to the poor he had been a kind benefactor. The domestic relations of life he had fulfilled irreproachably. Every heart bled for him; and the case of his son, Lord Macleod, who had espoused the same cause, excited universal commiseration.

On the Sunday following the trial, Lady Cromartie presented her petition to the King: he gave her no hopes; and the unhappy woman fainted when he left her.

It is pleasing to rest upon one action of clemency, before returning to the horrors of capital punishment. To the intercession of Frederick

Prince of Wales, Lord Cromartie eventually owed his life; that intercession is believed to have been procured by the merits and the attractions of Lady Cromartie, who was indefatigable in her exertions.

This Lady, the daughter of Sir William Gordon of Dalfolly, is said to have possessed every quality that could render a husband happy. Beautiful and intellectual, she manifested a degree of spirit and perseverance when called upon to act in behalf of her husband and children, that raised her character to that of a heroine. She was then the mother of nine children, and about to give birth to a tenth. During the period of suspense, her conduct presented that just medium between stoicism and excess of feeling, which so few persons in grief can command. [379]

At last, a reprieve for Lord Cromartie arrived on the eleventh of August; it was not, however, followed by a release, nor even by a free pardon. During two years, Lord Cromartie was detained a prisoner in the Tower, there, being condemned to witness the departure of his generous friends, Kilmarnock and Balmerino, to the scaffold. On February the eighteenth, 1748, he was permitted to leave his prison, and to lodge in the house of a messenger. In the following August he went into Devonshire, where he was desired to remain. A pardon passed the Great Seal for his Lordship on the twentieth of October, 1749, with a condition that he should remain in any place directed by the King. He died in Poland-street in London, on the twenty-eighth of September, 1766. [380]

On Thursday, the seventh of August, the Reverend James Foster, a Presbyterian minister, was allowed access to Lord Kilmarnock, to prepare him for a fate which now seemed inevitable. Great intercession had been made for the ill-fated prisoner, by his kinsman, James, sixth Duke of Hamilton, and husband of the celebrated beauty, Miss Gunning; but the friendly efforts of that nobleman were thought rather to have "hurried him to the block. "[381] When a report reached him that one of the prisoners would be spared, Lord Kilmarnock had desired, with the utmost nobleness of soul, that Cromartie should be preferred to himself. Balmerino lamented that he had not been taken with Lord Lovat; "for then, " he remarked, "we might have been sacrificed, and these two brave men have been spared. " But these regrets were unavailing, and Lord Kilmarnock and his friend prepared to meet their doom.

Mr. Foster, on conversing with Lord Kilmarnock, found him humbled, but not crushed by his misfortunes; contrite for a life characterized by many errors, but trustful of the Infinite mercy, to which we fondly turn from the stern justice of unforgiving man. And the reverend gentleman on whom the solemn responsibility of preparing a soul for judgment was devolved, appears to have discharged his task with a due sense of its delicacy, with fidelity and kindness.

Having introduced himself to Lord Kilmarnock with the premises that his Lordship would allow him to deal freely with him; that he did not expect to be flattered, nor to have the malignity of his crimes disguised or softened; —Mr. Foster told him, "that in his opinion, the wound of his mind, occasioned by his private and public vices, must be probed and searched to the bottom, before it could be capable of receiving a remedy. " "If he disapproved of this plan, " Mr. Foster thought "he could be of no use to him, and therefore declined attendance. " To this Lord Kilmarnock replied that, "whilst he thought it was not Mr. Foster's province to interfere in things remote from his office, yet it was now no time to prevaricate with him, nor to play the hypocrite with God, before whose tribunal he should shortly appear. "

This point being settled, the minister of the Gospel deemed it necessary to persuade the Earl, that he was not to be amused with vain delusive hopes of a reprieve; that he must view his sentence as inevitable; otherwise that his mind might be distracted between hope and fear; and that true temper of penitence which alone could recommend him to Divine mercy would be unattainable.

The unfortunate Earl touchingly answered, that indeed, when he consulted his reason, and argued calmly with himself, he could see no ground of mercy; yet still the hope of life would intrude itself. He was afraid, he said, that buoyed up by this delusive hope, when the warrant for his execution came down, he should have not only the terror of his sentence to contend with, but the fond delusions of his own heart: —to overcome the bitter disappointment—the impossibility of submission. He therefore assured Mr. Foster, that he would do all in his own power to repel that visionary enemy, and to fix his thoughts on the important task of perfecting his repentance, and of preparing for death and eternity.

In regard to the part which Lord Kilmarnock had taken in recent events, there seemed no difficulty in impressing his mind with a deep sense of the responsibility which he had incurred in helping to diffuse terror and consternation through the land, in the depredation and ruin of his country: and in convincing him that he ought to consider himself accessory to innumerable private oppressions and murders. "Yes, " replied Lord Kilmarnock, with deep emotion "and murders of the innocent too, " And frequently he acknowledged this charge with tears, and offered up short petitions to God for mercy.

But when Mr. Foster mentioned to him that the consequences of the "Rebellion and its natural tendency was to the subversion of our excellent free constitution, to extirpate our holy religion, and to introduce the monstrous superstitions and cruelties of Popery, " Lord Kilmarnock hesitated; and owned, at length, that he did not contemplate such mischiefs as the result of the contest; that he did not believe that the young Chevalier would run the risk of defeating his main design by introducing Popery; nor would so entirely forget the warnings which the history of his family offered, so far as to make any attacks upon the liberties and constitution of the country. His entering into the Rebellion was occasioned, as he then declared, by the errors and vices of his previous life; and was a kind of desperate scheme to extricate him from his difficulties. Humbled and penetrated by the remembrance of former levity, Lord Kilmarnock remarked, that not only was Providence wise and righteous, but to him, gracious; and that he regarded it as an unspeakable mercy to his soul, that he had not fallen at the battle of Culloden, impenitent and unreflecting; for that, if the Rebellion had been successful, he should have gone on in his errors, without ever entertaining any serious thought of amendment. "Often, " added the contrite and chastened man, "have I made use of these words of Christ, 'Father, if it be possible, let this cup pass from me: nevertheless, not as I will, but as thou wilt. '" But he had checked himself by the reflection, that it was not for him who had been so great a sinner, to address himself to God in the same language with his blessed Saviour, who was perfectly innocent and holy.

In time, aided by the representations of his spiritual attendant, the deepest remorse for a life not untainted by impurity of conduct, was succeeded by religious peace. It was then that the prisoner turned to that Bread of Life which Christ hath left for those who hunger and thirst after righteousness. But the Minister who led him into the fold of the Great Shepherd, would not consent to administer to him the

Holy Sacrament without a full confession made in the presence of the gentleman gaoler, of his past offences, and of his contrition for them. At that solemn moment, when the heart was laid open to human witnesses, Lord Kilmarnock professed the deepest penitence for his concurrence in the Rebellion, and for the irregularities of his private life: he declared his conviction that the Holy Sacrament would be of no benefit to him whatsoever, if his remorse and contrition were not sincere. This assurance was, in other words, yet, in substance the same, emphatically repeated. During the conversations held with Lord Kilmarnock, Mr. Foster perceived that the confessions of the penitent were free and ingenuous; that he examined his own heart with a searching and scrupulous care, sternly challenging memory to the aid of conscience. At last, he declared that he should rather prefer the speedy execution of his sentence to a longer life, if he were sure that he should again be entangled by the snares and temptations of the world. This was a few days before his death.

Gradually, but effectually, the spirit that had so much in it of a heavenly temper; the heart, so framed to be beloved, was purified and elevated; so that, a beautiful and holy calm, a heavenly disinterestedness, a patience worthy of him who bore the name of Christian, were manifested in one whom it were henceforth wrong to call unhappy. When Lord Cromartie's reprieve became known to Mr. Foster, he dreaded, lest this subdued, yet fortified mind, should be disturbed by the jealousies to which our worldly condition is prone: he trembled lest the sorrow of separation from a world which Lord Kilmarnock had loved too fondly, should be revived by the pardon of his friend. "Therefore, " relates Mr. Foster, "in the morning before I waited upon him, I prepared myself to quiet and mollify his mind. But one of the first things he said to me was, that he was extremely glad that the King's mercy had been shown to Lord Cromartie. " "My Lord, " inquired Mr. Foster, "I hope you do not think you have any injustice shown you? " Lord Kilmarnock's answer was, "Not in the least; I have pleaded guilty: I entirely acquiesce in the justice of my sentence; and if mercy be extended to another, I can have no reason to complain, when nothing but justice is done to me. "

With regard to some points upon which the public odium was directed to the young Chevalier and his party, Lord Kilmarnock was very explicit in his last conversations with Mr. Foster. We have already seen how far he was enabled to clear himself concerning his conduct to the prisoners at Inverness. A report having been industriously circulated, probably with a view to excuse the barbarities of the Duke of Cumberland, that an order had been issued in the Pretender's council at Inverness, to destroy the prisoners who might be taken at the battle of Culloden, Mr. Foster put the question to Lord Kilmarnock, Whether that statement were true? "I can most sincerely and freely answer, No, " was the satisfactory reply; and a similar contradiction was given by the dying man to every accusation of a similar tendency. [382]

On Monday the eleventh of August, General Williamson desired Mr. Foster, "in the gentlest terms that he could use, to apprize Lord Kilmarnock, that he had received the order for his, and for Lord Balmerino's execution. " Mr. Foster at first refused to undertake this office. "I was so shocked at it, " writes the good man "that I could not think of delivering the message myself, but would endeavour to prepare the unfortunate Lord for it, by divesting him, as far as I could, of all hope of life. " Such, indeed, had been the continual aim of all the reverend minister's counsels; and he had hoped to entrust the last mournful task of informing him of the order to other hands. On finding Lord Kilmarnock in a very resigned and calm state of mind, he ventured, however, to hint to him how necessary was that diligent and constant preparation for death which he had endeavoured to impress upon his mind. This was sufficient: the ill-fated prisoner immediately inquired, "whether the warrant for his execution was come down? " "I told him that it was, " relates Mr. Foster, "and that the day fixed upon was the following Monday. "

Lord Kilmarnock received this intimation with a solemn consciousness of the awful nature of its import; but no signs of terror nor of anxiety added to the sorrows of that hour. In the course of conversation, he observed to Mr. Foster, that "he was chiefly concerned about the consequences of death, in comparison of which he considered the 'thing itself' a trifle: with regard to the manner of his death he had, he thought, no great reason to be terrified, for that the stroke appeared to be scarcely so much as the drawing of a tooth, or the first shock of a cold bath upon a weak and fearful temper. " At the last hour, nevertheless, the crowd, —the scaffold, —the doom, upset that sublime and heavenly resignation, —the weakness of the flesh prevailed, although only for an instant.

In the silence and solitude of his prison, Lord Kilmarnock's recollection reverted to those whom human nature were shortly to be left to buffet with the storms of their hard fate. It reverted also to those who might, in any way, have suffered at his hands. The following touching epistle, addressed to his factor, Mr. Robert Paterson, written two days only before his execution, shows how tender was his affection for his unhappy wife: in how Christian a spirit towards others he died. His consideration for the poor shoemakers of Elgin is one of those beautiful traits of character which mark a conscientious mind. The original of this letter is still in existence, and is in the possession of the great-grandson of him to whom it was addressed. [383]

"Sir,

"I have commended to your care the inclosed packet, to be delivered to my wife in the manner your good sense shall dictate to you, will be least shocking to her. Let her be prepared for it as much by degrees, and with great tenderness, as the nature of the thing will admit of. The entire dependance I have all my life had the most just reason to have on your integrity and friendship to my wife and family, as well as to myself, make me desire that the inclosed papers may come to my wife through your hands, in confidence; but you will take all the pains to comfort her, and relieve the grief I know she will be in, that you and her friends can. She is what I leave dearest behind me in the world; and the greatest service you can do to your dead friend, is to contribute as much as possible to her happiness in mind, and in her affairs.

"You will peruse the State[384] before you deliver it to her, and you will observe that there is a fund of hers (I don't mention that of five hundred Scots a-year); as the interest of my mother-in-law's portion in the Countess of Errol's hands, with, I believe, a considerable arrear upon it; which, as I have ordered a copy of all these papers to that Countess, I did not care to put in. There is another thing of a good deal of moment, which I mention only to you, because if it could be taken away without noise it would be better; but if it is pushed it will be necessary to defend it. That is, a bond which you know Mr. Kerr, Director to the Chancery, has of me for a considerable sum of money, with many years interest on it, which was almost all play debt. I don't think I ever had fifty pounds, or the half of it, of Mr. Kerr's money, and I am sure I never had a hundred; which however I have put it to, in the inclosed declaration, that my mind may be entirely at ease. My intention with respect to that sum was to wait till I had some money, and then buy it off, by a composition of three hundred pounds, and if that was not accepted of, to defend it; in which I neither saw, nor now see anything unjust; and now I leave it on my successors to do what they find most prudent in it. Beside my personal debt mentioned in general and particular in the State, [385] there is one for which I am liable in justice, if it is not paid, owing to poor people, who gave their work for it by my orders; it was at Elgin in Murray; the regiment I commanded wanted shoes. I commissioned something about seventy pair of shoes and brogues, which might come to about three shillings, or three and sixpence each, one with another. The magistrates divided them among the shoemakers of the town and country, and each shoemaker furnished his proportion. I drew on the town for the price out of the composition laid on them, but I was told afterwards at Inverness, that it was believed the composition was otherwise applied, and the poor shoemakers not paid. As these poor people wrought by my orders, it will be a great ease to my heart to think they are not to lose by me, as too many have done in the course of that year; but had I lived, I might have made some enquiry after it; but now it is impossible, as their hardships in loss of horses, and such things which happened through my soldiers, are so interwoven with what was done by other people, that it would be very hard, if not impossible, to separate them. If you will write to Mr. Jones of Dalkinty, at Elgin, (with whom I was quartered when I lay there,) he will send you an account of the shoes, and if they were paid to the shoemakers or no; and if they are not, I beg you'll get my wife, or my successors, to pay them when they can.

"Receive a letter to me from Mrs. Boyd, my cousin Malcomb's widow; I shall desire her to write to you for an answer.

"Accept of my sincere thanks for your friendship and good services to me. Continue them to my wife and children.

"My best wishes are to you and yours, and for the happiness and prosperity of the good town of Kilmarnock, and I am, sir, your humble servant,

"KILMARNOCK. "

Tower of London, August 16th, 1746.

On the Saturday previous to the execution of Lord Kilmarnock, General Williamson gave his prisoners a minute account of all the circumstances of solemnity, and outward terror, which would accompany it. Lord Kilmarnock heard it much with the same expression of concern as a man of a compassionate disposition would read it, in relation to others. After suggesting a trifling alteration in the arrangements after the execution, he expressed his regret that the headsman should be, as General Williamson informed him, a "good sort of man; " remarking, that one of a rougher nature and harder heart, would be more likely to do his work quickly. He then requested that four persons might be appointed to receive the head when it was severed from the body, in a red cloth; that it might not, as he had heard was the case at other executions, "roll about the scaffold and be mangled and disfigured. " "For I would not, " he added, "though it may be but a trifling matter, that my remains should appear with any needless indecency after the just sentence of the law is satisfied. " He spoke calmly and easily on all these particulars, nor did he even shrink when told that his head would be held up and exhibited to the multitude as that of a traitor. "He knew, " he said, "that it was usual, and it did not affect him. " During these singular conversations, his spiritual attendant and the General, could hardly have been more precise in their descriptions had they been portraying the festive ceremonials of a coming bridal, than they were in the fearful minutiæ of the approaching execution. It was thought by them that such recitals would accustom the mind of the prisoner to the apparatus and formalities that would attend his death, and that these would lose their influence over his mind. "He allowed with me, " observes Mr. Foster, "that such circumstances were not so melancholy as dying after a lingering disorder, in a darkened room, with weeping friends around one, and whilst the shattered frame sank under slow exhaustion. " But experience and human feelings contradict this observation of the resigned and unhappy sufferer; we look to death, under such an aspect, as the approach of rest; but human nature shrinks from the violent struggle, the momentary but fierce convulsion, plunging us, as it were, into the abyss of the grave.

At this moment of his existence, when it was certain ruin at Court and in the army, to befriend the Jacobite prisoner, a friend, the friend of his youth, came nobly forward to attend Lord Kilmarnock in his dying moments. This was John Walkinshaw Craufurd, of Craufurdland in the county of Ayr, between whose family and that of the House of Boyd, a long and intimate friendship of several centuries had existed; "so much so, " observes a member of the present family of Craufurd, [386] "that a subterranean passage is said to exist between our old castles, of which we *fancy* proofs; but these are fire-side legends. "

"The family of Craufurd, " observes Mr. Burke, "is one of antiquity and eminence in a part of the empire where ancestry and exploit have ever been held in enthusiastic admiration. " By marriage, in the thirteenth century, it is allied anciently with the existing house of Loudon; and its connection and friendship with the House of Boyd was cemented by the death of one of its heads, Robert Craufurd, in 1487, in consequence of a wound received at the Wyllielee, from attending James Boyd, Earl of Arran, in a duel with the Earl of Eglintoun. In the days of Charles the First and Second, the Craufurds had been Covenanters, as appears in the history of that time: and in the year 1745, they were stanch Whigs; and Colonel Walkinshaw Craufurd had, when called upon to pay a mournful proof of respect to Lord Kilmarnock, attained the rank of Colonel in the British army. Besides the ancient friendship of the family, there had been several intermarriages; and the father of Colonel Craufurd had espoused, after the death of Miss Walkinshaw, Elenora, the widow of the Honorable Thomas Boyd, the brother of Lord Kilmarnock.

Colonel Walkinshaw Craufurd was a fine specimen of the true Scottish gentleman, and of the British officer. He was a very handsome, stately man, of high-bred manners, and portly figure, whom his tenantry both feared and honoured. He lived almost continually in the highest circles in London, except when in service, and also at the Court, visiting his Castle in Ayrshire only in the hunting season, for he kept a pack of hounds. To such a man the sacrifice of public opinion, then all against the Jacobites, —the sure loss of Court favour, —the risk of losing all military promotion, were no small considerations; yet he cast them all to the winds, and came nobly forward to pay the last respect to his kinsman and friend.

Already had he distinguished himself at the battle of Dettingen and Fontenoy; and he might reasonably expect the highest military honours: yet he incurred the risk of attending Lord Kilmarnock on the scaffold, and performing that office for him which that nobleman required. I almost blush to write the sequel; for *this* act, Colonel Craufurd was, immediately after the last scene was over, put down to the very bottom of the army list. [387] Such was the petty and vindictive policy of the British Government, influenced, it may be presumed, by the same dark mind that visited upon the faithful Highlanders the horrors of military law, in punishment of their fidelity and heroism. "The King, " observes Horace Walpole, referring to these and other acts, "is much inclined to mercy; but the Duke of Cumberland, who has not so much of Cæsar after a victory, as in gaining it, is for the utmost severity. "[388]

Whilst the mind of Lord Kilmarnock was thus gradually prepared for death, Lord Balmerino passed cheerfully the hours which were so soon to terminate in his doom. Fondly attached to his young wife, Balmerino obtained the boon of her society in his prison. So much were the people attracted by the hardihood and humour of this brave old man, that it was found necessary by the authorities to stop up the windows of his prison-chamber in the Tower, in order to prevent his talking to the populace out of the window. One only was left unclosed, with characteristic cruelty: it commanded a view of the scaffolding erected for his execution. [389] One day the Lieutenant of the Tower brought in the warrant for his death: Lady Balmerino fainted. "Lieutenant, " said Lord Balmerino, "with your d——d warrant you have spoiled my Lady's dinner. "

Lord Balmerino is said to have written to the Duke of Cumberland a "very sensible letter, " requesting his intercession with the King; but this seems to have been unavailing, from the well-known exclamation of George the Second, when solicited for the other prisoners, "Will no one speak a word to me for poor Balmerino? "

The day appointed for the execution was the eighteenth of August, at eight in the morning. Mr. Foster visited Lord Kilmarnock, and found him in a calm and happy temper, without any disturbance of that serenity which had of late blessed his days of imprisonment. He affected not to brave death, but viewed it in the awful aspect in which even the best of men, and the most hopeful Christians, must consider that solemn change. He expressed his belief, that a man who had led a dissolute life, and who yet believed the consequences of death, to affect indifference at that hour, showed himself either to be very impious, or very stupid. One apprehension still clung to his mind, proving how sensitive had been that conscience which strove in vain to satisfy itself. He told Mr. Foster "he could not be sure that his repentance was sincere, because it had never been tried by the temptation of returning to society. "

Lord Kilmarnock continued in a composed state of mind during the whole morning. After a short prayer, offered up by Mr. Foster, at his desire, he was informed that the sheriffs waited for the prisoners. He heard this announcement calmly; and said to General Williamson, with his wonted grace, "General, I am ready to follow you. " He then quitted his prison, and descended the stairs. As he was going down, he met Lord Balmerino; and the friends embraced. "My Lord, " said the noble Balmerino, "I am heartily sorry to have your company in this expedition. "[390]

The prisoners then proceeded to the outward gate of the Tower, where the Sheriffs, who had walked there in procession, received them: this was about ten o'clock in the morning of the eighteenth of August. The bodies of the two noblemen having been delivered with the usual formalities to the Sheriffs, they proceeded to the late Transport Office, a building near the scaffold. Two Presbyterian ministers, Mr. Foster and Mr. Home, accompanied Lord Kilmarnock, whilst the Chaplain of the Tower and another clergyman, attended Lord Balmerino. Three rooms, hung with black, were prepared; one for each of the condemned noblemen; another, fronting the scaffold, for spectators. Here, those who were so soon to suffer, had a short conference with each other, chiefly relating to the order, said to have been issued at Culloden, to give no quarter. This was a subject, not only of importance to Lord Kilmarnock's memory, but to the character of the Jacobite party generally.

"Did you, my Lord, " said the generous Balmerino, still anxious, even at the last hour, to justify his friends, "see or know of any order, signed by the Prince, to give no quarter at the battle of Culloden? "

"No, my Lord, " replied Kilmarnock.

"Nor I neither, " rejoined Balmerino; "and therefore it seems to be an invention to justify their own murderous scheme. "

To this Lord Kilmarnock answered, "No, my Lord, I do not think it can be an invention, because, while I was a prisoner at Inverness, I was told by several officers that there was such an order, signed 'George Murray, ' and that it was in the Duke of Cumberland's custody. " To this statement, (which was wholly erroneous) Lord Balmerino exclaimed, "Lord George Murray! Why then, they should not charge it on the Prince. " After this explanation, he bade Kilmarnock a last farewell: as he embraced him, he said, in the same noble spirit, that he had ever shown, "My dear Lord Kilmarnock, I am only sorry I cannot pay all this reckoning alone: once more, farewell for ever. "

Lord Kilmarnock was then left with the sheriffs, and his spiritual advisers. In their presence, he solemnly declared himself to be a Protestant, and said that he was thoroughly satisfied of the legality of the King's claim to the throne. He had been educated in these principles, and he now thoroughly repented having ever engaged in the Rebellion. He afterwards stated to his friends that he had within this week taken the sacrament twice in evidence of the truth of his repentance.

The hour of noon was now fast approaching, when the last act of relentless justice was to be performed. Mr. Foster, after permitting the Earl a few moments to compose himself, suggested that he should engage with him in prayer, and afterwards proceed to the scaffold. The minister then addressed himself to all who were present, urging them to join with him in this last solemn office, and in recommending the soul of an unhappy penitent to the mercy of God. Those who were engaged in this sad scene, sank on their knees, whilst, after a petition relating to the prisoner, a prayer was offered up "for King George, for our holy religion, for our inestimable British liberties. " This prayer, for the royal family, Lord Kilmarnock had often protested he would, at the latest moment, offer up to the throne of God.

After this solemn duty had been performed, Lord Kilmarnock bade an affectionate farewell to the gentlemen who had accompanied him, and here Mr. Foster's office ceased, the Rev. Mr. Home, a young clergyman, and a personal friend of Lord Kilmarnock, succeeding him in attendance upon the prisoner. Many reports prevailed of Lord Kilmarnock's fear of death, and of the weakness of his resolution; and Balmerino, it is said, apprehended that he would not "behave well, " an expression used, perhaps, in reference to his opinions, perhaps in anticipation of a failure of courage. As leaning upon the arm of his friend Mr. Home, Lord Kilmarnock saw, for the first time, that outward apparatus of death to which he had taken such pains to familiarise himself; "nature still recurred upon him; "—for an instant, the home of peace, to which he was hastening, was forgotten; —"the multitude, the block, the coffin, the executioner, the instrument of death, " appalled one, whose character was amiable, rather than exalted. He turned to his attendant, and exclaimed, "Home, this is terrible! " Yet his countenance, even as he uttered these words, was unchanged, and in a few moments, he regained the composure of one whose hope was in the mercy of his Creator. What else could sustain him in the agonies of that moment? "His whole behaviour, " writes Mr. Foster, "was so humble and resigned, that not only his friends, but every spectator, was deeply moved; the executioner burst into tears, and was obliged to use artificial spirits to support and strengthen him. " As the man kneeled down, after the usual custom, to pray for forgiveness, Lord Kilmarnock desired him to have courage, and placing a purse of gold in his hand, told him that the dropping of a handkerchief should be the signal for the blow.

Mr. Foster having rejoined Lord Kilmarnock on the scaffold, a long conversation, in a low voice, took place between them; for Lord Kilmarnock made no speech. "I wish, " said Mr. Foster, "I had a voice loud enough to tell the multitude with what sentiments your Lordship quits the world. " Again, the unfortunate nobleman embraced his friends; and bade Mr. Foster, who quitted the scaffold a few minutes before his execution, a last farewell. During all this time, which was more than half an hour, he took no notice of the multitude below: except, observing that the green baize over the wall obstructed the view, he desired that it might be lifted up that the crowd might see the spectacle of his execution.

A delay now took place, attributed by some to Lord Kilmarnock's "unwillingness to depart: "[391] but owing to a few trivial circumstances which, as Mr. Foster remarks, "are unnecessary to be mentioned in order to vindicate the noble penitent from the imputation of fear in the critical moment. " To the last, a scrupulous attention to decorum, and nicety in dress characterized Lord Kilmarnock. At his trial, he was described as having been a little too precise, and his hair "too exactly dressed for a person in his situation. " On the scaffold the same care was manifested. He appeared in a mourning suit, and his hair, which was unpowdered, was dressed according to the fashion of the day, in a bag, which it took some time to undo, in order to replace the bag by a cap. Even then, the cap being large, and the hair long, his lordship was apprehensive that some of the hair might escape, and intercept the stroke of the axe. He therefore requested a gentleman near him, to tie the cap round his head, that he might bind up the hair more closely. As this office was performed, the person to whom he had applied, wished his lordship a continuance of his resolution until he should meet with eternal happiness. "I thank you, " returned Lord Kilmarnock, with his usual courtesy and sweetness; "I find myself perfectly easy and resigned. "

There was also another impediment, —the tucking of his shirt under his waistcoat was next adjusted. Then Lord Kilmarnock, taking out a paper containing the heads of his last devotions, advanced to the utmost stage of the scaffold, and kneeled down at the block, on which, in praying, he placed his hands, until the executioner remonstrated, begging of him to let his hands fall down, lest they should be mangled, or should intercept the blow. He was also told that the neck of his waistcoat was in the way; he therefore arose, and with the help of Colonel Walkinshaw Craufurd, had it taken off. Near him were standing those who held the cloth ready to receive his head; among these Mr. Home's servant heard Lord Kilmarnock tell the executioner, that in two minutes he would give the signal. A few moments were spent in fervent devotion; then the sign was given, and the head was severed from the body by one stroke. It was not exposed to view according to custom: but was deposited in a coffin with the body, and delivered to his Lordship's friends. One peculiarity attended this execution. It is not required by law that the head of a person decapitated should be exposed; but is a custom adopted in order to satisfy the multitude that the execution has been accomplished. Since, by Lord Kilmarnock's dying request, this practice was omitted, the Sheriffs ordered that all the attendants on the scaffold should kneel down, so that the view of the execution might not be impeded[392] to those who were below.

The scaffold was immediately cleared, and put in order for another victim; and Mr. Ford, the Under-Sheriff, who had attended the first execution, went into the room in the Transport Office where Balmerino awaited his doom. "I suppose, " inquired the undaunted Balmerino, "that my Lord Kilmarnock is no more. " And having asked how he died, and being told the account, he said: "It is well done, and now, gentlemen, I will no longer detain you, for I desire not to protract my life. " He spoke calmly, and even cheerfully; Lord Kilmarnock had shed tears as he bade his friends farewell, but Balmerino, whilst others wept, was even cheerful, and hastened to the scaffold. His deportment, when in the room where he awaited the summons to death, was graceful and yet simple, without either any ostentation of bravery, or indications of indifference to his fate. He did not defy the terror, he rose above it. He conversed freely with his friends, and refreshed himself twice with wine and bread, desiring the company to drink to him, as he expressed it in his Scottish phrase, "ain degrae ta haiven; " but above all, he prayed often and fervently for support, and support was given.

True to the last to his professions, Lord Balmerino was dressed in what was called by a contemporary, "his Rebellious Regimentals, " such as he had worn at Culloden; they were of blue cloth, turned up with red; underneath them was a flannel waistcoat and a shroud. He ascended the scaffold, "treading, " as an observer expressed it, "with the air of a General, " and surveying the spectators, bowed to them; he walked round it, and read the inscription on his coffin, "Arthurus Dominus de Balmerino, decollatus, 18° die August. 1746, ætatis suæ 58°; " observed "that it was right, " and with apparent pleasure looked at the block saying, it was his "pillow of rest. " Lord Balmerino then pulling out his spectacles, read a paper to those who stood around him, and delivered it to the Sheriff to do with it as he thought proper. It was subsequently printed in a garbled form, much of it being deemed too treasonable for publication, and in that form is preserved in the State Trials. [393] It is now given as it was really spoken.

"I was bred in the anti-revolution principles, which I have ever persevered in, from a sincere persuasion that the restoration of the Royal Family, and the good of my native country, are inseparable. The action of my life which now stares me most in the face, is my having accepted a commission in the army from the late Princess Anne, who I knew had no more right to the crown than her predecessor, the Prince of Orange, whom I always considered as an infamous usurper.

"In the year 1715, as soon as the King landed in Scotland, I thought it my indispensable duty to join his standard, though his affairs were then in a desperate situation.

"I was in Switzerland in the year 1734, where I received a letter from my father acquainting me that he had procured me remission, and desiring me to return home. Not thinking myself at liberty to comply with my father's desire without the King's approbation, I wrote to Rome to know his Majesty's pleasure, and was directed by him to return home; and at the same time I received a letter of credit upon his banker at Paris, who furnished me with money to defray the expense of my journey, and put me in repair. I think myself bound, upon this occasion, to contradict a report which has been industriously spread, and which I never heard of till I was prisoner; that orders were given to the Prince's army to give no quarter at the battle of Culloden. With my eye upon the block, which will soon bring me unto the highest of all tribunals, I do declare that it is without any manner of foundation, both because it is impossible it could have escaped the knowledge of me, who was captain of the Prince's Life Guards, or of Lord Kilmarnock, who was colonel of his own regiment; but still more so, as it is entirely inconsistent with the mild and generous nature of that brave Prince, whose patience, fortitude, intrepidity, and humanity, I must declare upon this solemn occasion, are qualities in which he excels all men I ever knew, and which it ever was his desire to employ for the relief and preservation of his father's subjects. I believe rather, that this report was spread to palliate and excuse the murders they themselves committed in cold blood after the battle of Culloden.

"I think it my duty to return my sincere acknowledgments to Major White and Mr. Fowler, for their humane and complaisant behaviour to me during my confinement. I wish I could pay the same compliment to General Williamson, who used me with the greatest inhumanity and cruelty; but having taken the sacrament this day, I forgive him, as I do all my enemies.

"I die in the religion of the Church of England, which I look upon as the same with the Episcopal Church of Scotland, in which I was brought up. "

After delivering this speech, Lord Balmerino laid his head upon the block, and said, "God reward my friends, and forgive my enemies: bless and restore the King; preserve the Prince, and the Duke of York, —and receive my soul. "

The executioner then being called for, and kneeling to ask forgiveness, Lord Balmerino interrupted him. "Friend, you need not ask my forgiveness; the execution of your duty is commendable. " He then gave the headsman three guineas, saying, "this is all I have; I can only add to it my coat and waistcoat, " which, accordingly, he took off, laying them on the coffin for the executioner. After putting on a flannel jacket made for the occasion, and a plaid cap, he went to the block in order to show the executioner the signal. He then returned to his friends. "I am afraid, " he said, addressing them, "that there are some here who may think my behaviour bold: remember, sir, " he added, addressing a gentleman near him, "what I tell you; it arises from a just confidence in God, and a clear conscience. " Memorable, and beautiful words, distinguishing between the presumption of indifference, and the security of a living faith. When he laid his head on the block to try it, he said, "if I had a thousand lives I would lay them all down in the same cause. "

Lord Balmerino then showed the Executioner where to strike the blow; he examined the edge of the axe, and bade the man to strike with resolution; "for in *that*, friend, " he said, as he replaced the axe in the hand of the man, "will consist your mercy. " He asked how many strokes had been given to Lord Kilmarnock. Two clergymen coming up at that moment, he said, "no, gentlemen, I believe you have already done me all the service you can. " He called loudly to the warder, and gave him his perriwig; and instantly laid down his head upon the block, but being told that he was on the wrong side, he vaulted round, and extending his arms uttered this short prayer: "O Lord, reward my friends, forgive my enemies: "—he uttered, it has been stated, another ejaculation for king James; but that petition was suppressed in the printed accounts of his death: then, pronouncing these words, "receive my soul, " he gave the signal by throwing up his arm, as if he were giving the signal for battle. His intrepidity, and the suddenness of that last sign terrified the executioner, whose arm became almost powerless; the affrighted man struck the blow on the part directed, but though, it is hoped, it destroyed all sensation, the head was not severed, but fell back on the shoulders, exhibiting a ghastly sight. Two more strokes of the axe were requisite to complete the work. Then, the head having been received in a piece of scarlet cloth, the lifeless remains of the true, and noble hearted soldier were deposited in a coffin, and delivered to his friends.

A vast multitude viewed this spectacle, so execrable in its cruelty, so great in the deportment of the sufferers. Even on the masts of ships, in the calm river, were the spectators piled; all classes of society were interested in this memorable scene; and, for a few short weeks, the fashionable circles were diverted by the humours of Lady Townshend, and the witticisms of George Selwyn. During the imprisonment of Kilmarnock, it had been the fancy of the former to station herself under the window of his chamber in one of the dismal towers in which he was detained; to send messages to him, and to obtain his dog and snuff-box. But even this show of affected feeling failed to make compassion fashionable in the regions of St. James's. Calumny was busy at the grave of the beheaded Jacobites; and the accounts of those who attended them in their last hours were attacked by anonymous pamphleteers. It was said, among other things, that Balmerino uttered no prayer at the last moment; and his behaviour was contrasted with that of Kilmarnock. On this allegation, Mr. Ford, the Under-Sheriff, who was on the scaffold, observes, "the authors of these attacks being concealed are unworthy of other notice, since nothing is easier to an ingenious and unprejudiced mind, than to distinguish between the subject and the man: my Lord Kilmarnock was happily educated in right principles, which he deviated from, and repented; whereas, the great, though unhappy Balmerino, was unfortunate in his, —but, as he lived, he died. "[394]

The characters of these two noblemen, who, in life, held a very dissimilar course, until they coöperated in arms, are strongly contrasted. To Kilmarnock belonged the gentle qualities which enhance the pleasures of society, but often, too, increase its perils: the susceptible, affectionate nature, not fortified by self-controul; the compassionate disposition, acting rather from impulse than principle. Infirm in principle, his rash alliance with a party who were opposed to all that he had learned to respect in childhood; and whom he joined, from the stimulus of a misdirected ambition, cannot be justified. To this, it was generally believed, he was greatly incited by the persuasions of his mother-in-law, the Countess of Errol.

Whilst we bestow our cordial approbation on those who engaged in civil strife from a sense of duty, and from notions of allegiance, which had never been exterminated from their moral code, we condemn such as, attaching themselves to the Jacobite party, outraged their secret convictions, betrayed the trusts of Government, and violated the promise of their youth. Such a course must spring either from selfishness, or weakness, or from a melancholy union of both. In Lord Kilmarnock it was far more the result of weakness than of self-interest: his fortunes were desperate, and his mind was embittered towards the ruling government: his admiration was attracted by the gallantry and resolution of those who adhered to the Chevalier: his sense of what was due to his rank, and the consciousness of high descent, coupled with empty honours and real poverty, stimulated him to take that course which seemed the most likely to regain a position, without ever enjoying which a man may be happy, but which few can bear to lose. This was his original error; he joined the standard of Charles Edward, —but he was no Jacobite. He fought against his own convictions, the hereditary and ineffaceable prepossessions implanted in the heart by a parent.

From henceforth, until immured in the Tower, all in the career of Lord Kilmarnock was turbulence; and, it must be acknowledged, crime. For nothing can justify a resistance of sovereign power, save a belief in its illegality. "I engaged in the rebellion, " was Lord Kilmarnock's confession, "in opposition to my own principles, and to those of my family; in contradiction to the whole tenor of my conduct. " Such were his expressions at that hour when no earthly considerations had power to seduce him into falsehood.

By those historians who espouse the Jacobite cause, this avowal has been severely censured; and Lord Kilmarnock has been regarded as deserting the party which he had espoused. But, with his conviction, such a line of conduct as that which he pursued in prison, could alone be honest, and therefore alone consistent with his religious hopes, before he quitted life. Such censure has been well answered in Lord Kilmarnock's own words, "I am in little pain for the reflections which the inconsiderate or prejudiced part of my countrymen, (if there are any such whom my suffering the just sentence of the law has not mollified,) may cast upon me for this confession. The wiser or more ingenious will, I hope, approve my conduct, and allow with me, that next to doing right is to have the courage and integrity to avow that I have done wrong. " These sentiments were not, be it observed, made public until after his death.

If, in early life, the career of Lord Kilmarnock were tainted by dissolute conduct, his deep contrition, his sincere confession of his errors, his endeavours to amend them, redeem those very errors in the eyes of human judgment, as they will probably plead for him, with One who is more merciful than man. In his prison, his patience in suspense, his forbearance to those who had urged on his death, his generous sentiments towards his companions in misfortune, — his care for others, his trust in the mercy of his Saviour, present as instructive a lesson as mortals can glean from the errors and the penitence of others.

Contrasted with the gentle, unfortunate Kilmarnock, the gallant bearing of Balmerino rises to heroism. One cannot, for the sake of his party, help regretting that he had not taken a more prominent part in the councils of the young Chevalier, or held a more distinguished position in the field. His integrity, his strong sense, and moral courage might have had an advantageous influence over the wavering, and confirmed the indecisive. In the field, his would have been the desperate valour which suits a desperate cause; but his resources were few, and his influence proportionately small.

The soldier of fortune, driven at an early age from home, sent from country to country, serving, with little hope of advancement, under various generals, Balmerino had learned to view life almost as a matter of indifference, compared with the honest satisfaction of preserving consistency. His existence had been one of trial, and of banishment from all domestic pleasures, and in the perils of his youthful days, he had learned to view it as so precarious, that his final doom came not to him as a surprise, but seemed merely a natural conclusion of a career of danger and adventure. His heroism may excite less admiration even than the resignation of those who had more to lose; but his intrepidity, his courageous sincerity, his contempt of all display, his carelessness of himself, and the tender concern which he evinced for others, are qualities which we should not be *English* not to appreciate and venerate. His were the finest attributes of the soldier and the Jacobite: the firm, unflinching adherence; the enthusiastic loyalty; the utter repugnance to all compromising; and the lofty disregard of opinion, which extorted, even from those who endeavoured to ridicule, a reluctant respect.

For the relentless pretext of what was called justice, which sent this brave man to his doom, there is no possibility of accounting, except in the deep party hatred of the Government. Lord Kilmarnock is believed to have owed his death to the false report industriously spread of his having treated the English prisoners with cruelty; but no such plea could injure Balmerino. One dark influence, at that time all powerful at court, all powerful among the people, denied them mercy; —and the crowds which witnessed the death of Kilmarnock and of Balmerino, hastened to do homage to the Duke of Cumberland. Nothing can, in fact, more plainly show the effect of frequent executions upon the character of a people than the details of the year 1746. With the inhabitants of London, like the French at the time of the Revolution, the value of life was lowered; the indifference to scenes of horror formed a shocking feature in their conduct. In the great world, jests, and witticisms delighted the Satellites of power. It was the barbarous fashion to visit Temple Bar for the purpose of viewing the heads exhibited there; spying glasses being let out for the ghastly spectacle. And the coarse, unfeeling invectives of the press prove the general state of the public mind, in those days, more effectually than any other fact could do: —in the present times, the cruelty which pursues its victim to the grave would not be tolerated.

In his latest hours, the chief concern of Lord Kilmarnock seems to have been for his eldest son, to whom he addressed the following beautiful letter.

EXTRACT OF THE LATE EARL OF KILMARNOCK'S LETTER TO HIS SON LORD BOYD.

"Dated, Tower, 17th of August, 1746.

"Dear Boyd,

"I must take this way to bid you farewell, and I pray God may ever bless you and guide you in this world, and bring you to a happy immortality in the world to come. I must, likewise, give you my last advice. Seek God in your youth, and when you are old He will not depart from you. Be at pains to acquire good habits now, that they may grow up, and become strong in you. Love mankind, and do justice to all men. Do good to as many as you can, and neither shut your ears nor your purse to those in distress, whom it is in your power to relieve. Believe me, you will find more joy in one beneficent action; and in your cool moments you will be more happy with the reflection of having made any person so, who without your assistance would have been miserable, than in the enjoyment of all the pleasures of sense (which pall in the using), and of all the pomps and gaudy show of the world. Live within your circumstances, by which means you will have it in your power to do good to others. Above all things, continue in your loyalty to his present Majesty, and the succession to the crown as by law established. Look on that as the basis of the civil and religious liberty and property of every individual in the nation. Prefer the public interests to your own, wherever they interfere. Love your family and your children, when you have any; but never let your regard to them drive you on the rock I split upon; when, on that account, I departed from my principles, and brought the guilt of rebellion, and civil and particular desolation on my head, for which I am now under the sentence justly due to my Prince. Use all your interest to get your brother pardoned and brought home as soon as possible, that his circumstances, and bad influence of those he is among, may not induce him to accept of foreign service, and lose him both to his country and his family. If money can be found to support him, I wish you would advise him to go to Geneva, where his principles of religion and liberty will be confirmed, and where he may stay till you see if a pardon can be procured him. As soon as Commodore Burnet comes home, inquire for your brother Billie, and take care of him on my account. I must again recommend your unhappy mother to you. Comfort her, and take all the care you can of your brothers: and may God of His infinite mercy, preserve, guide, and comfort you and them through all the vicissitudes of this life, and after it bring you to the habitations of the just, and make you happy in the enjoyment of Himself to all eternity! "

PAPER DELIVERED BY THE LATE EARL OF KILMARNOCK TO MR. FOSTER.

"Sunday, 17th of August, 1746.

"As it would be a vain attempt in me to speak distinctly to that great concourse of people, who will probably be present at my execution, I chose to leave this behind me, as my last solemn declaration, appealing for my integrity to God, who knows my heart.

"I bless God I have little fear of temporal death, though attended with many outward circumstances of terror; the greatest sting I feel in death is that I have deserved it.

"Lord Balmerino, my fellow-sufferer, to do justice, dies in a professed adherence to the mistaken principles he had imbibed from his cradle. But I engaged in the Rebellion in opposition to my own principles, and to those of my family; in contradiction to the whole tenour of my conduct, till within these few months that I was wickedly induced to renounce my allegiance, which ever before I had preserved and held inviolable. I am in little pain for the reflection which the inconsiderate or prejudiced part of my countrymen (if there are any such, whom my suffering the just sentence of the law has not mollified,) may cast upon me for this confession.

"The wiser, or more ingenious, will, I hope, approve my conduct, and allow with me that, next to doing right, is to have the courage and integrity to own that I have done wrong.

"Groundless accusations of cruelty have been raised and propagated concerning me; and charges spread among the people of my having solicited for, nay, even actually signed orders of general savage destruction, seldom issued among the most barbarous nations, and which my soul abhors. And that the general temper of my mind was ever averse from, and shocked at gross instances of inhumanity, I appeal to all my friends and acquaintance who have known me most intimately, and even to those prisoners of the King's troops to whom I had access, and whom I ever had it in my power to relieve; I appeal, in particular, for my justification as to this justly detested and horrid crime of cruelty, to Captain Master, of Ross, Captain-Lieutenant Luon, and Lieutenant George Cuming of Alter.

"These gentlemen will, I am persuaded, as far as relates to themselves, and as far as has fallen within their knowledge as credible information, do me justice; and then, surely my countrymen will not load a person, already too guilty and unfortunate, with undeserved infamy, which may not only fix itself on his own character, but reflect dishonour on his family.

"I have no more to say, but that I am persuaded, if reasons of state, and the demands of public justice had permitted his Majesty to follow the dictates of his own royal heart, my sentence might have been mitigated. Had it pleased God to prolong my life, the remainder of it should have been faithfully employed in the service of my justly offended sovereign, and in constant endeavours to wipe away the very remembrance of my crime.

"I now, with my dying breath, beseech Almighty God to bless my rightful sovereign, King George, and preserve him from the attacks of public and private enemies.

"May his Majesty, and his illustrious descendants, be so guided by the Divine Providence as ever to govern with that wisdom, and that care for the public good, as will preserve to them the love of their subjects, and secure their right to reign over a free and happy people to the latest posterity. "

That Lord Boyd reciprocated the affection of his father appears from the following letter, which he addressed, a few days after the execution of Lord Kilmarnock, to Colonel Walkinshaw Craufurd, who was then at Scarborough.

"My Dear John,

"I had yours last post, and I don't know in what words to express how much I am obliged to you for doing the last duties to my unfortunate father; you can be a judge what a loss I have suffered; you knew him perfectly well, that he was the best of friends, the most affectionate husband, and the tenderest parent. Poor Lady Kilmarnock bears her loss much better than I could have imagined; but it was entirely owing to her being prepared several days before she got the melancholy accounts of it. I shall be here for some time, as I have a good deal of business to do in this country; so I shall be extremely glad to see you as soon as possible. I am, my dear John, your most sincere friend and obedient humble servant,

BOYD. "

"Kilmarnock (House) August 27th, 1746. "

Yet the young nobleman did not, it appears, entirely satisfy the expectations of those who were interested in his fate, and attached to his father's memory, as the following extract from a letter written by Mr. George Rosse, to Colonel Craufurd, shows. [395]

"Dear Sir,

"I am favoured with yours of the thirteenth from Scarborough, and had the honour of one letter from Lord Boyd since his father's execution, and sorry to tell you, it was not wrote in such terms as I could show or make any use of. If you had seen him, I dare say it would have been otherwise. However, I took the liberty of writing with plainness to him, in hopes of drawing from him, what may be shown to his honour and to his own immediate advantage.

* * * * *

"I put him in mind of writing to his cousin, Duke of Hamilton, and Mr. Home; an omission, which, with submission, is unpardonable, as he was apprised of their goodness to his father; and I gave him some hints with relation to himself, by authority of the ministry, which, if he continue in the army, may be improved upon. Those things I think proper to mention to you, as I know your friendship for Boyd, that you may take an opportunity of mentioning them to him, when you are with him, which I hope will be soon. He is appointed deputy

Captain-Lieutenant; but that I look upon as a step to higher preferment. I should like to hear from you; direct to (Crawfurdland) Kilmarnock, and I am, dear sir, your most obedient, humble servant.

"GEO. ROSSE. "

Leicesterfield, September 8th, 1746.

Notwithstanding these seeming acts of negligence, which may possibly have been explained, Lord Boyd became, in every way, worthy of being the representative of an ancient race. He was an improved resemblance of his amiable, unhappy father. Possessing his father's personal attributes, he added, to the courtesy and kindliness of his father's character, strength of principle, a perfect consistency of conduct, and sincere religious connections, both in the early and latter period of his life. His deportment is said to have combined both the sublime and the graceful; his form, six feet four inches in height, to have been the most elegant; his manners the most polished and popular of his time. In his domestic relations he was exemplary, systematic, yet with the due liberality of a nobleman, in his affairs; sagacious and conscientious as a magistrate; generous to his friends. "He puts me in mind, " said one who knew him, "of an ancient hero; and I remember Dr. Johnson was positive that he resembled Homer's character of Jaspedon. "[396] "His agreeable look and address, " observes that adorer of rank, Boswell, "prevented that restraint, which the idea of his being Lord High Constable of Scotland might otherwise have occasioned. "[397]

At the time of his father's execution, Lord Boyd was only twenty years of age. He claimed and obtained the maternal estate, and obtained it in 1751. In 1758 he succeeded Mary, Countess of Errol in her own right, his mother's aunt, as Earl of Errol, and left the army in which he had continued to serve. He retired to Slains Castle, where he passed his days in the exercise of those virtues which become a man who is conscious, by rank and fortune, of a deep responsibility, and who regards those rather as trusts, than possessions. He died at Calendar-house, in 1778, universally lamented, and honoured.

The Countess of Kilmarnock survived her husband only one year; and died at Kilmarnock in 1747. Two sons were, however, left, in addition to Lord Boyd, to encounter, for some years, considerable difficulties. Of these, the second, Charles, who was in the insurrection of 1745, escaped to the Isle of Arran, where he lay concealed, in that, the ancient territory of the Boyds, for a year. He amused himself, having found an old chest of medical books, with the study of medicine and surgery, which he afterwards practised with some degree of skill among the poor. He then escaped to France, and married there a French lady; but eventually he found a home at Slains Castle, where he was residing when Dr. Johnson and Boswell visited Scotland. He was a man of considerable accomplishment; but, as Boswell observed, "with a pompousness or formal plenitude in his conversation, " or as Dr. Johnson expressively remarked, "with too much elaboration in his talk. " "It gave me pleasure, " adds Boswell, "to see him, a steady branch of the family, setting forth all its advantages with much zeal. "

William Boyd, the fourth son of Lord Kilmarnock, was in the Royal Navy, and on board Commodore Burnet's ship at the time of his father's execution. He was eventually promoted to a company of the 14th foot, in 1761.

Lord Balmerino left no descendants to recall the remembrance of his honest, manly character. His wife, Margaret Chalmers, survived him nearly twenty years, and died at Restalrig, on the 24th of August, 1765, aged fifty-six.

The remains of these two unfortunate noblemen were deposited under the gallery, at the west end of the chapel in the Tower. Beside them repose those of Simon, Lord Lovat. "As they were associates in crime, so they were companions in sepulchre, " observes a modern writer, "being buried in the same grave. "[398] But the more discriminative judge of the human heart will spurn so rash, and undiscerning a remark; and marvel that, in the course of one contest, characters so differing in principle, so unlike in every attribute of the heart, and viewed, even by their enemies, with sentiments so totally opposite, should thus be mingled together in their last home.

FOOTNOTES:

[316] Wood's Peerage.

[317] Who, adds the same authority, carried azure, a fess chequé, argent and gules: and for their crest, a hand issuing out of a wreath, pointing with the thumb and two fingers: motto, *confido*; supporters, two squirrels collared or.

[318] Reay, 203.

[319] Reay, 203.

[320] Wood's Peerage. The defect of the title is the failure of issue male. The title of Livingstone was considered by the same authority as untouched.

[321] Ibid.

[322] Lockhart Papers, i. 138. Note. Calendar.

[323] Memoirs of Lord Kilmarnock. London, 1746, p. 19.

[324] Memoirs of the Earl of Kilmarnock, p. 20.

[325] MS. Letter presented to me by Mrs. Howison Craufurd, of Craufurdland Castle, Ayrshire.

[326] Memoirs of Lord Kilmarnock, p. 21.

[327] Horace Walpole's Letters, ii. p. 113.

[328] Foster's Account, p. 11.

[329] Grose, 214.

[330] Memoirs of Lord Kilmarnock, p. 23.

[331] Life of Colonel Gardiner, by Dr. Doddridge, *passim*.

[332] Doddridge. Life of Colonel Gardiner, p. 155.

[333] Henderson, p. 130.

[334] State Trials of George II.

[335] Maxwell, p. 60.

[336] Forbes's Account, p. 20.

[337] Maxwell, p. 50. This Nobleman was at the battle of Culloden.

[338] Henderson, p. 332.

[339] Henderson, p. 130.

[340] Note in Chambers, p. 89.

[341] History of the Rebellion, from the Scots' Magazine, p. 198.

[342] Chambers, p. 89. Henderson, p. 334.

[343] Observations on the Account of the Behaviour of Lords Kilmarnock and Balmerino, 1746.

[344] Ibid.

[345] Nesbitt, Heraldry, vol. i. p. 154.

[346] "Elphingstone, in the shire of Hadington, and in the parish of Tranent, a village at the distance of three miles S. S.W. from Tranent."—Edinburgh Gazetteer.

[347] Nesbitt, p. 154.

[348] Memoirs of Lord Balmerino. London, 1764.

[349] Wood's Peerage.

[350] Life of Lord Balmerino, p. 51. Buchan's Account of the Earls of Keith, p. 149.

[351] Scots' Magazine for 1746.

[352] Scots' Magazine for 1746.

[353] Georgian Era.

[354] Wood's Peerage.

[355] Maxwell, p. 59.

[356] Georgian Era.

[357] State Trials, vol. xviii.

[358] Edinburgh Gazetteer. Art. "South Leith. "

[359] History of the Rebellion from the Scots' Magazine, p. 302.

[360] Horace Walpole's Letters to Sir Horace Mann, vol. ii. p. 160.

[361] Georgian Era.

[362] Ibid.

[363] State Trials, vol. xviii. p. 466.

[364] Observations on the Account, &c., p. 23.

[365] Horace Walpole, vol. ii. p. 163

[366] Ibid. vol. ii. p. 115.

[367] Horace Walpole.

[368] See Scots' Magazine for 1746.

[369] State Trials.

[370] State Trials.

[371] Note. The plea was couched in these words: "July 29th, 1746. It is conceived that the late Act of Parliament, empowering his Majesty to transport such as are taken in arms from one county to another, where they may be tried by the course of the common law, did not take place till after that time, that the facts implying treason, were actually committed by the accused prisoners, and if so, the Grand Jury of Surrey, or of any other county whatsoever, where these acts of treason are not alleged to have been committed, could not, agreeable to law, find bills against such prisoners; and it may, on that score, be prayed, That the indictment be quashed, or that an arrest of judgment be thereupon granted. " What a bitter, though unavailing feeling of regret accompanies the reflection that this benevolent attempt to save the lives of these brave men, was fruitless.

[372] Letters to Sir H. Mann, vol. ii. p. 167.

[373] State Trials 18, p. 502.

[374] H. Walpole, p. 31. Letters to G. Montagu.

[375] Walpole's Letters to Montagu, p. 29. Folio.

[376] Letters to Sir H. Mann, vol. ii. p. 167.

[377] State Trials, by Hargreaves, pp. 18, 502.

[378] Memoirs of the Earl of Kilmarnock and Cromartie, and of Lord Balmerino, 1746.

[379] Life of Lord Cromartie, 1746.

[380] Buchan's Memoirs of the House of Keith, p. 143.

[381] Walpole's Letters to Sir H. Mann, vol. ii. p. 171.

[382] Foster's Account, p. 87.

[383] For a copy of this letter I am indebted to the kindness of Mrs. Craufurd of Craufurdland Castle, Kilmarnock. The original is in the possession of Martin Paterson, Esq. of Kilmarnock, and is endorsed "Copy of the last Instructions of Lord Kilmarnock to his factor, Mr. Robert Paterson. "

[384] Statement.

[385] Statement.

[386] Mrs. Howison Craufurd, the lady of William Howison Craufurd, Esq., of Craufurdland Castle, Ayrshire. To this Lady I am indebted for much of the information (afforded by her admirable letters) which has been introduced into this Memoir of Lord Kilmarnock. To this lady I addressed an inquiry respecting an original portrait of Lord Kilmarnock. Her efforts to obtain any intelligence of one have been wholly unavailing; and we have been led to the conclusion that, in the fire at Dean Castle, all the portraits of Lord Kilmarnock must have been destroyed; his resemblance, his name, his honour, and his Castle thus becoming extinct at once. At Craufurdland Castle there is a fine portrait of Lord Kilmarnock's brother, his widow and daughter, painted in oils, after a singular

fashion, black and white; giving it a ghastly hue. This perhaps accounts for the local tradition near Kilmarnock, "that on hearing of his brother's death, Mr. Boyd's colour fled, and never returned; nor was he ever seen to smile again. " A tradition not difficult of belief.

The present Mr. Craufurd, of Craufurdland Castle, represents also the family of Howison of Bræ-head. In Mrs. Howison Craufurd's family an amusing circumstance relative to Lord Lovat occurred. He was one evening in a ball-room, and was paying court to the great-grandmother of that lady. As he was playfully examining, and holding in his hand her diamond solitaire, a voice whispered in his ear, "that Government officers were in pursuit of him; and that he must decamp. " Decamp he did, taking with him, *perhaps* by accident, the costly jewel. The young lady was in the greatest trepidation, and her family were resolved to recover the ornament. Many years after, on his return from France, Lovat, whose character, in *no* respect, rose above suspicion, was taxed with the robbery, and refunded a sum which gave twenty pounds to each of a host of granddaughters, then in their girlhood.

[387] In a letter from Mrs. Craufurd of Craufurdland to the author, this fact is stated. It is mentioned as traditionary elsewhere, but is attested by the family.

[388] H. Walpole, vol. ii. p. 167.

[389] H. Walpole's Letters to Mr. Montagu.

[390] Foster's Account, p. 31.

[391] Walpole.

[392] Ford's Account in State Trials, p. 18, 522.

[393] For the original of Lord Balmerino's real speech, which is highly characteristic of its author, I am indebted to Charles Kirkpatrick Sharpe, Esq.

"I was brought up in true, loyal, and anti-revolution principles and I hope the world is convinced that they stuck to me. I must acknowledge I did a very inconsiderate thing, for which I am heartily sorry, in accepting a company of Foot from the Princess Anne, who I know had no more right to the Crown than her predecessor the Prince of Orange.... To make amends for what I had done I joined the... (Pretender) when he was in Scotland in 1715, and when all was over I made my escape, and lived abroad till the year 1734.

"In the beginning of that year I got a letter from my father which very much surprised me; it was to let me know he had a promise of a remission for me. I did not know what to do; I was then, (I think,) in the canton of Berne, and had nobody to advise with: but next morning I wrote a letter to the... (Pretender) who was then at Rome, to acquaint the... (Pretender) that this was come without my asking or knowledge, and that I would not accept of it without his consent. I had in answer to mine, a letter written with... (The Pretender's) own hand, allowing me to go home; and he told me his banker would give me money for my travelling charges when I came to Paris, which accordingly I got. When the... (the Pretender's son) came to Edinburgh I joined him, though I might easily have excused myself from taking arms on account of my age; but I never could have had peace of conscience if I had stayed at home.... I am at a loss when I come to speak of the... (Pretender's son,) I am not a fit hand to draw his character, I shall leave that to others. (Here he gives a fulsome character of the Pretender's son.)

"Pardon me if I say, wherever I had the command, I never suffered any disorders to be committed, as will appear by the Duke of Buccleugh's servants at East Park; by the Earl of Findlater's minister, Mr. Lato, and my Lord's servant, A. Cullen; by Mr. Rose, minister at Nairn, (who was pleased to favour me with a visit when I was prisoner at Inverness;) by Mr. Stewart, principal servant to the Lord President at the House of Culloden; and by several other people. All this gives me great pleasure, now that I am looking upon the block on which I am ready to lay down my head; and though it would not have been my own natural inclination to protect everybody, it would have been my interest to have done it for... (the Pretender's son) abhorred all those who were capable of doing injustice to any.... I have heard since I came to this place, that there has been a most wicked report spread, and mentioned in several of the newspapers that... (the Pretender's son) before the battle of Culloden, had given out orders that no quarter should be given to the enemy. This is such an unchristian thing, and so unlike... (the Pretender's son,) that nobody (the Jacobites) that knows him will believe it. It is very strange if there had been any such orders, that neither the Earl of Kilmarnock, who was Colonel of the regiment of the Foot Guards, nor I, who was Colonel of the second troop of Life Guards, should ever have heard anything of it; especially since we were both at the head-quarters the morning before the battle; I am convinced that it is a malicious report industriously spread to....

"Ever since my confinement in the Tower, when Major White or Mr. Fowler did me the honour of a visit, their behaviour was always so kind and obliging to me that I cannot find words to express it; but I am sorry I cannot say the same thing of a General Williamson: he has treated me barbarously, but not quite so ill as he did the Bishop of Rochester; and had it not been for a worthy clergyman's advice, I should have prayed for him in the words of David, Psalm 109, from the 6th to the 15th verse. I forgive him and all my enemies. I hope you will have the charity to believe I die in peace with all men; for yesterday, I received the Holy Eucharist from the hands of a clergyman of the Church of England, in whose communion I die as in union with the Episcopal Church of Scotland.

"I shall conclude with a short prayer. "—(Here a prayer is mentioned much the same as in Wm. Ford's account.)

[394] The account which I have given of Lord Kilmarnock's behaviour and fate, and also of Lord Balmerino's, is taken from the following works, to which I have not thought it necessary separately to refer. Foster's Account of the Behaviour of Lord Kilmarnock; and the Vindication of Foster's Account from the misrepresentations of some Dissenting Teachers: London, 1746. Account by T. Ford, Under-Sheriff at the Execution, in the State Trials, vol. xviii. p. 325. Horace Walpole's Letters to Geo. Montagu, and to Sir H. Mann. Scots' Magazine for 1746; and Buchan's Life of Marshal Keith; also a Collection of Tracts in the British Museum, relating to the Rebellion, 1746, and chiefly published during that year.

[395] For both these letters, hitherto unpublished, I am indebted for the courtesy of Mrs. Craufurd of Craufurdland Castle.

[396] Forbes's Life of Beattie, vol. ii. p. 351.

[397] Journey to the Hebrides, p. 108

[398] Bayley's History of the Tower, p. 122.

CHARLES RADCLIFFE.

The fate of Charles Radcliffe has been regarded as one of the most severe, and his death as one of the most unjustifiable acts inflicted on those who suffered for their adherence to the Stuart cause.

This unfortunate man was the third son of Francis Earl of Derwentwater, by the Lady Mary Tudor, the daughter of Charles the Second, and was born in 1693. He was the younger brother of James Earl of Derwentwater, who suffered in 1716, for his adherence to the Stuart cause. There was also another elder brother, Francis, who died unmarried, not taking any apparent interest in the politics of the day.

The family of Radcliffe were not regarded by the descendants of their common ancestor, Charles the Second, in the light of kindred whom the rules of decorum, and the usages of society might induce them to disclaim, or at all events, to acknowledge with shame or reluctance; the vitiated notions of the day attached a very different value to the parentage of royalty, even when associated with dishonour. The marriage of Sir Francis Radcliffe to the daughter of Mary Davis was that event which procured his elevation to the peerage; and this alliance, was considered as elevating the dignity of an ancient house. [399] The closest ties of friendship united the Stuarts and the Radcliffes, even from their earliest infancy. Educated, as well as his elder brother, James, chiefly at St. Germains, and with the Chevalier James Stuart, and brought up in the Roman Catholic faith, Charles Radcliffe, owing to the natural ardour of his disposition, imbibed much more readily than his brother the strong party views which characterized the Jacobites as a body.

In James, Earl of Derwentwater, the convictions of his faith, grounded as they are upon the belief of those great truths common to all Christians, worked healthfully; expanding the benevolence of his heart, teaching him mercy, moderation, and forbearance. On Charles, impetuous, zealous, stronger in intellect than his brother, but devoid of prudence, the same mode of culture, the same precepts acted differently. He became, even in early life, violent in his opinions, until the horror of what he deemed error, amounted to bigotry. Henceforth his destiny was swayed by those fierce resentments towards the opposite party by which not only his brother, but even the Chevalier himself, seem to have been so rarely actuated; a remarkable degree of moderation and candour raising the character of James Stuart, whilst Lord Derwentwater was the gentlest of opponents, the most honourable of foes.

In early life Charles Radcliffe appears to have been chiefly dependent upon his brother's kindness and bounty; whilst his pursuits and inclinations, characterized in a letter by Lord Derwentwater as his "pleasures, " were of an expensive description. But it was not long before other causes of concern besides want of money, or a love of dissipation began to disquiet those who were interested in the welfare of the Radcliffe family. About the year 1710, the young Earl of Derwentwater returned from the continent to his patrimonial property at Dilstone, in Northumberland, accompanied by his brother Francis, and by Charles who either frequently visited him, or wholly resided with him at his seat. During this period of the life of Charles Radcliffe, an insight into the general state of the family is afforded by several letters, addressed by the Earl of Derwentwater to Lady Swinburne of Capheaton, whom he styles his "cousin. " The relationship between these families originated in the marriage of Mrs. Lawson, daughter of Sir William Fenwick of Meldon, after the death of her first husband, with Francis, first Earl of Derwentwater, and grandfather of James Radcliffe, and of his brothers. Mrs. Lawson's daughter, Isabel, married Sir John Swinburne of Capheaton who was rescued from a singular fate by one of the Radcliffe family. When a child, he was sent to a monastery in France, where a member of that family accidentally saw him, and observing that he resembled the Swinburnes in Northumberland, he inquired his name, and how he came there? To these questions, the monks answered that they knew not his name; a sum of money was sent annually from England to defray his expenses; but of all other particulars they were wholly ignorant. On investigating the matter, it was found, however, that the child had been taught that his name was Swinburne; and that circumstance, coupled with the mysterious disappearance of the heir of that family from Northumberland induced the superior of the convent to permit his return home, where he identified himself to be the son of John Swinburne and of Jane Blount, by the description which he gave of the marks of a cat, and of a punchbowl, which were still in the house. [400] He was afterwards advanced by Charles the Second to the dignity of a baronet.

To Mary, the daughter of Anthony Englefield, of Whiteknights, Berks, and wife of Sir William Swinburne, of Capheaton, the son of that man whose childhood has so romantic a story associated with it, the following letters are addressed. Of these, the first is written by the celebrated John Radcliffe, Physician to Queen Anne. Dr. Radcliffe was probably a distant relation of the family, although no distinctive trace of that connection appears: he was a native of Wakefield, near Yorkshire; but when these letters were written, he had attained the highest eminence in his profession that could be secured by one man; and was in the possession of wealth which he eventually employed in the foundation of the Radcliffe Library, at Oxford. [401] The "Mr. Radcliffe" to whom he refers, and to whose malady his skill was called upon to administer, was Colonel Thomas Radcliffe, the uncle of Lord Derwentwater: the patient was at the time suffering from mental delusion, in consequence of a fever.

THESE TO SIR WILLIAM SWINBURNE AT CAPHEATON.

Dec. 6, 1709.

"Sir,

"Yours I received, and am very glad to hear that yourself and my lady is in so good health. I hope in a short time Mr. Radcliffe will be so too. He is recovered; but he had such a severe fever that he continues weak still. My Lord Derwentwater and his brother" (Francis) "and Mr. Fenwick, are all come safe from Holland, and are very well, and we shall drink your health together this night. He intends to be with you very speedily in the country. I do not doubt that you will extremely like his conversation: for he has a great many extraordinary good qualities, and I do not doubt but he will be as well beloved as his uncle. My most humble service to your lady and the rest of the good family, and I wish you a merry Christmas; and that I might be so happy as to take a share of it with you, would be a great satisfaction to him who is your most obliged and most faithful, humble servant,

"JOHN RADCLIFFE. "

The next letter is from Sir William Swinburne to his lady; in this he speaks of the pleasure with which Lord Derwentwater had returned to Dilstone, the seat of his ancestors, which he was, in so few short years, to forfeit.

TO MY LADY SWINBURNE, AT CAPHEATON.

Beaufort, 7th Feb. 1710.

"Dear Love!

"My Lord" (Derwentwater) "is very well pleased with Dilstone, and says it answers all that he has heard of it: but is resolved to build a new house, though Roger Fenwick told him he thought his lordship need not alter a stone of it. Upon Thursday my lord dines at Dilstone. Yours for ever,

"WILLIAM SWINBURNE.

"P. S. I understand my lord intends to be at Capheaton on Saturday, and then upon Tuesday at Witton, and so for Widdrington. My lord's leg is a little troublesome; but he intends to hunt the fox to-morrow, and it is a rule all to be abed at ten o'clock the night. Here is old Mr. Bacon and his son, Mr. Fenwick, of Bywell. My lord killed a squirl, and Sir Marmaduke a pheasant or two, and myself one, this morning—which is all, &c. "

The following letter from Lord Derwentwater, to Lady Swinburne, shows that the illness which occasioned so much uneasiness was obstinate: it affords a curious sample of the medical treatment of Dr. Radcliffe, who kindly, and perhaps wisely, humoured his patient in the desire to go to Newcastle.

"I have been just now with my dear uncle, and Jack Thornton was with me. He received us very well: but is yet unease about those people that disturb him, and he says that he must go down to Newcastle by sea, or else he will never get quitte of them. This is an ode fancy; but I believe we shall comply with it, for the doctor dous not sime very averce to it, and was for sending Joseph back with him; but I have taken the horse into my stable, for I feared it mit hurt the horse to return so soon. In fin, I fansed Sir William would like the value of the horse better than to have him sent back. I have been offered eighteen pound. I would have Sir William let me know by the next post whether he will have the horse or the money. I shall have the honor to whrit to him very soon. "

The two following epistles, one from Lady Derwentwater, the other from the Earl, speak of married happiness, alloyed, not only by the distempered fancies of an invalid uncle, but by the melancholy accounts of a brother's behaviour. It does not, however, appear certain which of the brothers, whether Francis or Charles, was thus alluded to.

FOR THE HONOURABLE LADY SWINEBURNE, JUNIOR, AT CAPHEATON.

"Hadcross, Aug. 17.

"I have manny thanks to returne your ladyship for the favour of your letter and oblidging congratulations. My Lord Darwenwater's great merit and agreable temper makes me think I have all the prospect imadgenable of being intierly happy. I desier the favour your ladyship will present my humble sarvise to Sir William. My father and mother joinse with me in this, and dessiers there complements to your ladyship, I beg you will be assured that I am, very much madam, your ladyship's most humble servant.

"A. DARVENWATAR. "

FOR MY LADY SWINBURNE, AT THE BLEW BALL, IN ST. JAMES'S PLACE, NEAR ST. JAMES'S, LONDON.

"Heatherope, Feb. 7.

"Madam,

"I fear'd the good news Miechal writ Gibson, might be false; because I have not heard anything of it from yourself, nor from my uncle, who, I flatter myself, would writ a line to give me so much satisfaction: but I hope all my doubts will vanish if your ladyship does me the favour to confirm what will be so great a content to us. If I could but be sure that my dear uncle avows all his fancys about the men he thought spoke to him, to be nothing but the unlucky effect of his favour, [402] and that he thinks to come over to manage his affairs, will be the most credeble and most kind way of proceeding, both as to himself and family, then I shall believe he was the same man he was befor, which, if you confirm, will be one of the most joyfull and the most unexpected good news that could befall your ladyship's humble, obedient servant, and affectionate kindsman,

"DARWENTWATER.

"I should have writ to your ladyship sooner, and really can have no good excuse: for I should have write to my dear cousen, though my head was full of fox-hunting: and though I had a mind to banish out of a new-married head some melancholic accounts of my brother's behaviour, which I suppose you have had intelligence of, or else of my dear wife's second miscarriage, which has been a great affliction to us, but I flatter myself with the hope of her having better luck another time. She presents her humble service, and so does my Lady Webb. I hope Sir William was well, and cosen Jacky, when you heard last. My brother Charles has been at Sir Marmeduke Constable's, and designs for London. Adieu! "

In May 1714, only one year before the fatal insurrection of 1715 broke out, the following letter, referring to different members of his family, was written by the Earl. What a pleasing picture of an affectionate nature does this correspondence afford. [403]

FOR MY LADY SWINBURNE, JUNIOR, AT CAPHEATON.

"Kathcrosse, May, 6, 1714.

"Now I write with pleasure to your ladyship, since I hope to be so happy as to enjoy your good companie in a few months, I mean immediately after York Races, for my two years will be out here the tenth of July. Indeed Sir John has behaved himself wonderfully well to us quite the holl time, really performing in everything more than I could have expected from a man of honnor, as indeed I had reason to believe him. My lady is not of so steady a temper; but however, we agree very well: and she is mighty fond of my wife, which I take very kindly, since as yet we are but one. Never any body could be so desirous to goe to the North as my wife is, especially just comming from the divertions of London, except your ladyship or myself, who longs to be established there, that we may at least be out of the way of such inhuman proceedings as we saw, upon all accounts, this year at London. My poor dear uncle's case may serve for one instance. After getting the better in all the courts, and, that lastly, the Lord Chancellor and eleven Judges had given there decree in favor of Will. Constable, and my uncle, a factious party, most young rakes, have reversed the decree, and given it for Roper, by a divition of fifty-three against twenty-three torrys, who were resolute enough to appear in a good cause, being forsaken by their brethren, who were afraid to be caled favourers of Poperie. I long to hear what my uncle will say to this news. If he be well, it will nettle him in spite of resignation. Gibson writes word they are at Doway; but he does not know when my uncle will sett forwards. I do not know where to wish him: for I really don't know how he is. For in one letter Gibson writes, he tells me my uncle is as well as ever he was in his life; and at the end of the letter he tells me his honnor is afraid of being pursude. 'Tis certain my uncle writes in another stille than usuall: for, in letters of business he continually mentions God Almighty, the Blessed Virgin, and the Saints. All I say is, God send him over a comfort to his friends, which he must be if he is well. Brother Frank is recovered, but is the very same man. Brother Charles is mighty uneasie: he is no ritcher, though I doe what I can to help him in his pleasures.

"Pray my duty to my uncle and aunt, to whom I will write soon, and kind services to all other relations.

"If your ladyship will tell Tom Errington that I have executed the leases, and that I wonder cousin Tom Errington is not in for a quarter part of Redgroves, and that, supposing there were some such valuable reason as my cousin Tom's not being willing to accept of it, or having resigned it to one of those mentioned in the lease, which by the bye I should take very ill, then that lease of Redgrove's may stand good: but otherways I would have the lease altered, and my cousin Tom Errington to come in for a quarter part, as I promised him he should. In letting him know this, your ladyship will oblige your humble and obedient servant and kinsman,

"DERWENTWATER.

"My dear wife presents her humble service to your ladyship, and desires the same may be made acceptable to all with you. We expect Lord Wald and my lady to make my sister happy, who will do the same by them. "

The felicity which Lord Derwentwater enjoyed was of brief duration. According to tradition among his descendants, he was urged on to those steps which ended in his death by the violent counsels of his brother Charles, whose impetuosity the unfortunate earl often regretted, expressing, in his private correspondence, how much his rash and intemperate spirit distressed and alarmed him. Of the progress, and the principal features of the insurrection of 1715, and of the part which Lord Derwentwater took in that event, an account has already been given. [404] "Happy, " observes the biographer of Charles Radcliffe, "had it been for him, happy for his lady, and happy for his family, had the earl staid at home, and suffered himself to be withheld from that fatal expedition. "[405]

Charles Radcliffe was at that time twenty-two years of age; he had no experience in military affairs, but was full of spirit and courage, ready to offer himself for every daring, and even hopeless enterprise, and seeming to set no value on his life where honour was to be won. Such a character soon became popular with the leaders of the movement in the north; and Lord Derwentwater gave the conduct of his tenantry into his brother's hands, Captain Shaftoe commanding under Mr. Radcliffe.

The behaviour of this young commander throughout the whole of the expedition was consistent with this character of intrepidity; but that which surprised many persons in a man who had never before engaged in war, was the judgment, as well as courage, which he displayed. And perhaps, had his counsels been followed, the result of that ill-starred rising, in which so many brave men perished, might have been less disastrous to the party whom he espoused. When the insurgents were at Hexham, and intelligence was brought that General Carpenter was approaching, Mr. Radcliffe proposed that the Jacobite troops should go out and fight the English before they had recovered from their long march; but his opinion was overruled. His was that description of mind which gleans much from observation; he studied the countenances of those around him, and formed his own conclusion of their characters. When any false alarm happened to be given that the king's troops were near, it was his practice, undaunted himself, to watch the countenances of his officers, when they were ordered to head their corps, and march against the enemy. Some of them, he observed, turned pale, and looked half-dead with fear; the eyes of others flashed with fire and fury: on these, he was certain that a dependence might be placed in the time of action, whilst he forbore from placing the others in any post of responsibility. Nor were his own party the only subjects of his curiosity. Until this eventful period of his life, he had seen but little of the world, "and now, " observes his biographer, "he fancied himself on his travels. " He therefore passed over no object of interest cursorily; at every town he visited, he inquired what were the customs of the place—what monuments of celebrated men, or other objects of antiquity were to be found there; and of these he made written notes; whilst in the council and the camp, he studied the tempers and passions of men.

When, upon the forces arriving at Hawick, the Highlanders mutinied, and going to the top of a rising ground declared that they would not stir a step farther, but would march with Lord Wristoun to the west of Scotland, Mr. Radcliffe thought their views reasonable, and advocated the endeavour to strike a bold stroke in Scotland, and to aim at the entire conquest of that kingdom. His opinion, which events justified, was overruled, and the leaders of his party were resolute in continuing their fatal and rash project of proceeding to England. Mr. Radcliffe, on finding that his representations were ineffectual, begged that he might have an hundred horse given to him, that with them he might try his fortune with the Highlanders: this was also denied him, for fear of weakening the force; and he was constrained to proceed with his confederates in arms to Preston.

In the action at that place, Mr. Radcliffe behaved with a heroism that deserved a happier fate. It was a fine sight to behold him and his brother Lord Derwentwater, endeavouring to animate their men, by words and example, and maintaining their ground with unequalled bravery, obliging the king's forces to retire. During the action Mr. Radcliffe encountered the utmost danger, standing in the midst of the firing, and doing as much duty as the lowest soldiers in the ranks. But his life was spared only to encounter a more disastrous termination, after a long and wearisome exile. When, being invested on all sides by the enemy, the insurgents proposed a capitulation, the gallant young man exclaimed, "that he would rather die, with his sword in his hand, like a man of honour, than be dragged to the gallows, there to die like a dog. " These exclamations fell unheeded; and he was obliged to submit with the rest; soon afterwards, this fine, high-spirited youth, was carried to Newgate, there to await his trial, in company with his companions in error and misfortune.

In Newgate, Mr. Radcliffe witnessed a scene of desperation, accompanied with the ordinary circumstances of licentiousness, and reckless misery, which, unchecked by adequate regulations, the prisons of that day afforded. Until after the execution of Lord Derwentwater and of Lord Kenmure had taken place, hopes of a reprieve sustained the unhappy prisoners in Newgate, and, "flaunting apparel, venison pasties, " wine, and other luxuries, for which they paid an enormous price, were the ordinary indulgences of those who were incarcerated in that crowded receptacle. [406]

Contributions were made from many different quarters for the prisoners; and the friends of the "rebels" were observed to be also very generous to the turnkeys. Numbers of ladies visited the prison, and a choice of the most expensive viands was daily proffered by the lavish kindness of their fair enthusiasts. Of course much scandal followed upon the steps of this dangerous and costly kindness; and escapes were facilitated, perhaps, not without connivance on the part of Government. On the fourteenth of March an attempt was made by some of these unfortunate people to get out of the press-yard, by breaking through a part of the wall, from which they were to be let down by a rope; but they were discovered, and, in consequence, heavily ironed. Nevertheless, on the twenty-third of March almost all of the prisoners were released from their fetters, an indulgence which was a proof of the lenity of the Government, as the ordinary keepers of the prison would not have dared to have allowed it. [407] After this, Mr. Forster and others amused themselves with the game of shuttlecock, at which, relates the author of the Secret History of the Rebels in Newgate, the "valiant Forster beat every one who engaged him: so that he triumphed with his feathers in the prison, though he could not do it in the field. " On the tenth of April that gentleman made his escape: and henceforth, a lieutenant, with thirty of the Foot Guards, was ordered to do constant duty at Newgate. Meantime, crowded as the building was, a spotted fever broke out, and seemed likely to relieve the civil authorities from no small number of the unfortunate prisoners.

On the eighth of May, Mr. Radcliffe was arraigned at the Exchequer Bar, at Westminster, for High Treason: to this he pleaded not guilty. In a few days afterwards he was brought there again, and tried upon the indictment; he had no plea to offer in his defence, and was found guilty.

He soon afterwards was carried to Westminster, accompanied by eleven other prisoners, to receive sentence of death. They were conveyed in six coaches to the Court. As the coach in which Mr. Radcliffe was seated, drove into Fleet Street, it encountered the state carriage in which George the First, who was then going to Hanover for the first time since his accession, was driving. This obliged Mr. Radcliffe's coach to stop; and, perceiving that he was opposite to a distiller's shop, he called for a pint of aniseed, which he and a fellow-prisoner, with a servant of Newgate, drank, and then proceeded to Westminster.

Mr. Radcliffe was several times reprieved; and it was thought he might have been pardoned; but affrighted, perhaps, by his brother's fate, and probably weary of imprisonment, he now began to project a plan of escape, to which he was emboldened by the great success of several similar attempts. Greater vigilance was, indeed, resorted to in the prison, after the flight of Brigadier Mackintosh, who had knocked down the turnkey, and ran off through the streets: and all cloaks, riding-hoods, and arms, were prohibited being brought in by the visiters who came to visit the prisoners. It is amusing to hear, that a certain form of riding-hoods acquired, at this time, the name of a Nithsdale, in allusion to the escape of the Earl of Nithsdale. [408]

On the day appointed for Mr. Radcliffe's escape, the prisoners gave a grand entertainment in Newgate: this took place in a room called the Castle, in the higher part of the prison. Mr. Radcliffe, when the party were at the highest of their mirth, observing a little door open in the corner of the room, passed through it followed by thirteen of the prisoners; and succeeded in finding their way, unmolested, to the debtor's side, where the turnkey, not knowing them, and supposing them to be visiters to the prisoners, allowed them to pass on. Mr. Radcliffe was dressed in mourning, and had, according to his own subsequent account to a fellow prisoner in Newgate, a "brown tye-wig. " In this way, without any disguise, but wearing his ordinary attire, did he escape, leaving within the prison walls, his friend, Basil Hamilton, nephew of the Duke of Hamilton, who, as it was deposed on his trial, was his chum, or companion, living with him in a room, the windows of which looked upon the garden of the College of Physicians. After remaining concealed for some time, Mr. Radcliffe took the first opportunity of getting a passage to France. [409] He lived, for many years, in Paris, in great poverty, tantalized with promises of assistance from the French Court, yet witnessing the ungenerous treatment of the Chevalier by that Court. His nephew, John Radcliffe, who was killed accidentally, assisted him with remittances in 1730 for some time, and James Stuart gave him a small pension: his difficulties and privations must have been considerable; yet they never lessened his ardour in the cause for which he had sacrificed every worldly advantage.

Either to amend his ruined fortunes, or to gratify a passion long unrequited, Mr. Radcliffe was resolved upon marriage. The object of his hopes was Charlotte Maria, Countess of Newburgh, the widow of Hugh, Lord Clifford of Chudleigh, and the mother of two daughters by that nobleman. This lady was about a year older than himself, being born in 1694. It is a tradition in the family of Lord Petre, the lineal descendant of James, Earl of Derwentwater, that Charles Radcliffe offered his hand twelve times to the Countess of Newburgh, and was as often refused. Wearied by his importunity, Lady Newburgh at last forbade him the house. But the daring character of Mr. Radcliffe, and his strong will, suggested an expedient, and he was resolved to obtain an interview. To compass this end, he actually descended into an apartment in which the Countess was sitting, through the chimney; and taking her by surprise, obtained her consent to an union. Of the truth of this curious courtship, there is tolerably good evidence, not only in the belief of the Petre family, but from a picture representing the fact, which is at Thorndon. [410] The nuptials took place at Brussels, in the church of the Virgin Mary, on the twenty-fourth of June, 1724, [411] and in 1726, James Bartholomew, who became, after the death of his mother, third Earl of Newburgh, was born at Vincennes. [412]

Lady Newburgh had every reason, as far as prudence could be allowed to dictate to the affections, for her reluctance to a marriage with Mr. Radcliffe. He was, at this time, an outlawed man, with a sentence of death passed upon him, and no hope could ever be revived of his regaining, even after the death of his nephew, the family honours and estates. Yet, in the ardour and fearlessness of Charles Radcliffe's character there must have been much to compensate for those circumstances, and to win the fancy of the young. There seems no reason to suppose that the union thus strangely formed was infelicitous; and indeed, from family documents, it is evident that the family so marked out by fate for sorrow, were happy in their mutual affection. Of the two daughters of Lady Newburgh's first marriage, Anna, the eldest, was married to the Count de Mahony, whose descendants, the Gustiniani might claim the title of Newburgh, were they not debarred by being born aliens. Another was Frances, who died unmarried. This lady is mentioned in a letter written by Charles Radcliffe, recently before his death, when he was confined to the Tower, with peculiar affection, as "that other tender mother of my dear children. "[413]

In the year 1733, Mr. Radcliffe visited England, and resided several months in Pall Mall; yet the ministry did not consider it necessary to take any notice of his return, nor, probably, would they ever have concerned themselves on that subject, had not a second insurrection brought the unfortunate man into notice. In 1735, he again returned, and endeavoured by the mediation of friends to procure a pardon, but was unsuccessful in that attempt. [414]

Irritated, perhaps, by that refusal, and still passionately attached to the cause which he had espoused; undeterred by the execution of his brother, or by the sufferings of his friends, from mixing himself in the turmoils of a second contest, Charles Radcliffe, on the breaking out of the insurrection of 1745, again ventured his life on the hazard. He had no lands to lose, no estates to forfeit; but he had all to gain; for the death of his nephew made him the head of the unfortunate house of Radcliffe. After that event, he assumed the title of Earl of Derwentwater, and it was of course assigned to him at the court of St. Germains, and indeed always insisted upon by him; but the estates were alienated, and there appeared no hope under the present government of ever recovering those once enviable possessions. Under these circumstances, Mr. Radcliffe was naturally a likely object for the representations of the sanguine, or the intrigues of the designing to work upon; and in this temper of mind he met, in the year 1743, with John Murray of Broughton, at Paris, where that gentleman remained three weeks; and became intimately acquainted with Mr. Radcliffe, who is described among others, as a "wretched dependant on French pensions, with difficulty obtained, and accompanied with contempt in the payment. "

While the fashionable world were diverting themselves with epigrams upon the Rebellion, a small expedition was fitted out, consisting of twenty French officers, and sixty Scotch and Irish, who embarked at Dunkirk on board the Esperance privateer; among these was Charles Radcliffe and his eldest son. At this time nothing was spoken of in London except the daring attempt in Scotland, —sometimes in derision, —sometimes in serious apprehension: "the Dowager Strafford, " writes Horace Walpole (Sept. 1745), "has already written cards for my Lady Nithesdale, my Lady Tullebardine, the Duchess of Perth and Berwick, and twenty more revived peeresses, to invite them to play at whist, Monday three months: for your part, you will divert yourself with their old taffetys, and tarnished slippers, and their awkwardness the first day they go to Court in clean linen. "[415] "I shall wonderfully dislike, " observes the same writer, "being a loyal sufferer in a threadbare coat, and shivering in an attic chamber at Hanover, or reduced to teach Latin and English to the young princes at Copenhagen. Will you ever write to me in my garret at Herenhausen? I will give you a faithful account of all the promising speeches that Prince George and Prince Edward make whenever they have a new sword, and intend to reconquer England. "

One of the first adverse circumstances that befel the Jacobites in 1745, was the capture of the vessel in which Mr. Radcliffe hoped to reach the shores of Scotland. It was taken during the month of November by the Sheerness man-of-war; and Mr. Radcliffe and his son were carried to London and imprisoned in the Tower.

On the twenty-first of November he was conveyed, under a strong guard from the Tower, to Westminster; he was brought to the bar, by virtue of a Habeas Corpus, and the record of his former conviction and attainder was at the same time removed there by Certiorari. These being read to him, the prisoner prayed that counsel might be allowed him; and named Mr. Ford and Mr. Jodrel, who were accordingly assigned to him as counsel. A few days were granted to prepare the defence, and on the twenty-fourth of the month the prisoner was again brought up; he pleaded that he was not the person named in the record, who was described as Charles Radcliffe, but maintained that he was the Earl of Derwentwater. He also requested that the trial might be put off, that two witnesses, one from Brussels, the other from St. Germains, might be summoned. This was refused. The prisoner then challenged one of the jury, but that challenge was overruled. During these proceedings the lofty, arrogant manner, and the vehement language of Mr. Radcliffe drew from his counsel the remark that he was disordered in his senses. The judge, Mr. Justice Foster, who tried the case, bore his contemptuous conduct with great forbearance. When brought into Court, to be arraigned, he would neither hold up his hand, nor plead, insisting that he was a subject of France, and appealing to the testimony of the Neapolitan Minister, who happened to be in Court. But not one of these objections was allowed, and the trial proceeded.

No fresh indictment was framed, and the point at issue related merely to the identity of the prisoner. The award in Mr. Radcliffe's case was agreeable to the precedent in the case of Sir Walter Raleigh, and execution was awarded on his former offence, judgment not being again pronounced, having been given on the former arraignment. This mode of proceeding might be law, but no one after the lapse of thirty years, and the frequent communications of the prisoner with the English Government, can regard such a proceeding as *justice*: and, as in the case of Sir Walter Raleigh, it brought odium upon the memory of James the First, so it excited in the reign of George the Second almost universal commiseration for the sufferer, and disgust at the course adopted.

The evidence in this case was far from being such as would be accepted in the present day.

Two Northumberland men were sworn to the fact that the prisoner at the bar was the younger brother of the Earl of Derwentwater, and that they had seen him march out from Hexham, in Northumberland, at the head of five hundred of Lord Derwentwater's tenantry; they recognized him, as they declared, by a scar on his face; they had been to see him in the Tower, to refresh their memories, and could swear to him, as Charles Radcliffe, brother of the Earl of Derwentwater. After this deposition, Roger Downs, a person who had acted in the capacity of barber to the State prisoners, in 1715, was called.

To him Mr. Radcliffe thus addressed himself: [416] "I hope, sir, you have some conscience; you are now sworn, and take heed what you say. "

To this Downs replied; "I shall speak nothing but the truth. I well remember that I was appointed close shaver at Newgate, in the year 1715 and 1716, when the rebels were confined there, and shaved all those who were close confined. "

The Counsel then asked, "Pray, sir, did you shave Charles Radcliffe, Esquire, the late Earl of Derwentwater's brother, who was confined in Newgate for being concerned in the rebellion in the year 1715, or who else did you shave of the said rebels at that time? And pray, sir, who was keeper, or who were turnkeys of the said gaol of Newgate."

The answer of Downs was couched in these words, "William Pitt, Esq. was head keeper, and Mr. Rouse, and Mr. Revel, were head turnkeys, who appointed my master to be barber, to shave the prisoners; and I attended in my master's stead, and used to go daily to wait on the rebel prisoners, and I particularly remember that I shaved Basil Hamilton, a reputed nephew of the late Duke of

Hamilton, and Charles Radcliffe, Esq., brother to the late Earl of Derwentwater, who I perfectly remember were chums, or companions, in one room, in the press-yard, in Newgate, that looked into the garden of the College of Physicians, and for which service I was always very well paid. "

The Counsel then desired him to look at the prisoner and inform the Court if that gentleman were the very same Charles Radcliffe that he shaved in Newgate, at the aforesaid time, and who after escaped out of Newgate.

To this Downs returned the following reply: "I cannot on my oath say he is. "

Then the head keeper of Newgate was called, and he produced the books belonging to the gaol, wherein were the names of Charles Radcliffe, and other rebels, who had been condemned, and were respited several times. This gentleman said, that the books produced then in Court were in the same condition that he found them: but as to the person of the prisoner he knew nothing, his confinement having taken place several years before he belonged to the gaol.

Abraham Mosely, a servant of the head keeper, was then called, but he was not sworn; another gentleman was afterwards brought to the bar; as the book was handed to him to be sworn, Mr. Radcliffe, looking earnestly at him, inquired what book it was that he was going to be sworn upon: the officer answered it was the New Testament. Mr. Radcliffe replied, "He is no Christian, and believes neither in God nor devil. " The evidence of this witness, whose name is suppressed, was, however, received, and it seems not to have been inconsistent with his alleged character. It was the disclosure of a confidential conversation on the part of Mr. Radcliffe, who had imparted to the witness in what manner he had escaped from Newgate in 1715. The witness was asked whether the prisoner was drunk when he made this confession: he answered that he was. Then being asked if he were drunk himself, he replied that he never got drunk; upon which Mr. Radcliffe said hastily, that "some people would get drunk if at free cost. "

The prisoner examining no witnesses, the Chief Justice summed up the case, and in ten or fifteen minutes the jury, who had retired, brought in a verdict of guilty. A Rule was then made for the proper writ for the execution of the prisoner, on the eighth of December, and he was remanded to the Tower. When informed by the Court of the time fixed for his doom, Mr. Radcliffe said he wished they had given him a longer time, that so he might have been able to acquaint some people in France, and that his brother, the Earl of Morton, and he might "have set out on their journey together. "

The unhappy Mr. Radcliffe returned to his prison. Much has been written of the arrogance and intemperance of his conduct and language, but much must be allowed for the subservience of the contemporary writers, as well as for the irritated feelings of the man. Considering himself as a nobleman, and meeting with disrespect, and, perhaps, harsh usage, a quick temper was aggravated almost to madness. To his inferiors the passion and pride of his character were so offensive that the warders of the Tower could be scarcely induced to give him their attendance; and this inconvenience was the more severely felt as a man named McDermont, who had been his equerry for twenty-three years, was sent to Newgate on the very day when Mr. Radcliffe entered the Tower.

At the hour of his last earthly trial, this man, whose eventful and singular life was brought to a close at the age of fifty-three, redeemed the errors of the last few weeks of anguish, and of bitter disappointment. He submitted calmly to his doom. The sullen sorrow, and the intolerable haughtiness of his manner, were exchanged for a composure, solemn and affecting, and for a courtesy which well became the brother of Lord Derwentwater.

Between eight and nine on the morning of the eighth of December, the Sheriff, driving in a mourning coach to the east gate of the Tower, demanded the prisoner. The gate was opened, and in about ten minutes a landau, in which Mr. Radcliffe was seated, drove out at the east gate, towards Little Tower Hill. He was accompanied by the Under-Sheriffs, and by the officers of the Tower: the landau was surrounded by a party of Foot Guards, with their bayonets fixed. The street was lined with horse soldiers, from the iron gate of the Tower, to the scaffold, which was encompassed also with horse soldiers. At the foot of the stairs of the scaffold a booth was erected, for the reception of the prisoner.

Like Lord Balmerino, Mr. Radcliffe wore his regimentals, which were those of the French army; and consisted of a scarlet coat, with gold buttons, the sleeves faced with black velvet; a scarlet waistcoat, trimmed with gold lace; and white silk stockings. His hat was encircled with a white feather.

As the prisoner alighted from the landau, he saw some of his friends standing near the booth; he paid his compliments to them with the grace of a well-bred man; and, smiling, asked of the sheriffs, who had preceded him in the mourning-coach, "if he was to enter the booth? " He was answered in the affirmative. "It is well, " he replied; and he went in, and there passed about ten minutes in his devotions.

The scaffold had been provided early that morning with a block, covered with black, a cushion, and two sacks of sawdust; and the coffin of the unhappy prisoner, also covered with black, was placed on the stage.

Mr. Radcliffe ascended the scaffold with great calmness, and asked for the executioner. "I am but a poor man, " said the unfortunate man, "but there are ten guineas for you: if I had more, I would give it you; do your execution so as to put me to the least possible misery. " He then kneeled down, and folding his hands, uttered a short prayer. He arose, and was then assisted by two of the warders in the last preparations for his doom, taking off his coat and waistcoat, and substituting for his wig a white cap. Having taken a respectful leave of the sheriffs, he was about to kneel down, when it was discovered that it would be necessary to tuck back the collar of his shirt. That office was performed by the executioner. Then, after saying a short prayer, and crossing himself several times, he laid his head upon the block. In less than half a minute afterwards, he gave the signal, by spreading out his hands: his head was severed at one blow, and the body fell upon the scaffold. The executioner, searching his pockets, found in them a silver crucifix, his beads, and half-a-guinea. No friend attended the man who had been so long exiled from his own country, on the scaffold; but four undertakers' men stood, with a piece of red cloth, to receive the head of the ill-fated Charles Radcliffe. His body, being wrapt in a blanket, was put into the coffin, with his head, and conveyed to the Nag's Head, in Gray's Inn Lane, and thence, in the dead of the night, to Mr. Walmsbey's, North Street, Red Lion Square, whence it was removed to be interred in the church-yard of St. Giles's-in-the-Fields, where a neglected stone alone marks his burial-place. The following is the inscription on the coffin: —"Carolus Radcliffe, comes de Derwentwater, decollatus, die 8vo. Decembris, 1746, ætatis 53. " To this were added the words, so appropriate to the close of an adventurous life, "Requiescat in pace. "

Desolate as these last hours appear to have been, and uncheered by the presence of a friend, some tender care was directed to the remains of the unfortunate sufferer. His head was afterwards sewn on to the body by a dependant of Lord Petre's family, a woman of the name of Thretfall, whose grandson, a carpenter, who lived for many years at Ingatestone Hall, Essex, a seat of Lord Petre's, used to relate to the happier children of a later generation (the descendants of James, Earl of Derwentwater), the circumstances, of which he had heard in his childhood. The Countess of Newburgh was afterwards buried by the side of her husband; and the sexton of St. Giles's Church, some years since, on the lid of the coffin giving way, perceived some gold lace in a state of preservation; so that it seems probable that the blanket in which the bleeding remains were removed, was superseded by the costly and military attire worn by the prisoner.

Previous to his death Mr. Radcliffe wrote to his family. His letters, and all the memorials of his brother, and of himself, have been sedulously preserved by the family to whom they have descended. Lady Anna Maria Radcliffe, the only daughter of James, Earl of Derwentwater, married in 1732, James, eighth Baron Petre, of Writtle, county Essex. A connexion had already subsisted between the families, a sister of Lord Derwentwater having married a Petre of the collateral branch, seated at Belhouse, in Essex, which branch is now extinct.

Lady Anna Radcliffe appears to have entertained the deepest reverence for her father's memory, and to have held all that belonged to him, or that related to his fate, sacred. She caused a large mahogany chest to be made to receive the clothes which he wore on the scaffold, and also the covering of the block; likewise, a cast of his face taken after death: and having deposited these relics in the chest, she added a written paper with her seal and signature, *Anne Petre*, authenticating the said apparel and documents, and solemnly forbidding any of her descendants or other persons to make use of the chest for any other purpose, but "to contain her father's clothes, unless some other receptacle more costly be by them provided. " This box is deposited in a room at Thorndon Hall, with letters and papers relating both to *James*, Lord Derwentwater, and to his brother *Charles*.

The eldest son of Mr. Radcliffe, called the Lord Kinnaird, in right of the Barony of Kinnaird, remained a prisoner in the Tower at the time of his father's execution; and the uncertainty of that young man's fate must greatly have added to the distress of his father. In the spring of 1746, he was suffered to return to France, on a cartel, an exchange of prisoners including him as a native of France. The circumstance to which the youth owed his long imprisonment, was a report which gained ground that he was the second son of James Stuart, Henry Benedict, whom the English political world believed, at that time, to be on the eve of going to Ireland, and under this impression, the mob followed the young man as he was conveyed from the vessel to the Tower with insults. Before returning to France, he was received by the Duke of Richmond, his mother's relative, with great consideration, and entertained at what Horace Walpole terms "a great dinner. "[417] Such was what the same author calls the *Stuartism* in some of the highest circles.

Lord Kinnaird afterwards put in a claim for the reversion of the Derwentwater estate, but without success, for it had already been sold by the Commissioners. A scene of iniquitous fraud, in the sale of the forfeited estate belonging to Lord Derwentwater was afterwards detected by Lord Gage, for which Dennis Bond, Esquire, and Sergeant Birch, Commissioners of the sale, were expelled the House. [418] In 1749, an Act was passed vesting the several estates of James, Earl of Derwentwater in trustees, for the benefit of Greenwich Hospital; but, out of the funds thus arising, 30,000*l.* was appropriated to the widowed Countess of Newburgh, and the interest of the remaining 24,000*l.* , was to be paid to James Bartholomew, Lord Kinnaird, during his life, and after his death the principal to revert to his eldest son. [419] From the Chevalier, the widowed Countess of Newburgh received, as the following letter will shew, much kindness and sympathy; the conduct of James to his fallen and powerless adherents, appears to have been almost invariably marked by compassion and generosity. The Countess of Newburgh survived her husband ten years, during which time the affection of the Chevalier, and of his sons, for her husband's memory was evinced by kindness to his widow, as the following letter testifies: —

LADY DERWENTWATER TO THE CHEVALIER DE ST. GEORGE.[420]

Sir,

I received the honour of our Majesty's most gracious letter, and beg leave to return my grateful thanks. Your Majesty is very good in commending my dear Lord who did but his duty: he gave his life most willingly for your Majesty's service, and I am persuaded that your Majesty never had a subject more attacht to his duty than he was. The Prince of Wales and the Duke of York have been so good to show a great concern for my loss, and recommended most strongly to the King of France my famyly. His Majesty has been most extremely good and gracious to them. My son, that was Captain in Dillon's, has now the Brevet of Colonel reform'd with appointments of 1800 livres a-year; his sisters have 150 livres a-year each of them, with his royal promis of his protection of the famyly for ever. The Marquise de Mezire, and her daughter the Princess de Monteban have been most extremely friendly to my famyly in this affair.

I am, your Majesty's most dutyfull subject,

CHARLOTTE DERWENTWATER. St. Germains, February, ye 10th, 1747.

Of the Countess's two younger sons, one, James Clement Radcliffe, an officer in the French service, survived till 1788, the other, who bore his father's name, Charles, died in 1749. Three of her daughters died unmarried, but Lady Mary, the fourth, married Francis Eyre, Esq., of Walworth Castle, Northamptonshire. On the failure of the issue of three sons, in 1814 the title of Newburgh passed into the family of Eyre through the marriage of the above Mary, and devolved upon Francis Eyre, the grandson of Charlotte Countess of Newburgh, and of Charles Radcliffe, father of the present Earl of Newburgh.

By the marriage of Lady Anne Radcliffe, the only daughter of James, Earl of Derwentwater, in 1732, to Robert James, eighth Baron Petre, the present Lord Petre is the rightful representative of that attainted nobleman, being the third in direct descent from Lady Anne Radcliffe, whose only brother, John, [421] was killed accidentally abroad, having never been married. [422]

In concluding this account of the unfortunate Charles Radcliffe, a reflection naturally arises in the mind, how different would have been the spirit of administration in the present day to that which the government of that period displayed: —how great would have been the horror of shedding the blood of honourable and valiant men; how universal the sentiment of mournful commiseration; and how strong the conviction, that men, so true to an ill fated cause, would have been faithful to any engagements which required them to abandon their efforts in that cause; had clemency, but too imperfectly understood in those turbulent and merciless times, excited their gratitude, and for ever ensured their fidelity.

FOOTNOTES:

[399] "Genuine and Impartial Memoirs of the Life and Character of Charles Radcliffe, wrote by a Gentleman of the Family, (Mr. Eyre,) to prevent the public being imposed on by any erroneous or partial accounts, to the prejudice of this unfortunate gentleman. " London, printed for the Proprietor, and sold by E. Cole, 1746.

[400] Hodgson's Hist. of Northumberland, vol. ii. p. 227, note.

[401] Ibid. p. 233.

[402] Fever.

[403] At Thorndon, the seat of Lord Petre, in Norfolk, are other original letters of Lord Derwentwater, referring to his wife. In most touching terms he thanks the mother of Lady Derwentwater for having "given her to him. " This, and other interesting documents, are highly prized, and consequently carefully preserved by the ancient and noble family to whom they have descended.

[404] See Life of Lord Derwentwater, vol. i.

[405] Ibid. 14.

[406] Secret History of the Rebels in Newgate, 3rd edition, London, 1716.

[407] Ibid. p. 8.

[408] Secret History.

[409] State Trials.

[410] For this anecdote, and also for a considerable portion of the materials of this Memoir, I am indebted to the great kindness and intelligence of the Hon. Mrs. Douglas, daughter of the present Lord Petre.

[411] Wood's Peerage.

[412] MS. Letter.

[413] I must again refer to the information supplied by the Hon. Mrs. Douglas.

[414] Life of Charles Radcliffe, p. 25.

[415] Letter to G. Montagu, p. 18.

[416] State Trials; quoted from the Impartial History of the late Charles Radcliffe, written at the time.

[417] Letter to Sir H. Mann, vol. ii. p. 140.

[418] A review of the reign of Geo. II. London. 1762.

[419] Douglas's Peerage, Edit. by Wood.

[420] Brown's Hist. Highlands, (Stuart Papers, Appendix) page 491.

[421] In my first volume, I have stated that the Earl of Newburgh was the direct representative of James Earl of Derwentwater. (See p. 280, vol. i.) Into this error I was betrayed by an obscure passage in Burke's Extinct Peerage.

I am indebted to the Hon. Mrs. Douglass, to whom I have before expressed my obligations, for a correction of this mistake, and also for the copy of the pedigree in the Appendix. This lady has also explained the reason why so many accounts have stated that the body of James Earl of Derwentwater was interred in St. Giles's Church-yard. His body was privately removed to Dagenham Park, in Essex, a house his Countess had hired in order to be near London. A report, meanwhile, was circulated by his friends that he had been buried in St. Giles's; and, when no further danger of tumult was to be apprehended, the remains of the Earl were deposited with his ancestors in the vaults of the chapel at Dilstone.

The mother of the present Mr. Howard, of Corby Castle, and sister of Sir Thomas Neave, Bart., has often related to her young relations, that when she and her sisters were children, they were afraid to pass at night along the gallery at Dagenham, it being popularly supposed that Lord Derwentwater still walked there, carrying his head under his arm. This must have been, at least, seventy years after his death.

[422] See Appendix, No. 2, also note.

APPENDIX

No. I.

This letter was addressed by the Rev. Joseph Spence, author of "Polymetus, " and of "Spence's Anecdotes, " and prebend of Durham, to his father, who had forbidden him to enter into the society of the Chevalier, at Rome.

The Rev. Joseph Spence left this letter, with other MSS. and books, to the late Mrs. Coltman, mother of Samuel Coltman, Esq., of Darley Dale. It is not dated, but undoubtedly refers to the Chevalier, James Stuart.

"Sir,

"About a month ago, Mr. —— and I being in search of some of the antiquities of your place, we became acquainted with an English gentleman, very knowing in this kind of learning, and who proved of great use to us; his name is Dr. Cooper, a priest of the Church of England, whom we did not suspect to be of the Pretender's retinue, but took him to be a curious traveller, which opinion created in me a great liking for his conversation. On Easter eve, he made us the compliment, that as he supposed us bred in the profession of the said Church, he thought it incumbent on him to invite us to divine service, next day being Easter Sunday. Such language, at Rome, appeared to me a jest. I stared at the Doctor, who added that the Pretender (whom he called king), had prevailed with the late pope, to grant licence for having divine service according to the rules of the Church of England, performed in his palace, for the benefit of the Protestant gentlemen of his suite, his domestics, and travellers; and that Dr. Berkley and himself were appointed for the discharge of this duty; and that prayers were read as ordinarily here as in London. I should have remained of St. Thomas's belief, had I not been a witness that this is a matter of fact, and as such, have noted it down, as one of the greatest wonders of Rome. This was the occasion of my first entrance into the Pretender's house: I became acquainted with both the Doctors, who are sensible, well-bred men. I put several questions to them about the Pretender, and, if credit can be given them, they assure me he is a moral, upright man, being far from any sort of bigotry, and most averse to disputes and distinctions of religion, whereof not a word is admitted in his family. They described him in person very much to the resemblance of King

Charles II., which they say he approaches more and more every day, with a great application to business, and a head well turned that way, having only some clerks, to whom he dictates such letters as he does not write with his own hand. In some days after, my friend and I went to take the evening air, in the stately park called Villa Ludovici, there we met, face to face, on a sudden, with the Pretender, his Princess, and court; we were so very close before we understood who they were, that we could not retreat with decency, common civility obliged us to stand side-ways in the alley, as others did, to let them pass by. The Pretender was easily distinguished by his star and garter, as well as by his air of greatness, which discovered a majesty superior to the rest. I felt at that instant of his approach, a strange convulsion in body and mind, such as I never was sensible of before, whether aversion, awe, or respect occasioned it, I can't tell: I remarked his eyes fixed on me, which, I confess, I could not bear—I was perfectly stunned, and not aware of myself, when, pursuant to what the standers-by did, I made him a salute; he returned it with a smile, which changed the sedateness of his first aspect into a very graceful countenance; as he passed by I observed him to be a well-sized, clean-limbed man. I had but one glimpse of the Princess, which left me a great desire of seeing her again; however, my friend and I turned off into another alley, to reason at leisure on our several observations: there we met Dr. Cooper, and, after making some turns with him, the same company came again in our way. I was grown somewhat bolder, and resolved to let them pass as before, in order to take a full view of the Princess: she is of a middling stature, well-shaped, and has lovely features: wit, vivacity, and mildness of temper, are painted in her look. When they came to us, the Pretender stood, and spoke a word to the Doctor, then looking at us, he asked him whether we were English gentlemen; he asked us how long we had been in town, and whether we had any acquaintance in it, then told us he had a house, where English gentlemen would be very welcome. The Princess, who stood by, addressing herself to the Doctor in the prettiest English I think I ever heard, said, 'Pray, Doctor, if these gentlemen be lovers of music, invite them to my concert, to-night; I charge you with it; ' which she accompanied with a salute in the most gracious manner. It was a very hard task, sir, to recede from the honour of such an invitation, given by a princess, who, although married to the Pretender, deserves so much in regard to her person, her house, and family. However, we argued the case with the Doctor, and represented the strict orders we had to the contrary; he replied, there would be no prohibition to a traveller against music, even at the ceremonies of the Roman Catholic Church;

that if we missed this occasion of seeing this assembly of the Roman nobility, we might not recover it while we stayed in Rome; and, that it became persons of our age and degree to act always the part of gentlemen, without regard to party humours. These arguments were more forcible than ours, so we went, and saw a bright assembly of the prime Roman nobility, the concert composed of the best musicians of Rome, a plentiful and orderly collation served; but the courteous and affable manner of our reception was more taking than all the rest. We had a general invitation given us whilst we stayed in town, and were desired to use the palace as our house, we were indispensably obliged to make a visit next day, in order to return thanks for so many civilities received; —those are things due to a Turk. We were admitted without ceremony; the Pretender entertained us on the subject of our families as knowingly as if he had been all his life in England: he told me some passages of myself and father, and of his being against the followers of King Charles I. and II., and added, "that if you, sir, had been of age before my grandfather's death, to learn his principles, there had been little danger of your taking party against the rights of a Stuart. "

"He then observed how far the prejudices of education and wrong notions of infancy are apt to carry people from the paths of their ancestors: he discoursed as pertinently on several of our neighbouring families as I could do, upon which I told him I was surprised at his so perfect knowledge of our families in England; his answer was, that from his infancy he had made it his business to acquire the knowledge of the laws, customs, and families of his country, so that he might not be reported a stranger when the Almighty pleased to call him thither. These and the like discourses held until word was brought that dinner was served; we endeavoured all we could to withdraw, but there was no possibility for it after he had made us this compliment, "I assure you, Gentlemen, I shall never be for straining man's inclinations; however, our grandfathers, who were worthy people, dined, and I hope there can be no fault found that we do the same. " There is every day a regular table of ten or twelve covers well served, unto which some of the qualified persons of his court, or travellers, are invited: it is supplied with English and French cooking, French and Italian wines; but I took notice that the Pretender eat only of the English dishes, and made his dinner of roast-beef, and what we call Devonshire-pie: he also prefers our March beer, which he has from Leghorn, to the best wines: at the dessert, he drinks his glass of champagne very heartily, and to do him justice, he is as free and cheerful at his table as any man I know; he spoke much in favour of our English ladies, and said he was persuaded he had not many enemies among them; then he carried a health to them. The Princess with a smiling countenance took up the matter, and said, "I think then, Sir, it would be but just that I drink to the cavaliers. " Sometime after, the Pretender begun a health to the prosperity of all friends in England, which he addressed to me. I took the freedom to reply, that as I presumed he meant his own friends, he would not take it ill that I meant mine. "I assure you, Sir, " said he, "that the friends you mean can have no great share of prosperity till they become mine, therefore, here's prosperity to yours and mine. " After we had eat and drank very heartily, the Princess told us we must go see her son, which could not be refused; he is really a fine promising child, and is attended by English women, mostly Protestants, which the Princess observed to us, saying, that as she believed he was to live and die among Protestants, she thought fit to have him brought up by their hands; and that in the country where she was born, there was no other distinction but that of honour and dishonour. These women, and particularly two Londoners, kept such a racket about us to make us kiss the young Pretender's hand that to get clear of them as soon as we could, we were forced to comply: the Princess laughed very heartily, and told us that she did not question but the day would come that we should not be sorry to have made so early an acquaintance with her son. I thought myself under a necessity of making her the compliment, that being hers, he could not miss being good and happy. On the next post day, we went, as commonly the English gentlemen here do, to the Pretender's house for news. He had received a great many letters, and after perusing them he told us that there was no great prospect of amendment in the affairs of England; that the Secret Committee and several other honest men were taking abundance of pains to find out the cause of the nation's destruction, which knowledge, when attained to, would avail only to give the more concern to the public without procuring relief; for that the authors would find means to be above the reach of the common course of justice: he bemoaned the misfortune of England groaning under a load of debts, and the severe hardships contracted and imposed to support foreign interests: he lamented the ill-treatment and disregard of the ancient nobility; and said it gave him great trouble to see the interest of the nation abandoned to the direction of a new set of people, who must at any rate enrich themselves by the spoil of their country: "some may imagine, " continued he, "that these calamities are not displeasing to me, because they may, in some measure, turn to my advantage; I renounce all such unworthy thoughts. ""[423]

FOOTNOTE:

[423] The rest of the letter not being material, is omitted.

No. II. —THE PEDIGREE OF THE DERWENTWATER FAMILY.

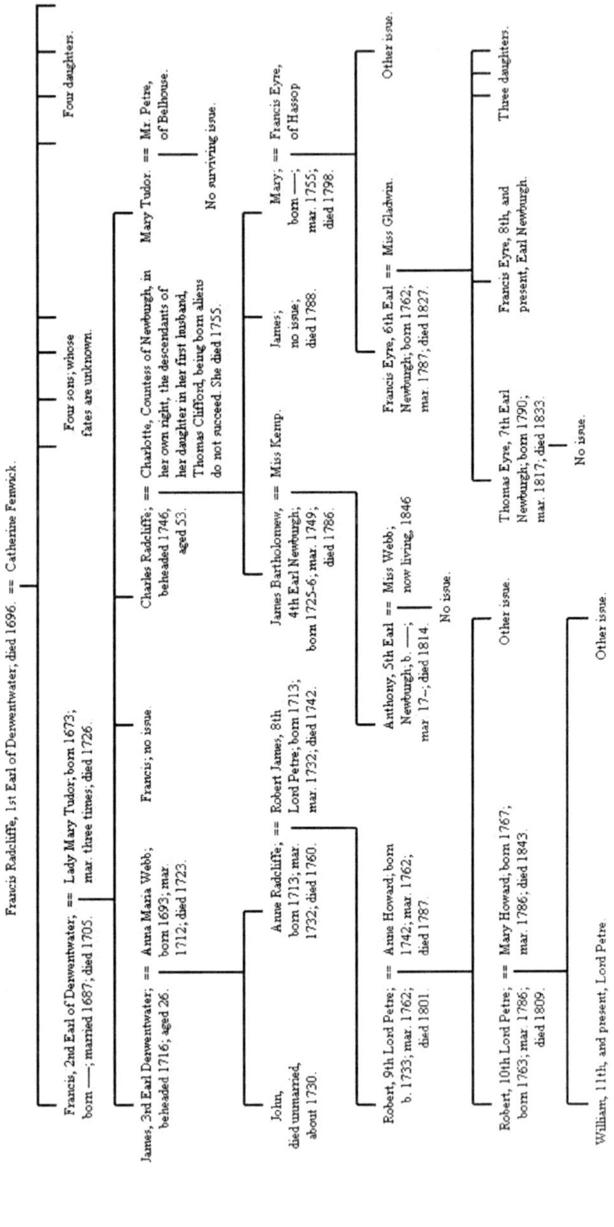

No. III.

The following address affords a curious specimen of the subtlety of Lord Lovat, and the mode usually adopted by him of cajoling his clan. It was copied by Alexander Macdonald, Esq., from an old process, in which it was produced before the Court of Session, and it is preserved in the Register House, Edinburgh; the signature, date, and address are, holographs of Lord Lovat.

THE HONOURABLE THE GENTLEMEN OF THE NAME OF FRASER.

My dear Friends,

Since, by all appearances, this is the last time of my life I shall have occasion to write to you, I being now very ill of a dangerous fever, I do declare to you before God, before whom I must apear, and all of us at the great day of Judgement, that I loved you all, I mean you and all the rest of my kindred and family who are for the standing of their chief and name; and, as I loved you, so I loved all my faithful Commons in general more than I did my own life or health, or comfort, or satisfaction; and God to whom I must answer, knows that my greatest desire and the greatest happiness I proposed to myself under heaven was, to make you all live happy and make my poor Commons flourish; and that it was my constant principle to think myself mutch hapier with a hundred pounds and see you all live well at your ease about mee than have ten thousand pounds a year, and see you in want or misery. I did faithfully desire and resolve to make up, and put at their ease Allexander Fraser of Topatry, and James Fraser of Castle Ladders and their familys; and whatever disputs might ever be betwixt them and me which our mutual hot temper occasioned, joyned with the malice and calomny of both our ennemies, I take God to witness, I loved those two brave men as I did my own life for their great zeal and fidelity they showed for their chief and kindred; I did likewise resolve to support the families of Struy Foyers and Culdithels families, and to the lasting praise of Culdithel and his familie. I never knew himself to sarwe from his faithfull zeal for his chief and kindred, nor none of his familie, for which I hope God will bless him and them and their posterity. I did likewise desyring to make my poor Commons live at their ease and have them always well clothed and well armed after the Highland maner, and not to suffer them to wear low country cloths, but make them live like their forefathers with the use of their arms, that they might always be in condition to defend themselves against their ennemies, and to do service to their friends, especially to the great Duke of Argile, and to his worthy brother the

Earl of Illay, and to that glorious and noble famyly who were always our constant and faithful friends; and I conjure you and all honest Frasers to be zealous and faithfull friends and servants to the family of Argile and their friends, whilst a Campbell and a Fraser subsists. If it be God's will that for the punishment of my great and many sins and the sins of my kindred, I should now depart this life before I put these just and good resolutions in execution; yet I hope that God in his mercy will inspire you and all honest Frasers to stand by and be faithfull to my cousin Inverlahie and the other heirs male of my family, and to venture your lives and fortunes to put him or my nearest heirs male named in my Testament written by John Jacks, in the full possession of the estate and honours of my forefathers, which is the onely way to preserve you from the wicked designs of the family of Tarbat and Glengary joyned to the family of Athol: and you may depend upon it, and you and your posterity will see it and find it, that if you do not keep stedfast to your chief, I mean the heir male of my famyly; but weakly or falsely for little private interest and views abandon your duty to your name, and suffer a pretended heiresse, and her Mackenzie children to possess your country and the true right of the heirs male, they will certainly in les than an age chasse you all by slight and might, as well Gentlemen, as Commons, out of your native country, which will be possessed by the Mackenzies and the Mackdonalls, and you will be, like the miserable unnatural Jews, scattered, and vagabonds throughout the unhappy kingdom of Scotland, and the poor wifes and children that remains of the name, without a head or protection when they are told the traditions of their familie will be cursing from their hearts the persons and memory of those unnaturall cowardly knavish men, who sold and abandoned their chief, their name, their birthright, and their country, for a false and foolish present gain, even as the most of Scots' people curs this day those who sold them and their country to the English by the fatal union, which I hope will not last long.

I make my earnest and dying prayers to God Almighty, that he may, in his mercy, thro the merits of Christ Jesus, save you and all my poor people, whom I always found honest and zealous to me and their duty, from that blindness of heart that will inevitably bring those ruins and disgraces upon you and your posterity; and I pray that Almighty and Mercifull God, who has often miraculously saved my family and name from utter ruin, may give you the spirit of courage, of zeal, and of fidelity, that you owe to your chief, to your name, to your selves, to your children, and to your country; and may the most mercifull, and adorable Trinity, Father, Son and Holy Spirit, three persons, one God, save all your souls eternally, throu the blood of Christ Jesus, our Blessed Lord and Saviour, to whom I heartily recommende you.

I desire that this letter may be kept in a box, at Beaufort, or Maniack, and read once a-year by the heir male, or a principale gentleman of the name, to all honest Frasers that will continue faithfull to the duty I have enjoined in this above-written letter, to whom, with you and all honest Frasers, and my other friends, I leave my tender and affectionat blessing, and bid you my kind, and last farewell.

LOVAT.

London, the 5 of Aprile, 1718.

Not being able to write myself, I did dictat the above letter to the little French boy, that's my servant. It contains the most sincere sentiments of my heart; and if it touch my kindred in reading of it, as it did me while I dictat it, I am sure it will have a good effect, which are my earnest prayers to God.

IV.

Allusion having been made often, in the course of these memoirs, to the process of "serving oneself heir" to an estate, in Scotland: the following document, [424] shewing the form of such a process, may not be deemed uninteresting.

Claim for William Maxwell, Esq. of Carruchan, who served heir-male in general of Robert, Fourth Earl of Nithisdale.

"Honourable persons and good men of Inquest: I, William Maxwell, of Carruchan, who was son of Captain Maxwell of Carruchan, who was son of Alexander Maxwell, of Yark and Terraughty, who was son of the Honourable James Maxwell, of Breckonside, immediate younger brother of John, third Earl of Nithisdale, who was father of Robert, fourth Earl of Nithisdale, say unto your wisdoms, that the said Maxwell of Nithisdale, nephews of my great-great-great-grandfather, died in the faith and peace of our Sovereign Lord the King then reigning, and that I am nearest and lawful heir male in general to the said Robert, fourth Earl of Nithisdale, the nephew of my great-great-great-grandfather, and that I am of lawful age. Therefore I beseech your wisdoms to serve and cognesce me nearest and lawful heir male in general to the said deceased Robert, fourth

Earl of Nithisdale, and cause your clerk of the Court to return my service to your Majesty's Chancery. Under my seal,

"According to justice and your wisdom's answer, &c. &c. "

Le Toque, pinx. *S. Freeman, sc.*

PRINCE CHARLES EDWARD.

COMMONLY CALLED THE YOUNG PRETENDER.

A. Ramsay, del. S. Freeman, sc.

FLORA MCDONALD.

S. Freeman, sc.

ARTHUR, LORD BALMERINO.

FROM A VERY SCARCE CONTEMPORARY PRINT.

FOOTNOTE:

[424] I am indebted for a copy of this process to Sir John Maxwell, Bart. Pollok.

Printed in the United Kingdom
by Lightning Source UK Ltd.
134525UK00002B/108/P

9 781409 906605